S. G. Frankland

8th December 1991

# WARSHIP 1991

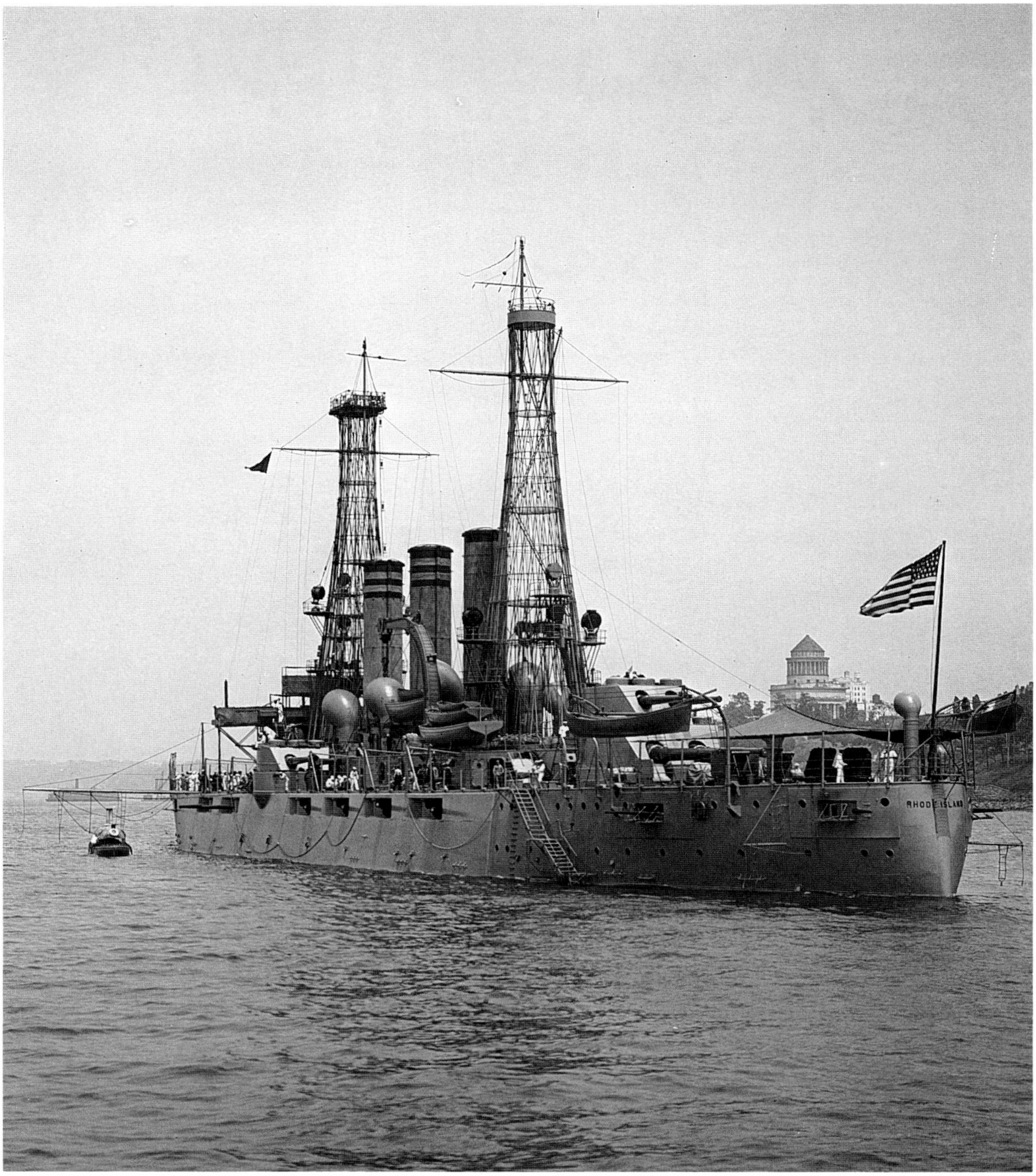


*USS* Rhode Island *(BB-17) lying off the New York Navy Yard, 22 July 1910. (*USN*).*

# WARSHIP 1991

*Edited by Robert Gardiner*

CONWAY MARITIME PRESS

First published in Great Britain by
Conway Maritime Press Ltd
101 Fleet Street
London EC4Y 1DE



*British Library Cataloguing in Publication Data*
Warship . .
1991 –
1. Warships
623.825

ISBN 0–85177–582–9

Designed by Beverley Rigby
Typesetting and page make-up by
The Word Shop, Bury, Lancashire
Printed and bound in Great Britain by
Butler & Tanner Ltd, Frome

# CONTENTS

# EDITORIAL

The last twelve-month has been dominated by the Gulf crisis and ensuing war, and of course we give the main maritime events due prominence in Ian Sturton's review of the year. It was not essentially a maritime war, and there was no real ship-to-ship combat, but naval units were the first on station and the flexibility of sea power was demonstrated yet again. However, some of the less committed members of the allied coalition discovered that 'sending a gunboat', so often more acceptable than direct military action in peacetime, could also satisfy the same conditions in a shooting war. Luckily this heterogeneous armada of reluctant volunteers was not required to go in harm's way.

The brilliant victory is unlikely to mean any lasting benefits to the services involved. The West's politicians are determined to be paid the 'Peace Dividend' promised by the end of the Cold War, and just like the stark contrast between the decisiveness of the military action and the political vacillation following the ceasefire, inter-service cooperation is already being displaced by savage in-fighting. In a world of radical reductions in defence expenditure, the Gulf War will be subject to much far from objective analysis: the air force lobby in the US is already claiming that air power won the war more or less single-handed, so all the early books about the 'lessons of the war' will need to be treated with circumspection. To those with any historical perspective – and this should include every *Warship* reader – it all sounds very familiar.

Looking somewhat further back, this year has also been marked by a number of significant anniversaries, including the 75th of Jutland and the 50th of Pearl Harbor. This latter seemed important enough to give over a large proportion of this issue to Japanese subjects. Of particular note are two articles devoted to major Japanese assets, the naval air force and the oxygen torpedo. In the first, Robert Mikesh, a leading authority on early Japanese aviation, attempts a unique overview of developments across a quarter century, taking in the strategic, economic and political factors that inspired what was undoubtedly the world's best naval air arm by 1941. The second, by the familiar team lead by Hans Lengerer, is a more technical analysis of oxygen torpedoes and their history, which is matched by a similar article on IJN anti-aircraft guns and gunnery.

For historians, the post-*Glasnost* information dividend is definitely beginning to pay out. We are pleased to welcome to our pages a Romanian naval authority, Cristian Crăciunoiu, whose interests were necessarily pursued with great discretion under the Ceaucesceu regime. We all remember stories of 'harmless' aviation or rail enthusiasts being arrested by the authorities of the old Communist East, and in these countries modelmaking was regarded as virtually the only legitimate reason for taking an interest in things military. As the editor of the main Romanian modelling magazine, Cristian was in a position to collect both information and photographs on Romanian wartime naval activity against the Soviets, but it is only now that he can consider publishing some of it. We hope his article on minelaying will be the first of many.

Last year's editorial had occasion to mention the problems of commenting on contemporary, and even recently disposed of, ships, since documentation is so slow to be released. One answer to this difficulty is convincingly demonstrated by Robert Largess and Harvey Horwitz in their piece on the experimental submarine *Albacore*. This boat's work was so important to the nuclear submarine programme that information on many aspects have never been fully released, and the authors were obliged to undertake numerous interviews with ex-crew members in order to piece together the main outline of her career. It may not have quite the authority of primary source material, but it is far more original than anything previously published, and must be preferable to endless reworking of material on well-documented warships.

In this issue we are fortunate to have a second fine article on a relatively modern subject, the Swedish cruisers of the *Tre Kronor* class. Neutral Sweden has not been any more forthcoming about defence matters than the bigger powers, and although these ships were a wartime design, their long postwar service ensured continuing security. Two mysteries surrounding these ships are satisfactorily cleared up by Dan Harris – namely their curious combination of twin and triple main turrets, and why a coast defence navy like Sweden's should build cruisers at all. In neither case did conventional design considerations play any part, and it would be interesting to know if the author, without the benefit of his personal knowledge, would have been able to deduce the political inspiration for these ships from surviving official records.

Beyond the main features, the review section follows the pattern of previous years, although there are fewer but longer Warship Notes. One of these concerns the intriguing if little considered matter of warship names, so often consigned to the level of trivia quizzes ('Which historical character, religious figures excepted, has had major warships named after him in four different navies on opposite sides of contemporary alliances?'). This note reveals the conscious myth-building behind British naming policy and in the process solves one small conundrum, to the editor's satisfaction at least: a few RN 'Captains' class frigates were renamed, apparently to avoid confusion with similar sounding USN ships, but this did not apply to the *Drury*, ex-*Cockburn*; if Andrew Lambert is right and the Admiralty was sensitive enough not to send the *Waterloo* to be Anglo–French flagship during the Crimea, then Their Lordships' descendants must have realised that it showed little gratitude to name a Lend-Lease ship after the man who burnt down the White House.

**Robert Gardiner**

# THE LAST MANILA GALLEON

Of all the major sailing fleets the Spanish Navy in the eighteenth century is probably the least well known, despite the survival of copious documentation. In this article David F Marley uses Mexican sources to decribe the curious provenance and design of the last great Manila Galleon: not only an interesting vessel in its own right but an exception that proved the rule of Spanish warship building in the 1700s.

On 9 June 1764, the inhabitants of Plymouth were witness to an extraordinary sight. Fully eighteen months after the conclusion of the Seven Years War, there stood into the Sound a formation of Royal Navy vessels from Madras in distant India, bringing in a huge prize. This was Admiral Samuel Cornish's Far Eastern Squadron returning to England after prolonged service on the far side of the globe, highlighted by their successful expedition against Manila two years before. During this same campaign, they had captured the Acapulco-bound galleon *Santísima Trinidad*, which was now being led into the Hamoaze. Immediately, she created a sensation. The Spanish vessels which plied the Pacific Ocean between Manila and Acapulco were legendary for their wealth and shroud of mystery. Seamen had hunted them since the times of Drake, and succeeded in taking four; but this was the first which had actually been sailed back to England for the public to view. Clearly the crowds lining the seashore were not disappointed by her appearance, for the prize was everything a galleon should be – massively large, and most unusual in her design. In fact, she was quite unlike any ship they had ever seen.

To begin with, she measured 167ft 6in along her gun deck, the same as a 74-gun ship. But in contrast to the leaner ship of the line, the Spaniard was some 4ft wider at 50ft 6in, and her bulk was truly prodigious. From the poop quarterdeck, her hold measured 30ft 6in in depth, exceeding that of a British Third Rate by more than 10ft, and she rode a full fathom deeper in the water as well, drawing 28ft as she ploughed through the Channel waves. [When taken fully laden out in the Philippines, her captors later reported, she had been drawing 37ft of water, despite the fact she was missing both her fore and main

*Return of a British squadron to Plymouth with a prize. As this Dominic Serres painting was executed in 1766, it has sometimes been suggested that it might represent Admiral Cornish's return with the captive* Santísima Trinidad, *although this cannot be confirmed.* (National Maritime Museum)

masts at the time.] Her 2000 tons burthen was being propelled by disproportionately large top hamper, and the pronounced sheer of her lines gave her a faintly oriental look. There was also the curious matter of her armament, for the *Santísima Trinidad*, unlike a regular man of war, had a lower deck which was completely unpierced and unarmed. Her main battery was upon the upper deck, with lighter pieces on quarterdeck and forecastle. This, of course, was the classic frigate layout, which was only then being introduced into the British service; but the Spanish prize was obviously no frigate. Her dimensions were altogether those of another class of vessel.

Indeed, it was her vast size as much as her exotic reputation which people came to see. The *Scots Magazine* described her as 'one of the largest [ships] ever seen in Britain'. The *Annual Register* said 'she lay like a mountain in the water'. People flocked into Plymouth from as far away as London to gaze upon the captive galleon, and wonder at her strange design.

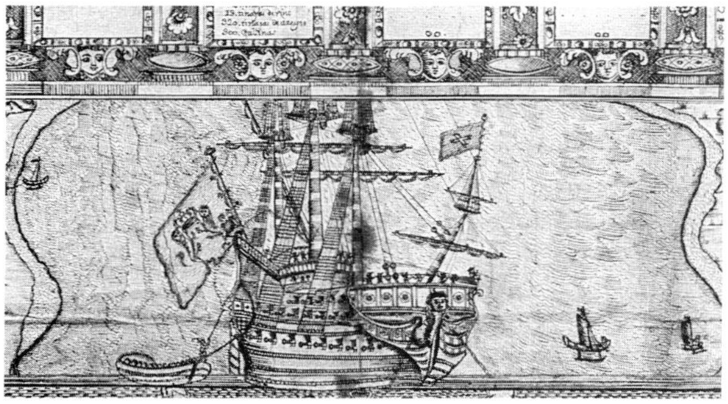

*Drawing of the* Santísima Trinidad *as she appeared in 1752, after completing her maiden voyage to Acapulco* (Archivo General de la Nación, México)

## *Spanish naval architecture*

During the first half of the eighteenth century, Spain had started to resurrect her neglected navy. However, the country's enfeebled finances did not permit her naval strategists to contemplate a grand ocean-going battle fleet. Instead, they had to allocate their funds more modestly, opting for what the Royal Navy would regard as Fourth Rate ships of the line, of from 50 to 60 guns apiece. These, it was hoped, would allow the Spanish Navy to keep communications open with the overseas empire in times of war, although they would be outgunned in any line of battle proper. Ideally, the new warships would be swift enough to evade heavier enemy squadrons, and stout enough to resist smaller pursuers or privateers. They were to be employed singly or in pairs on convoy duty, and in transporting the King's silver.

In the years 1714–1749, the Spanish Navy acquired slightly more than one hundred ships of the line, of which eighty-one were Fourth Rates. Fifty-six of these were 60-gun ships, the most prevalent design. This particular configuration was favoured by the Ministry of Indies, in the years immediately following the War of the Spanish Succession, as best suited for sailings to and from the Americas. The ships developed according to this programme were to be characterized by very heavy hulls, which in turn required them to have outsized masts and yards as well, in order to achieve the requisite speeds. The Spanish naval establishment of 1713 described the typical 60-gun ship as being 143ft in length, 39½ft in breadth, and drawing 18ft of water. Her tonnage was to be fixed at 990 tons, and her armament consist of twenty-four 24pdrs on the lower deck, twenty-four 18pdrs on the upper deck, ten 6pdrs on quarterdeck and forecastle, plus two bow- or sternchasers. Her complement was to be 380 men.

However, these norms only ever served as recommendations, never rigid specifications. The Spanish Crown owned very few shipyards throughout this period, and was thus obliged to obtain its vessels through private contractors. Naturally, there was a great deal of variety in the designs employed by individual shipwrights, so the 1713 parameters were intended as a guideline for the King's officers in the placing of shipbuilding orders. It was not until the middle part of the eighteenth century that the Spanish Government was at last able to begin constructing vessels to its own standardized series of plans. Prior to this date, there was considerable latitude in the development of His Catholic Majesty's warships – and nowhere was this more apparent than in Spain's remotest dominion, the Philippine Islands.

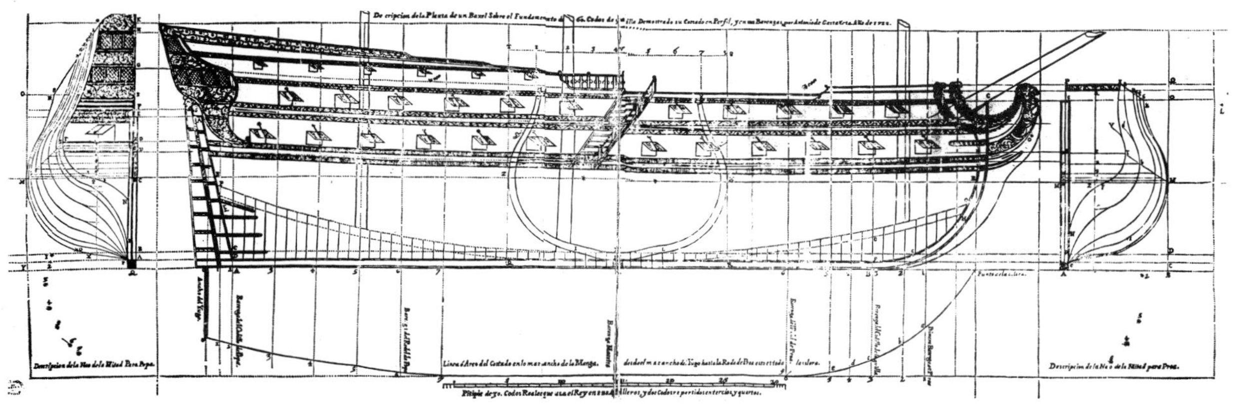

*Sheer and half-breadth plan for a 60-gun Spanish ship of the line, by the naval architect Don Antonio Gaztañeta, 1722.* (Archivo General de Indias, Sevilla)

*Drawing of an early eighteenth century Spanish Fourth Rate.* (Museo Naval, Madrid)

*Prototype for a 60-gun ship of the line, from the Spanish naval reconstruction programme of 1750. The ideal royal warship, as envisioned by the King's ministers in Madrid. Contrast her with the 60-gun* Santísima Trinidad, *launched this very same year in the Philippines.* (Museo Naval, Madrid)

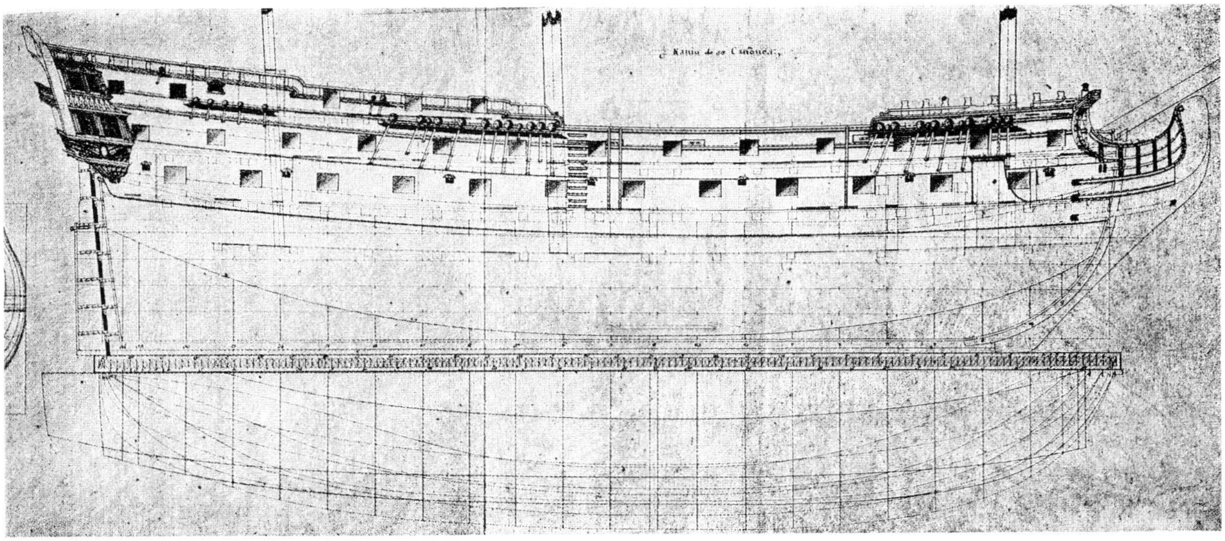

## *Pacific lifeline*

In theory, the galleons which made the yearly crossings between Manila and Acapulco were supposed to be royal warships, not unlike any others in the Spanish naval establishment. Their primary function, insofar as the Crown was concerned, was to carry monies, supplies, and reinforcements to the Spanish colony in Asia, as they had done ever since the first expeditions set forth in the sixteenth century. Only as a secondary consideration were they to bring back cargoes of private goods to be sold in Acapulco, and the King's ministers regarded this as a mere favour granted to the settlers by an indulgent Crown. The principal purpose remained that of logistics.

However, to the Spaniards living in Manila, the priorities were the reverse: the shipping of their trade goods to New Spain quickly became paramount, as it constituted their sole outlet for commerce. By law, all private vessels were prohibited from making the crossing to Mexico, and European traders were discouraged from visiting the Philippines. As a result, the King's galleons were the only means for the colonists to conduct any business. Every Spanish citizen in the Islands was entitled to an equal share in the cargo space of a galleon, to be used or sold as the holder saw fit. Those who chose to consign cargoes naturally sought the highest possible return on their money, packing the hold with such luxury items as Chinese silks, ivory, spices, and gold, which commanded fantastic prices in Mexico. Soon the King's warships were being crammed with more and more trade goods, to the point where they began to change in nature. From royal warships, they became transformed into East Indiamen.

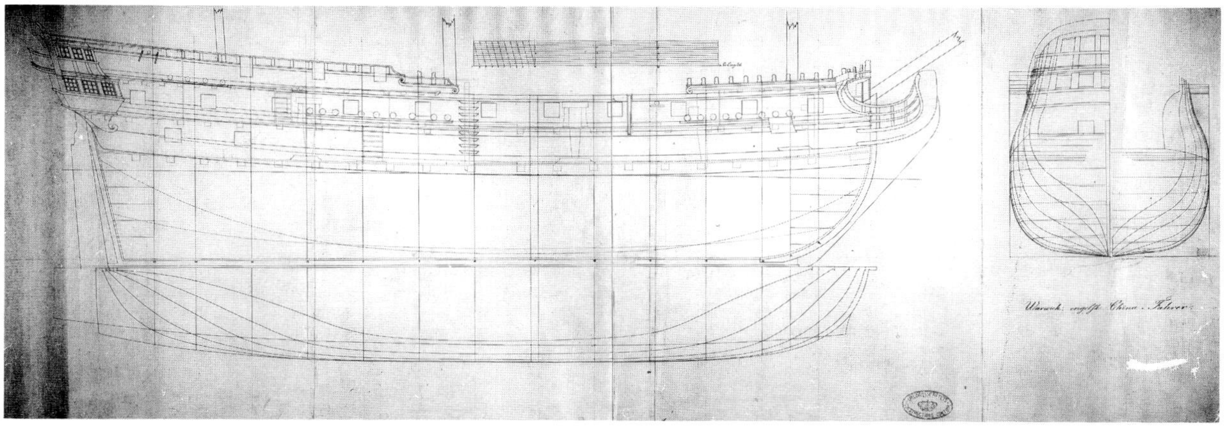

*Sheer plan of the English East Indiaman* Warwick, *built in 1750. Like the* Santísima Trinidad, *her lower deck was largely unarmed, so as to be used for cargo space.* (Rigsarkivet, Copenhapen)

Since the vessels themselves were also built in the Philippines, this evolution was reflected in their architecture. Gradually they began to grow in length and breadth, in order to accommodate more cargo. They dispensed with their lower batteries, in order to provide more passenger space. They reduced the calibre of their weapons, so as not to become too top-heavy, nor make it difficult to transfer guns into the hold in case of need. For their defence, they relied increasingly upon the thickness of their hulls, and the remoteness of their travel route. They were manned by large crews of 'seamen', many of whom were nothing more than merchants or private citizens travelling in disguise, and officers who were well-connected sons of local officials.

In vain did the Spanish Crown attempt to legislate against this deviation. By a royal decree of 1734, the total value of private goods shipped out of Manila aboard the galleons could not exceed 500,000 *pesos* a year, nor could the proceeds brought back from their sale in Acapulco be more than a million; but the wily Philippine merchants routinely flouted this restriction, with the open connivance of customs officers on both sides of the Pacific. Another edict declared the galleons could not be of more than 560 tons burthen; but this too was conveniently ignored, as both the local contractors who laid them down, and the Crown officials who approved them, had a vested interest in providing for as large a bottom as possible. The financial well-being of virtually everybody in the Islands depended upon this, in spite of what some faceless bureaucrat might say in far-off Madrid.

## *Preceding galleons*

In 1743, Commodore Anson captured the homeward-bound *Nuestra Señora de Covadonga* off Cape Espíritu Santo with his *Centurion*, 60 guns. When the British first began to close against their much larger opponent, they were surprised to see she bore no lower tier of guns. In the words of one of Anson's officers, 'we were amazed to think what he could propose against our weight of metal', and indeed the Spaniard was soon beaten into submission. Upon taking possession of their prize, the British found she only had 32 cannon cleared for action, with another 4 between decks that were not used, and 8 others stowed in her hold. All in all, the *Covadonga* carried 44 guns, and these mere 6-, 8-, and 12pdrs, much lighter than the British ordnance, so 'it must be confessed we engaged the enemy with great advantages on our side'. Furthermore, the officer added, the Spanish ship was so shot through that it 'may serve to refute a ridiculous opinion which has been handed down amongst all seafaring people as a certain tradition, that the sides of the galleons were always built shot proof; but we found by experience that they were not strong enough to resist our grapeshot, much more our 24pdr balls.'

The *Covadonga*, of course, was an older ship, having spent at least a dozen years in the trade. She was taken with considerable ease, despite the advance warning her commander had received of a British presence in the Pacific, and the 550 men she carried to Anson's 227. Obviously, the galleon's lighter armament and poor handling contributed more to her defeat than the relative thickness of her bulwarks. Within days, the British transferred 1,313,843 *pesos* in silver coin out of her into the *Centurion*, along with 35,862 ounces of bullion. As the two vessels then made their way to Macao, more treasure was discovered below, hidden in hundreds of different places. So much bullion was eventually removed from the galleon that her upper deck guns had to be stowed in the hold as ballast. Upon reaching China, the Spanish prisoners were released, and the *Covadonga*'s hulk sold to a private merchant for 6000 *pesos*.

Two years later, before they had even had a chance to recover from this loss, the Spaniards in Manila suffered a second setback at the hands of the neutral Dutch. The wily Governor of Batavia sent false reports into the Philippines that another British force had arrived in the Far East, in search of the galleon. Fully as the Dutchman anticipated, the Spaniards cancelled their Acapulco sailing for 1745, which allowed the Governor to dispatch his own Dutch East Indiamen across the Pacific in their stead, in the hopes of gaining access to the rich Mexican market. This Dutch overture eventually failed of its purpose, but not before it cost the Spaniards at Manila another year's trade.

During the winter of 1745/46, a new galleon was launched in the Philippines to replace the lost *Covadonga*. Her name was *Nuestra Señora del Rosario y los Santos Reyes*, and she very much reflected the local citizen's ideal of a large vessel. The on-going naval war with Britain prevented regular consultations between Manila, Mexico, and Spain, so the Philippine officials enjoyed a relatively free hand. There had not even been a governor in office throughout most of this period, the previous one having died after a long illness, and the Bishop of Ilocos assuming his duties on an interim basis. As a result, the royal restrictions were conveniently ignored, and an outsized vessel produced. The new galleon measured 188ft overall, 156ft on the keel; she was extremely broad at 56ft, while the depth of her hold measured 26ft, and her burthen was put at 1710 tons. The *Rosario* was better armed than her predecessors [doubtless as a consequence of Anson's raid], being pierced for 70 guns instead of the 44 carried by the *Covadonga*. The construction of the new vessel cost the King's Exchequer 95,857 *pesos*, at the usual usurious rates charged by the Philippine contractors.

But just as the *Rosario* perpetuated the previous galleons' enormity, she also retained their notoriously bad sailing qualities as well. On her maiden voyage to Acapulco in 1746, she (along with the older *Nuestra Señora del Pilar*, 44) made an unusually slow crossing, slower still than those of the sixteenth century. And on her second departure from the Philippines in 1748, the new galleon, according to a contemporary chronicler, 'was driven back by contrary winds, because it was poorly constructed and difficult to manage.'

The problem, it was suggested, lay in the outmoded and faulty design of the vessels, which not only made them sluggish, but unable 'to sail to windward, and to keep clear of the land or run away from storms'. The *Rosario*, in particular, had even 'had the after-piece of her rudder increased until it was so wide that it required eight men to handle it, working with two wheels and a pair of hawsers. The distribution of storage space in the hold is no less to be condemned, particularly the location of the powder magazine in the fore part of the ship.' These and other opinions were relayed back to Spain by the Marqués de Ovando, the new Governor-designate of the Philippines, when he travelled out to Manila aboard the *Rosario* in 1750. By this time, the Anglo-Spanish hostilities were finally at an end, but the Islands' economy continued to suffer.

There had been missed crossings in 1743, 1745, and 1748, and the cargo brought over by the *Rosario* in 1749 was unsold at Acapulco. Therefore, the galleon was forced to sail back to Manila the following year without any commercial profits, although she did transport out 1,200,000 *pesos* in royal payrolls. But even as the *Rosario* was drawing near the Philippines with the new Governor, one last disaster remained to befall the trade: for that summer marked the departure from Cavite of the aged *Pilar*, a vessel by now too decayed to attempt the crossing, were it not for the Manileños's desperate desire to revive their fortunes. The *Pilar* began leaking even before she cleared Manila Bay, and her passengers begged the captain to turn back. This he refused to do, and the galleon sailed on to her doom. The only trace of her that was ever found was some wreckage washed up on the eastern shore of Luzon many months later.

## *Launch of the Trinidad*

The *Pilar* would not have had to sail on her final ill-fated voyage if the new galleon being built at Bagatao had been ready in time. However, the construction of this new vessel was such a vast undertaking that she could not be completed until the autumn of 1750. Her name was the *Santísima Trinidad y Nuestra Señora del Buen Fin* – literally, the 'Most Holy Trinity and Our Lady of the Good End' – also known as the *Poderoso*, the 'Powerful', as she was the largest ship ever built in the Philippines. As with the *Rosario* before her, the Island authorities had enjoyed almost complete autonomy in her design, and the vessel was virtually finished by the time the new Governor arrived.

The result was the monstrously oversized *Santísima Trinidad*, larger still than the huge *Rosario*. On paper, the latest galleon was supposed to conform to the Spanish navy's guidelines for a Fourth Rate ship of the line, having a heavy hull and lofty superstructure, and being rated at 60 guns [although only pierced for 27 a side, plus bow- and sternchasers]. However, as she also incorporated the classic Philippine feature of an unarmed lower deck, the rest of her dimensions were totally absurd. The vessel had apparently been designed by Don Domingo Nebra, the only shipwright in the Islands judged competent enough to build for the Acapulco trade, and who was 70 years of age. His newest creation, although narrower than the *Rosario* by almost six full feet, rode both higher, and deeper, in the water.

In fact, the *Santísima Trinidad*'s upper works were gigantic, with a towering poop of seventeenth century proportions which made her leewardly and crank. Her hull reached far below the waterline as well, in part because of its shape, in part because of the dense tropical hardwoods used in the ship's construction. Traditionally, the framing of all the galleons was of teak, while the hard *molave* wood was employed for beams, knees, keel, other inside work, and rudder. The outer planking and wales were usually of *lanang*, a wood of great toughness which the Spaniards believed would absorb smaller shot, while repulsing heavier rounds. The massive weight of all these timbers made the *Santísima Trinidad* ride deep in the water, although they also gave her a hull of immense strength and resistance to the elements.

The distribution of her armament was scarcely as well planned, though, for in addition to the missing lower battery, the *Santísima Trinidad* had five of her gunports in the waist. Few if any cannon could be borne at this point, as the gangways were normally too narrow, and the skid beams too flimsy, to support any but the lightest ordnance. It is therefore unlikely that the *Santísima Trinidad* ever mounted any guns in these positions. As for the rest of her artillery, she was only pierced for thirteen pieces along either side of her gun deck, instead of the

*Eighteenth century Spanish panoramic view of the Bay of Manila. The city is in the immediate foreground, with the naval base of Cavite ten miles away in the middle distance, to the left. In 1762, it took the* Santísima Trinidad *more than a month to clear the bay.* (Museo de América, Madrid)

more usual fourteen for its length. Such ample spacing of her main battery may have been prompted by the testimony of the *Covadonga*'s survivors, who complained that Anson's *Centurion* benefited from wider gunports, and hence better play for his artillery. The broader spacing of the *Santísima Trinidad*'s heavy ordinance would therefore allow more room for her gunners (as well as passengers), and help reduce her top weight.

For it was her poor sailing qualities which most distressed the Spaniards. These became evident even as the vessel was being taken from Bagatao to Cavite for her final arming and commissioning. Nevertheless, the next year the *Santísima Trinidad* made her debut in the trans-Pacific service, setting sail for New Spain in the summer of 1751. She completed the crossing successfully, if somewhat ploddingly, and created a huge stir when she finally crawled to her anchorage in Acapulco. Usually the Mexican officials were willing to accommodate to the venality of the Philippine traffic, but the colossal size of the new galleon was impossible to overlook. She seemed custom-built for carrying excess cargoes, and the matter was duly reported to the King's ministers in Madrid.

On 14 November 1752, an angry rebuke was sent back from El Escorial, deploring the many irregularities in the Manila trade which are 'caused, in the most part, by the excessive size of her ship'. Ferdinand VI himself proposed to remedy this situation by instructing the next governor of the Philippines, Don Pedro Manuel de Arandia, as to 'this very grave matter'. Upon taking up his new posting, the Governor was to 'devise a method for reducing and moderating the vessel to that which is permitted (reforming the existing galleon, and disposing the construction of another, arranged to more proper and convenient measures).' In this, His Majesty added, De Arandia was to be guided by the principle that the ships were to have sufficient burthen 'for conducting the permitted cargo of the Islands, and no more'. They were also to be properly armed, not just 'as in time of peace, but for what might occur in war, and various encounters with pirates'.

In the long run, it would be decided to replace the galleons with smaller frigates, which were not only better suited to the Pacific service, but not 'as up to the present, apt only for receiving more and more cargo'. Eventually this plan was agreed to, and the Mexican Exchequer was instructed to set aside 50,000 *pesos* for the construction of two new royal frigates in Manila. However, as so often happened with orders destined for that particular corner of the empire, these did not have the expected result.

## *Conversion of the Trinidad*

While the matter was being debated, the *Santísima Trinidad* continued with her trans-Pacific crossings. Both her second and third voyages were remarkably slow, especially the latter. On 22 July 1755, the galleon departed Cavite, with 435 people aboard. It took her a full day to clear Manila Bay, and another month to exit the San Bernardino Strait. In early October, she was struck by a

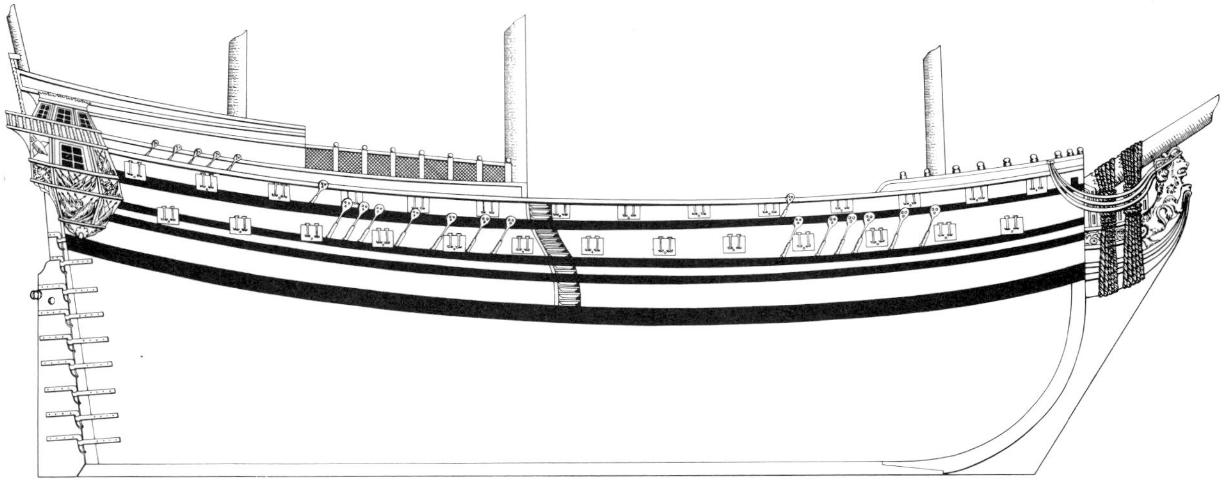

*Draught of the original configuration of the* Santísima Trinidad, *1750–57. Note crowned lion figurehead, emblematic of all Spanish royal warships.* (Archivo General de la Nación, México) ▲

*The* Santísima Trinidad *after her conversion, 1757–63. Note nine sets of rudder pintles, indicative of the great depth of her hold.* (Archivo General de la Nación, México) ▼

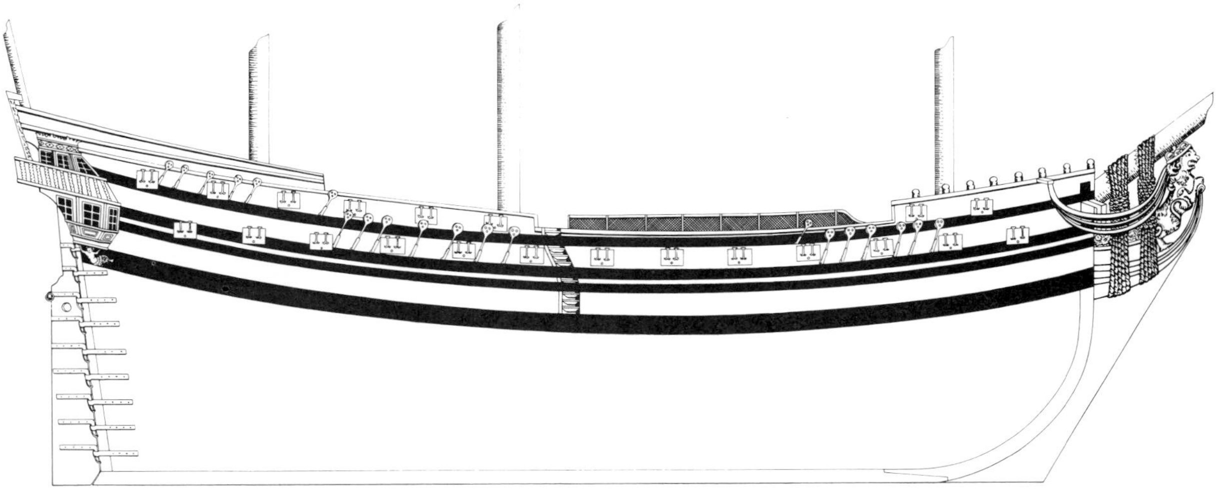

gale in mid-ocean, and almost sank; but what was even worse was the agonizingly slow process which then ensued across the North Pacific wastes, as one by one her passengers began to succumb to scurvy. On 1 October, there were 20 people sick; by 30 November, 60; by 21 December, more than 80; by 4 January, 102; by 13 January, 150.

Finally, on 1 February 1756 – more than a month and a half overdue – the ship managed to stagger into Cabo San Lucas, at the tip of Baja California; 82 of her passengers had died before land was sighted, including the former Governor of the Philippines, the Marqués de Ovando, who was retiring now that this term of office had expired. More than 200 other people were transferred ashore sick at the Jesuit mission of San José del Cabo, to be nursed back to health while the vessel continued her voyage to Acapulco. Only 27 crew members were left standing by the time the galleon finally came to anchor on 29 February of that year. This seven-month odyssey had been one of the longest and most terrible in the annals of the trade, and did much to solve the question of the *Santísima Trinidad*'s fate – although not in a way that might have been anticipated.

For ironically, when the ship completed the return leg to Manila in October of that year, she brought back the 50,000 *pesos* earmarked for the two new royal frigates. However, these funds were never used for this purpose. Instead, they were diverted by the Philippine officials into alterations to the *Santísima Trinidad* herself. The legal basis for their action was the King's comment of 14 November 1752, that he wished to have the huge vessel reduced in size. This option was of course much more palatable to the local authorities than the alternative, of having her large bottom replaced by that of a smaller frigate. Furthermore, the galleon obviously needed improving anyway, in light of her dreadful crossing to Mexico the previous year. Therefore, it was more convenient for the Manileños to obey His Majesty's initial injunction, and ignore the subsequent one of constructing two new royal frigates.

As a result, the *Santísima Trinidad* spent the year 1757 being overhauled at the Cavite dockyard. In effect, she was razed by almost an entire deck. Her forecastle was only slightly reduced, but the bulwarks above her waist were eliminated altogether, and replaced by rails. Her quarterdeck and poop were fully cut down as well, thus reducing her profile, and the cabins in her stern were rearranged. However, her hull remained unaffected by these changes from the main deck down, and the vessel thus retained her ample cargo-carrying capacity. The same could not be said about her armament. Five of her gunports vanished on either side with the reduction of her waist, and another was sealed off on each quarter of the bows. Thus the *Santísima Trinidad*'s broadsides decreased from 27 to 21 guns, although the Philippine authorities continued to rate her as a 60 in all their official correspondence. Evidently this fiction allowed them to maintain her quarterbill virtually intact, and still charge the Mexican Exchequer for a full complement, despite her diminished size.

The reconstruction of the *Santísima Trinidad*, and other sundry labours associated with this project, came to 53,656 *pesos*. The newly redesigned vessel then made her next voyage to Acapulco in 1758–59, and another in 1760–61. Both were relatively satisfactory, the crossing averaging five months to complete, instead of the seven immediately prior to her conversion. However, the galleon still remained quite slow and clumsy, her sailings being aided more by favourable winds and moderate weather on these occasions, than any dramatically improved handling qualities.

This was most forcefully driven home to the Spaniards on the sixth departure of the vessel, in 1762. First, her sailing was postponed well past the usual date, because her consort the *Rosario* had not yet reappeared from Acapulco. Eventually the *Santísima Trinidad* could wait no longer, and she got under way from Cavite on 1 August of that year. However, her commanders had delayed just a bit too long, for even as she began making for the entrance of Manila Bay, the winds shifted around to the south-west. These were the autumnal winds called *vendavales*, which continued to blow so steadily that the galleon could not claw her way out of the bay until 3 September, more than a month later. The vessel then paused at San Jacinto Bay from 7 to 12 September, to take on water and wood, and replenished her provisions from a large sampam sent out from Manila.

Thus resupplied, the *Santísima Trinidad* resumed her voyage and exited the San Bernardino Strait. Some 900 miles out at sea, as she was approaching the Mariana Islands, the galleon was struck by a fierce north-easterly gale the night of 2 October. By 0700 the next morning, the storm had reached such a pitch that her fore mast toppled over the side, followed fifteen minutes later by the main mast. Her crew frantically cut away the debris, but not

*The Spanish naval base of Cavite, about 1762. 'I' marks the spot where galleons were careened, and 'N' where new masts were stepped from timber yard 'L'.* (Archivo General de Indias, Sevilla)

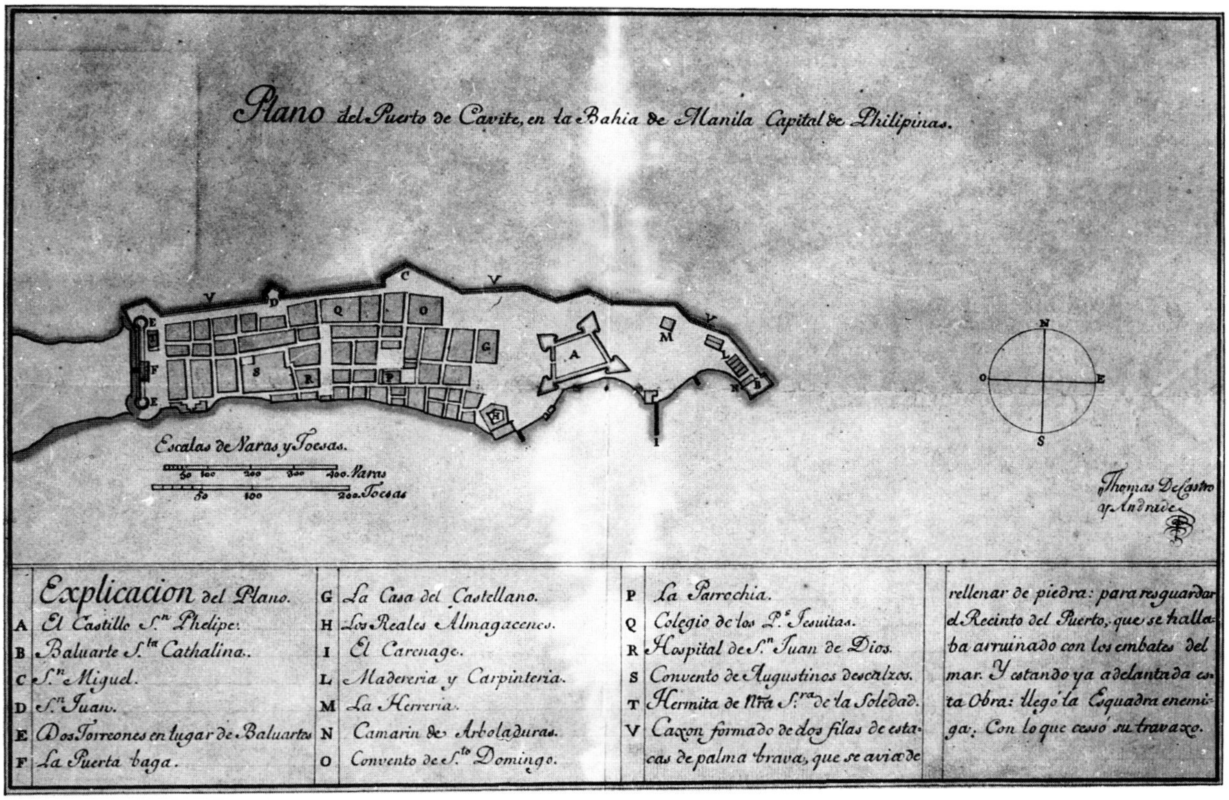

before it battered the hull and started some leaks. By the time the typhoon blew itself out on 6 October, the ship was in no condition to proceed. With pumps going and a jury rig set up, she reversed course to the Philippines.

Cape Espíritu Santo was sighted on 28 October, and the Spaniards thought about putting into Palapag to effect repairs. However, the narrow approaches to the harbour were judged too difficult for the galleon to attempt in her precarious state, so the *Santísima Trinidad* pressed on towards Bagatao. This was a fateful decision, for if the damaged vessel had entered Palapag, she would have found the *Rosario* inside recuperating from her own Pacific crossing. But more important still, the *Santísima Trinidad*'s officers would have learned that war with England had broken out back in Europe, that Manila had fallen to a sudden British attack, and that two Royal Navy warships were preparing to exit the Sibuyan Sea in search of Spanish prey.

## *Capture of the Trinidad*

As the crippled galleon emerged from the San Bernardino Strait on the evening of 29 October [30 October in the British records], her lookouts spotted a strange sail off Capul Island. They were unable to identify her further in the gloom, but she was actually HMS *Panther*, 60, Captain Hyde Parker commanding. The British, too, had seen the Spaniard, and directed their anchored consort, the frigate *Argo*, 28, Captain Richard King commanding, to make sail and intercept. The three ships lost sight of each other with nightfall, but by 2000 hrs the *Argo* came up with the chase opposite the Naranjos. The Spanish saw the frigate at the same time, and belatedly realized their danger.

Typically, the galleon was not prepared for action. Having sailed at a time when Spain was still believed to be at peace, she only had seven guns mounted, the rest being stowed in her hold. The *Santísima Trinidad* was also heavily loaded with trade goods, and crowded with more than 800 people, the vast majority of them non-combatants. Nevertheless, the Spaniards stood to their few cannon, commended themselves to '*María Santísima*', and hoped for the best. Shortly before 0100 in the morning, they hailed the advancing frigate, which had now closed in on their stern quarter, but received no reply.

The *Argo* opened fire about half an hour later, but the Spaniards refrained until the frigate had overhauled them, and their guns could bear. There then ensued a brisk cannonade between the two, as the *Argo* flailed impotently against her huge opponent, and received very much the worst of it. Although they could not see in the dark, the British were unable to penetrate the *Santísima Trinidad*'s thick sides with their 9pdrs, and the Spanish could reply undaunted. After more than two hours of this unequal contest, the *Argo* put up her helm and broke off the action. She fell behind to carry out repairs, and attend to her dead and wounded, while the galleon sailed on unscathed.

The next morning, though, the *Panther* was able to rejoin her consort, having been prevented the night before by a strong counter-current. Together the two vessels closed in on the slow moving galleon, one on either flank. The Spaniards had spent the night hoisting six more guns out of their crammed hold, and now mounted thirteen pieces. The engagement was resumed at 0900, and lasted almost two hours. Parker, who had served as a junior officer aboard Anson's *Centurion*, brought his two-decker 'within half musket shott' range of the lumbering *Santísima Trinidad*, and crashed heavy broadsides into her. However, unlike what had occurred a generation earlier with the *Covadonga*, the Spanish vessel was able to resist the British shot. The quarry, Parker said, 'made but little resistance, trusting [to the] immense thickness of the sides of their ship, which the *Panther*'s shott was not able to penetrate excepting her upper works.'

*Contemporary chart published in the* London Magazine *(1763), showing the track of the Manila Galleon. Reproduced in Blair & Robertson,* The Philippine Islands, *Vol 49.*

But the galleon's defence depended upon the courage of a few hardy men, principally the master's mate (*segundo piloto*). When this individual was severely wounded by a British round, the heart went out of the rest of the crew and passengers. Frightened and confused in their beleaguered ship, the Spaniards decided to haul down their colours – much to the surprised relief of the British, who could plainly see what little effect their fire had had upon the enemy's hull. When they went aboard the *Santísima Trinidad* to take possession of their prize, they found she had only suffered 28 total casualties (18 killed, 10 wounded) compared to 72 in both Royal Navy warships (35 dead, 37 injured). Still, the galleon was theirs, and fairly won.

The *Panther* took the *Santísima Trinidad* in tow, and

the three vessels sailed back to Manila, arriving outside the British-occupied port on 3 November 1762. The bulk of the Spanish prisoners were deposited ashore on Corregidor Island, and the galleon painstakingly warped to her mooring at Cavite. There she came to anchor on 12 November, and was repaired over the winter months by Filipino workmen.

*Contrast between Spanish and English style masting and rigging. Note how much loftier the Spanish one is (top), as evinced by the narrow tapering shrouds.* (Museo Naval, Madrid)

## *Disposal by the British*

When most of the Royal Navy force departed Manila on 2 March 1763, they took the refitted galleon along with them. The *Santísima Trinidad* represented a unique problem as a prize of war. Potentially, she was very valuable, but only if her cargo of trade goods could be sold at a high profit. The *Covadonga*, of course, had been taken returning from Mexico with the proceeds of such a sale; but the *Santísima Trinidad* had been captured outward-bound, with her luxury items still intact. These could not be sold in Manila, whose economy was devastated following the invasion. Consequently, the only solution was to carry the goods away, still packed in the galleon's hold, to be disposed of elsewhere.

Madras, however, was not much better as a market, as the British discovered once they brought their prize into the Roads. Chinese silks and ivories were relatively plentiful there. As a result, her captors decided to sail the galleon all the way back to England once the squadron was ordered home at the conclusion of the Seven Years War. This decision was not arrived at lightly, for they had already noticed the *Santísima Trinidad*'s 'heavy sailing' during the voyage from Manila to the Coromandel Coast. To convey such an ungainly vessel around the Cape of Good Hope would require epic patience and endurance. Indeed, Captain Hyde Parker, in a letter to his son, even expressed the doubt whether the prize could 'be got home' at all.

Nevertheless, the galleon was sailed to Plymouth, albeit with great difficulty, by her prize-master Lieutenant Mainwaring Wilding. There then arose another complication, when the Advocate-General reported that the vessel might not constitute a legitimate capture, because of the late date on which she had been taken. The High Court of the Admiralty upheld this opinion, which was eventually overturned by the Lords of Appeal on 14 August 1765. The *Santísima Trinidad* was shortly thereafter sold at Plymouth, where she had lain ever since her arrival. In light of her vast size and poor handling, it is unlikely she was ever put into service, but rather broken up for her wood. It is believed Captain Hyde Parker and Richard King received £30,000 apiece as their share of her value, principally from the sale of her cargo. This was a great deal of money, but only a tenth as much as Anson had received from the *Covadonga*'s capture.

Meanwhile, in the Philippines, the other great galleon – the *Rosario* – had been hunted down and destroyed at her hiding place in Palapag by the British forces. The Spaniards had stripped their vessel of her treasure and other valuables, and abandoned the hulk when the British approached, who then put her to the torch. Consequently, there were no ships left to resume the trans-Pacific crossings once Manila was restored to Spanish rule. These would have to be built anew; but this time, the government in Madrid refused to fall into the errors of the past. Henceforth, only frigates were ever used in the Acapulco–Manila trade.

**Sources**

A great deal of original information on the *Santísima Trinidad*, including the two draughts of her conversion, can be found in the Mexican National Archives, Series *Correspondencia de Virreyes (Primera Serie)*, Vol 1, and *Segunda Serie*, Vols 1, 3–4, and 6; *Filipinas*, Vols 3–6; *Marina*, Vols 1, 5, 10–11, 18–19, and 23–24; and *Reales Cédulas (Originales)*, Vols 72–74, 76–77, and 79.

Secondary sources include William L Schurz, *The Manila Galleon* (1959); Blair and Robertson, *The Philippine Islands*, Vols 48–49 (1907); Nicholas P Cushner, *Documents Illustrating the British Conquest of Manila* (1971); and Manera and Moya, *El buque en la armada española* (1981).

# THE ARMOURED CRUISER USS BROOKLYN

With her ram bow and extreme tumblehome reflecting the French origins of the armoured cruiser concept, the *Brooklyn* was nevertheless the first major US steel warship to be built with largely domestically manufactured equipment. William C Emerson has assembled a fine collection of contemporary plans and photographs which he accompanies with a brief outline of the ship and her career.

A TWIN screw armoured cruiser, the *Brooklyn* was of about 9,270 tons displacement. She was built from Navy department plans by the famous yard of William Cramp and Sons of Philadelphia, Pa, and was launched in 1896. Total cost of the hull and machinery was $2,986,000. The contract required that the vessel be able to maintain a speed of 20kts, but she exceeded this by nearly 2kts, winning her builder a premium of $350,000.

While authorized to be of the same general type as the *New York* the displacement was increased by about 1000 tons, improving sea-keeping qualities, endurance (greater coal stowage), and disposition and weight of armament. A forecastle deck was added, the freeboard forward was increased 8ft, and the forward 8in gun turret correspondingly raised. The greater freeboard increased materially the seagoing efficiency of the ship, permitted the working of the guns in the forward turret in almost any condition of sea, and secured greater comfort for the crew by providing a large additional berthing space. Her maximum draught aft at lowest point of the keel, when she was ready for sea and all bunkers were filled, was 26ft 2in.

## *Hull*

In the early days of what was then referred to as the 'New Navy', the US steel industry was not yet capable of producing the armour plates and steel forgings needed for its armoured warships. As late as 1888 the US was entirely dependent on European manufacturers for its supply of large steel forgings suitable for engines, large cannon, or armour plate. The industry had matured sufficiently that the contract for the *Brooklyn* specified that the entire vessel and major components were to be of domestic manufacture.

At just over 400ft in length, the *Brooklyn* was the second longest ship in the US navy when commissioned. Because of the need for great speed, cruisers of the day were significantly longer than battleships, and not until the *Virginia* class of 1902 was a US battleship longer. The hull was constructed of mild steel with frames spaced 4ft apart in the midships space allocated for machinery. Elsewhere, frame spacing was 3ft 6in. The ship was divided into 242 watertight compartments, including 13 within the double bottom. Between the protective and berth decks and running along the inner shell of the vessel was a cofferdam, 3ft 6in wide, which extended the entire length of the ship. This cofferdam, filled with a dense cellulose material, was intended to provide added protection from projectiles and to self-seal penetrations of the hull. Popular in US warships of the day, this method of protection was ineffective and was soon discarded.

Inboard of the cofferdams was a passageway on each side, 2ft wide and extending most of the length of the ship. Below the protective deck there was a somewhat wider passageway extending the length of the engine and boiler rooms. Trim tanks were located at the extreme ends of the vessel.

Within the hull were a total of 55 coal bunkers, with 19 below the protective deck and 36 above; 43cu ft of bunker capacity was provided for each of the 1693 tons of coal the *Brooklyn* was capable of carrying. Her coal supply at normal displacement was 20 per cent greater than that of the *New York*, and she could easily have gone from New York to San Francisco, around the Cape, without recoaling.

## *Armament*

The *Brooklyn* was more heavily armed than most contemporaries. Rather than two, she had four armoured turrets, each mounting two 8in guns. The fore and aft turrets had an angle of fire of 145° on each side of the bow and stern, respectively. The two midship turrets, using the tumblehome to advantage, had a very wide arc of fire; they could fire from right ahead to dead astern, a total angle of fire of 180°. Thus, while most of her contemporaries could fire only two of their largest guns ahead or astern, and only four on the broadside, the *Brooklyn* could fire six ahead, astern or to the side. And because the axis of the guns in the forward turret was higher than that of

*Sailors removing ash from the* Brooklyn's *fire room furnaces.* (Library of Congress)

the corresponding guns on many contemporaries, the *Brooklyn* was able to fight in severe weather.

Additional heavy armament carried comprised twelve 5in rapid fire guns in segmental shields. Eight of these guns were mounted on the berth deck in side mounted sponsons which bulged out from the sides of the hull. The other four were mounted at main deck level, two in side sponsons forward and the other two inboard, just abaft the main military mast.

As was standard with pre-dreadnought vessels, the *Brooklyn* was also armed with a wide array of smaller calibre weaponry. This included twelve 6pdrs, all save two of which were mounted behind segmental shields within the hull and four 1pdr rapid fire cannon, which along with the four Colt machine-guns, were mounted on the military masts. Additional armament were four above-water torpedo tubes for the 18in diameter Whitehead torpedoes.

*Massive equipment used to operate steam windlass.* (Library of Congress)

*Hammocks strung on berth deck. Most of the personnel on the* Brooklyn *slept in this manner.* (Library of Congress)

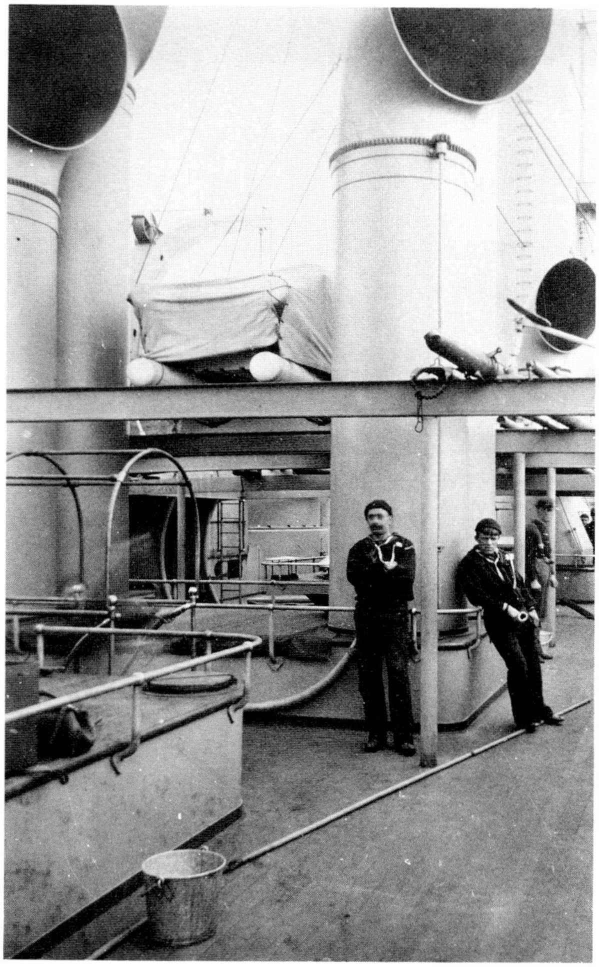

*View of spar deck. Notice punt, used for side cleaning, on superstructure deck skids.* (Library of Congress)

◀ *The stately armoured cruiser* Brooklyn *in peacetime colours about 1896.* (US National Archives)

## Brooklyn *CONTRACT TRIALS (FULL POWER, FORCED DRAUGHT)*

| | |
|---|---|
| Date of trial | 27 August 1896 |
| Duration of trial | 4 hours |
| Place of trial | New England coast |
| Condition of sea and weather | Smooth, fine |
| Draught, mean, on trial | 21ft 10in |
| Displacement | 8150 tons |
| Immersed midship section | 1225sq ft |
| Cylinder, diameters | |
| High pressure | 32in |
| Intermediate pressure | 47in |
| Low pressure | 72in |
| Stroke of pistons | 42in |
| Number and type of boilers | 5 double-ended<br>2 single-ended |
| Length of boilers | 18ft (four double-ended)<br>20ft (one double-ended)<br>9ft 5in (all single-ended) |
| Diameter of boilers | 16ft 3in (all) |
| Number of furnaces (each boiler) | 10 (double-ended), 5 (single-ended) |
| Grate surface (total) | 1016sq ft |
| Heating surface (total) | 33,432sq ft |
| Screw propellers | |
| Material | Manganese bronze |
| Diameter | 16ft 6in |
| Pitch, mean | 20ft 11in |
| Pitch, adjustable | Between 19ft 6in and 22ft 3in |
| Area developed | 232sq ft (one screw) |
| Number of blades each | 3 |

| | Starboard | | Port |
|---|---|---|---|
| Forward engine steam pressure, (psi) | | | |
| High pressure cylinder | 61.1 | | 60.2 |
| Intermediate pressure | 33.6 | | 29.9 |
| Low pressure | 14.5 | | 13.1 |
| Equivalent on low pressure | 40.5 | | 37.4 |
| Forward engine indicated horsepower | | | |
| High pressure | 1384 | | 1372 |
| Intermediate pressure | 1662 | | 1462 |
| Low pressure | 1694 | | 1565 |
| Total, forward and aft engines | | | |
| Aggregate both engines | 9230 | | 9019 |
| Collective, four main engines | | 18,249 | |
| Air-pump engines | 8.2 | | 8.3 |
| Circulating pump engines | 37.4 | | 40.6 |
| Feed pumps (6) | | 82.0 | |
| Blowers (12) | | 269.1 | |
| Other auxiliaries | | 75.7 | |
| Aggregate of all machinery | | 18,769.6 | |
| Speed in knots | | 21.91 | |
| Slip of propeller (mean) | | 18.67 per cent | |

Warship/Armoured Cruiser
SSU 36

*Lowering Commodore Schley's flag after the battle of Santiago de Cuba, 3 July 1898. Note the 5in gun position.* (Library of Congress)

*Gun deck view with details of one of the 5in gun positions.* (Library of Congress)

## Brooklyn *TECHNICAL SPECIFICATION*

*Construction data*

| | |
|---|---|
| Builder | William Cramp and Sons, Philadelphia, Pa |
| Contract awarded | 11 February 1893 |
| Contract price | $2,986,000 (hull and machinery) |
| Laid Down | 2 August 1893 |
| Launched | 2 October 1895 |
| Commissioned | 1 December 1896 |

*Design particulars*

| | |
|---|---|
| Rig | Two military masts |
| Displacement (tons) | 9215 |
| Gross tonnage | 6097 |
| Net tonnage | 3470 |
| Total weight of machinery | 1334 tons |
| Tons immersion at normal draught | 41.19 per inch |
| Design speed | 20 kts |
| Trial speed | 21.91kts |
| Length load waterline | 400ft 6in |
| Max breadth | 64ft 8in |
| Mean draught | 24ft 0in |
| Max draught aft at lowest point of keel, ship ready for sea with bunkers full | 26ft 2in |
| Coal capacity | 900 tons (normal)<br>1460 tons (bunker capacity) |
| Endurance | 5110nm at 10kts |

Armament
- 8–8in breech loading rifled guns
- 12–5in rapid fire guns
- 12–6pdr
- 4–1pdr rapid fire
- 4 Colt machine-guns
- 2–3in rapid fire field guns
- 4–18in Whitehead torpedo tubes

Armour

| | |
|---|---|
| Sides | 3in |
| 8in turrets | 5½in |
| 8in barbettes | 8in in front<br>4in in back |
| Conning tower | 7½in |
| Protective deck | 6in (slopes), 3in (flat) |
| Waterline protection | Obturating material (cocoa) |
| Volume | 24,789cu ft |

Machinery

| | |
|---|---|
| Boilers | 5 double-ended (cylindrical)<br>2 single-ended (cylindrical) |
| Engines | 4 vertical triple expansion reciprocating |
| Max indicated hp | 18,770 |
| Propellers | 2 |
| Diameter of propellers | 16ft 6in |

| | |
|---|---|
| Complement | 46 officers<br>470 men |

*General muster on main deck aft, with detail of steam driven winch.* (Library of Congress)

*View of 6pdr rapid fire gun on after deckhouse deck.* (Library of Congress)

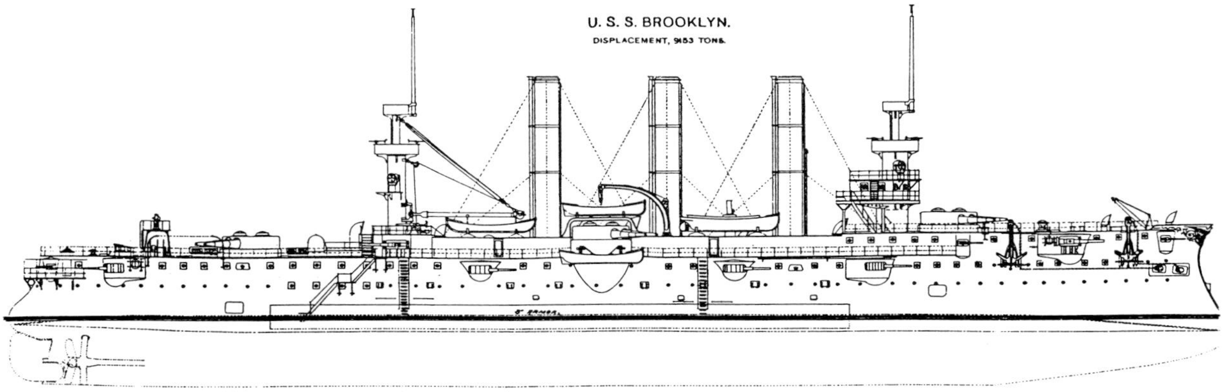


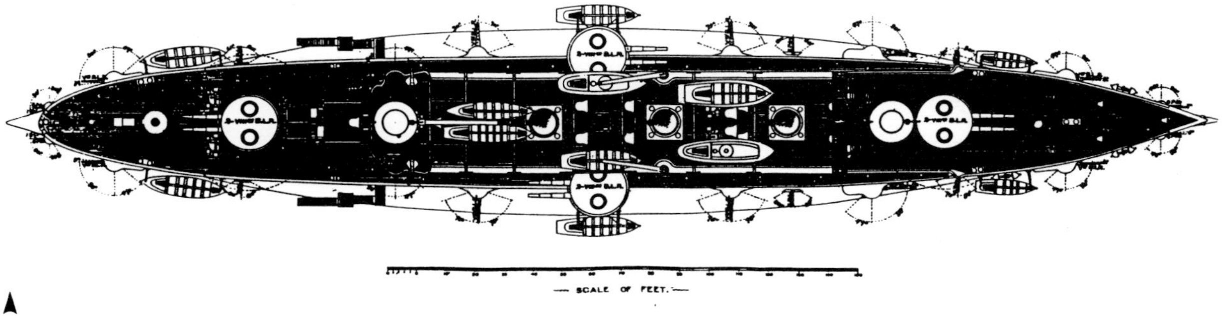


▲

*Outboard profile and plan view of* Brooklyn *from an 1893 publication. Her narrow beam and tall smoke stacks are clearly evident.* (Society of Naval Architects and Marine Engineers)

*Midship section. Shown are coal storage areas and the layout of side and protective deck armour.* (Society of Naval Architects and Marine Engineers) ►

*Body plan of* Brooklyn. *Her fine lines and exaggerated tumblehome are clearly evident.* (US National Archives)

▼

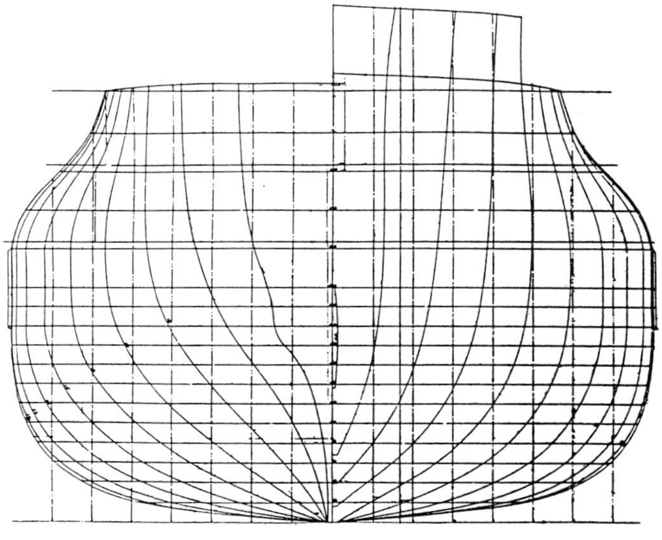

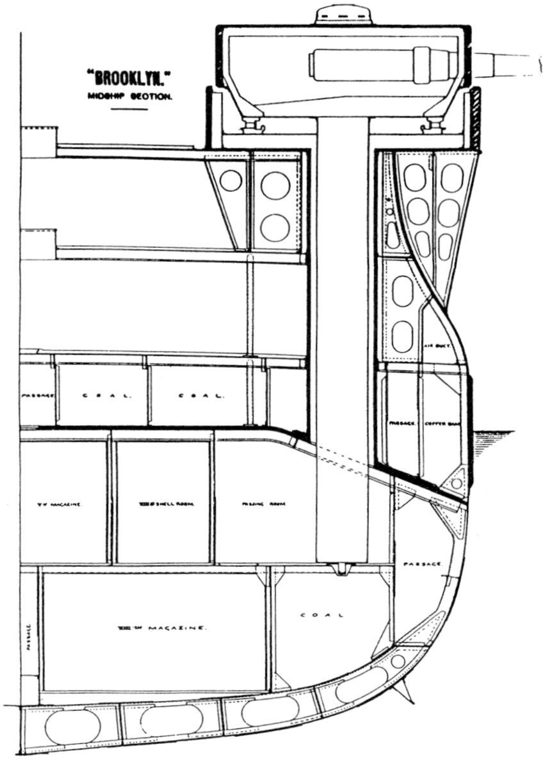

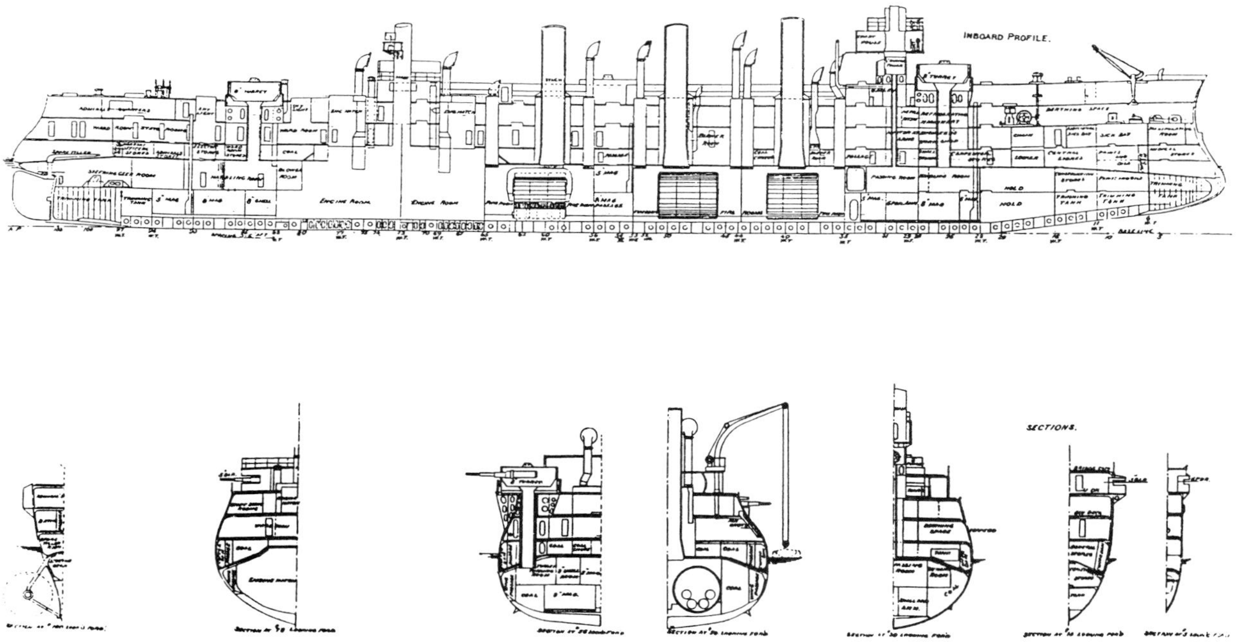


*Inboard profile and cross section views of the* Brooklyn. (American Society of Naval Engineers)

*Sketches of the gun deck and hold. Note the arrangement of the boilers and propeller shafts.* (American Society of Naval Engineers)

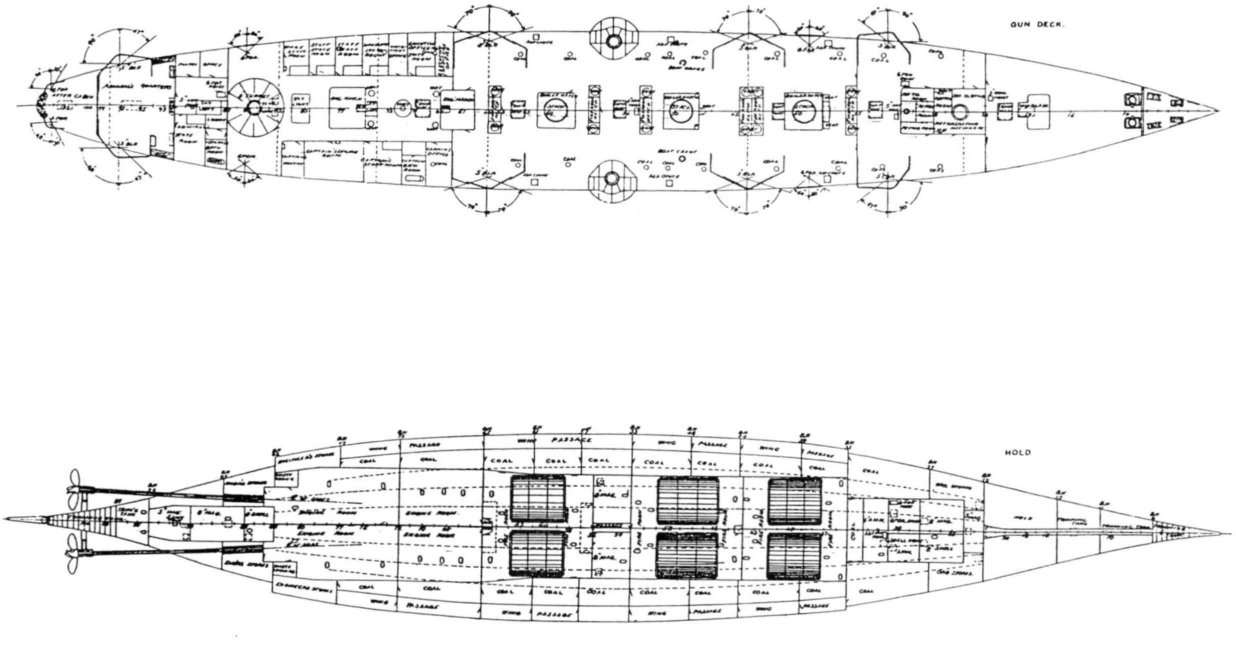

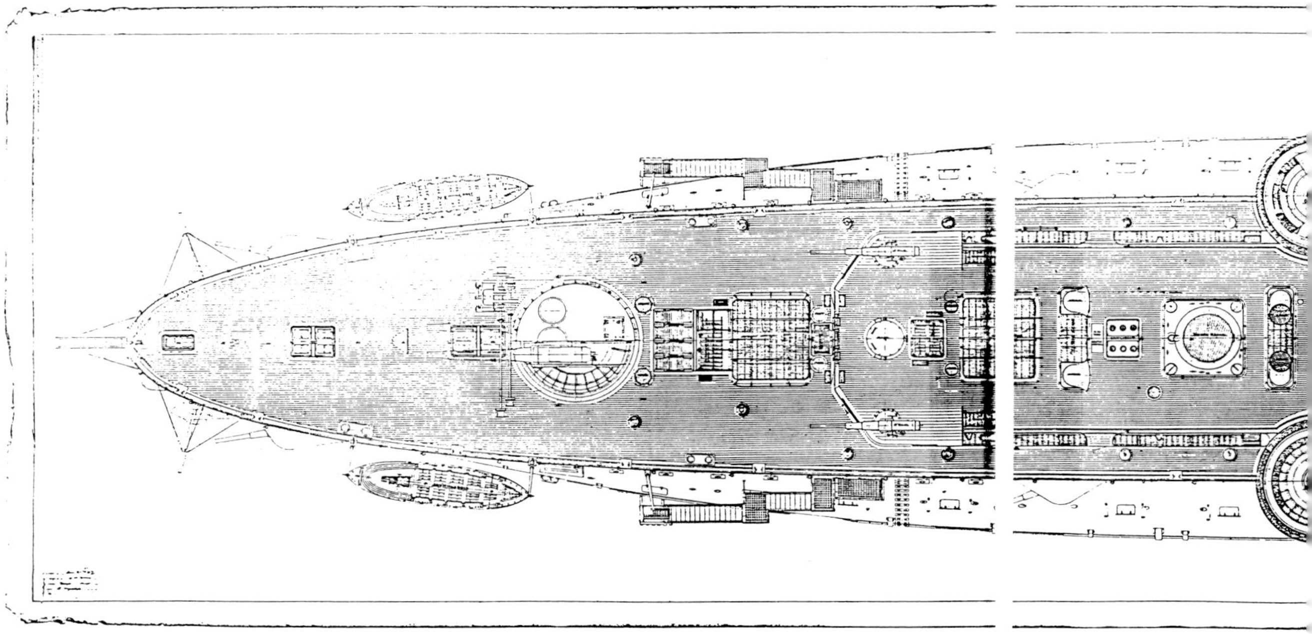

*Original Navy plan of main deck.* (US National Archives)

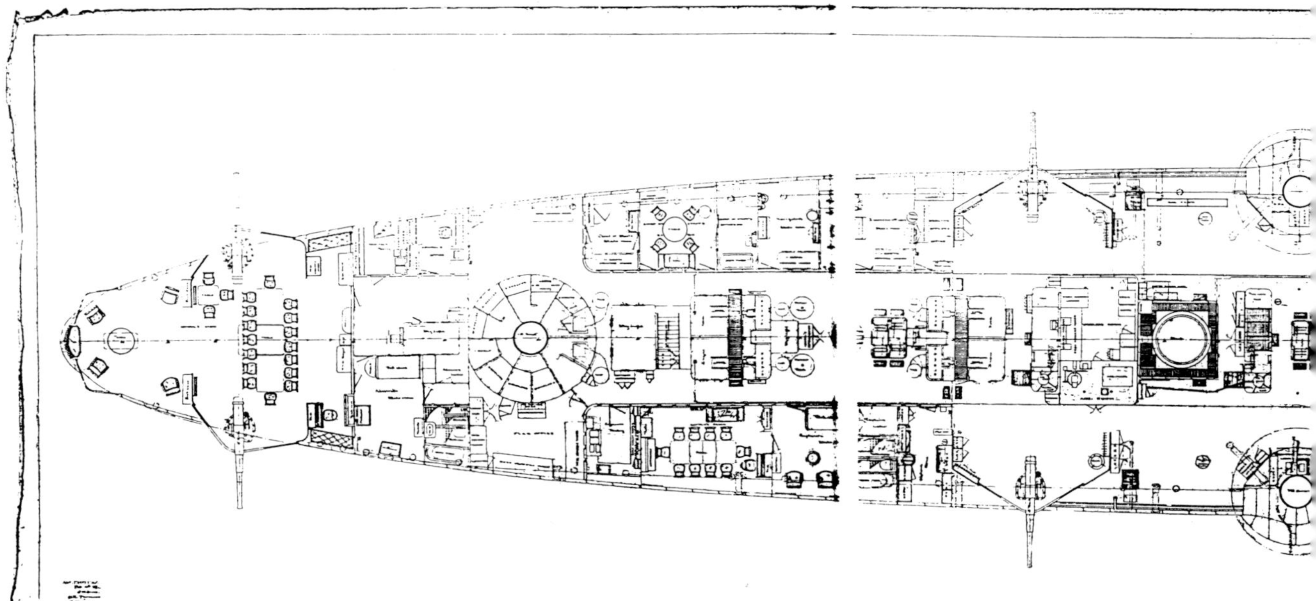

*Gun deck plan. Visible is the layout of the* Brooklyn*'s 5in gun sponsons and light armour shields.* (US National Archives)

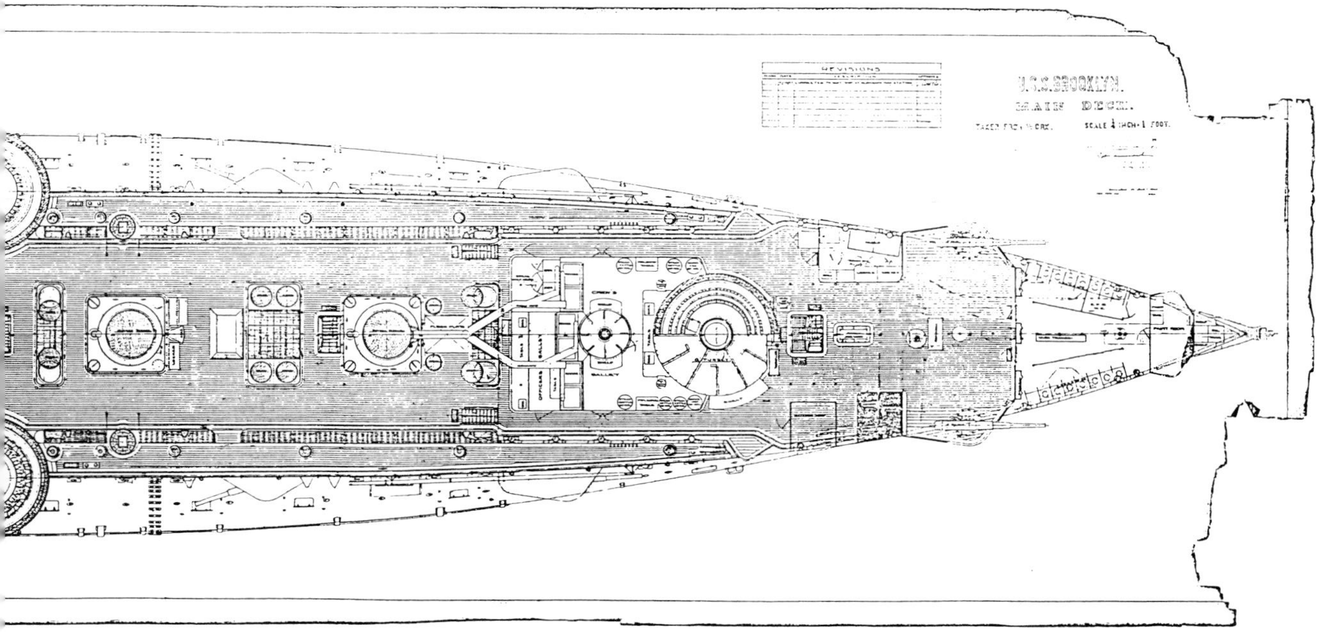

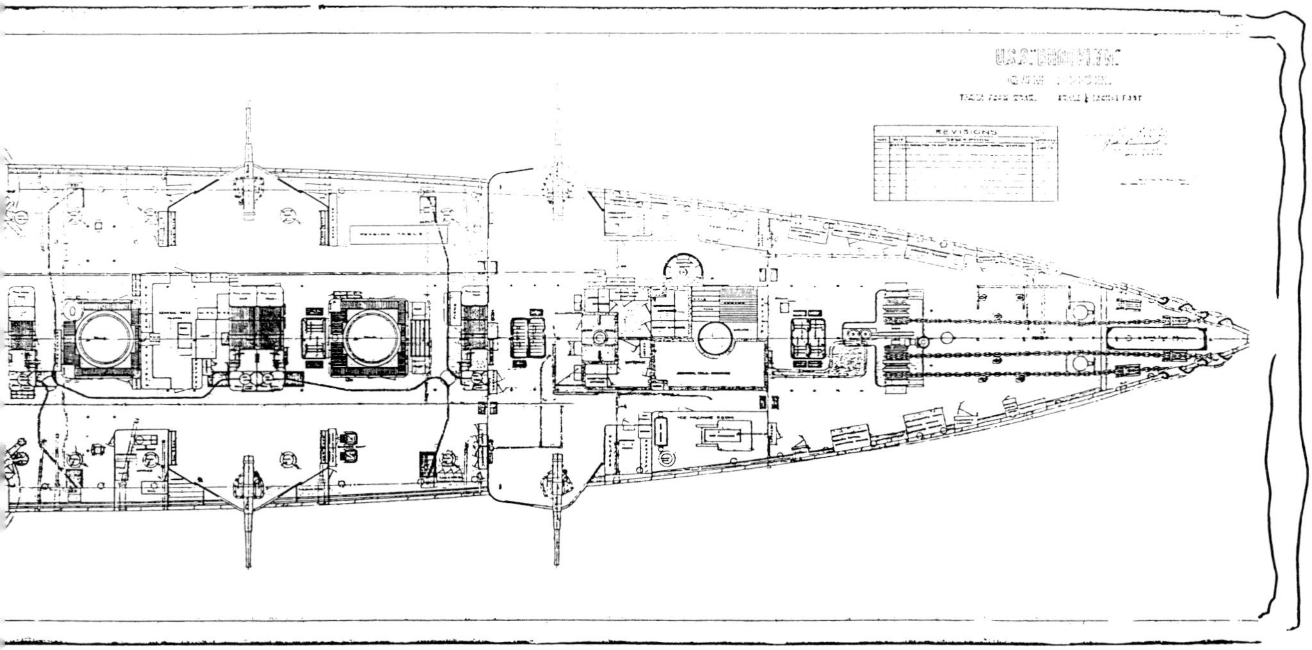

Brooklyn's *stern 8in gun turret and emergency steering gear.* (Library of Congress)

## Armour

Despite their name, armoured cruisers were only lightly protected, with allocations of armour much less than that of battleships. The armour was arranged to give maximum protection against shell fire from weapons equal to or less powerful than those carried aboard. Should she meet an equal she could stand and fight; should she meet a more powerful ship such as a battleship, her superior speed would carry her safely away.

The bands of side armour, which reached 4ft above and 4ft below the 24ft waterline, extended 194ft along the sides but were just 3in thick. This armour was intended to protect against shots entering the machinery or ammunition storage areas.

The *Brooklyn*, as did most battleships, had an armoured cap covering virtually the entire ship just above the waterline. This cap, known as a protective deck, extended the full length of the ship and was supported by heavy beams. Below it was the propelling machinery, steering gear, magazines, shell rooms, and most other vitals of the warship. It was flat over most of the ship and sloped down near the edges to meet the ship at the bottom of the side armour. The flat portions of the protective deck were at waterline level and were 3in thick. The sloped areas met the sides of the ship some 5ft 6in below the waterline, and were 6in thick. The armour on the sloped portions was heavier to protect from side penetrations in those days before plunging shot.

The turrets were armoured with 5½in on the sides, and the barbettes surrounding the turrets were 8in thick in front, 4in at the back. All these armour plates were of a nickel steel hardened with a process known as Harveyizing, a face hardening method named after its inventor. The 5in gun sponsons were armoured with 4in thick plates. For further protection against fragments from shells exploding between decks, splinter bulkheads 1½in thick were worked between the 5in gun stations.

The conning tower, located just below the charthouse, was made of forged steel 7½in thick. An armoured shaft, for voice tubes and electrical cable, lead from the conning tower into the forward handling room and was armoured with 5in of steel.

## Machinery

In the years before *Dreadnought* introduced the turbine engine, the standard high performance engine was of the vertical triple expansion type. The *Brooklyn* had four

▲
*The* Brooklyn *during the fleet review in New York harbour in 1898. Near sister-ship* USS New York *in the background.* (US Naval Historical photo)

*Starboard view of* Brooklyn *with steam cutter pulling away. Note the peacetime colour scheme.* (US National Archives photo)
▼

such engines in separate rooms, two for each shaft. The two engines which drove each shaft were mounted in such a way that one engine could be disconnected. This was of great value when steaming at slow speeds, or any time when stoking furnaces in all boilers was unpractical. However, this had a serious downside. In order to re-couple the engines, the ship had to stop engines – a difficulty in battle. This nearly caused embarrassment during the battle of Santiago de Cuba, when the Spanish unexpectedly fled and the ship could not pause to couple the engines.

There were seven boilers, placed in three compartments. Five were double-ended and two were single-ended. In each end of the double-ended boilers there were five furnaces, with five total in the single-ended boilers – under full power, there were some sixty furnaces being stoked! The boilers were 16ft 3in in diameter and the longest was nearly 20ft long. Steam pressure was 160psi. Mechanical shaking grates were mounted in each furnace to improve the removal of ash from the fires. The smoke pipes attached to each boiler were routed to the three distinctive funnels on the *Brooklyn*. These were more than 100ft high and were the tallest in the navy. Firebox draught was said to be noticeably improved with these high stacks.

Up to this time, turrets had been turned by either steam or hydraulic power. Steam was the most popular, but the vulnerability of steam lines, the heat generated, and the difficulties of fine control made it less than ideal. Electric motors were suggested as an alternative, and the *Brooklyn* became a trial case, with a head to head test of the two competing methods. The forward and starboard turrets were turned by electicity, and the port and after turrets by steam. The many advantages of electric power were quickly evident and the navy made a permanent switch to electric power in turrets after the results were in. In addition to the four main engines, there were a total of 77 additional steam engines on the *Brooklyn* running everything from ash hoists to an ice machine, distillers, and boat cranes.

With all machinery working, the *Brooklyn* was very fast for her day. During her speed trial over the Government official trial course off Cape Ann, Massachusetts, she covered 83 nautical miles in less than 4 hours, with a trial speed of nearly 22kts.

## Boats

The *Brooklyn* carried some thirteen boats plus two side cleaning punts. The largest boats carried were 33ft in length, and she carried two, a steam launch and a sailing launch. Also carried was a 30ft steam cutter, two 30ft whaleboats, one 30ft whaleboat gig, one 30ft barge, four 28ft sailing cutters, two 20ft dinghies, and the two punts. Eight boats were carried on davits located at the bow, waist and aft; five were stowed on skids over the superstructure deck, and the two punts were stored on either the deck or on skids. The boats stored on the skids were lowered into the water via the large gooseneck cranes located amidships both port and starboard.

## Career

The *Brooklyn*, designated AC-3, was launched on 2 October 1895, and commissioned on 1 December 1896, with Captain F A Cook in command. Her first voyage was to Great Britain with representatives of the United States for the Diamond Jubilee of Queen Victoria. Returning to US waters, she soon became flagship of the Flying Squadron under Commodore W S Schley, on 28 March 1898.

Upon war with Spain, the Flying Squadron joined Admiral Sampson's fleet. The Americans had blockaded a weak Spanish fleet, under Admiral Cervera, in the port of Santiago, Cuba. Advancing ground forces armed with artillery eventually forced the Spanish to leave, and at 0930 on 3 July they steamed out in a desperate attempt to escape.

It was a Sunday morning and sailors aboard the *Brooklyn* were preparing for an inspecton. In the ensuing excitement and confusion, the *Brooklyn* nearly rammed the USS *Texas* as she steered a course West, parallel to the escaping Spanish. As the lead ship that day, the *Brooklyn* was instrumental in destroying the enemy fleet, which consisted of four armoured cruisers and two torpedo-gunboats. A fifth cruiser was destroyed the next day. Although struck over 20 times, there was little real damage to the *Brooklyn* and the only American death was a man aboard her. In contrast, the Spanish lost 350 men killed. With this overwhelming victory, the naval war was over.

A few more high points marked the rest of the *Brooklyn*'s career. In 1902 she was in Havana, Cuba for the ceremonies to transfer the authority of that Island from the United States Government to the Cuban Government. In 1905 she returned from France the remains of the American naval hero John Paul Jones. In 1907 she was part of the display at the Jamestown Exposition, in Jamestown, Virginia. By the First World War she was totally unsuited for warfare, and played only a minor role in Asian waters. Taken out of commission in March 1921, she was sold on 20 December 1921.

**Sources**

*Conway's All the World's Fighting Ships 1860–1905* (Conway Maritime Press, London 1979).

*Dictionary of American Naval Fighting Ships* (Naval History Division, Navy Department, Washington 1959).

*Journal of the American Society of Naval Engineers*, 8 (August 1896).

Library of Congress, Washington DC 20540 (for photos).

National Archives, Record Group 19, Cartographic & Architectural Branch, Washington DC 20408 (for plans).

Naval Historical Center, Washington Navy Yard, Washington DC 20374 (for photos).

Still Pictures Branch (NNSP), National Archives, Washington DC 20408 (for photos).

*Transactions of the Society of Naval Architects and Marine Engineers* (1893 edition).

*Annual Report of the Secretary of the Navy* (Government Printing Office, Washington, DC 1898).

Ivan Musicant, *US Armored Cruisers*, (Naval Institute Press, Annapolis 1989).

*USS* Brooklyn *leading naval parade at New York, following return of the fleet from Cuban waters in August 1898.* (US Naval Historical Center)

*The* Brooklyn, *in peacetime colours, being assisted into drydock about 1902.* (US National Archives)

*Stern quarter of* Brooklyn *in 1898, flying the one-star flag of Commodore Schley.* (US Naval Historical Center)

*In drydock in 1898. Note the precarious and very dangerous position of workmen cleaning the side.* (US Naval Historical photo)

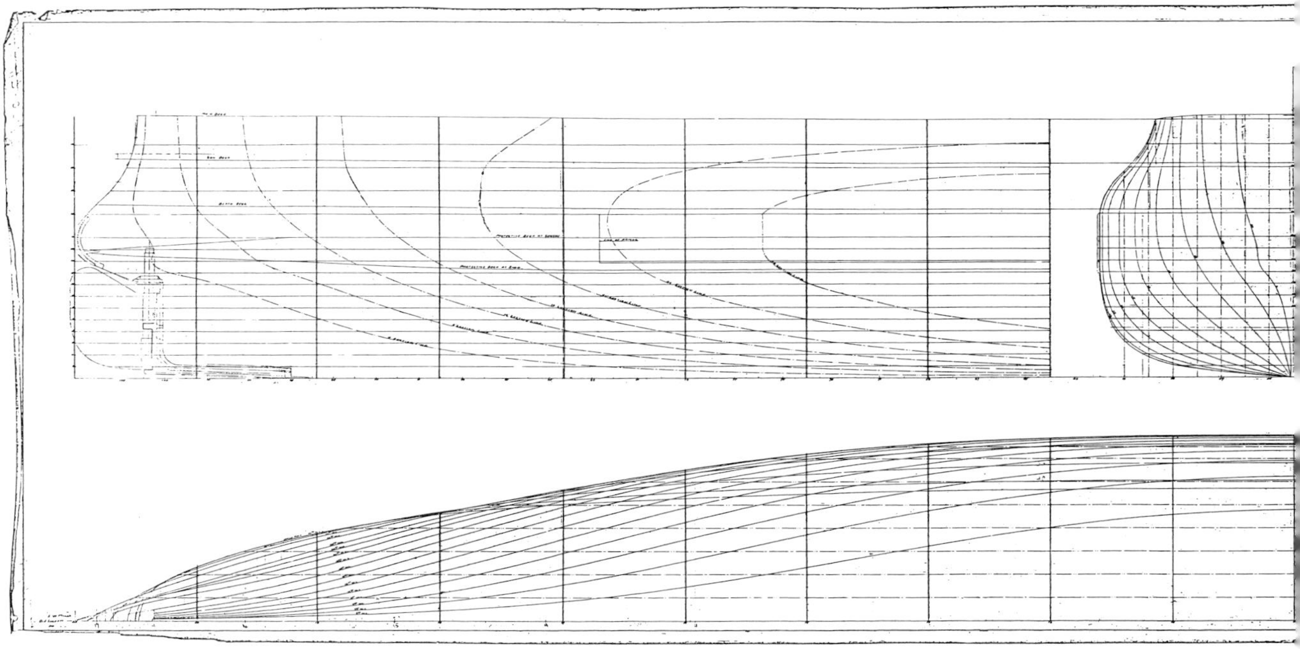

*Original US Navy sheer, half-breadth, and body plan.* (US National Archives)

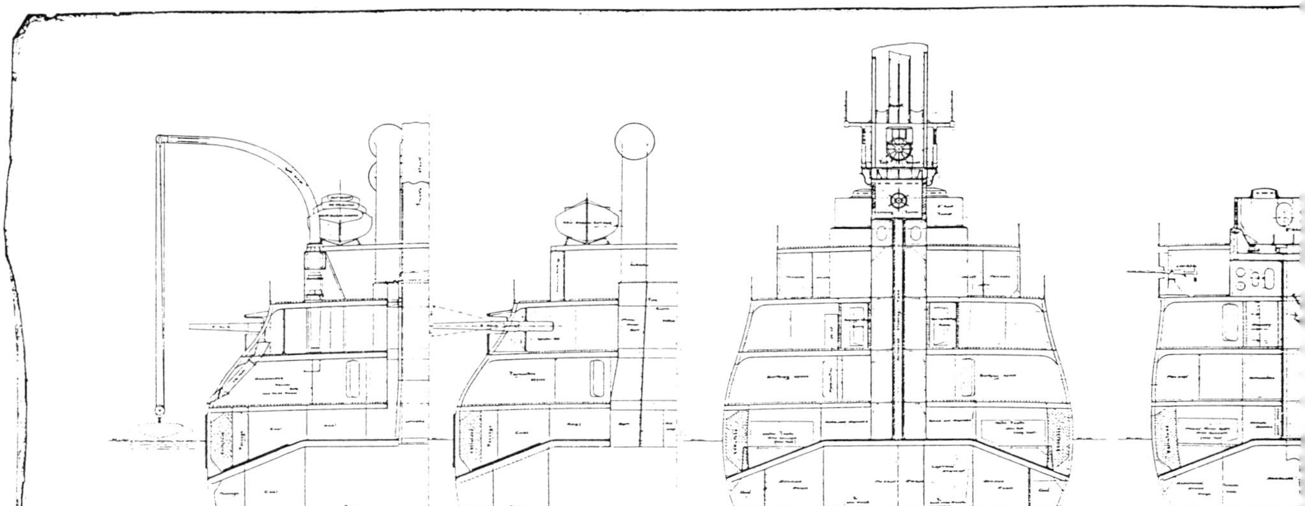

*Original plan of 'US Armored Cruiser No 3' with 'cross sections at numerous frames'.* (US National Archives)

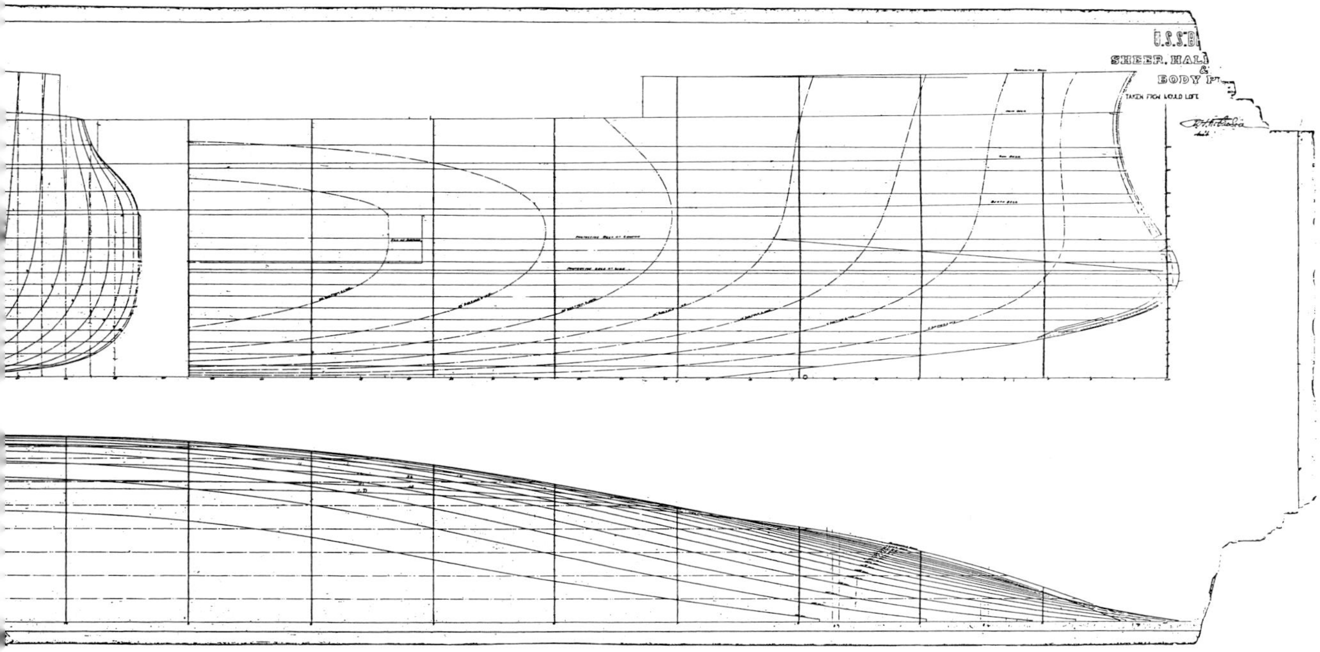
TAKEN FROM MOULD LOFT

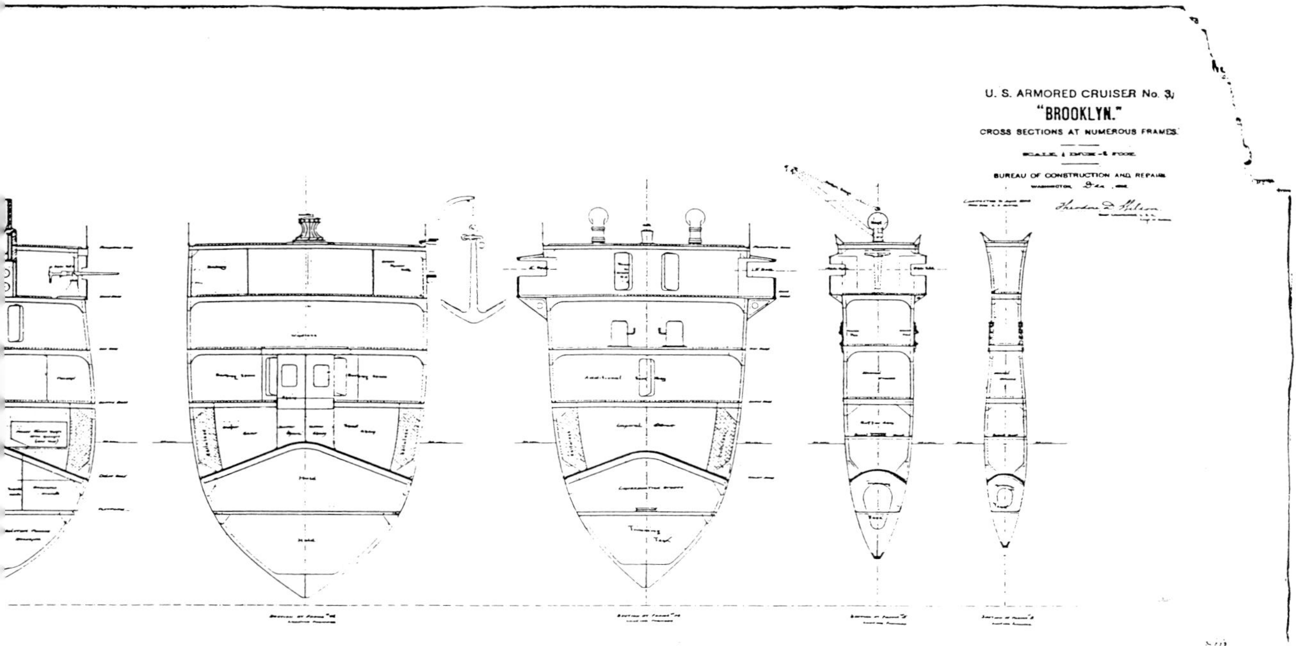
U. S. ARMORED CRUISER No. 3.
"BROOKLYN."
CROSS SECTIONS AT NUMEROUS FRAMES.
BUREAU OF CONSTRUCTION AND REPAIR

# BRITISH 'M' CLASS DESTROYERS OF 1913–14

Although most attention has been reserved for the 'Tribal's at the beginning and the 'V&W's at the end of the Great War, in reality the workhorses of the British fleet were the 'M's. The nearest thing to a war-standard design, this important, numerous (and varied) class is profiled by Keith McBride.

THE first British torpedo boat destroyers, the '27-knotters' of 1893–95, and their immediate successors, the '30-knotters' of 1897, were not built in classes. The Admiralty laid down very broad characteristics and left a great deal of freedom to the builders, of whom the leaders – Yarrow, Thornycroft and J S White – were in many respects the originators of the type. Abroad, such builders as Normand and Herreshoff filled a similar role. It was not until 1913 that a division into alphabetical classes was made; the few '27-knotters' becoming the 'A's, the '30-knotters' becoming the 'B's, 'C's and 'D's. The 1911–12 destroyers became the 'K's[1]; a set of 'K' names, some rather silly, was drawn up but not adopted. Tonnage had by now grown to 898/1000 tons compared with about 275 tons for the earliest boats.

The 'K's benefited from extensive weapon tests against torpedo craft, carrying three 4in on the centreline; the original proposal was for two 4in and four or five 12pdrs. Other innovations were spare torpedoes for the two tubes and an increase of speed to 29–32kts.

The order of priority laid down for them by the Captain Superintendent of Torpedo Boat Destroyers (CSTBD) – in effect the Admiralty 'Destroyer Desk Officer' – ran: good gun armament, speed and seaworthiness, low cost, good radius of action. He doubted if destroyers could steam at 30kts on one day in three in the North Sea.

## *Status*

Even at this late stage, destroyers were still not regarded as 'ships', but considered rather as MTBs or landing craft were in the Second World War. Their officers were considered as a sort of naval hippies, who wore seaboots, went ashore every afternoon, married early, and paid insufficient attention to the Great God Gunnery. One big ship officer was heard to refer to his destroyer colleagues as 'Decent enough fellows, but socially quite impossible'. Thereafter, the destroyer men delighted to refer to themselves as the SQIs. A further mark of the lowly status of destroyers was that the Sovereign did not have to be consulted about their names, nor were they christened, though sometimes the builders would lay on a meal for the shipyard workers, crew, relatives and visitors.

Peterel, *a Palmer-built '30-knotter' of 1899 reclassified as the 'B' class (four funnels); other '30-knotters' became the 'C' class (three funnels) and 'D' class (two funnels).* (CMP)

Sheldrake, *a Denny-built 'H' class boat during the war.* (CMP)

## 'Admiralties' and 'Specials'

From the 'H's of 1909–10 onward, an 'Admiralty' design was drawn up annually for the use of 'Good Ordinary Builders' (bad ordinary builders would not have been let loose on destroyers; nor was any destroyer built in a Royal Dockyard before the 1930s!) but, from the following year, the leading builders were allowed to build 'Specials', variations on the 'Admiralty' theme, for which they set and guaranteed their own performance figures, trying their utmost to outdo one another and the DNC's Office.

## 1912 – Churchill and Fisher

By the time plans were being drawn up for the 1912–13 Programme, Winston Churchill was First Lord and was much under the influence of Lord Fisher, who, of course, wanted more speed. First thoughts were of a reduced version of the 1909–10 *Acorns*, the most recent boats completed, but soon the idea of an improved 'K' took over. Gun armament and speed – 29kts trial – remained unchanged from the 'K's. However, it was felt that it was better to have all torpedoes 'up the spout' and ready to fire. Twin tubes, which had been used in 14in calibre in some torpedo-boats, were therefore reintroduced for the 'L' class.

## Naming policy

A random collection of traditional names was prepared for the 'L's, as for previous destroyers. These suggested speed and liveliness and many came from Shakespeare and Scott, but soon after completion they were given alphabetical ones, the first time this was actually done for destroyers.

The 'L's fell into two groups: the two-funnelled, derivatives of the 'K Special' *Ardent*, and the three-funnelled boats based on the 'K Special' *Fortune*, both lost at Jutland. The former had longitudinal framing, but came out heavy, so the 'L's reverted to the transverse arrangement; longitudinal framing did not reappear till the 'J's of 1936. Speed went up to about 29½kts in practice, a trifle faster than the 'K's. They were laid down early in the financial year, and were in service as the 3rd Destroyer Flotilla at the outbreak of war. *Lance* was delivered on 1 August and fired the first British shot of the war at the *Koningin Luise* on the 5th. On 29th August, crowds were waiting at Harwich to cheer in the victors – including the 'L's – of the previous day's Battle of Heligoland. The first recipients of their enthusiasm were the *Meteor* and *Miranda*, straight from the builders. The 'M's had arrived.

Laurel, *a two-funnelled 'L', built by J S White.* (CMP)

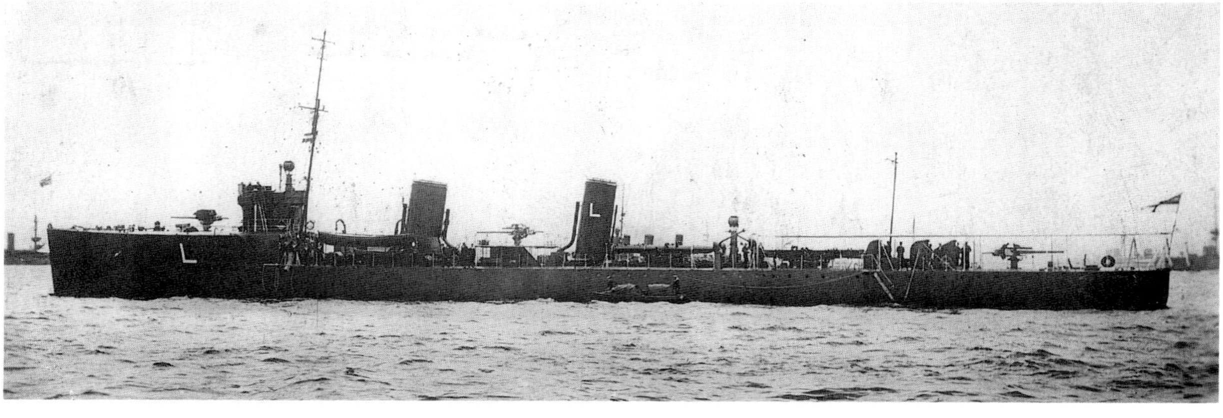

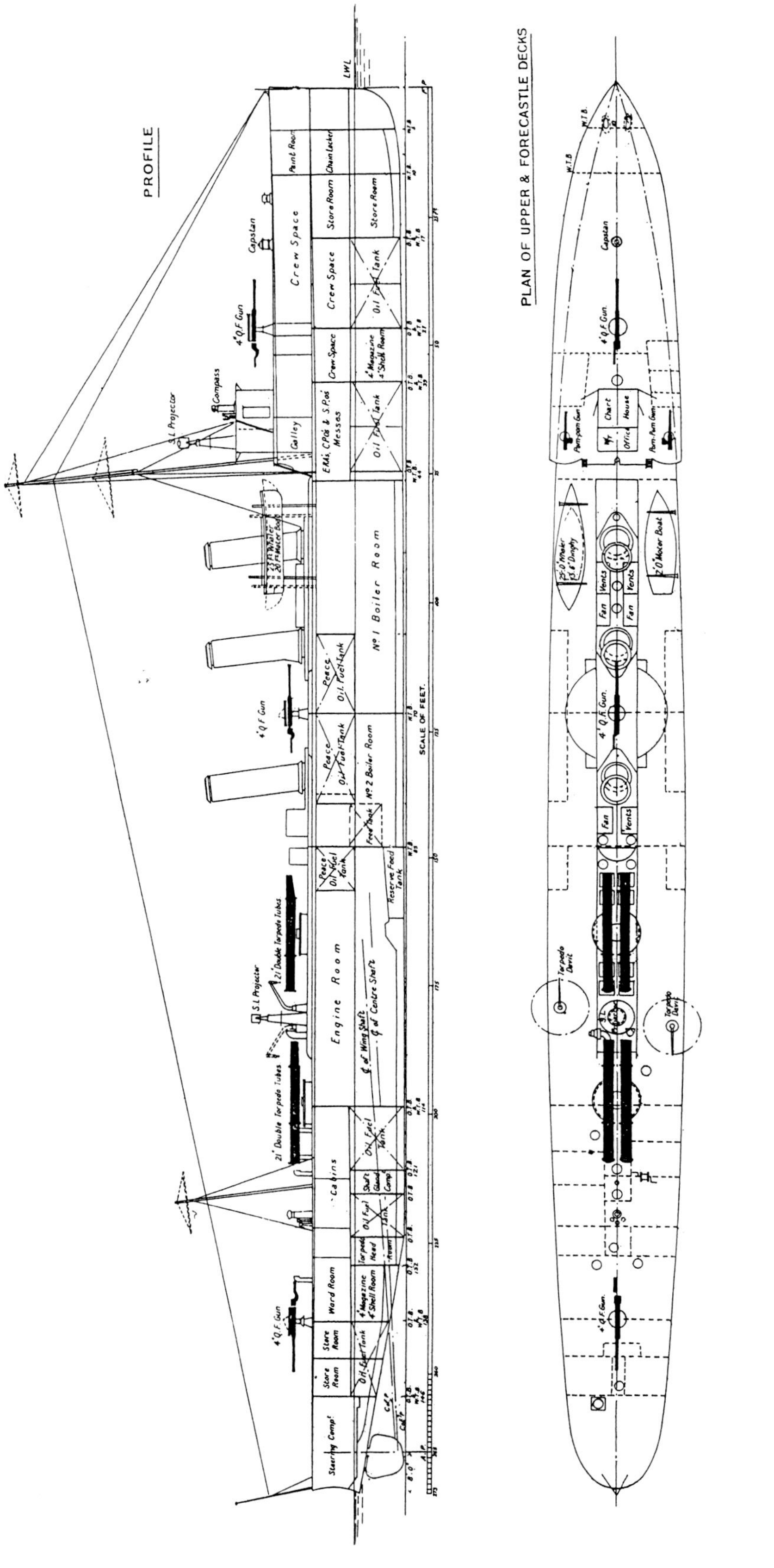


*General arrangement of the Admiralty 'M' class.* (RINA Transactions 1919)

## *Design of the 'M's*

Design work on the 'M's began in June 1912, by which time further news of the high speed – both 'trial' and 'service' – of German destroyers had been received. Detailed figures showed that ARA *Tucuman*, built by Schichau for the Argentine Navy, had done 34.53kts over six hours in deep water, and 36.4 in shallow. It was felt that the 'L' armament was adequate, but that 34 to 36kts on trial were needed. Winston Churchill wrote 'I cannot say how important this matter seems to be', but in fact, in *The World Crisis* he seems to have confused the 'L's and the faster 'M's. Top priority went to battleships and light cruisers so funds for destroyers were short.

The Controller, Sir Archibald Moore, wanted more 'Specials', to exploit the skills of the leading builders, and also an 'Admiralty' design for the 'good ordinary ones'; but his intentions were not clear initially. At first a 275ft design with 33,000shp was considered; the Engineer-in-Chief advised that this power would require 490 tons machinery weight while 30,000shp would need 455 tons, against 375 for 24,500 in the 'L's (according to the 'cube law', something like 40,000shp would be required to drive an 'L' at 34kts.)

Apart from the shortage of funds, it seems that early model tests were unpromising. Meetings took place on 22 July and 14 August to consider the problem. A further one, referred to by the DNC staff in anticipation as a 'performance', was set for the 21st. There had been much discussion of the very light and fast Yarrow Special 'I' *Firedrake*, on trial but not yet delivered, which gained great speed from her light hull and high propulsive coefficient. However, Mr Pethick, the head of the destroyer design section, doubted if others could duplicate Yarrow's success.

The meeting decided to reduce requirements, and to revert to the 'K's' triple-screw, 24,500shp machinery, which was more economical and might produce more power than twin screws. A fudge factor was introduced by reducing the trial fuel load to 75 tons from 150 and the trial to six hours from eight, for a displacement of 880 tons at the start of the trial. Length was reduced from 275ft to 265ft for the 'Admiralty' design and the whole ship scaled down accordingly. Freeboard at the bow was only 15ft 1in against 16ft 3in in the 'L's. A trial speed of 33½/34kts and a radius of action of 2200nm at 15kts were called for, which would require 250 tons fuel capacity. It was hoped to carry the reserve feed water below the boilers and fuel below the engines. Steering was to be improved and scantlings were to be to recent Admiralty standards, not the *Firedrake*'s lighter ones. The 'Admiralty' design was to be pencilled in by the end of September, so that the 'Special' builders could order parts and set up framing. No money could be paid until after the 1913–14 Naval Estimates were passed in March 1913, and in theory the builders would be laying down boats 'on spec'. They were allowed to retain 275ft length and would it was hoped, exceed the required speed.

Various modifications to the 'Admiralty' design inevitably followed; the turbine change allowed the dynamo to be moved into the engine room, which permitted the ERA's mess to be moved away from the officers' accommodation, a drying room and a cabin to accommodate a sick or badly injured man were provided, as well as space for an extra Petty Officer. By adding 3in to hull depth, arching of the beams was avoided over all but the foremost boiler. Because of the fan power required, the coaming over the boilers had to be enlarged. However, hammock space remained at 18in, despite hopes of 20in. Curiously, eight weeks' provisions were carried against a month's for big ships – possibly destroyers were expected to spend a lot of time in out-of-the-way ports.

By great efforts, the 'Admiralty' sketch design was ready by 20 September; trial displacement was expected to be 870/880 tons, and 950 tons in service. The double floating dock at Harwich, the main destroyer base, had 1920 tons lift, so in order to dock two at a time meant a maximum of 960 tons. The 'Admiralty' design was passed on to Yarrow, Thornycroft and for the first and last time, to Hawthorn Leslie, for guidance. J S White received no orders, possibly because they were busy with flotilla leaders for Chile, which eventually became the *Broke* class.

## *The 'M' 'Specials' and the Admiralty 'M's*

The 'Specials' comprised three two-funnelled Yarrows with longer forecastles; two Thornycrofts with three rounded funnels, the centre one being noticeably thicker, and a higher freeboard; and the two Hawthorn Leslies, *Mansfield* and *Mentor*, the last four-funnelled destroyers to be ordered for the RN, though not, of course, the last to serve in it.

After 1 April 1913, nine 'Admiralties' (later reduced to six for lack of funds) and, for the first time, two 'Leaders' were authorized. In general, the 'M's were faster editions of the 'L's. The triple-screw direct-drive turbines, with geared cruising turbines on the outer shafts, were expected to give a little more power than in the 'K's. Stresses were higher than expected and exceeded those in the 'L's, but the 'M's proved notably tough ships. The machinery spaces were 119ft long, and it was thought that the ships would float with the engine room and one boiler room open to the sea. This would mean 140ft of the upper deck being submerged. The double boiler room was placed forward of the single one to reduce the effect of a hit near the forward engine room bulkhead.

## *War and mass construction*

For the 1914–15 estimates, serious consideration was given to the 750-ton *New Firedrake*; not until August, after the outbreak of war, did Winston Churchill authorize a further batch of 'M's; sixteen 'Admiralties' and four Yarrows. This was actually earlier than the normal peacetime building cycle and the eight 'Admiralties' with cruising turbines were probably 'peacetime' with the others forming part of the first wartime order. Yarrow laid down an 'M' 'on spec' *after* the outbreak of war, for lack of work, but this situation (partly due to the 'M's being delivered well ahead of schedule) soon changed. The need for destroyers exceeded all expectations, and batch after batch were laid down.

*A Thornycroft 'Special'*, Patrician, *launched in 1916.* (CMP)

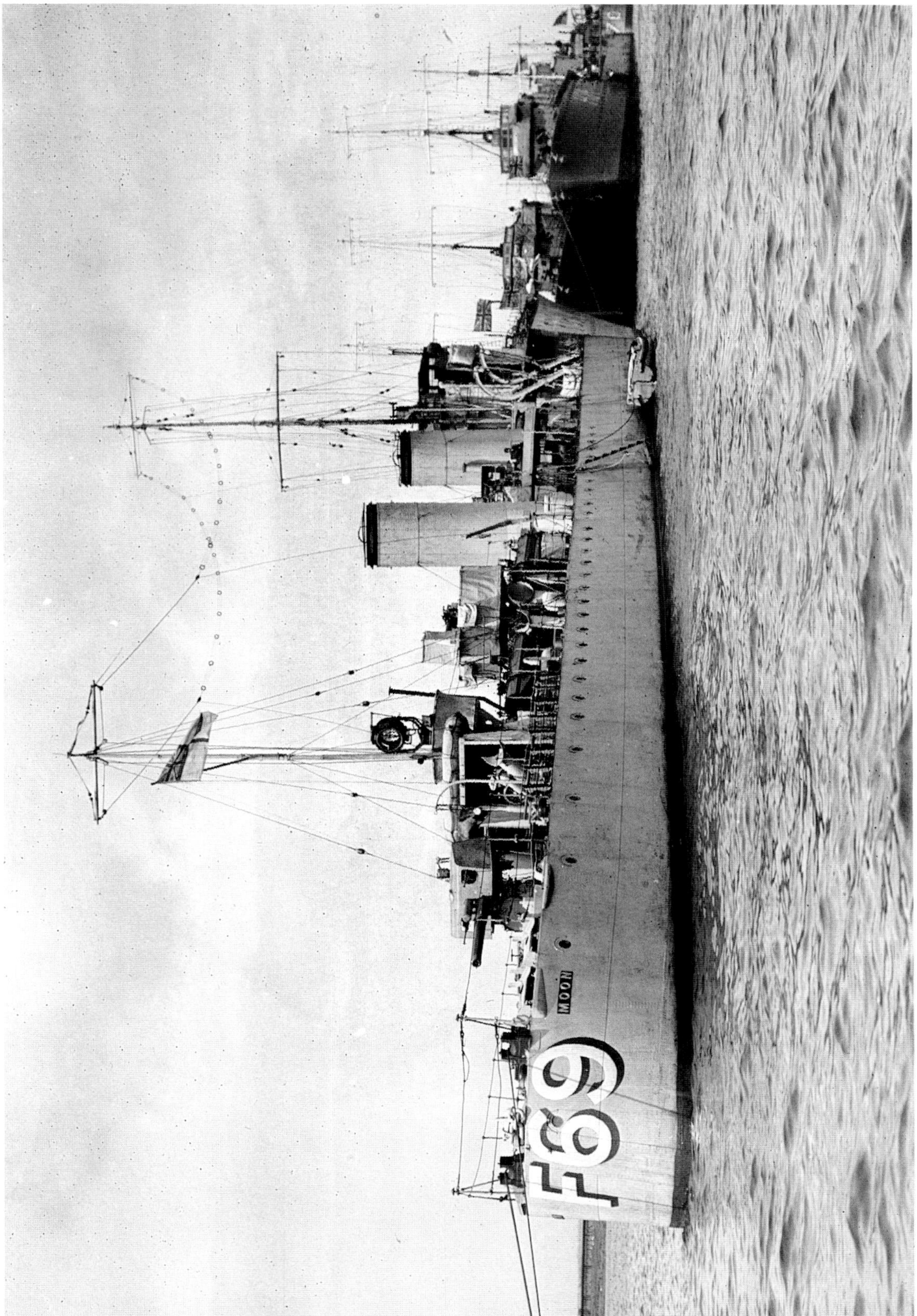


*One of four Yarrow 'Specials', the* Moon. (National Maritime Museum)

Meteor, *one of the two Thornycroft 'Specials'; possibly a commissioning portrait.* (National Maritime Museum)

Marmion, *Repeat 'M', of the first order (September 1914).* (CMP)

As more 'M's came from the builders, they joined the Grand Fleet and Battlecruiser Force. By the time of Jutland, two of the four Grand Fleet flotillas, the 11th and 12th, and the Battlecruiser Force's 13th, were made up of 'M's. Of the 78 British destroyers and flotilla leaders present, 37 were 'Admiralty' and 4 Yarrow 'M's. Their extra speed proved vital in the battle, especially when working with battlecruisers. The 'I's of the 1st Flotilla, which accompanied the *Queen Elizabeths* to Jutland, and even the 'L's, proved too slow and accomplished little. Of the 'M' flotillas, the 13th made a determined attack on the German battlecruisers, fighting a fierce mini-battle with the German IX flotilla and their supporting craft, the 11th protected the van of the battlefleet and helped to repel German destroyer attacks, while the 12th guarded the rear. During the night, the 11th and 13th encountered the enemy without much success. The 12th, thrown off course by the wandering 13th, sighted the German battleships at daybreak, when their searchlights were ineffective, attacked, and blew up the *Pommern*. The German official historian, who was present, wrote that this showed what a well-organized destroyer attack could do.

Two 13th Flotilla 'M's, the *Nestor* and *Nomad*, were lost, hit in the machinery spaces during the attack on the German battlecruisers and finished off by the German battleships. Several 'M's were damaged, but in return they accounted for the *Pommern, V-27, V-29* and possibly the *V-4*, claimed shares in the *Weisbaden* and *V-48*, and made a torpedo hit on the *Seydlitz*.

could reach. The builders accomplished prodigies, many boats being delivered well ahead of schedule in spite of shortages of skilled labour and much else.

Many of the highly skilled prewar craftsmen had joined up or been conscripted, of whom thousands died in the mud of Flanders. The 'diluted' wartime workers did their best and in general their handiwork stood up well to the raging of the sea and the violence of the enemy. There were complaints of bad workmanship and finish, but these do not seem to have been serious. Galvanizing was omitted in many cases, for lack of skilled staff. Beardmore's had to finish three boats after the firm of A Stephen proved unable to do so, but this was unique.

## *Wartime experience*

As early as January 1915, the 'M's extra speed came into use; at the Dogger Bank, seven of them pushed well ahead of the speeding British battlecruisers, to protect them from German destroyers, and got close enough to be driven off by the *Blücher*'s secondary battery. A torpedo attack from astern would have been futile, and the North Sea wasn't big enough for them to overtake. In the final stage, they helped to finish off the *Blücher*, *Meteor* receiving an 8.2in hit in her boiler room.

Nicator, *an Admiralty Repeat 'M', from the same batch as* Offa. (National Maritime Museum)

It was decided to standardise on the 'M' design for wartime construction; as a curious sidelight on conditions, the production of actual drawings was slow and laborious. It happened that Beardmore still had sets of 'L' plans so to save time they were ordered to build two repeat 'L's, *Lochinvar* and *Lassoo*, while additional 'M' plans were being prepared. If more of the builders had retained the 'L' plans, would the 'L's have become the standard wartime type?

## *The Greek 'M's*

Four Greek 'M's, differing in their boiler room arrangements, were taken over from the builders, and were given classical names. Four Hawthorn Leslie boats, allegedly for Turkey and hence potential enemies of the Greek 'M's, but probably laid down 'on spec', were also taken over; they were enlarged 'M's with extra guns, and were given 'T' names.

Nine additional 'Admiralties' and one Yarrow were ordered in November 1914, twenty-two 'Admiralties' at the end of that month and forty in the spring of 1915. Some had cruising turbines and some not; their lack was severely felt. Prewar, the specified endurance had been eight hours at full speed and 2000 miles at 15kts, which proved totally inadequate. The submarine menace proved even worse than had been feared and required an escort for battleships and cruisers in any area which submarines

Offa, *another Repeat 'M', of the February 1915 fourth order.* (CMP)

Lightfoot *towing* Medusa *(an ex-Greek 'M') on 25 March 1916 after her collision with* Laverock*; she had to be abandoned and later sank. The incident is described by 'Taffrail', whose* Murray *was in company.* (National Maritime Museum)

## The 'M' class
*TECHNICAL AND CONSTRUCTION DATA*

*1913–14 'Admiralties'*
265ft bp, 273ft 4in oa × 26ft 8in × 16ft 3in hull depth, 900 tons trials displ.

Legend Weights: hull 368 tons, machinery 362 tons, oil 75 tons, armament 33½ tons, reserve feed water 15½ tons, general equipment 46 tons; total 900 tons.

| *Name* | *Builder* | *Displ* | *Launched* | *Cont Price(£)* | *Machinery* |
|---|---|---|---|---|---|
| Matchless | Swan Hunter | 1154 deep | 5 October 1914 | 118,581 | |
| Murray | Palmer | 806 light | 6 August 1914 | 115,260 | P |
| Myngs | Palmer | | 24 September 1914 | 113,524 | P |
| Milne | John Brown | | 5 October 1914 | 110,415 | |
| Moorsom | John Brown | | 20 December 1914 | 107,490 | BC |
| Morris | John Brown | | 19 November 1914 | 106,710 | BC |

*1913–14 'Specials'*
265ft bp, 271ft 6in oa × 27ft × 16ft 9in depth, 1055 tons trials, 27,000shp, 750 revs, twin screws, 4 Yarrow boilers, 250psi, 35kts.

| | | | | | |
|---|---|---|---|---|---|
| Mansfield | Hawthorn Leslie | 1055 | 3 December 1914 | 125,882 | P |
| Mentor | Hawthorn Leslie | 1037 | 21 August 1914 | 126,952 | P |

265ft bp, 274ft 3in oa × 27ft 3in × 16ft 9in depth, 980 tons trials, 26,500shp, 680 revs, twin screws, 4 Yarrow boilers, 250psi, 35kts, 2100nm at 15kts.

| | | | | | |
|---|---|---|---|---|---|
| Mastiff | Thornycroft | 985 | 5 September 1914 | 124,585 | P |
| Meteor | Thornycroft | 980 | 24 July 1914 | 127,060 | P |

260ft 3in bp, 269ft 6in oa × 25ft 7½in × 16ft 3in depth, 883 tons trials, 23,000shp, 635 revs, twin screws, 3 Yarrow boilers, 250psi, 35kts, 3060nm at 15kts, 278 tons oil.

| | | | | | |
|---|---|---|---|---|---|
| Miranda | Yarrow | 895 | 27 May 1914 | 132,646 | BC |
| Minos | Yarrow | 883 | | 125,021 | BC |
| Manly | Yarrow | 883 | | 118,221 | BC |

*First War Order (& 1914–15 Estimates ?), August – September 1914*

Cruising turbines only in Fairfield, Swan Hunter and J S White boats, no peace tanks, midships gun on bandstand, stem and ram cast in one piece. Barr & Stroud receivers and voice pipes at each gun, improved towing slips.

| *Name* | *Builder* | *Trials (tons)* | *Launch* | *Trials (kts)* | *Machinery/shp/revs* |
|---|---|---|---|---|---|
| Mons | John Brown | 890 | 1 May 1915 | 33.91 | BC/26,810/778.7 |
| Marne | John Brown | | 29 May 1915 | 34.152 | BC/?/739 |
| Mystic | Denny | 957 | 26 June 1915 | 33.41 | P/26,627/805 |
| Maenad | Denny | 962 | 10 August 1915 | 33.43 | P/26,901/732.1 |
| Manners | Fairfield | 886 | 15 June 1915 | 34.32 | BCGR/?/743.3 |
| Mandate | Fairfield | 980 | 27 April 1915 | 32.06 | BCGR/?/? |
| Magic | J S White | 1015 | 10 September 1915 | 33.5 | PGR/?/723 |
| Moresby | J S White | 1004 | 20 November 1915 | 33.7 | PGR/?/717 |
| Marmion | Swan Hunter | 1028 | 28 May 1915 | | P/?/708.7 |
| Martial | Swan Hunter | | 1 July 1915 | | P/?/? |
| Mary Rose | Swan Hunter | 1014 | 8 October 1915 | | BCGR/?/712.3 |
| Menace | Swan Hunter | | 9 November 1915 | | BCGR/?/? |
| Michael | Thornycroft | | 19 May 1915 | 33.54 | P/24,500/? |
| Milbrook | Thornycroft | 976 | 12 July 1915 | 32.75 | P/22,750/711.4 |
| Minion | Thornycroft | | 11 September 1915 | 33.88 | P/25,250/? |
| Munster | Thornycroft | | 24 November 1915 | 34 | P/25,000/? |

## The 'M' class
*TECHNICAL AND CONSTRUCTION DATA, CONTINUED*

*Yarrow Specials, August – September 1914*

Two funnels, sloping stern, raked stem 2ft longer.

| | | | | | |
|---|---|---|---|---|---|
| Moon | Yarrow | 776 | 23 April 1915 | 37.86 | ?BC/?/694.6 |
| Morning Star | Yarrow | 791 | 26 June 1915 | 36.73 | ?BC/?/663 |
| Mounsey | Yarrow | 826 | 11 September 1915 | 39.01 | ?BC/?/692.7 |
| Musketeer | Yarrow | 886 | 12 November 1915 | 35.61 | ?BC/?/680.5 |

*'Admiralties', Second Wartime Order, Early November 1915*

| | | | | | |
|---|---|---|---|---|---|
| Mameluke | John Brown | 955 | 14 August 1915 | 34.45 | BC/?/741 |
| Marvel | Denny | | 7 October 1915 | 32.44 | P/25,424/716.8 |
| Mischief | Fairfield | 890 | 12 October 1915 | 33.51 | BC/?/742 |
| Mindful | Fairfield | 911 | 24 August 1915 | 33.54 | BC/?/737 |
| Nonsuch | Palmer | 1026 | 8 December 1915 | | PGR/26,030/705 |
| Negro | Palmer | | 8 March 1916 | | PGR/?/? |
| Nessus | Swan Hunter | 1000 | 24 August 1915 | | P/25,280/726 |
| Nepean | Thornycroft | 992 | 22 January 1916 | 32.65 | PGR/?/738 |
| Nereus | Thornycroft | | 24 February 1916 | 35.47 | PGR/29,300/738 |

*Yarrow, Second Wartime Order, Early November 1914*

| | | | | | |
|---|---|---|---|---|---|
| Nerissa | Yarrow | 782m | 9 February 1916 | 36.63 | BC/?/701.8 |

*'Admiralties', Third Wartime Order, End November 1914*

| | | | | | |
|---|---|---|---|---|---|
| Noble | A Stephen | 948 | 25 November 1915 | 35.26 | BC/27,800/749.5 |
| Nizam | A Stephen | 925 | 6 April 1916 | 34.69 | BC/?/724.7 |
| Nomad | A Stephen | 918 | 7 February 1916 | 33.45 | BC/?/689.8 |

(Above three all finished by Beardmore, who built their engines)

| | | | | | |
|---|---|---|---|---|---|
| Nonpareil (Launching trouble) | A Stephen | | 16 May 1916 | | BC/?/? |
| Norman | Palmer | | 20 March 1916 | | PGR/?/? |
| Northesk | Palmer | | 20 March 1916 | | PGR/?/? |
| North Star | Palmer | | | | PGR/?/? |
| Nugent | Palmer | | 21 January 1917 | | PGR/?/? |
| Obedient | Scott | 937 | 5 November 1915 | 34.97 | P/?/769 |
| Obdurate | Scott | 950 | 21 January 1916 | 33.89 | P/?/745 |
| Onslaught | Fairfield | 940 | 4 December 1915 | 34.31 | BCGR/?/750.4 |
| Onslow | Fairfield | 920 | 15 February 1916 | 33.94 | BCGR/?/745 |
| Opal | Doxford | 1020 | 11 September 1915 | | P/?/701.6 |
| Ophelia | Doxford | | 13 October 1915 | | P/?/? |
| Opportune | Doxford | | 20 November 1915 | | P/?/? |
| Oracle | Doxford | | 23 December 1915 | | P/?/? |
| Orestes | Doxford | | 21 March 1916 | | P/?/? |
| Orford | Doxford | | 19 April 1916 | | P/?/? |
| Orpheus | Doxford | | 17 June 1916 | | P/?/? |
| Octavia | Doxford | | 21 June 1916 | | P/?/? |
| Ossory | John Brown | 943 | 9 October 1915 | 35.12 | BCGR/?/760 |
| Nestor | Swan Hunter | | 22 December 1915 | | BCGR |

## The 'M' class

*TECHNICAL AND CONSTRUCTION DATA, CONTINUED*

*Fourth Wartime Order, February 1915*

All raked stems except Scott's.

| | | | | | |
|---|---|---|---|---|---|
| Napier | John Brown | 948 | 27 November 1916 | 34.42 | BCGR/?/756 |
| Narborough | John Brown | 957 | 2 March 1916 | 34.7 | BCGR/?/758.4 |
| Narwhal | Denny | 963 | 3 December 1915 | 34.25 | PGR/28,214/771.5 |
| Nicator | Denny | 954 | 3 February 1916 | 35.44 | PGR/28,569/792.2 |
| Norseman | Doxford | | 15 August 1916 | | P/?/? |
| Oberon | Doxford | | 29 September 1916 | | P/?/? |
| Observer | Fairfield | | 1 May 1916 | | BCGR/?/? |
| Offa | Fairfield | | 7 June 1916 | | BCGR/?/? |
| Orcadia | Fairfield | | 26 July 1916 | | BCGR/?/? |
| Oriana | Fairfield | | 23 September 1916 | | BCGR/?/? |
| Oriole | Palmer | | 31 July 1916 | | PGR/?/? |
| Osiris | Palmer | | 26 September 1916 | | PGR/?/? |
| Paladin | Scott | 914 | 27 March 1916 | 33.88 | PGR/?/745.4 |
| Parthian | Scott | 938 | 21 April 1916 | 35.09 | PGR/?/768.1 |
| Partridge | Swan Hunter | | 4 March 1916 | | BCGR/?/? |
| Pasley | Swan Hunter | | 15 April 1916 | | BCGR/?/? |

*Thornycroft Specials, Ordered February 1915*

Straight stems.

| | | | | | |
|---|---|---|---|---|---|
| Patrician | Thornycroft | | 5 June 1916 | 35.6 | BC/32,125/? |
| Patriot | Thornycroft | | 20 April 1916 | 37.34 | BC/32,350/? |

*Fifth Wartime Order, May 1915*

| | | | | | |
|---|---|---|---|---|---|
| Plucky | Scott | 898 | 3 July 1916 | 33.97 | PGR/?/740.4 |
| Portia | Scott | 906 | 10 August 1916 | 34.83 | PGR/?/771.8 |
| Pheasant | Fairfield | | 23 October 1916 | | BCGR/?/? |
| Phoebe | Fairfield | | 20 November 1916 | | BCGR/?/? |
| Pigeon | Hawthorn Leslie | | 3 March 1916 | | P/?/? |
| Plover | Hawthorn Leslie | | 19 April 1916 | | P/?/? |
| Penn | John Brown | | 8 April 1916 | 34.0 | BCGR/?/746 |
| Peregrine | John Brown | | 29 May 1916 | 34.5 | BCGR/?/750 |
| Pelican | Beardmore | 950 | 18 March 1916 | 34.82 | P/?/746.8 |
| Pellew | Beardmore | | 18 May 1916 | | P/?/? |
| Petard | Denny | | 24 March 1916 | 35.32 | PGR/29,897/791.9 |
| Peyton | Denny | | 2 May 1916 | 35.83 | PGR/29,605/793.6 |
| Prince | A Stephen | | 26 July 1916 | | BC/?/? |
| Pylades | A Stephen | | 28 September 1916 | | BC/?/? |
| (completed by Beardmore) | | | | | |
| Medina | J S White | 937 | 8 March 1916 | 33.5 | P/?/745 |
| Medway | J S White | | 19 April 1916 | 33.5 | P/?/730 |

*Thornycroft Specials, Ordered May 1915*

| | | | | | |
|---|---|---|---|---|---|
| Rapid | Thornycroft | | 15 July 1916 | 35.46 | BC/28,900/? |
| Ready | Thornycroft | | 26 August 1916 | 34.37 | BC/?/? |

*Yarrow Specials, Ordered May 1915*

| | | | | | |
|---|---|---|---|---|---|
| Relentless | Yarrow | 774m | 15 April 1916 | 36.93 | BC/?/689 |
| Rival | Yarrow | 779m | 14 June 1916 | 36.83 | BC/?/657 |

## The 'M' class
*TECHNICAL AND CONSTRUCTION DATA, CONTINUED*

*The Greek 'M's*

Higher fore funnel, main topmasts, different boiler layout, different accommodation. 4in originally Mk VII QF on PXIII mountings; changed 1918 to Mk IV on PIX.

| | | | | |
|---|---|---|---|---|
| Medea ex-Crite | John Brown | 3 January 1915 | abt 33 | BC/25,893/749 |
| Medusa ex-Lesbos | John Brown | 27 March 1915 | abt 33 | BC/25,897/757 |
| Melampus ex-Chios | Fairfield | 16 December 1914 | | BC/?/? |
| Melpomene ex-Samos | Fairfield | 1 February 1915 | | BC/?/? |

Machinery notes
PGR = Parsons turbines with geared cruising turbines.
BCGR = Brown-Curtis turbines with geared cruising turbines.
P & BC = Parsons and Brown-Curtis turbines, respectively, without cruising turbines.

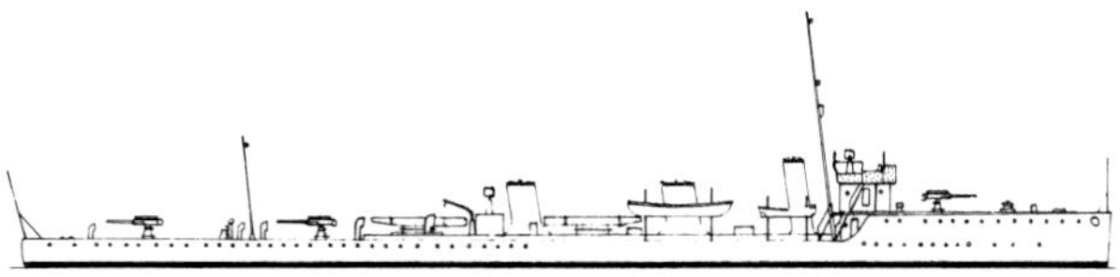
*i*

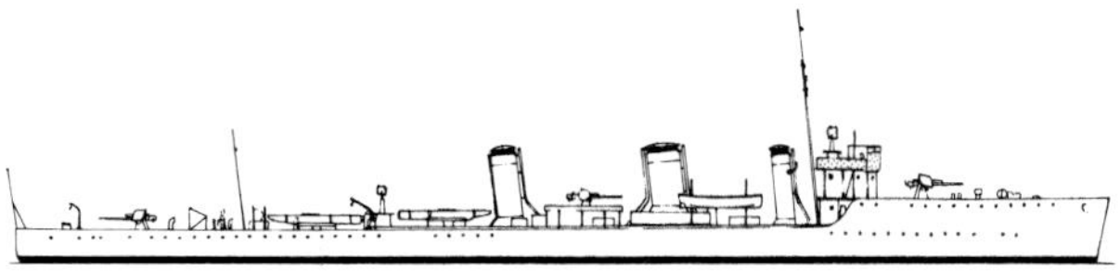
*ii*

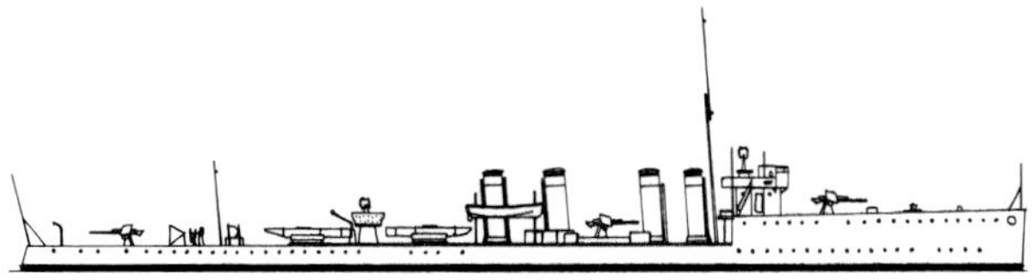
*iii*

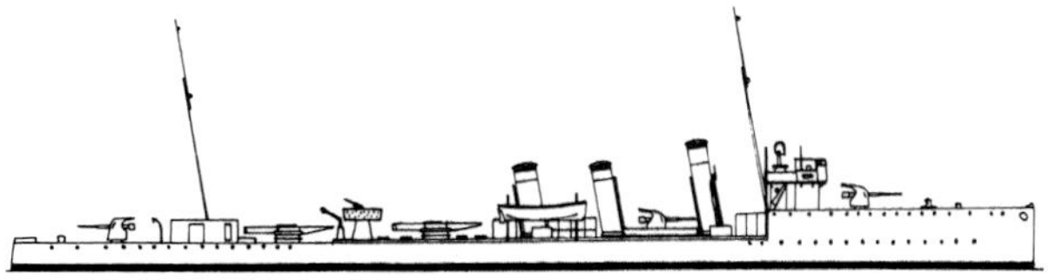
*iv*

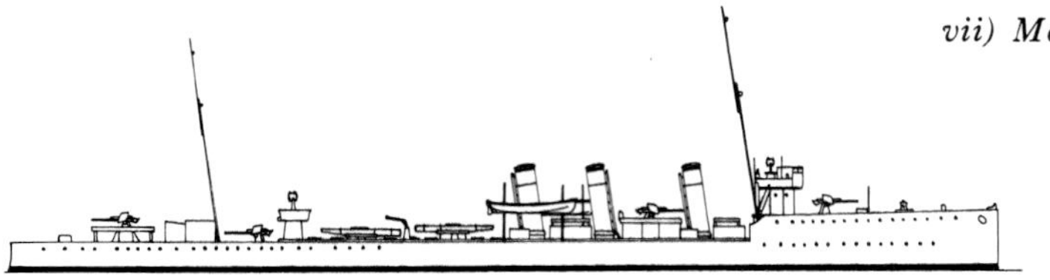
*v*

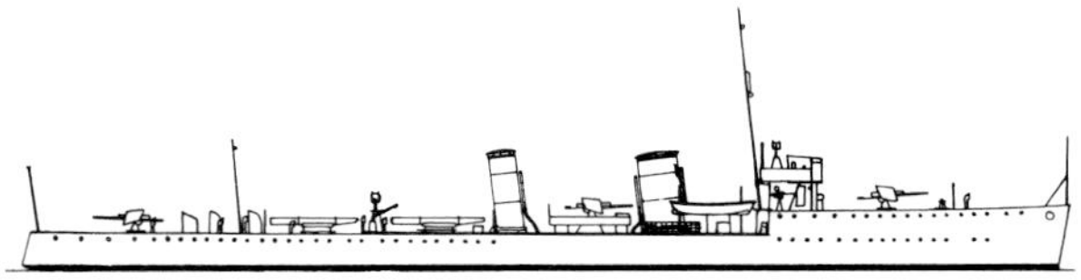
*vi*

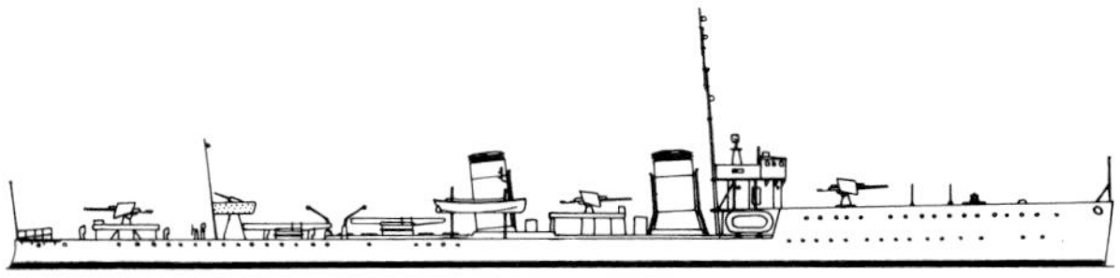
*vii*

*Development of the 'M' class design.*

*i)* Garland, *a Parsons 'Special' of the* Acasta *or 'K' class, 1911–12 programme.*

*ii)* Lochinvar, *'L' class, 1912–13 programme (this vessel was actually a 'Repeat' ordered in 1914).*

*iii)* Mansfield, *Hawthorn Leslie Special 'M', 1913–14 programme.*

*iv)* Melampus, *an ex-Greek 'M', 1914.*

*v)* Termagant, *reputedly ex-Turkish 'M'. 1914.*

*vi)* Musketeer, *a Yarrow Special Repeat 'M', 1914.*

*vii) Modified 'R' class design.*

Peyton *in very heavy weather demonstrates the meaning of 'wet' when applied to 'M' class destroyers.* (Imperial War Museum)

## *The U-boat threat*

As the U-boat threat to shipping built up, destroyers were slowly shifted onto it, at first mostly on ineffective patrols and searches, then, from 1917, on convoy work. Towards the end, 'M's were leaving the fleets for anti-submarine and escort duties. The destroyer seemed to both sides to be the natural enemy of the U-boat. Ramming was effective against U-boats, but required a hardened spike to pierce their stout pressure hulls. From 1916, depth charges became available, at first only 4 per destroyer but 30 to 40 by the end of the war. As yet, there was no effective means of aiming them, but they sank some U-boats and scared many more. Wartime service required greatly increased endurance and in July 1915, this led to the 'R's, which were in effect twin-screw geared-turbine 'M's and had about 25 per cent more endurance, though their gears were often rough and noisy. They were not at first regarded as a separate class, later; several names were exchanged to fit boats into their correct classes – quite apart from the fact that the 'M's had taken over a great deal of the alphabet in the meantime. Oddly enough, many of the 'traditional' names rejected for the 'L's reappeared in the ranks of the wartime destroyers: 'Tradition packs a heavy wallop'. The vital need for increased endurance led to peace tanks being used in wartime, despite the fire risks, and tankage was increased where possible.

## *Later war experiences*

By the latter part of the war, experienced captains and crews from older destroyers were being transferred bodily to later boats as the old ones came in for major refit, for example from the *Mischief* to the *Pellew*. The last 'M's to take part in major battles seem to have been the *Medway* and *Nerissa* on 17 November 1917, when they kept up with 'V's and Modified 'R's at 33.3kts in spite of the latter bursting a manoeuvring valve, and *Morris* in the action off Dunkirk on 20/21 March 1918.

It was found that in smooth water, German destroyers (officially 'Fleet Torpedo Boats') could usually outrun British ones in a chase, but pure speed proved of limited value. Long-range shooting by destroyers proved inaccurate, but the outfit of 120 rounds per gun proved adequate. Experience of torpedo attacks showed that single shots were very inaccurate – 'Never fire torpedoes in penny packets' became the torpedoman's maxim, and four tubes proved the minimum battery; the 'W's introduced six. There were complaints that in close-range night actions, 21in torpedoes often dived under the enemy before taking up their proper depth; old 14in were fixed on deck and the 'S's were given pairs of 18in under the bridge, which proved useless. By contrast, the Germans were taking the fixed forward tubes out of their boats just as the British and Japanese were putting extra tubes in much the same place; none was much use. Paravanes, minesweeping gear, kite balloons and dazzle painting were other wartime innovations. Some 'M's were fitted as minelayers, offensive minelaying proving a very effective strategy.

The most frequent enemy was the weather. The 'M's stood up to it well, but more comfortable bridges, moved aft, proved necessary, and the lack of a protected fore-and-aft gangway cost many good men washed overboard. Guns were once more raised on 'bandstands'. In combat, the 'M's did well, though like all destroyers they were vulnerable to hits in their long machinery spaces. Many were brought back to port, some more than once, after mine or torpedo hits. They kept the sea in conditions and for periods which had never been contemplated, and gained a number of successes against U-boats.

## *Aftermath*

By the end of the war, many were showing signs of their long, hard service, and most had gone to the breakers by the early 1920s. Though they left successors in the 'R's, the Modified 'R's and the 'S's, the future lay with the 'V's and their many descendants; but, unlike some more prestigious vessels, the 'M's had done their job.

**Notes**

[1] There was no 'J' class; it may have been a 750-ton *New Firedrake* design with two 12pdrs and five tubes which was under discussion for some time.

**Sources**

The Ships' Covers (mostly ADM 138/437, the first of several, which covers the rationale of the design, as far as anyone committed such ideas to paper).

Edgar J March, *British Destroyers 1892–1953*. This is magnificent but it does cover a huge field. I was inclined to criticise him for getting swamped by his material – but that was before I started looking into the Ships' Covers.

'Taffrail', *Endless Story*. This gives the operational and human side.

# THE FATHER OF THE FLAT-TOP?

Credit for devising the concept of the flight-deck aircraft carrier has been claimed by many individuals, but none was more persistent than a now-obscure American marine engineer and naval architect, John Lawrence Bogert. During a long dispute with the US Navy, he steadfastly insisted he was 'the father of the flat-top plane-carrier' – a slogan emblazoned on his business letterhead during the later years of his long and diverse career. R D Layman and Stephen McLaughlin analyse his claims.

BOGERT (1858–1956), a descendant of a Dutch family settled in what became Long Island, NY, was the son of a prominent New York lawyer and the brother of a well-known chemist. Upon graduation from Columbia College (which later formed the core of Columbia University) in 1878 he embarked on a career in mechanical engineering that lasted nearly to his death at the age of 97. After working for a locomotive-building firm and the Morgan Iron Works, he formed a partnership for the manufacture of machine tools. In 1884 he left this venture to establish his own firm, continuing to produce machine tools and later expanding into internal combustion engines. In 1913, as a consulting engineer for the New York Engine Company[1], he was instrumental in acquiring the American rights for Krupp diesel engines, and reincorporated his own firm as the American System Krupp-Diesel Engine Company.

Although Bogert continued to be active in many phases of engineering for the next several decades, the diesel became a main preoccupation; many of the forty or so US patents he received concerned various improvements to diesel engines, and he argued its merits ceaselessly at meetings of the American Society of Naval Architects and Marine Engineers, of which he was an articulate member of long standing. His formal qualifications as a naval architect are obscure, although he indicated in later years that he had studied shipbuilding under John Roach.[2] Whatever his qualifications may have been, there is no doubt that Bogert was well-versed in many aspects of maritime construction and propulsion. A man of many parts, he was also a leading tenor with the New York Oratorical Society for more than fifty years, an avid swimmer who until late in life took a daily dip in the waters off New York, and an associate editor of *Marine News*, a now-defunct New York-published maritime and engineering journal (not to be confused with the modern *Marine News*, the journal of the World Ship Society).

He was also a man occasionally ahead of his time; at the 1938 meeting of the American Society of Naval Architects and Marine Engineers, he advanced the concept of the container ship, and at the 1943 session he advocated the gas turbine engine. Therefore it is not surprising to find him arguing in 1917 that the defence of merchant ships against submarines could best be accomplished by aircraft carriers – a judgement the next war would prove correct. He proceeded to draw up two schemes for such vessels.

*John Lawrence Bogert in his late 50s or early 60s.* (By courtesy of Helen F Emery).

## The Kaiser Wilhelm II conversion

One was for conversion of the interned German liner *Kaiser Wilhelm II*[3] into a 'Bogert mothership for airplanes'. He published a description of this proposal in *Marine News* in a 1933 article illustrated by a sketch that shows the vessel retaining her centreline superstructure, including all four funnels. A 253ft landing deck has been added aft and a 153ft take-off deck forward; at the stern there is a hint of an odd arresting gear system that will be described a bit further on.

This drawing conflicts strangely with another of the same project in a 1941 issue of the same journal, which shows plan as well as elevation; although retaining the separate fore and aft aircraft decks, this version removes half the engines and boilers, eliminates two funnels and offsets the remaining two to starboard to create a nearly clear deck. There is a small centreline deckhouse forward and trainable catapult immediately aft of it. The caption notes that the vessel is to be fitted with blisters (bulges) and armed with 5in guns and depth charge mortars.

The immediate impression of this drawing is that it is an updated version of the earlier scheme. But it is specifically dated 'July 1917'. Various features, however, prove it could not possibly have been done that year. The catapult is a typical 1940s affair; there was no such device anywhere in the world that Bogert could have used as a model for it in 1917.[4] The aircraft in the 1933 drawing are apparently floatplanes, whilst those in the 1941 rendering are clearly biplane amphibian flying boats, quite unlike any aircraft Bogert could have seen in 1917 – in fact they strongly resemble the Supermarine Walrus, which entered service in 1936.

The conclusion is inescapable that the drawing published in 1933 was the original 1917 design. As such, it was logical but undistinguished, mirroring arrangements fitted to British merchantmen that had been converted to aviation vessels (although it is highly improbable that Bogert could have been acquainted with these). For some reason, Bogert updated this sketch to produce a more modern-looking version in 1941.

In 1917, Bogert sent plans for the proposed conversion of the *Kaiser Wilhelm II* to the Navy Department, and they were eventually referred to the National Advisory Committee for Aeronautics – possibly because of the design, possibly because the committee chairman, William F Durand, was a distinguished and experienced naval and mechanical engineer. In a letter dated 30 November 1917, Durand told Bogert that 'the whole subject [of aviation vessels] has been covered very carefully by officers of the Shipping Board and present opinion is that tonnage is much more important for freight carrying purposes than for use as mother ships for airplanes.' Although conceding the feasibility of such a vessel, Durand concluded: 'So long as the present opinions regarding strategy and the significance of tonnage prevail, it does not seem likely that it will be considered justifiable to use tonnage for the purpose indicated [by Bogert].'

There was ample reason for this somewhat unimaginative position; 1917 was the crisis year of the submarine war, and at the time of US entry into the conflict merchant tonnage was being sunk faster than it was being built. By November, adoption of convoy was reversing this situation, but there was still urgent need to use every available ton to keep Britain supplied with vital commodities and to transport and maintain American troops abroad.

## Anticipating the MAC ship

Undetered, Bogert pressed another scheme, more original than the *Kaiser Wilhelm II* idea and perhaps predating it – 'a mothership for airplanes and submarine destroyer' that was a combined cargo vessel and flight-deck aircraft carrier. A 15,000-ton craft, it was to be powered by three diesel engines producing a total of 7500bhp for a speed of 16kts. Bogert wanted to provide an upper deck as clear as possible of obstacles, so the thin exhaust pipes for the diesels could be folded down, as could the radio masts. All hatches – including six on each beam for access to cargo holds – were flush with the deck. The deck was broken only by a deckhouse topped by an upward-curving ramp – startingly similar in appearance to the V/STOL 'ski jump' of some modern carriers – over which aircraft were to take off. Bogert thought this would help the machines get airborne, but in fact it would have had a retarding effect on the low-powered aircraft of 1917; a downward-sloped platform, as Bogert had shown in his *Kaiser Wilhelm II* design, would have been more useful.

Although the vessel lacked any form of hangar, it was to carry three bomb-laden amphibious floatplanes. They were to be assisted in take-off and landing by midships 'accelerating and retarding belts' – treadmill-type devices flush with the upper deck, they would add to velocity during takeoff and, reversed, would help slow landing aircraft to a halt.[5]

The ship's underwater protection was to consist of 'a double wall of anti-torpedo compartments,' each 7ft 6in wide, 10ft deep and 30ft long, to be filled with 'special kinds of cargo' resistant to explosions. At various times Bogert suggested the use of baled cotton, coal, grain or even corn [maize] cobs.

Bogert armed his ship with four 5in guns (4 x 1) mounted in sponsons fore and aft on each beam; he specified this calibre in the correct belief that the larger German submarines then under construction would mount 5.9in (15cm) guns; he noted that 'The 4-inch gun is not sufficient' to counter U-boats armed with such guns in a surface action.

Save for the oddities of the ramp and endless belts, the overall external appearance of the design seems quite reasonable, suggestive of the later escort carriers (CVEs) or, more presciently, the British merchant aircraft carriers (MAC ships) of the Second World War which did exactly what Bogert proposed his ship should do – protect convoys from submarine attack while carrying useful cargo. Bogert dubbed his paper vessel *Democracy*, and in April or May 1917 (the exact date cannot be determined) personally took its plans to the Navy Department in Washington and then filed a patent application for it. He waited several weeks for a reply; when none came, he began an extensive publicity campaign to call attention to *Democracy*, writing articles that appeared in more than

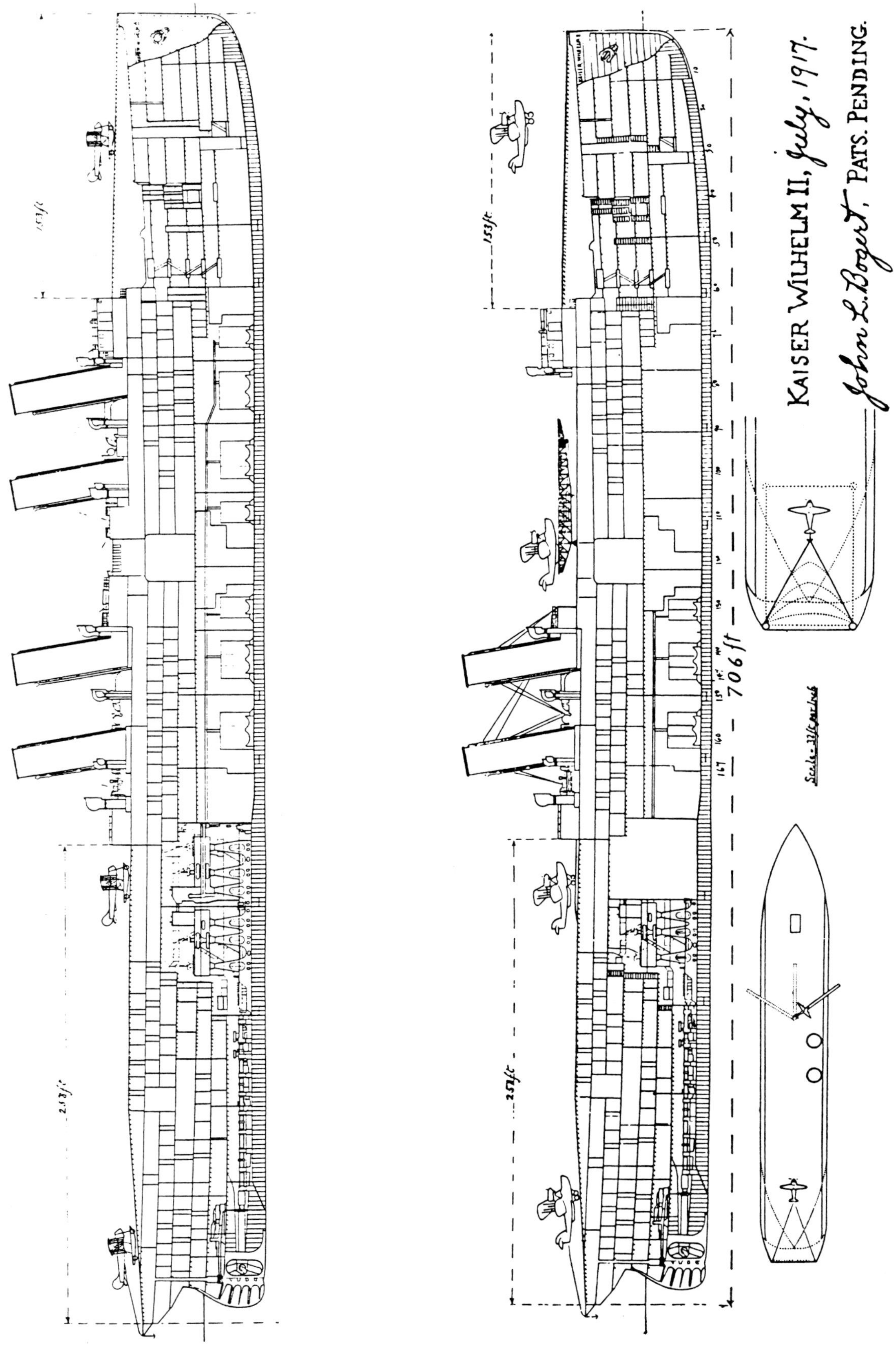
KAISER WILHELM II, July, 1917.
John L. Bogert, PATS. PENDING.
153 ft
706 ft
257 ft

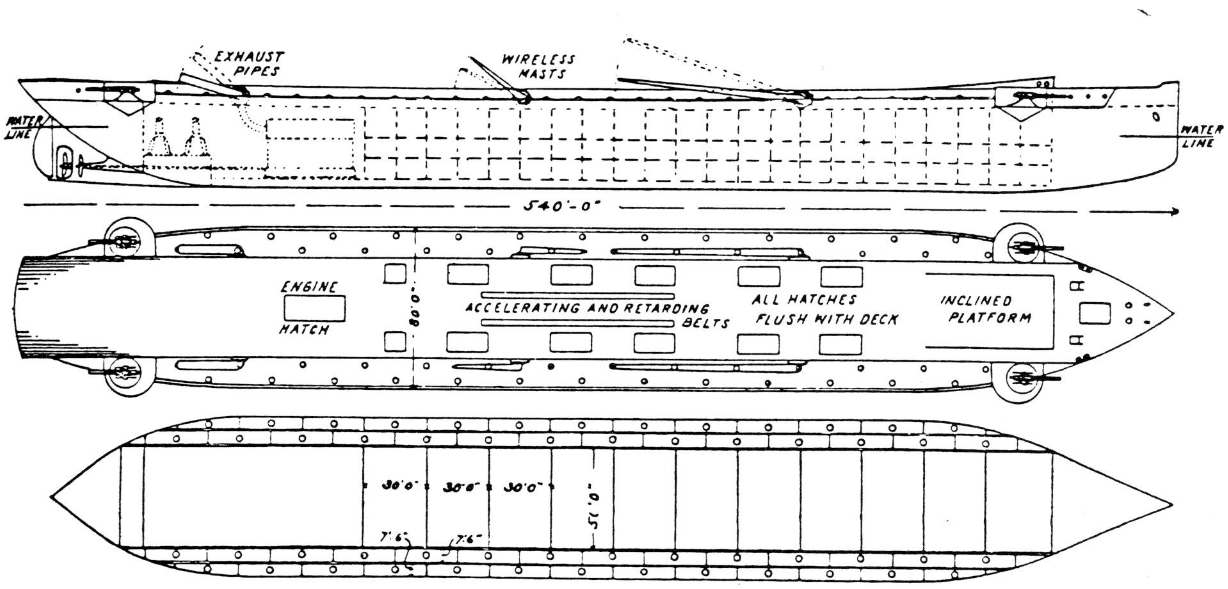


*John L Bogert's 1917 design for what he termed a 'mothership for airplanes and submarine destroyer' to which he gave the name* Democracy.

thirty publications (including *Scientific American*). He also wrote letters to a large number of political, governmental and military officials. He commissioned an oil painting showing *Democracy* defending a convoy, with one of its aircraft attacking a submerged U-boat, and arranged for the painting to be prominently displayed in a New York City store window; in later years it was reproduced periodically in *Marine News* to reinforce Bogert's pronouncement that the combination of armed

◄◄ *Bogert's plan for converting* Kaiser Wilhelm II *into an aviation vessel, as published in the October 1933 issue of* Marine News. *This apparently was the original design as presented to the Navy Department.*

◄ *This plan for conversion of* Kaiser Wilhelm II *was published in* Marine News *in 1945, and although it is dated July 1917 it includes design features that, as noted in the text, Bogert could not have been aware in that year. In addition to the aircraft arresting device at the stern, the vessel, according to Bogert's caption, was to mount 5in guns and 'depth bomb mortars', although their locations are not indicated on the drawing. The mention of 'depth bombs' is another indication that this design long postdated 1917, for until the first American vessels arrived in European waters after US entry into the war most US naval officers were unaware of even the existence of this weapon. It is unlikely, therefore, that an American civilian would have had knowledge of it.*

freighter and bomb-carrying aircraft could have ended the submarine menace.

Bogert also tried to interest Britain in the idea, sending plans to Lord Northcliffe, chief of the British War Mission to the United States, and to Lord Pirrie, head of the shipbuilding firm of Harland & Wolff and later Controller-General of Merchant Shipbuilding. The response from both was that the scheme had been referred to the appropriate departments; no more was heard.

Official US rejection finally came with a letter from Captain Robert Stocker, acting chief of the Bureau of Construction and Repair, in July 1918. Stocker informed Bogert that 'other considerations which have entered into the development of the present aircraft program make it inadvisable to undertake the development of your method of handling these machines at the present time. The Bureau has given consideration to the question of motherships, but does not regard it essential that the airplane land directly on the ship.' Bogert would in later years make great use of that last sentence, citing it as stupid lack of interest in the 'flat-top plane-carrier'.

Unmentioned in Stocker's letter but undoubtedly a factor was the fact that in 1917 the Navy had no aircraft capable of the kind of high-seas operation envisioned by Bogert. Lacking the stimulus of war experienced by the European powers, the United States was years behind in aeronautical technology and design, and would not catch up until too late. Thus the Navy was unwilling to experiment with an aviation vessel until it had aircraft able to work from it.'[6]

The armistice that ended the war also brought a temporary truce to Bogert's battle with the Navy, although he continued to snipe at it from time to time over the years in the pages of *Marine News* while pursuing his varied occupations as a maritime and transportation engineer and consultant.

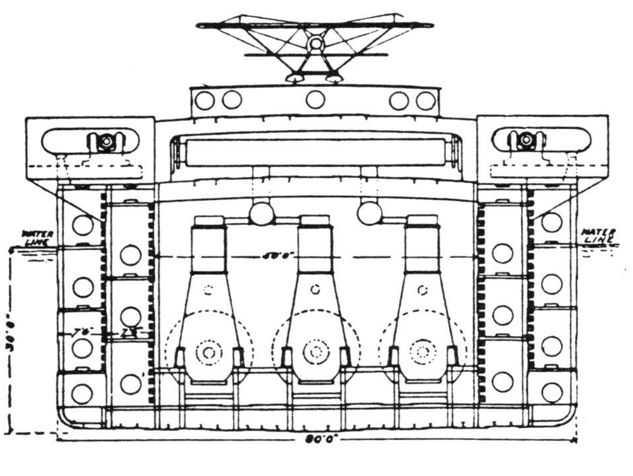


*This sectional view of* Democracy *as drawn by Bogert shows the 'double wall of anti-torpedo compartments'.*

## *Aircraft arresting gear*

One of the inventions Bogert returned to again and again between the wars shows up in his sketches for the *Kaiser Wilhelm II* conversion, where there is an unusual 'arresting gear' – the landing aircraft trails a line with a grappling hook dangling over the stern of the ship. This apparently is the genesis of a device Bogert would be touting as late as 1945; his inspiration, he wrote, was the system used aboard the US cruiser *Pennsylvania* when Eugene Ely landed an aircraft aboard her in 1911. Ely's aeroplane had hooks which snagged athwartship lines anchored at each end by sandbags; astonishingly, Bogert actually believed (for he stated it in print several times) that sandbags continued to be used as braking devices aboard US carriers as late as 1941, specifically citing *Lexington* and *Saratoga*. He therefore believed his own system to be far more advanced than that used aboard contemporary carriers, and described it in some detail in a 1933 article:

> Projecting at an angle from the landing deck are two triangular frames, one at the extreme starboard and the other at the extreme port side of the ship. Between these two frames is stretched the bight of a cable or rope, whose two standing parts passing through blocks are led round a drum on the deck below. The axle of this drum or pair of drums is controlled as to rotation by a suitable braking mechanism, whose torque factor is capable of adjustment to suit the weight and size of plane landing . . . [A] grapnel is attached to a rope that can be raised or lowered from the airplane . . . Retracted while flying, this grapnel can be lowered sufficiently to ensure certain contact with the bight of the rope stretched across the stern of the ship.

Bogert also 'contemplated winding the grapnel rope round a drum in the fusilage [*sic*] of the airplane, controlling the rotation of the drum frictionally when landing. This would constitute a perfect braking device, permitting the operator to determine just how quickly he desired to stop the speed of his plane.'

Whatever the theoretical merits of Bogert's system, it was a practical impossibility under normal conditions. Bogert naively believed the grapnel would inevitably snag the raised line on the first pass and that the connection of the two lines would automatically steady the aeroplane in a straight path. He took no account of ship motion or wind currents that might cause the aircraft (or the hook) to dip or swerve, and failed to realize the highly precise control that would be required to halt an aeroplane at a safe height before it reached stalling speed (the speed at which aerodynamic lift is lost and gravity takes over). Nor did he acknowledge the unfortunate result should the dangling hook snag anything *other* than the rope.

*Bogert's scheme for an aircraft arresting device, in which a grapnel-fitted line trailed from an aeroplane would snag a line suspended between two braking drums at a ship's stern. This sketch by Stephen McLaughlin, based on a drawing by Bogert in* Marine News, *shows the reciprocal braking drum proposed for installation within the aircraft.*

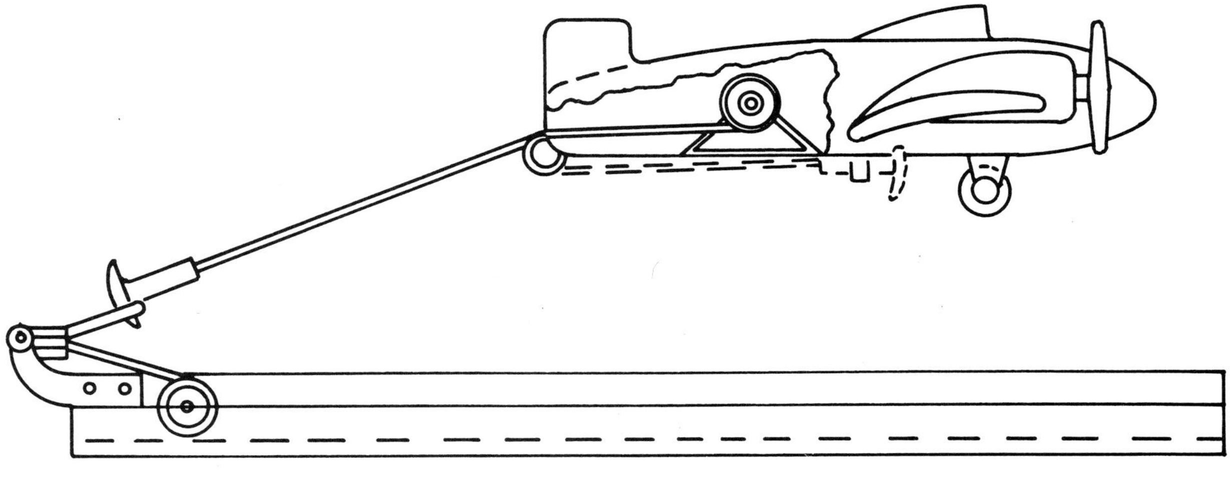

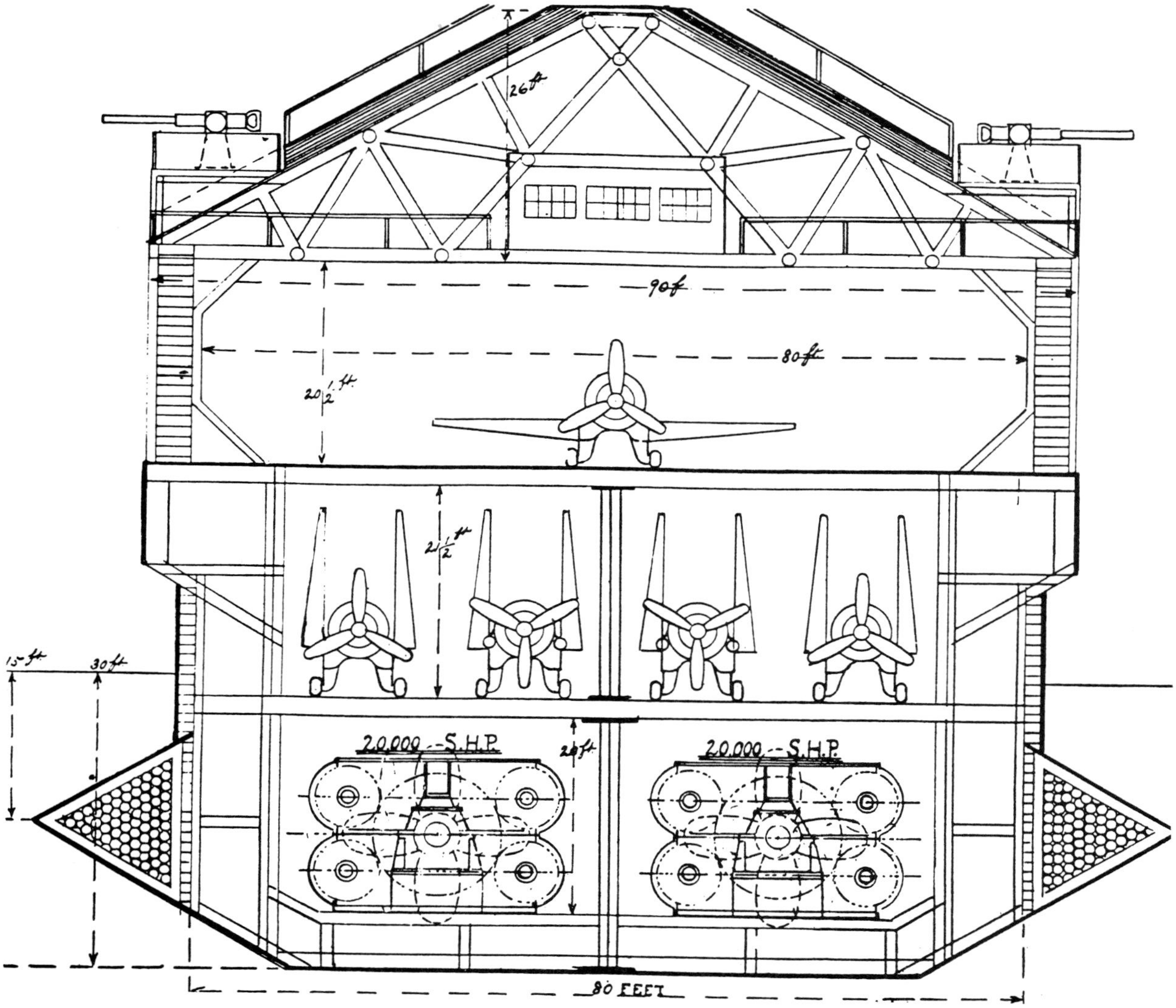


*A sectional view of Bogert's 1945 design. It was captioned 'Bogert's unsinkable freight ship & submarine destroyer of May 1917. Roof & blisters added June 1945'. However, a comparision with sectional view of* Democracy *shows considerable change, notably the addition of a hangar deck and a great increase in horsepower.*

## Protection schemes

Like the First World War, the Second World War inspired Bogert to naval innovations. In 1942 he proposed triangular blisters (bulges) for anti-torpedo protection. The idea, as described by Bogert, involved 'taking the bow of a ship and turning it through 90 degrees and stretching it along the hull. If the bow of a destroyer will deflect the torpedo, why shouldn't the triangular blister do the same in the larger vessel?' This rationale ignores the fact that a destroyer's bow gains some immunity from torpedo attack not because it 'deflects' the torpedo, but simply because it forms such a narrow target.

Not content with the protection he believed the triangular form would provide, Bogert recommended putting cylinders of compressed air inside, which would 'serve as the finest spring in the world to relieve the blow of an exploding torpedo and take the blow away from the structure of the ship.' It seems more likely that a torpedo explosion would have shattered the heavy compressed air cylinders, sending fragments at high velocity tearing through the vitals of the ship.

A new variation on the triangular blister was incorporated in Bogert's 1945 attempt at 'Making the Plane Carrier Immune to Suicide Attack'. To counter Japanese kamikaze attacks, he proposed a device 'that will be vastly superior . . . to anything now afloat as far as suicide bombing planes are concerned.' This was 'a roof [over the flight deck] that will shed bombs. A bomb that falls vertically, nose down, may be able to penetrate a horizontal deck, but not a chilled steel slanting roof, especially if that roof is supported by an elastic backing that can absorb the force of the blow . . .'

Drawings of a ship so protected accompanied the article. It is *Democracy* all over again in most respects, but tarted up with the 'roof' that extends over all but about 170ft of the vessel, triangular blisters (this time filled with pine logs) and a row of nine anti-aircraft guns on each beam. Other refinements are a hangar deck and an increase in horsepower to 40,000shp. At the stern is Bogert's pet grapnel-on-a-rope arresting device, and forward on the flight deck is once again the endless belt accelerator.

While the 1917 *Democracy* design was in many respects quite reasonable, this successor is hopelessly flawed. The impossibility of operating high-performance aircraft from what was in essence a tunnel 20ft high and 80ft wide was alone enough to put it beyond the pale of feasibility.

## *Bogert versus the US Navy*

Earlier, Bogert had fired the first shots of a new war with the Navy. As a later Navy document put it,

> In 1940 Mr Bogert re-opened his campaign for the adoption of his 1917 design for a carrier and for 'blisters' of a doubtful design to be fitted to all cargo vessels. Six times in a little over two years, he took the Government to task for not adopting his plan; then, when the escort-carriers [CVEs] came into service, he asked to be given credit for their successful work.

The Navy tried to quiet him with a laudatory rejection of his claims. In a letter of 16 December 1943, the Navy Office of Inventions wrote

> . . . your proposals on a tactical use of ships and aircraft, made before the airplane had grown up to the job you prescribed for it, was [*sic*] indeed most far sighted on your part and a successful prediction of things to come. While it is felt that the present use of the airplane for anti-submarine work is the natural development of an inherently valuable weapon rather than as a result of your suggestion or that of anyone else, the Navy Department does wish to express its appreciation of the interest you have shown in combatting the submarine problem . . .

Far from placating Bogert, this letter only enflamed him the more. Pressing his campaign, he instigated a patent search to prove that his patent application for *Democracy* predated any others. It was carried out by patent attorney D H Haskell, who on 2 November 1944 informed Bogert that 'None of the patents [relating to aviation vessels] indicate anything approaching the design of a real "flat-top" until years after your generous and public spirited presentations and offers of a practical flat-top design to the government.'

Thus armed, Bogert returned to the fray with another barrage of letters to officials ranging from the President of the United States on down. Finally, in an effort to settle the matter once and for all, the Navy Inventions Section made a study of all the accumulated correspondence and issued a lengthy report which arrived at the hardly unexpected conclusion that Bogert's claims were unjustified.[7]

The report began by quoting a statement by Bogert in 1917 that 'the combination of the bomb-dropping airplane with the armed freight ship is the fundamental idea of the Bogert invention', and then noted 'if the [Navy] Department were inclined to stand on technicalities, this contemporary statement of his "fundamental idea" would dispose of his claim, as no such combination has ever been used by the Navy'. A basic difference between *Democracy* and the CVEs, it pointed out, was that the latter 'happened to have merchant hulls but were not in fact cargo-carrying vessels. They were men-of-war in every sense, the only difference being that commercial hulls were used simply for speedy construction and economy.'

Turning to Bogert's belief that he originated the tactic of defending convoys with carrier-borne aircraft, the report said: 'As the combination of surface vessels and airplanes for convoy work had been the subject of much thought in naval circles, the adoption of the system was not in any way due to his efforts, but was a natural development, only awaiting the necessary carriers.'

Later on, the document brings up a point alluded to earlier as a probable reason for lack of US naval interest in carriers in 1917:

> At that time, the Navy had only a handful of planes and was experiencing difficulty in acquiring more suitably reliable ones for overwater flight. Our coastal anti-submarine air patrols, as fast as they could be supplied with planes, were organized and extended . . . Those familiar with this work, and the limitations imposed by the necessity of returning to land bases, were by no means blind to the advantages of [aviation vessels]. The obstacle lay in the lack of availibility of suitable planes.

As to Bogert's claim to have devised the flight-deck carrier:

> Ships combining the essential features of the Bogert plans had been designed and one was nearing completion [a reference to HMS *Argus*]. When he described himself as the 'Inventor of the Flat-top Plane-carrier', he is claiming credit which is not his due. From the time . . . when [Eugene] Ely had flown a plane off a warship, and had landed a plane on a warship, the idea of a ship on which planes could land and from which they could take off, was open to all comers. Who first had the idea is not known, and may never be known. It is likely that it was in many minds as it was a perfectly natural development of a new and important weapon. But so far as known the credit for putting this idea into concrete form must be to the British designers of HMS *Argus*.

This evaluation could probably stand for all time as the answer to the question of who invented the flight-deck carrier. However, the report muddied waters by stating that *Argus* was designed in 1912; this error probably grew out of the fact that William Beardmore & Co, which built *Argus* on the hull of an incomplete Italian liner, had in 1912 drawn up plans for a combined aeroplane/seaplane carrier-destroyer tender. This vessel never existed save on paper, but it is easy to see how a misinterpretation could have been made.[8]

Bogert's reaction to this report was predictable. On 15 August 1946 he sent to Navy Secretary James Forrestal a 14-page, single-spaced letter of attempted refutation – a meandering, repetitious opus analyzing the report paragraph by paragraph, each page headed 'John L Bogert vs United States Navy'.

To counter the assertion that the Navy had never made use of a combined cargo vessel and aircraft carrier, Bogert insisted that the CVEs *were* cargo carriers because they were built on hulls of the Maritime Commission's C-3 freighter design. *'Once a cargo vessel, always a cargo vessel'* he declared (his emphasis) and the CVEs' cargo consisted of their fuel, ordnance, fresh water and stores.

> Replacing their shelter deck with a heavy flight deck, installing catapults and elevators reduced their carrying capacity materially, nevertheless they were still cargo carriers, and had to stow either cargo or ballast to float at their proper waterline, and still have their proper metacentric height.

By this reasoning, any warship could be called a cargo vessel. Bogert would have been on more logical ground had he compared his cargo-carrying flat-top to the British MAC ships, which operated aircraft while at the same time transporting grain or petroleum. Perhaps he was unaware of the existence of these vessels; had he been, his plaints might have been directed to London instead of Washington.

Another more telling argument Bogert might have employed was the fact that the CVEs were originally conceived as aircraft transports, intended to take fully assembled, flight-ready aeroplanes to areas of combat – a function they did in fact perform even after becoming combatants themselves – but apparently he was ignorant of this aspect of their design history.

Bogert dismissed the primacy of *Argus* on two grounds, the first based on American law as relating to his patent application of 1917. The resemblance of *Democracy* to *Argus*, he argued, 'has no relevancy whatsoever, even if preliminary drawings were made by a British firm for that vessel [*Argus*] in 1912' (thus accepting the Navy's error about her design date). 'It is a well established principle of patent law that only foreign publication of *workable drawings* can establish a date in anticipation of the claims of an American filing date.' No such drawings of *Argus* had been published, of course, because she was designed and constructed under conditions of wartime secrecy.

Bogert's second reason for rejecting *Argus* as the first 'flat-top' carrier was a bizarre belief, which he repeated several times both in this letter and in articles, that aircraft could not and did not land directly on her deck. 'She was equipped,' he wrote, 'to catapult airplanes into the air, but recover them [by crane] when they alighted in the water alongside. She was not adapted for airplane flight in, over the stern, since she was fitted with ducts for discharging smoke and funnel gases at the stern.'

These sentences were written the year *Argus* was broken up after a 28-year career during which thousands of landings had been made on her deck by at least forty different types of aircraft. One wonders if Bogert was ever disabused of his fantastic notion; perhaps not, for there seems to have been no reply to this final and futile plea for official recognition.

He did receive private recognition five years later. During Maritime Day celebrations in New York City on 22 May 1951, he was presented with the Admiral William A Moffett Maritime Aviation Trophy by the National Maritime & Aeronautical Association.[9] It was awarded, the New York *World-Telegram and Sun* uncritically told its readers, for Bogert's 'invention 33 years ago of the

*Bogert published this design for an aircraft carrier with armoured 'roof' in the July 1945 issue of* Marine News.

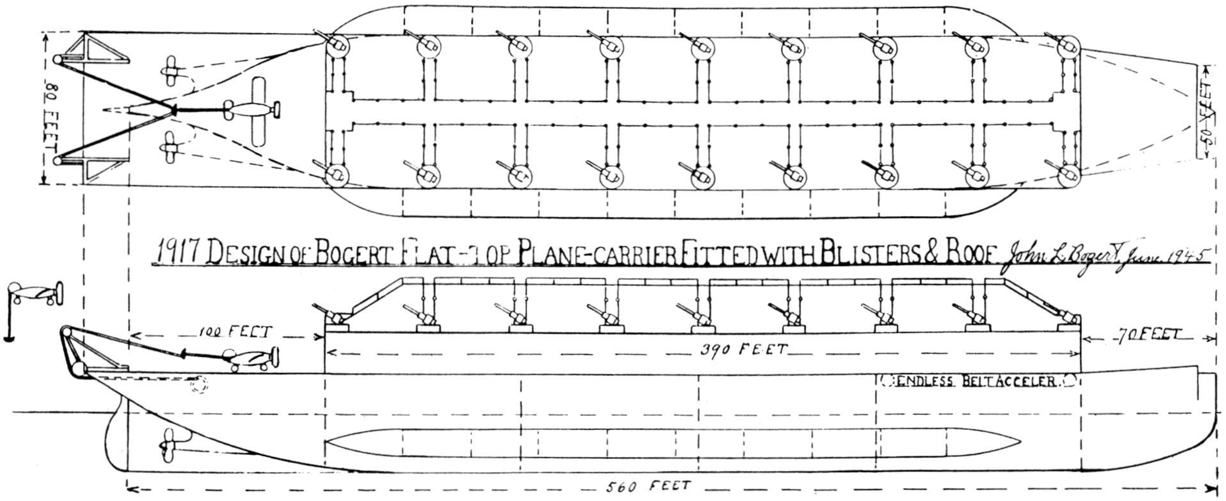

flat-top airplane carrier.' 'Thirty-four years is a long time to have to wait for recognition,' Bogert wrote a few days later. 'However, better late than never.'

Bogert remained active professionally to nearly the end of his life, and continued to be interested in aircraft carriers. In 1955 he advocated protection of the Greater New York area from Soviet nuclear attack by a system of standing fighter patrols based on stationary carriers anchored at various points seaward of the city.

He died the next year, undoubtedly still convinced, as he wrote to Forrestal in 1946, 'Just as every school boy knows that John Ericsson's *Monitor* saved the Capitol from being shelled, so every school boy is going to learn that John L Bogert's ideas licked the German U-boats and won the "Battle of the Atlantic".'

**Notes**

1 One of whose partners was John Rodrigo Dos Passos Sr, father of the novelist.

2 Specifically, Bogert said at the 1938 meeting of the American Society of Naval Architects and Marine Engineers (hereafter abbreviated as ASNAME), 'I practically learned my trade from Roach'; 'I worked for him before the United States had a metal warship, before the *Atlanta*, the *Boston*, the *Chicago* and the *Dolphin* were contracted for.' Presumably this would have been while Bogert was associated with the Morgan Iron Works, which had engined ships for John Roach & Son. The four vessels cited by Bogert – the so-called ABCD ships of the American 'New Navy' of the 1880s – were also engined by Morgan. Roach received the contract for them in 1882 but before they were completed, Roach, who had made a substantial financial contribution to the Republican Party during the 1884 presidential election campaign, came under investigation by the new Democratic administration of President Grover Cleveland and the vessels' design and construction were severely criticized. Subsequently, the contract was abrogated, the ships completed in government yards, and Roach's firm collapsed into bankruptcy. During the same 1938 ASNAME meeting Bogert vigorously defended the design of the ABCD ships and charged that Roach was entirely the victim of an act of political revenge.

3 This 19,361grt vessel was taken over in August 1917 for use as a troop transport by the American Expeditionary Force under the name *Agamemnon*. Her conversion to an aviation vessel was proposed again in 1920 by Brigadier General William Mitchell of the US Army Air Service. Nothing came of the idea.

4 Three US armoured cruisers carried catapults for a time in 1917 but these fixed, stern-mounted structures bore no resemblance whatever to the catapult in Bogert's drawing. The only other vessel to have a catapult in 1917 was the British trials ship *Slinger*, converted from a steam hopper while under construction and not completed until two months after the date given for the drawing. Her catapult also was totally dissimilar in appearance.

5 This was another idea that Bogert was to advocate over and over again during the next three decades. It was not as original a scheme as he probably thought – Winston Churchill had suggested a somewhat similar device in 1914.

6 This was basically the reason for the rejection in 1917 of an aircraft carrier proposal advanced by Lieutenant Kenneth Whiting. See R D Layman, *Before the Aircraft Carrier: The Development of Aviation Vessels 1849–1922* (Conway Maritime Press, London, 1989), p116.

7 Navy Inventions Section, EXOS:ORIEN 1–9, 1946.

8 For the design history of *Argus*, see Norman Friedman, *British Carrier Aviation: The Evolution of the Ships and Their Aircraft* (Conway Maritime Press, London, 1988).
The 1912 Beardmore design is described and illustrated in Layman, *Before the Aircraft Carrier*, pp33–4.

9 Rear Admiral Moffett, for whom the trophy was named, was chief of the US Navy's Bureau of Aeronautics from 1921 until his death in 1933. The authors have been unable to find any information relating to the National Maritime & Aeronautical Association.

**Bibliography**

The authors are grateful to Mrs Helen F Emery and Dr Bruce P Bogert, both grandchildren of John L Bogert, for their help in gathering material for this article. Also valuable was a collection of papers held by the New York Public Library.

*Transactions of the American Society of Naval Architects and Marine Engineers*, 1922–43.

Articles in the *New York Times, New York Daily Mirror* and *New York World-Telegram and Sun*, 1943–56.

*National Cyclopaedia of American Biography*, 1918.

'The Merchantship as a Submarine Destroyer', *Scientific American*, 22 September 1917.

Articles by John L Bogert in *Marine News*:

'Another Page or Two in the History of Aviation,' October 1933.

'A Powerful Offense – Best Defense Against Submarines,' October 1933.

'Flight Acceleration and Retardation,' July 1941.

'Making the Plane Carrier Immune to Suicide Attack,' July 1945.

'Convoy Protection by Plane Carriers: the Lesson of Both Wars,' September 1945.

'One Man's Contribution to Victory,' February 1956.

'Adapting Hull Structures to Overcome Bombs and Torpedoes,' date unknown.

Edward C Moore, 'Strategic Crossroads,' unpublished manuscript, 1953.

'The Bogert Method,' *New Yorker*, 5 September 1953.

# FRENCH SUBMARINE DEVELOPMENT BETWEEN THE WARS

An early leader in submarine technology, France was to devote considerable resources to the underwater arm of the *Marine Nationale* between 1919 and 1939. During this period new operational concepts were developed which in turn influenced design, a process here analysed by John Jordan.

FRANCE'S love affair with the submarine dates from the Napoleonic era, when the Emperor saw in the ingenious 'secret weapon' proposed by the American Robert Fulton the answer to close blockade of French ports and harbours by the Royal Navy. Throughout the nineteenth century France was to be in the vanguard of underwater developments, pursuing both the single-hull *sous-marin pur* powered excusively by batteries (some combined steam propulsion with batteries) and, in the wake of Laubeuf's *Narval* of 1899, the double-hulled *submersible*.

Not only was France well to the fore in submarine technology, but many French naval officers felt that the submarine was destined to break the mould of traditional maritime strategy. The *Jeune Ecole*, led by the influential Admiral Aube, proposed that rather than attempt to match the British battlefleet with a force of comparable vessels, which would be beyond French financial capabilities, the Navy should construct a large force of torpedo-boats, operating both above and below the surface. Such a force would be inexpensive to build, too numerous to destroy, and would effectively prevent the Royal Navy from imposing its traditional blockade on French ports.

Despite the care and expense lavished on the development of these underwater weapons and the favour with which they were regarded, the performance of the numerically-impressive French submarine force in the First World War was disappointing, and by 1918 the *Marine Nationale* not only had fewer submarines in service than Britain, Germany, the United States and even Italy, but its early lead in submarine technology had evaporated, so that the latest foreign types were far superior in a number of important respects to their French counterparts.

The physical effects of the First World War on France must bear a large part of the responsibility for this relative decline. The ambitious programme of 1912 which envisaged a force of 46 ocean-going boats (*sous-marins de haute mer*) and 48 coastal submarines (*sous-marins défensifs*) failed to materialise because of the occupation of Northern France, labour problems caused by mobilisation, and the shifting of the workload of the naval *arsenaux* to production related to the war on land. Private shipyards had not been admitted to the prewar submarine construction programmes for security reasons, which effectively precluded an important alternative source of supply.

However, the virtual moratorium on French submarine construction imposed by the critical situation on the Western Front served to conceal more fundamental problems affecting the development of its underwater arm. The French love-affair with submarine technology, which found its most literary expression in Jules Verne's *20,000 Leagues Under the Sea*, favoured a 'science fiction' approach which inspired a succession of famous *ingénieurs*. French submarine designs were often strikingly innovative, but there was no single line of development and little operational evaluation which might have benefited future designs. Personal rivalries between *ingénieurs*, and the consequent obsession with improvements in performance which might glorify the name of a particular individual, resulted in the development of factions within the *Marine Nationale*; theory came to be placed at a higher level than practice. The fleet abounded with imaginative prototypes which failed to spawn a successful production model.

Moreover, the brilliance of conception of the designs was rarely matched by the execution of the dockyards; detail work was poor, and the designers were always ahead of the technology of the day. Failure to produce a reliable diesel engine was a fundamental reason for the poor performance of French submarines in the First World War.

Last, but by no means least, the obsession with technological theory was accompanied by weaknesses in strategic thinking. French submarine development appears to have taken no account of the *Entente Cordiale*

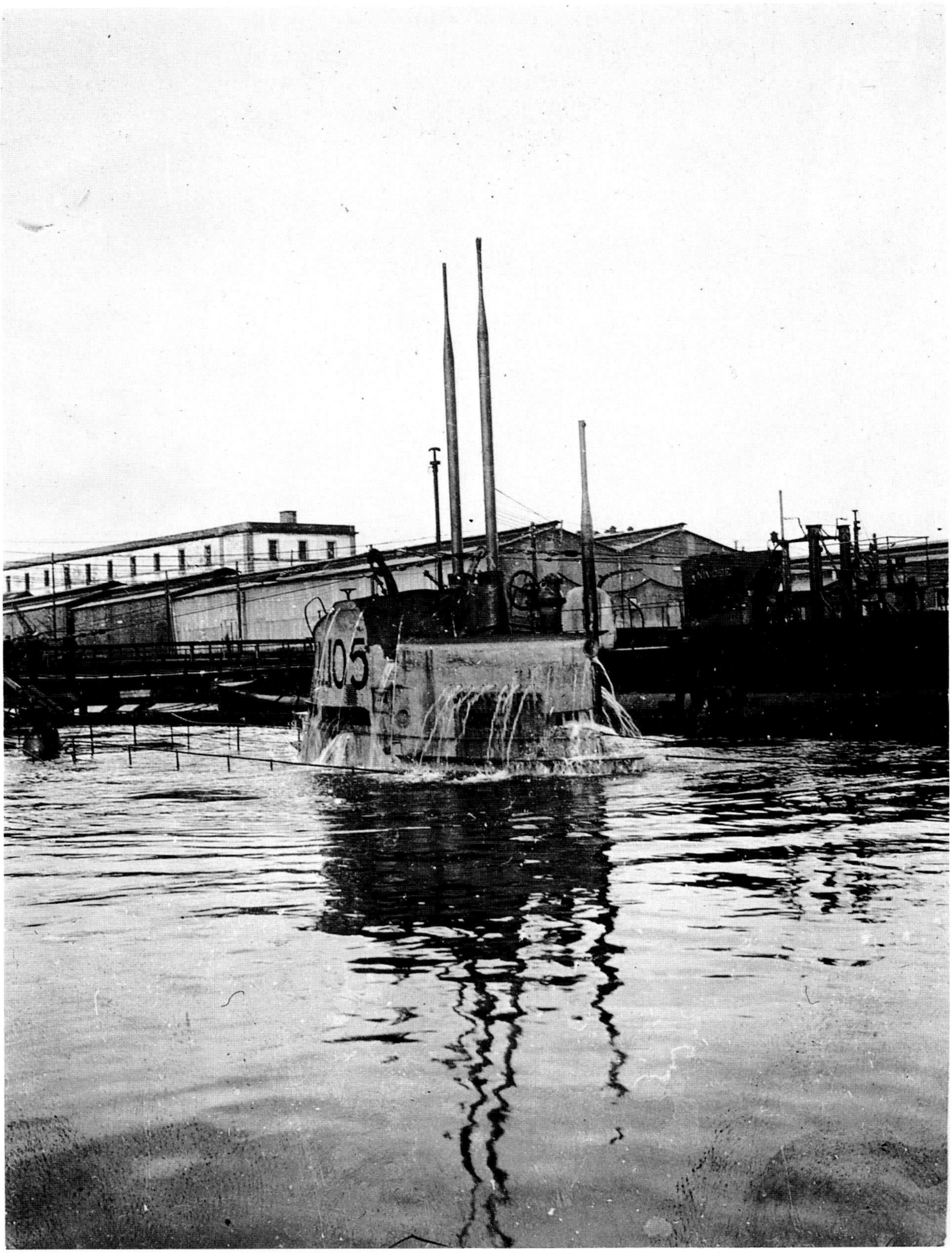


Jean Autric, *ex*-U-105, *during initial diving trials under the French flag.* (CMP*)*.

of 1904 and the increasing closeness of France's alliance with Great Britain. The continued predominance of the *sous-marin défensif* over the *sous-marin de haute mer* (the 1910 programme established a ratio of 73 to 21!) is indicative of a failure to appreciate the importance of the fundamental changes taking place in France's political allegiances, and of the need for a new rationale for the operational employment of the French submarine force.

There would be no significant threat to French harbours in the First World War. On the contrary, the *Marine Nationale* would be called on to mount its own blockades on the ports of far-off Austria-Hungary and Turkey – operations for which even the *sous-marins de haute mer* were to prove manifestly unsuited.

## The CEPSM Report

In the wake of the First World War a committee with the title *Commission d'Etudes Pratiques des Sous-Marins* (CEPSM) was set up to evaluate French experience of submarine operations under wartime conditions and to make recommendations for the future. Its report, delivered in 1919, was critical of many aspects of French submarine design. The boats completed in the prewar period had proved subject to frequent mechanical breakdowns and were difficult to maintain. They had not been designed for long patrols; they carried insufficient fuel (in part because the *Marine Nationale* disliked the idea of locating fuel tanks between the two hulls), and living conditions were crowded and inadequate. Conning towers were too close to the water and cramped, and periscopes were of poor quality compared with those in service with foreign navies. Finally, the number and placing of torpedo tubes was unsatisfactory, as war experience had proved the value of being able to launch salvoes of torpedoes against a manoeuvring target.

In view of these criticisms it is unsurprising that the report established the priorities for future submarines as robustness, endurance, and habitability, together with the ability to fire four torpedoes *in any direction* (author's italics). A larger calibre of 550mm (21.7in) was proposed for submarine torpedoes, as the 450mm (17.7in) model then in use was felt to be inadequate against major naval surface units. With the unreliability of current French diesel engines firmly in mind, the report recommended the adoption of a 2-stroke 1800bhp diesel with the relatively high weight ratio of 40kg per bhp for future construction.

Very specific recommendations were made regarding the two mainstream submarine types required. The *sous-marin de grande patrouille* was to be a large ocean-going boat of 1800 tonnes submerged, with a 20 per cent reserve of bouyancy and a diving depth of 60m (200ft), 90m (300ft) max. It was to have the comparatively high speed of 16.5kts on the surface and 10kts submerged. Endurance on diesels was to be 12,000nm at 9kts (or 60 days), while endurance on batteries alone was to be 90nm at 5kts or 150nm at 4kts. The powerful armament would comprise a single 100mm (3.9in) gun, and no fewer than twelve torpedo tubes with six reserve torpedoes.

The layout of the torpedo tubes reflected the recommendation that future submarines should be able to launch salvoes of four torpedoes in any direction. There were thus four fixed tubes in the bow, four in the stern, and a further four tubes in external trainable twin '*tourelles*' mounted directly beneath the deck casing amidships. This novel feature, which was to be adopted for all interwar French submarine construction, was intended to provide for four-torpedo salvoes at any angle on the beam. The concept derived from the Drzewiecki torpedo drop collar favoured by the French for many of their prewar submarine designs. Trainable tubes, which were electrically operated, were potentially a neater solution to the problem of launching torpedoes on the beam, and created less drag when the boat was submerged.

The trainable tube did not find favour with other navies, which considered them too complex and too vulnerable to shock damage, corrosion and mechanical/electrical breakdown. However, these navies had managed to develop good-quality gyros for their torpedoes whereas the French, cushioned by the dubious benefits of the Drzewiecki torpedo drop collar, had neglected this area of development.

The smaller counterpart to the ocean-going submarine proposed by the committee was the *sous-marin de moyenne patrouille*, a 700-tonne submarine designed for blockade and shallow-water operations, and armed with four bow and two stern torpedo tubes (but, somewhat surprisingly, no gun). Again great emphasis was to be placed on robustness and reliability.

Whereas the ocean-going submarine could be considered the linear successor to the prewar French *sous-marin de haute mer*, it is important to note that the smaller boat was no longer to be a *sous-marin défensif*, designed purely to protect French ports and harbours against hostile blockade or bombardment (the term, however, persisted in popular usage and even in naval circles). War experience had finally brought home to the *Marine Nationale* that this was an outdated concept, inextricably linked with traditional Anglo-French rivalry. The model for the *sous-marin de moyenne patrouille* was to be the German UB III, which proved its capabilities in British coastal waters in the last years of the war.

In addition to these two mainstream types, the CEPSM committee envisaged two new classes of minelaying submarine, which presumably approximated in size to the ocean-going and *moyenne patrouille* types. However, no firm specifications were laid down for these.

## War prizes

Following the conclusion of the First World War, France made strenuous efforts to acquire German U-Boats as war prizes, against strong British opposition.

The history of German submarine development stood in direct contrast to that of the French. The Germans had arrived late on the scene – the first U-boat, *U-1*, was launched only in August 1905, and only twenty submarines were in full operational service by the outbreak of war. However, the creation of the *Inspektion des U-Bootwesens*, an independent administrative body charged with evaluation and development, in the prewar period ensured that early lessons were rapidly assimilated. The German wartime construction programmes were characterized by long production runs, with incremental improvements being made to each successive design, and by 1918 the Germans were acknowledged to be world leaders in submarine technology.

### *FRANCE'S EX-GERMAN WAR PRIZES*

| *Originally* | *French name* | *Displ (surf/sub)* | *Fate* |
|---|---|---|---|
| U-CRUISER | | | |
| U-139 | Halbronn | 1150t/2500t | BU 1935 |
| OCEAN-GOING TYPE | | | |
| U-105 | Jean Autric | 798t/1000t | BU 1937 |
| U-108 | Léon Mignot | 798t/1000t | BU 1935 |
| U-162 | Pierre Marrast | 820t/1000t | BU 1937 |
| U-166 | Jean Roulier | 820t/1000t | BU 1935 |
| COASTAL TYPE | | | |
| UB-94 | Trinité-Schillemans | 520t/640t | BU 1935 |
| UB-99 | Carissan | 520t/640t | BU 1935 |
| UB-155 | Jean Corre | 525t/650t | BU 1936 |
| MINELAYERS | | | |
| U-79 | Victor Réveillé | 750t/830t | BU 1933 |
| U-119 | René Audry | 1165t/1510t | BU 1937 |

The qualities of the war-built German submarines were precisely those lacking in the French prewar designs: robust construction coupled with reliable diesel engines, high endurance, rapid diving (as little as 35 seconds for some U-boats), and a powerful, well-balanced armament.

Following a Conference of Ambassadors on 25 June 1920 it was finally agreed to distribute the surviving German U-boats among the victorious allied powers. Ten submarines duly arrived in the summer of 1920 to be refurbished for service in the *Marine Nationale*, together with a further 36 boats for breaking up. All were in poor condition, due not only to the neglect of the past two years, but to the sabotage of much of their equipment by their former German crews. It was to take between two and four years, and considerable German (and, ironically, English!) assistance before they were ready for service again. Nevertheless, early inspection of the hulls, machinery and control systems provided invaluable assistance in the preparation of new submarine designs.

The German prizes provided a useful cross-section of the types designed and completed during the First World War. There was a single large U-cruiser (ex-*U-139*), four ocean-going U-boats (designated *de grande patrouille* by the French in accordance with the system of classification recommended by the CEPSM), three coastal submarines of the UB III type (designated *de moyenne patrouille*), and two minelayers (one large, one of medium size).

The foundations for French submarine development in the postwar era had now been laid, and all seemed set for a period of consolidation and steady progress. However, the political manoeuvring which inevitably accompanies the end of a great war had not yet run its course, and the *Marine Nationale* would soon be faced by a threat from a totally unexpected quarter.

## *The Washington Conference*

The Washington conference which took place between November 1921 and February 1922 is generally remembered for the limitations which it imposed on the battlefleets of the major world naval powers. What is perhaps less well known is that Britain, which had hitherto shown herself recalcitrant and obstructive regarding the distribution of the surviving German U-boats as prizes, attempted to obtain from the conference the total abolition of submarines from the naval inventory, mounting a strong verbal assault on the French in the process. Quoting from a treatise on submarine warfare by a French naval officer and academic (Castex, *Synthèse de la Guerre Sous-Marine de Pontchartrain à Tirpitz*, published in 1920), the British delegation accused France of preparing for a submarine war on commerce.

The French delegates, although taken by surprise by the vehemence of this assault, nevertheless put up a determined resistance to the British proposal, which eventually foundered for lack of support from the United States and Japan. Both the Americans and the Japanese wanted submarines which could scout for their respective battlefleets in the vast expanses of the Pacific, and neither was prepared to abandon such a key piece in the strategic game of chess which would develop during the postwar period. A resolution to prohibit the employment of submarines against merchant vessels was adopted by the Conference, but came to nothing when the French refused to ratify the clause.

The French nation was most unhappy with the outcome of the Washington Conference. It felt particularly aggrieved that the ratios for capital ship construction had been established on the basis of *existing* fleets, given the catastrophic effect on French naval construction programmes of the German occupation of Northern France. The ratios took no account either of the ambitious 1912 programme or of France's position as the world's second colonial power, with overseas commitments stretching from the Caribbean to the Pacific. French pride was hurt by being relegated to fourth place after Japan, and by parity with Italy, now seen as her major rival in the Mediterranean.

The response of the French parliament shows clearly the strength of national feeling regarding the conference. The Washington Treaty was ratified only in July 1923, and many *députés* felt that France should circumvent the restrictions imposed on capital ship construction by reviving the 'small-ship' naval strategy advanced by the *Jeune Ecole* of the late nineteenth century. Thus when the *Marine Nationale* requested 96,000 tons of submarines (including 65,000 tons *de haute mer*) in 1924–25, the parliamentary commissions responded by raising this figure to 124,800 tons (96,000 tons *de haute mer*).

It goes without saying that news of these figures was not well-received in Britain, where France was still suspected of planning a trade war against the British merchant fleet. These suspicions were to endure even into the early 1930s, and were only reinforced by the construction of the large corsair submarine *Surcouf* in the late 1920s. The irony of the situation is that while the French parliament was voting funds for large programmes of submarine construction as a reflex action against Anglo-Saxon arrogance, the *Marine Nationale* was using the largest part of those funds to pursue a project of long standing which offered little or no threat to the British merchant fleet, the *sous-marin d'escadre* or 'fleet submarine'.

## New construction programme

At the same time that these political controversies were raging, the chief constructor Léon Roquebert was supervising the plans for the new generation of submarines. Whereas French submarine development before the war had been piecemeal and fragmented Roquebert, who was to be chief constructor from 1916 until 1936, gave to the postwar programmes stability and continuity, and was subsequently referred to as the 'father' of the submarine fleet.

Various submarine projects were considered during 1920–21, of which perhaps the most interesting were design 'J', a 3000-tonne boat armed with a 305mm (12in) gun similar in conception to the British 'M' class, and design 'K', a 4000-tonne troop-carrying submarine. However, the only designs seriously pursued during this period were drawn up within the tight framework of the CEPSM recommendations, and six *sous-marins de grande patrouille* of the *Requin* class and six *sous-marins de moyenne patrouille* were duly authorized in 1922.

### *Requin* Class

| | | | |
|---|---|---|---|
| Auth 1922 | Q115 Requin | Auth 1923 | Q127 Caïman |
| | Q116 Souffleur | | Q128 Phoque |
| | Q117 Morse | | Q129 Espadon |
| | Q118 Narval | | |
| | Q119 Marsouin | | |
| | Q120 Dauphin | | |

| | |
|---|---|
| Displacement: | 1150t surfaced; 1441t submerged |
| Dimensions: | 78.3m × 6.8m × 5.1m<br>256ft 10in × 22ft 4in × 16ft 9in |
| Propulsion: | 2 shafts, 2 Sulzer/Schneider diesels, 2 electric motors, 2900bhp/1800hp = 15kts/9kts |
| Oil Fuel: | 116t (+51t in ballast tanks) |
| Torpedo tubes: | 10–550mm (+6 reserve); 4 bow, 2 stern, 2 twin trainable |
| Guns: | 1–100mm/40 cal Mod 1925, 2–8mm MG (2 × 1) |
| Complement: | 51 |

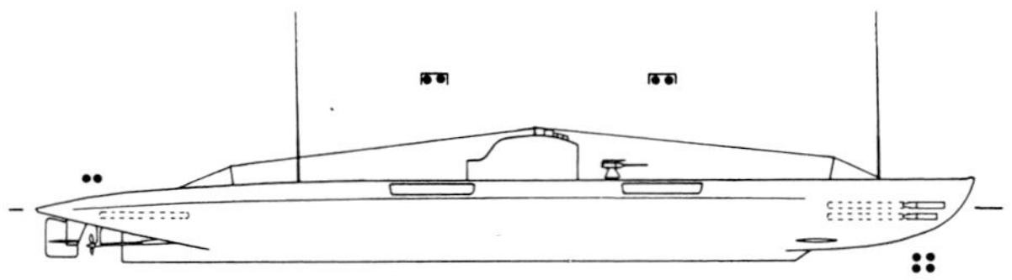

*Requin* class, general arrangement. (Author)

The *Requin* was a relatively conservative design, based closely on the German U-boats of the *U-93/U-127* classes acquired by the *Marine Nationale* in 1920. Smaller than the 1800-tonne type recommended by the CEPSM, these boats had only two thirds the endurance (7700nm at 9kts), and failed to make their designed surface speed on their Sulzer/Schneider diesels. In spite of strong CEPSM recommendations to the contrary, the designers could not resist the attractions of lightweight machinery and construction, and regular equipment failures resulted. The conning tower was again too cramped, and had to be rebuilt in the late 1930s. Handling characteristics were less than satisfactory, and there were defects in the layout of the auxiliary machinery, with poor access for maintenance.

Nevertheless these boats constituted a major improvement over the prewar designs; they were fast-diving and well-armed. By comparison with the ocean-going type proposed by the CEPSM there was a reduction to two stern torpedo tubes, but this was in part compensated for by the trainable external mountings, which could supplement the fixed tubes on after bearings. In line with the committee's recommendations six reserve torpedoes were provided, giving a total of sixteen weapons.

### 600 Tonnes Type

| | | | |
|---|---|---|---|
| Auth 1922 | Q121 Ondine (N) | Auth 1923 | Q130 Eurydice (N) |
| | Q122 Ariane (N) | | Q131 Danaë (N) |
| | Q123 Sirène (L) | | Q132 Galatée (L) |
| | Q124 Naïade (L) | | Q133 Nymphe (L) |
| | Q125 Circé (S) | | Q134 Thétis (S) |
| | Q126 Calypso (S) | | Q135 Doris (S) |

| | |
|---|---|
| Displacement: | 626ft surfaced; 787t submerged* |
| Dimensions: | 66.0m × 4.9m × 4.1m<br>216ft 6in × 16ft 1in × 13ft 6in |
| Propulsion: | 2 shafts, 2 Normand-Vickers diesels, 2 electric motors, 1200bhp/1000hp = 14kts/7.5kts |
| Oil Fuel: | 60t |
| Torpedo tubes: | 7–550mm (+1 reserve): 3 bow, 2 stern, 1 twin trainable |
| Guns: | 1–100mm/40cal Mod 1925, 2–8mm MG (2 × 1) |
| Complement: | 41 |

(N) = Normand; (L) = A C de la Loire; (S) = Schneider
* details for *Ondine* sub-group (N)

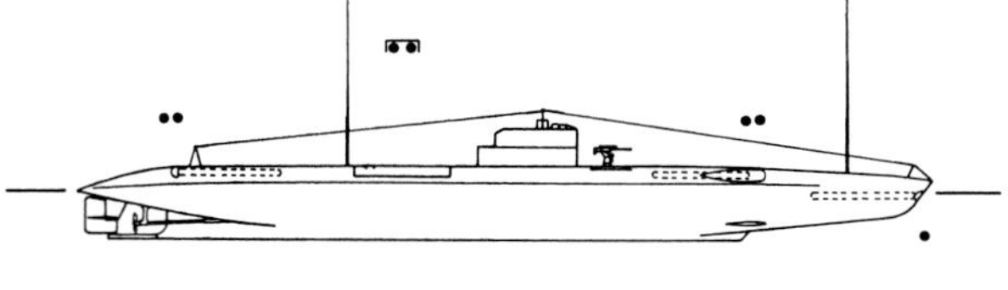

600 tonnes *type, general arrangement.* (Author).

Morse, *of the* Requin *class, as she appeared in 1930. Note the distinctive trainable torpedo tubes fore and aft of the conning tower. The deck gun is a 100mm Model 1925.* (Marius Bar)

*The 600t submarine* Danaë *of the Normand-Fenaux sub-group. She has the 75mm Model 1928 deck gun, and the external bow tubes are less prominent than in the Schneider-Laubeuf sub-group.* (Marius Bar)

*The 600t submarine* Thetis, *of the Schneider-Laubeuf sub-group, shortly after completion in 1930. She has the 100mm Model 1925 in place of the 75mm Model 1928 fitted in most submarines of the class. Note the prominent external* tubes canons *on either side of the bow.* (Marius Bar)

The 600-tonne *sous-marins de moyenne patrouille* (also termed *'de défense côtière'*) represented a radical departure from previous practice in that they were designed and built by private shipyards on the basis of specifications laid down by the *Service Technique des Constructions Navales*. Three shipyards were each responsible for a sub-group of four boats (the second half of the order was authorized in 1923), and drew up their own plans under the aegis of former constructors employed as consultants. Augustin-Normand was advised by Fenaux, Schneider by Laubeuf, and A C de la Loire by Simonot.

They were well-armed for their size, the arrangement adopted being a single internal bow tube with two external fixed tubes (designated *tubes-canons*) forward of the conning tower, two fixed stern tubes, and a trainable twin mounting immediately abaft the conning tower, for a total of seven ready-use torpedoes plus a reserve torpedo for the single bow tube. There was also a 75mm (3in) deck gun, although several units received a 100mm (3.9in).

The *600 tonnes* were manoeuvrable and well-adapted to operations in shallow waters. However, French persistence with the double hull (also a feature of the German UB III on which these boats were closely modelled) meant that crew accommodation was particularly cramped. They were not good divers, experienced stability problems, and had a maximum underwater speed of only 7.5kts. They also shared many of the defects of the *Requin* class with regard to the layout and reliabilty of their machinery.

The Normand-Fenaux sub-group proved to be the most successful of the three, but the *Marine Nationale* clearly considered the experiment of putting out contracts to three competing shipyards worth repeating, as it was to adopt the same procedure with the next class of *sous-marins de moyenne patrouille*.

## The 1500 tonnes

It would be some years before the operational limitations of the *Requin* class would become apparent. A further three units were authorized under the 1923 programme, but already the conception of the type was being questioned. Derived as it was from the German U-boats, the *Requin* was well-suited to anti-commerce warfare on the high seas, but this type of warfare was an appropriate mission for the *Marine Nationale* only if Britain were the enemy. In spite of all the quarrelling and harsh words at the Washington Conference this seemed an unlikely eventuality. The hypothesis on which the French had based its 20-year postwar reconstruction programme had been war against Italy, with war against Germany being a secondary, more remote possibility.

If this game-plan were to be adhered to, it made little sense to build submarines to attack merchant ships on the high seas. The blockade of ports and attacks on coastal shipping in the shallow waters of the Mediterranean, or even the North Sea, could be performed more effectively by the *sous-marins de moyenne patrouille*, which were designed with precisely this function in mind. Rather than the general-purpose ocean-going type represented by the *Requin*, the *Marine Nationale* required a 'fleet submarine' which could attack enemy warships and which could scout for its own battlefleet.

The concept of a *sous-marin éclaireur d'escadre* was by no means new to the *Marine Nationale*. It had been a dream of the Naval Staff since 1914, when it was first proposed as an answer to the problem of scouting for the battlefleet. Not only would the *sous-marin d'escadre* provide the intelligence which would set up a fleet engagement in the most favourable circumstances, but it would also intervene in the battle on its own account.

Such a concept was all the more relevant now that the balance between the French and Italian battlefleets was so finely poised. In the wake of the Washington Treaty the

### *1500 TONNES TYPE*

| | | | |
|---|---|---|---|
| AUTH 1924 | Q136 Redoutable | AUTH 1927 | Q153 Phénix |
| | Q137 Vengeur | | Q154 Persée |
| | | | Q155 Protée |
| AUTH 1925 | Q138 Pascal | | Q156 Pégase |
| | Q139 Pasteur | | Q157 Prométhée |
| | Q140 Henri Poincaré | | |
| | Q141 Poncelet | AUTH 1928–9 | Q167 L'Espoir |
| | Q142 Archimède | | Q168 Le Glorieux |
| | Q143 Fresnel | | Q169 Le Centaure |
| | Q144 Monge | | Q170 Le Héros |
| | | | Q171 Le Conquérant |
| AUTH 1926 | Q147 Achille | | Q172 Le Tonnant |
| | Q148 Ajax | | |
| | Q149 Actéon | AUTH 1930 | Q178 Agosta |
| | Q150 Achéron | | Q179 Béveziers |
| | Q151 Argo | | Q180 Ouessant |
| | | | Q181 Sidi Ferruch |
| | | | Q182 Sfax |
| | | | Q183 Casabianca |

| | |
|---|---|
| Displacement: | 1570t surfaced; 2084t submerged |
| Dimensions: | 92.3m × 8.2m × 4.7m<br>302ft 10in × 26ft 11in × 15ft 5in |
| Propulsion: | 2 shafts, 2 Sulzer/Schneider diesels, 2 electric motors, 6000–8000bhp/2000hp = 17–20kts (see text) |
| Oil Fuel: | 95t (+117t in ballast tanks) |
| Torpedo tubes: | 9–550mm (+2 reserve): 2–400mm: 4 bow 550mm, 1 trainable triple 550mm, 1 trainable quadruple 550/400mm. |
| Guns: | 1–100mm/50cal Mod 1925, 2–13.2mm AA (1 × 2) |
| Complement: | 61 |

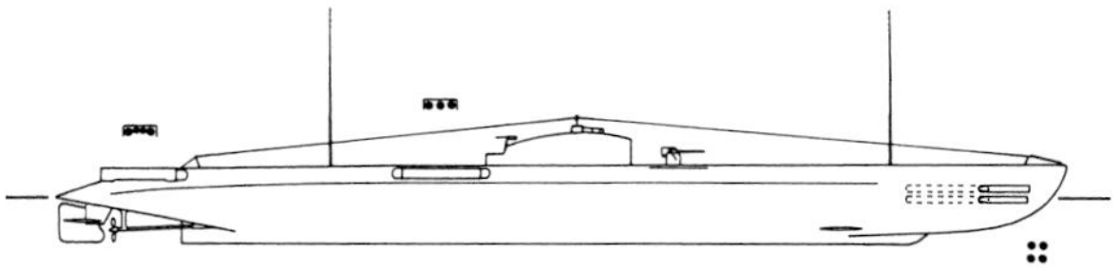

1500 tonnes *type, general arrangement.* (Author).

Pasteur, *one of the early boats of the 1500t series. The triple trainable torpedo mounting abaft the conning tower houses three 550mm tubes, while the stern mounting comprises two 400mm tubes inside two 550mm tubes.* (Marius Bar)

*The 1500t submarine* Protée *with hinged radio masts in the raised position. The photo dates from 1937. The tricolore panel was painted on the conning tower as a recognition feature for the duration of the Spanish Civil War.* (Marius Bar)

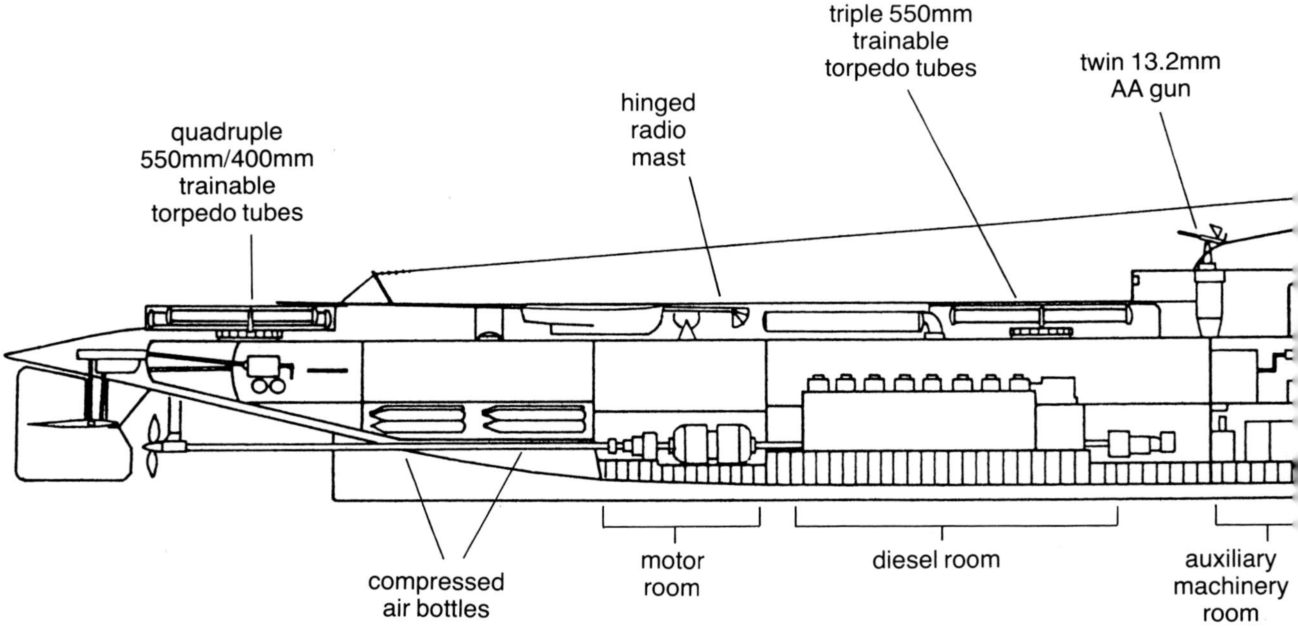


1500 tonnes *type, inboard profile.* (Author)

French battle line comprised only six battleships, and the absence of one or two ships for refit or repair could swing the balance in favour of the enemy unless other means were available to reduce his material superiority prior to the major fleet action.

The *Marine Nationale* was much influenced by British thinking of the time, and took a close interest in both the diesel-powered 'J' class and the steam-powered 'K' class of the late war period. In December 1922, before even the first boat of the *Requin* class was laid down, the *Conseil Supérieur de la Marine* requested a preliminary design for a diesel-powered submarine with a surfaced speed of 18kts, capable of operations in concert with the surface fleet. This was duly presented in February 1923 as Project M², but was immediately rejected. The designers had attempted to fulfil the requirements on a hull of 1000–1080 tonnes displacement, and the resulting design was cramped, with suspect endurance.

The major problem was undoubtedly that of building a diesel engine powerful enough to provide the high surface speed required. With the British 'J' class Vickers had to go to twelve cylinders and three shafts to provide the 3600bhp necessary for a design speed of 19.5kts. The longer engine resulted in torsional vibration, and the machinery spaces occupied 36 per cent of the boat's length, thereby precluding the installation of stern torpedo tubes. The Sulzer/Schneider diesels employed in the *Requin* were rated at only 1450bhp, yet these were by far the most powerful units yet built in France. The relatively low displacement of the M² design was therefore dictated by the maximum brake horsepower available from current diesels, as in theory a smaller boat could be driven at a higher speed by prime movers with a fixed output.

Nevertheless the *Conseil*, no doubt aware that the German submarine cruisers of the *U-142* type (none of which had been completed before the termination of hostilities) were to have been powered by MAN diesel units rated at 3000bhp, was not satisfied that the STCN designers had explored every possible avenue with Project M². It responded by tightening up the performance specifications and by inviting private shipyards to contribute to the studies, while at the same time removing all restrictions on displacement.

It was specified that the new submarines should be armed with four bow torpedo tubes (with four reserve torpedoes) and two trainable twin mountings, complemented by a single 100mm (3.9in) gun, an anti-aircraft gun and two machine-guns. Speed would be 17kts *sustained* (a 48-hour trial was demanded!), with an endurance of 4000nm (or 30 days) at 10kts on diesels and 100nm at 5kts on batteries. The submarine should be capable of diving in less than 60 seconds, would have a maximum diving depth of 80m (260ft) and a 25 per cent reserve of bouyancy. Displacement was to be the *minimum* compatible with these requirements.

The demand for 17kts sustained was undoubtedly the most difficult requirement; it was to be achieved, although at some cost in terms of size, complexity and reliability. Other interesting features of the draft requirements are the abandonment of fixed stern torpedo tubes, thereby releasing internal volume at the after end of the boat for high-powered propulsion machinery – they were

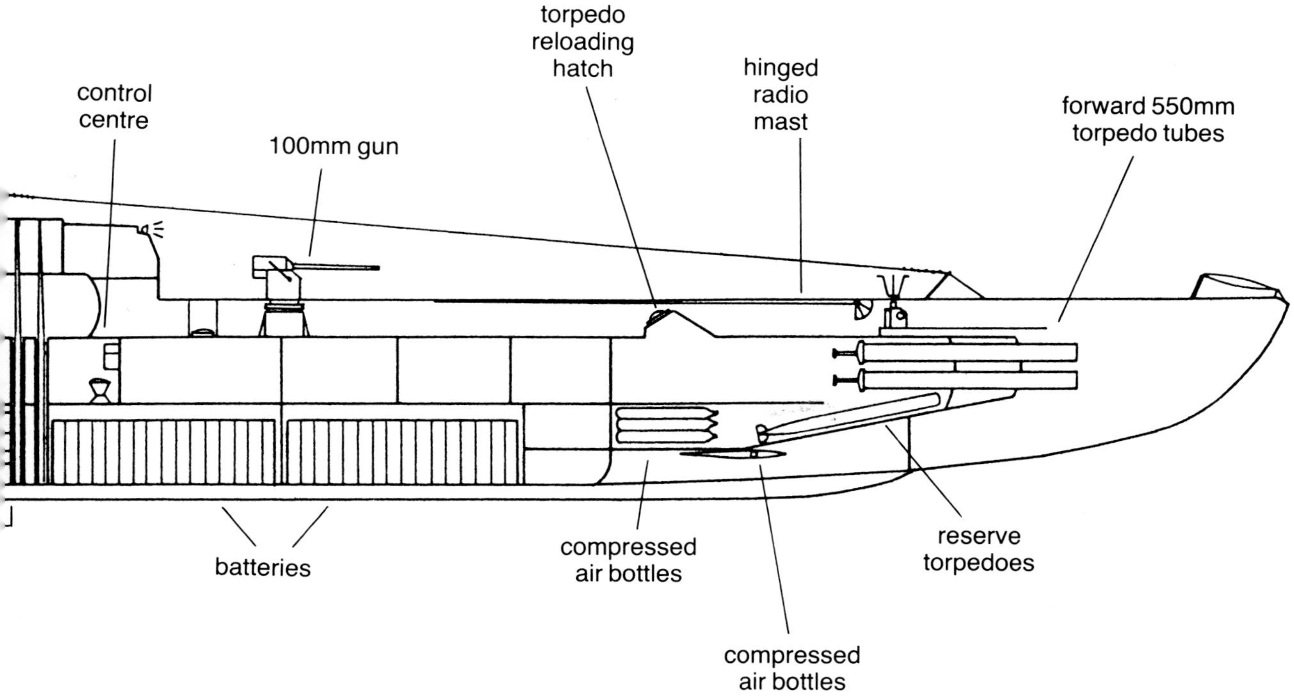


to be effectively replaced by locating one of the two trainable mountings directly above the stern – and the substantial AA armament.

The apparently limited endurance is a reflection of the submarine's primary mission in support of the battlefleet, a mission which required less bunkerage than the anti-commerce role. The *Marine Nationale* disliked the idea of using external fuel tanks, as they were subject to tell-tale oil leaks which threatened the security of the boat – this proved to be a constant problem for the Royal Navy's large 'overseas' patrol submarines of the 1920s. However, in order to ensure that the submarines could be deployed to protect French interests in distant waters, external tanks could be used to double the bunkerage for a maximum range of 8000nm.

The resulting design was the *1500 tonnes*, a type which was to dominate French submarine construction between the wars. The first two units, *Redoutable* and *Vengeur* were authorized in 1924, and twenty-nine further units, forming four different sub-groups, followed between 1925 and 1930. By the outbreak of war in 1939 the *1500 tonnes* made up 40 per cent of the French submarine fleet.

All units of the class had a hull of similar dimensions. Differences between the various sub-groups were largely concerned with improvements in performance, characterized by ever-more-powerful diesels exhibiting a steady increase in power/weight ratio. The power/weight ratio for the diesels installed in *Requin* had been 32kg/bhp (despite CEPSM recommendations that it should be at least 40kg/bhp in order to secure reliability); in *Redoutable* this figure was reduced to 27kg/bhp, and in *Agosta*, the lead boat of the last series, to 20kg/bhp.

In terms of available horsepower this gave the boats of the *Redoutable/Pascal* sub-groups a total of 6000bhp for a maximum surface speed of 18kts, while the diesels of the *L'Espoir* sub-group (authorized 1928–29) were rated at 7200bhp for 19kts, and those of the *Agosta* (authorized 1930) at 8000bhp for 20kts. Some boats of the *Agosta* series even sustained 21kts on trials, although this speed was never to be attained in operational service.

In order to reduce the stress on their high-technology diesels the *1500 tonnes* were restricted to 75 per cent of maximum power during peacetime, giving them a maximum surfaced speed of 14–15kts. Moreover, the critical speed of the diesels relative to vibration had to taken into account when grouping the *1500 tonnes* into divisions of four, as mixing units from different sub-groups resulted in problems when the submarines operated in formation.

Of the submarines built overseas during the 1920s only the Japanese fleet boats of the 'KD' (*Kaidei*) type can be adequately compared with the French *1500 tonnes*, and it is by no means clear that the French were aware of Japanese developments. A further attempt at producing a fast, high-powered fleet submarine was made by the Royal Navy in the 1930s with the three *Thames* class boats, which had a surfaced displacement of 1850 tons, a length of 345ft (105m), and were driven by two large turbo-charged diesels each rated at 5000bhp, but construction of this class (originally projected as twenty units), was quickly terminated and only three boats were completed.

The large size of the *1500 tonnes* enabled the designers

*Orion, one of only two 630t boats built to a Loire-Simonot design. The conning tower is reminiscent of the 1500t. The photo dates from 1934.* (Marius Bar)

to make incremental improvements to each sub-group without a corresponding increase in dimensions. Nevertheless, there was still inadequate attention to habitability, and the *1500 tonnes* never attained their designed 30-day patrol. There was insufficient ventilation in the early boats, supplies of bottled oxygen were inadequate, and fresh stores were provided for the equivalent of 2½ days! (This last defect was corrected by the installation of additional refrigeration power at later refits.)

Despite double hull construction the *1500 tonnes* could dive in 40–45 seconds. Handling when dived was excellent, and they could stay submerged for 18 hours consecutively, surfacing only at night to replenish batteries. Sea-keeping on the surface was adjudged superior to that of the torpedo-boats of the *Bourrasque* class (also designated *1500 tonnes*), although there were problems with the forward diving planes, which were mounted low and close to the bow, when running on the surface in heavy seas.

Wartime experience was to reveal that insufficient attention was given to protecting the submarines against the shocks experienced during depth-charging. Problems were experienced with water-tight hatches and battery integrity. Electrically-operated systems such as lighting circuits and the external torpedo mountings frequently failed because switchboards and control systems were not seated on flexible mountings. The *1500 tonnes* were inferior in this respect to the earlier *Requin* because a greater proportion of their equipment was located between the pressure hull and the outer casing.

The armament of the *1500 tonnes* as completed differed in one important respect from that specified by the *Conseil Supérieur*. The 550mm (21.7in) heavyweight torpedo, which had a 315kg (695lb) warhead, was considered unnecessarily powerful for use against small surface targets. The *Marine Nationale* therefore embarked on the development of a lightweight 400mm (15.75in) torpedo with a 144kg (317lb) warhead. Maximum range at 44kts was 1800m as compared with 3000m for the 550mm torpedo.

It proved possible to accommodate triple trainable torpedo mountings in place of the twin mountings specified by the *Conseil Supérieur*, and with the advent of the lightweight 400mm torpedo it was decided that the stern mounting should comprise two 400mm tubes inside two outer tubes of 550mm calibre. This made for a total of eleven tubes (nine of 550mm plus two of 400mm) in place of the eight 550mm tubes originally specified. In compensation, only two reserve torpedoes were carried for the bow tubes.

For the British Admiralty the development of a 400mm torpedo was further evidence that the French were preparing for a commerce war against merchant shipping. In this it was entirely mistaken. The 400mm tubes of the *1500 tonnes* were intended for targets of opportunity. Had they been intended for a sustained campaign against merchant shipping the ratio of 400mm to 550mm tubes would have been different, and reloads would have been essential. Not only were the French 400mm tubes always in an external mounting, but of the entire submarine fleet only the large corsair submarine *Surcouf* carried reserve 400mm torpedoes, and these had to be reloaded via a hoist

*The 630t submarine* Amazone, *of the Normand-Fenaux sub-group. Note the telescopic signals mast used to communicate with other boats in her division (submarines operated in tactical groupings of four).* (Marius Bar)

*The 630t submarine* Oréade *of the Normand-Fenaux sub-group. The radio masts are hinged down onto the deck casing.* (Marius Bar)

and a crane while the boat was running on the surface.

The 400mm torpedo proved ultimately unsuccessful, and many failures were experienced in action. In 1943–44 the surviving *1500 tonnes* had their stern trainable tubes replaced by a second triple 550mm mounting.

### *630 TONNES TYPE*

| | | | |
|---|---|---|---|
| AUTH 1926 | Argonaute (S) | AUTH 1928 | Q163 Orphée (N) |
| | Aréthuse (S) | | Q164 Oréade (N) |
| | Diane (N) | | Q165 Orion (L) |
| | Méduse (N) | | Q166 Ondine (L) |
| AUTH 1927 | Q159 Amphitrite (N) | AUTH 1929 | Q174 La Psyché (N) |
| | Q160 Antiope (N) | | Q175 La Sybille (N) |
| | Q161 Amazone (N) | | Q176 La Vestale (S) |
| | Q162 Atalante (S) | | Q177 La Sultane (S) |

| | |
|---|---|
| Displacement: | 630t surfaced; 798t submerged* |
| Dimensions: | 63.4m × 5.2m × 4.2m<br>208ft × 17ft 0in × 13ft 9in |
| Propulsion: | 2 Schneider-Carel diesels, 2 electric motors, 1300bhp/1000hp = 14kts/9kts |
| Oil Fuel: | 65t |
| Torpedo tubes: | 6–550mm (+1 reserve): 2–400mm: 3 bow 550mm, 1 trainable twin 550mm, 1 trainable triple 550/400mm. |
| Guns: | 1–75mm/35cal Mod 1928,<br>1–8mm MG |
| Complement: | 41 |

* details for Argonaute sub-group (S)

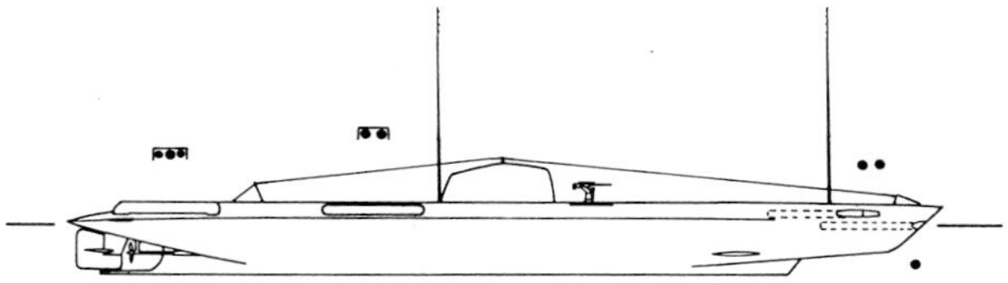

630 tonnes *type, general arrangement.* (Author)

## *The 630 tonnes and Amirauté types*

The twelve 600-tonne submarines of the *Sirène/Ariane/Circé* series were superseded by a new class of sixteen slightly larger boats authorized 1926–29. The *630 tonnes* were, like their predecessors, designed and built in private shipyards to a specification provided by the STCN. Nine were completed to a Normand-Fenaux design with Normand-Vickers 4-stroke diesels, five to a Schneider-Laubeuf design with 2-stroke Schneider-Carel diesels, and two to a Loire-Dubigeon design with 2-stroke Sulzer diesels. Five different shipyards participated in the construction programme.

The *630 tonnes* were better divers than their predecessors. The stability problems experienced with the *600 tonnes* were corrected, and the hydraulically-operated control surfaces proved more reliable than the electric controls of the latter. Underwater speed was increased from 7.5kts to 9kts, and the trainable torpedo mounting above the stern incorporated two 400mm tubes outside a single 550mm. However, the *630 tonnes* suffered from the traditional French vice of over-elaboration in the pursuit of high performance, and the sheer quantity of new equipment meant that they were more cluttered and less habitable than the *600 tonnes*.

With the termination of the *630 tonnes* programme the *Marine Nationale* clearly felt that private competition had delivered as much as could reasonably be expected in terms of innovation and improvements in performance, and that it was time to incorporate the lessons learned in a simpler, standard design. The next class, authorized in 1930 (a further two boats would follow in 1936), was designed by the STCN and was to be known as the *Amirauté* type.

### *AMIRAUTÉ TYPE*

| | | | |
|---|---|---|---|
| AUTH 1930 | Q185 Minerve | AUTH 1936 | Q189 Pallas |
| | Q186 Junon | | Q190 Cérès |
| | Q187 Vénus | | |
| | Q188 Iris | | |

| | |
|---|---|
| Displacement: | 662t surfaced; 856t submerged |
| Dimensions: | 68.1m × 5.6m × 3.7m<br>223ft 5in × 18ft 5in × 12ft 2in |
| Propulsion: | 2 shafts, 2 Normand-Vickers diesels, 2 electric motors, 1800bhp/1230hp = 14.5kts/9kts |
| Oil Fuel: | 60t |
| Torpedo tubes: | 6–550mm, 3–400mm: 4 bow 550mm, 2 stern 550mm, 1 trainable triple 400mm. |
| Guns: | 1–75mm/35cal Mod 1928,<br>1–13.2mm AA, 2–8mm MG |
| Complement: | 42 |

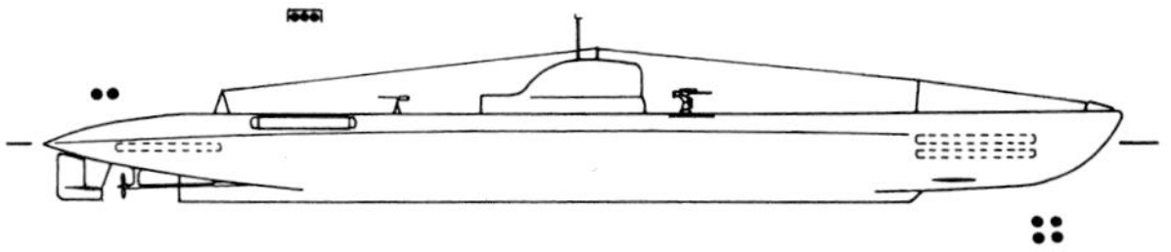

Amirauté *type, general arrangement.* (Author)

The armament of these boats was greatly simplified. There were four 550mm internal bow tubes (for the first time in a *sous-marin de moyenne patrouille*), two 550mm internal stern tubes, and a triple 400mm trainable mounting abaft the conning tower. No reserve torpedoes were carried in order to maximise internal volume. Other performance parameters were similar to the *630 tonnes*, the 4-stroke Normand-Vickers diesel being preferred to the Sulzer/Schneider units.

Authorised at the rate of 1–2 per year between 1925 and 1930, the six minelayers of the *Saphir* class were contemporaries of the *630 tonnes*. Designed to lay mines in the shallow waters of the Mediterranean and the North Sea, they were relatively small submarines with a surfaced displacement of 760 tonnes. Performance was unremarkable, but they proved robust and reliable, and their relatively small size made them particularly well-suited to operations in shallow waters. *Rubis*, which served with the FNFL (Free French naval forces) from June 1940, was the outstanding minelaying submarine of the Second World War.

### *Saphir Class*

| | |
|---|---|
| Auth 1925 Q145 Saphir<br>Q146 Turquoise | Auth 1927 Q158 Rubis |
| Auth 1926 Q152 Nautilus | Auth 1929 Q173 Diamant |
| | Auth 1930 Q184 Perle |

| | |
|---|---|
| Displacement: | 761t surfaced; 925t submerged |
| Dimensions: | 65.9m × 7.1m × 4.3m<br>216ft 2in × 23ft 4in × 14ft 1in |
| Propulsion: | 2 shafts, 2 Normand-Vickers diesels, 2 electric motors, 1300bhp/1100hp = 12kts/9kts |
| Oil Fuel: | 95t |
| Mines: | 32 HS 4 |
| Torpedo tubes: | 3–550mm (+2 reserve): 2–400mm: 2 bow 550mm, 1 trainable triple 550/400mm. |
| Guns: | 1–75mm/35cal Mod 1928, 1–13.2mm AA, 2–8mm MG |
| Complement: | 42 |

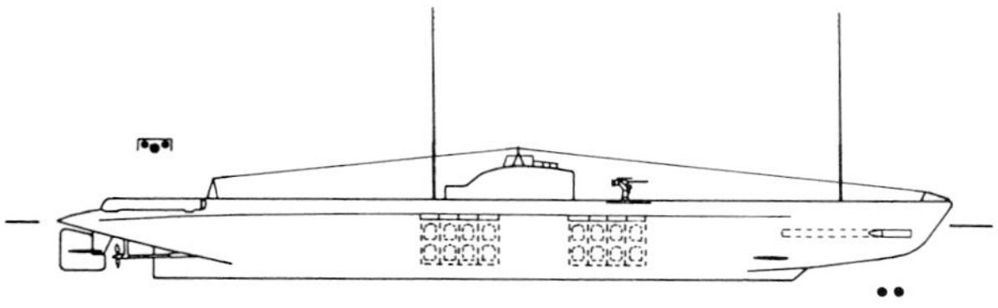

Saphir *class, general arrangement.* (Author)

## *Surcouf*

The *Surcouf*, classified by the *Marine Nationale* as a *croiseur corsaire submersible*, was authorized in 1926. Laid down in the following year, she was to take some seven years to build and on completion was the world's largest submarine – a position she was to hold until 1942.

In conception she derived from the German U-Cruisers of the First World War, although the design was also undoubtedly influenced by the British X-1 cruiser submarine, completed in September 1925. On a standard displacement of 2880 tonnes she was armed with twin 203mm (8in) 50cal guns in a fully-enclosed, water-tight rotating turret. In contrast to the *1500 tonnes* the torpedo armament was weighted in favour of the smaller 400mm torpedo, which was considered more than adequate against mercantile targets. There were four bow tubes of 550mm, and two triple trainable mountings each of one 550mm tube and two 400mm tubes set into the after deck casing. Not only were there eight reserve torpedoes for the internal bow tubes, but a reload magazine containing four 400mm torpedoes was located within the pressure hull beneath the trainable mountings, the tubes being reloaded by the crew via a hoist and deck crane while the boat was surfaced.

Two large Sulzer diesels each rated at 3800bhp provided a maximum speed of 18.5kts on the surface, and the designed endurance was 10,000nm at 10kts, stores sufficient for a 90-day patrol being carried. A floatplane intended to locate potential targets on the high seas was carried in a watertight hangar abaft the conning tower, and there was accommodation for 40 prisoners.

### *Surcouf*

| | |
|---|---|
| Auth 1926 | Surcouf |

| | |
|---|---|
| Displacement: | 3304t surfaced; 4218t submerged |
| Dimensions: | 110.0m × 9.0m × 7.3m<br>360ft 10in × 29ft 6in × 24ft 0in |
| Propulsion: | 2 shafts, 2 Sulzer diesels, 2 electric motors, 7600bhp/3400hp = 18.5kts/8.5kts |
| Oil Fuel: | 272t (+88t in ballast tanks) |
| Torpedo tubes: | 6–550mm (+8 reserve): 4–400mm (+ 4 reserve): 4 bow 550mm, 2 trainable triple 550/400mm. |
| Guns: | 2–203mm/50cal Mod 1924 (1 × 2), 2–37mm AA (2 × 1), 4–8mm MG (2 × 2) |
| Complement: | 118 |

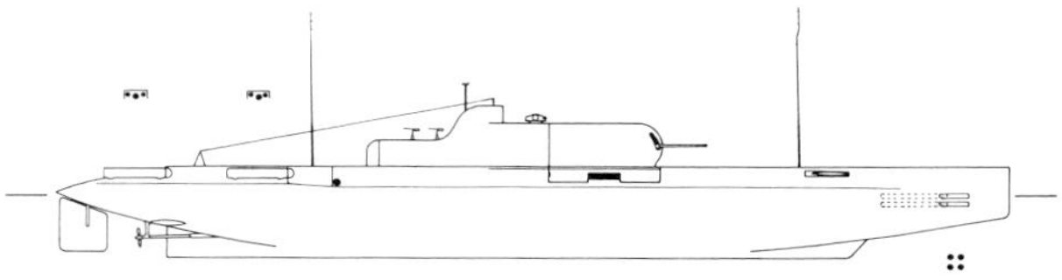

Surcouf, *general arrangement.* (Author)

The construction of *Surcouf*, with the prospect of a new generation of commerce-raiding cruisers – two sisters were projected by the *Marine Nationale* – could not fail to cause concern on the other side of the Channel, and the British made a second attempt to secure the abolition of the submarine as a weapon of war at the London Conference of 1930. On this occasion, however, the French delegation came better prepared, and a compromise was reached whereby France would be permitted to complete the *Surcouf* in return for an agreement to limit future submarines to 2000 tons standard displacement and 5.1in (130mm) guns.

The most serious weaknesses of the *Surcouf* design were conceptual rather than technical. By the time the submarine was completed France was again in a close

Rubis *under FNFL colours, seen after a particularly successful patrol, in August 1941.* (CMP). ▲

*The minelaying submarine* Nautilus, *third of the* Saphir *class. The vertical mine-chutes were set into the saddle tanks on either side of the conning tower.* (Marius Bar) ▼

Surcouf, *the largest and most impressive submarine of her generation. The 203mm guns were in a watertight rotating turret. At the after end of the conning tower was a hangar for a 'collapsible' Besson MB.411 scout seaplane. (*Marius Bar*)*

*A close-up of the* Surcouf*'s 8in guns. (*CMP*).*

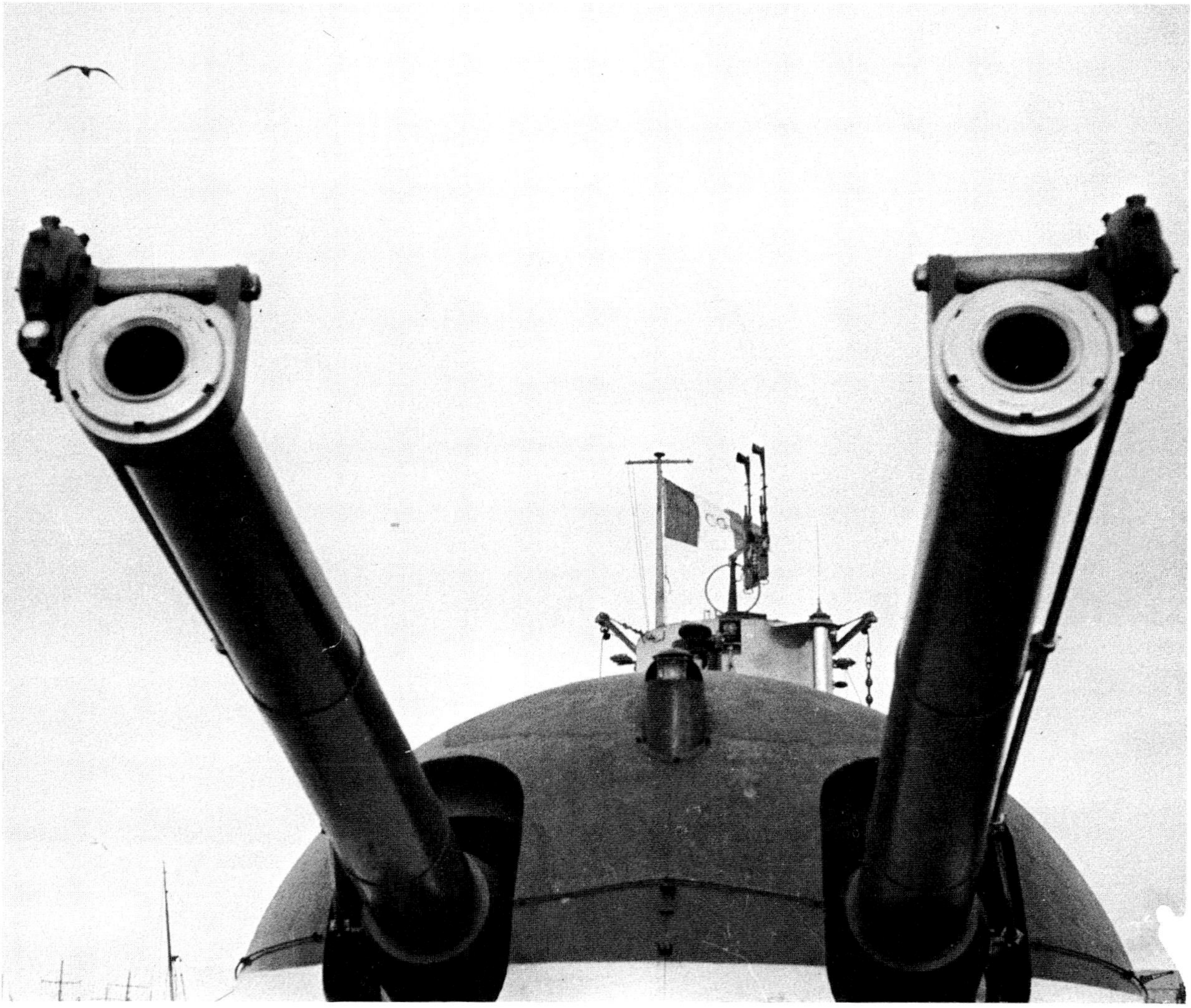

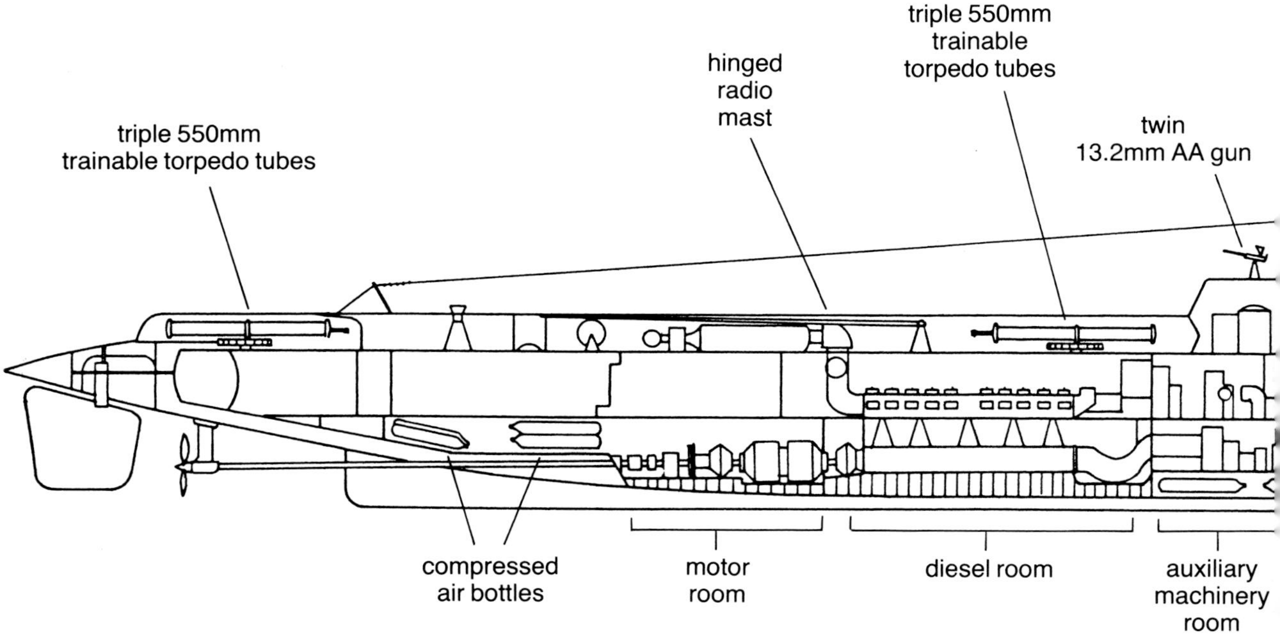


Roland Morillot *class, inboard profile.* (Author)

political alliance with Britain, and the potential enemies were Germany and Italy. Italy's mercantile trade was focused on the Mediterranean, while the trans-Atlantic operations of the small German merchant fleet would be quickly and effectively snuffed out by a Royal Navy blockade, leaving few worthwhile targets for a large commerce-raiding submarine.

When ultimately war broke out in 1939 *Surcouf* was a submarine in search of a mission and, by a supreme irony, was to spend a not-inconsiderable part of her remaining service life as a trans-Atlantic convoy escort.

## *The new generation*

The fascination which *Surcouf* held for foreign observers in her day has led to an over-estimation of her importance to French submarine development in the interwar period. Not only was the design ultimately a one-off in the Jules Verne tradition, but the very conception of the submarine as a commerce-raider places it outside the mainstream of French submarine development between the wars, which was primarily concerned with submarines which could support the French surface fleet. This preoccupation was further reaffirmed in 1934, the same year which saw the completion of *Surcouf*, with the authorization of the lead-boats of two new types, the *Roland Morillot* and the *Aurore*.

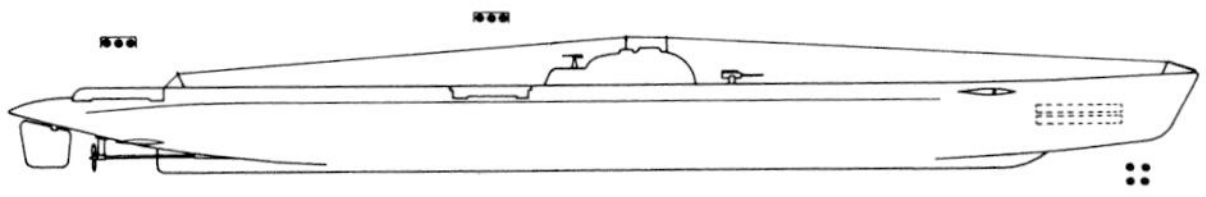

Roland Morillot *class, general arrangement.* (Author)

### *ROLAND MORILLOT CLASS*

AUTH 1934 Q191 Roland Morillot
AUTH 1937 Q198 La Praya
AUTH 1938 Q199 La Martinique, Q204 La Guadeloupe, Q205 La Réunion

| | |
|---|---|
| Displacement: | 1810t surfaced; 2417t submerged |
| Dimensions: | 102.5m × 8.3m × 4.6m<br>336ft 3in × 27ft 3in × 15ft 0in |
| Propulsion: | 2 shafts, 2 Sulzer diesels, 2 electric motors, 12,000bhp/2300hp = 22kts/ 9.5kts |
| Oil Fuel: | 93t (+85t in ballast tanks) |
| Torpedo tubes: | 10–550mm (+8/4 reserve): 4 bow, 2 trainable triple |
| Guns: | 1–100mm/40cal Mod 1936, 2–13.2mm AA. (1 × 2) |
| Complement: | 70 |

*Roland Morillot* was the linear successor to the *1500 tonnes*, and was to be the ultimate *sous-marin éclaireur*. With a length of 102.5m (336ft 3in) – 10m longer than the *Redoutable* – and a surface displacement of 1810 tonnes, the *Morillot* was to be powered by two Sulzer diesels, each producing a massive 6000bhp for a maximum speed of 22–23kts even at three-quarters power.

Other improvements were largely incremental, but there were attempts to iron out some of the more obvious defects of the *1500 tonnes*. The 400mm torpedo tubes were eliminated, giving the submarine a homogeneous armament of ten 550mm tubes (four fixed bow tubes, plus two triple trainable mountings abaft the conning tower). There were eight spare torpedoes for the bow tubes as compared to only two in the *1500 tonnes*. Internal fuel

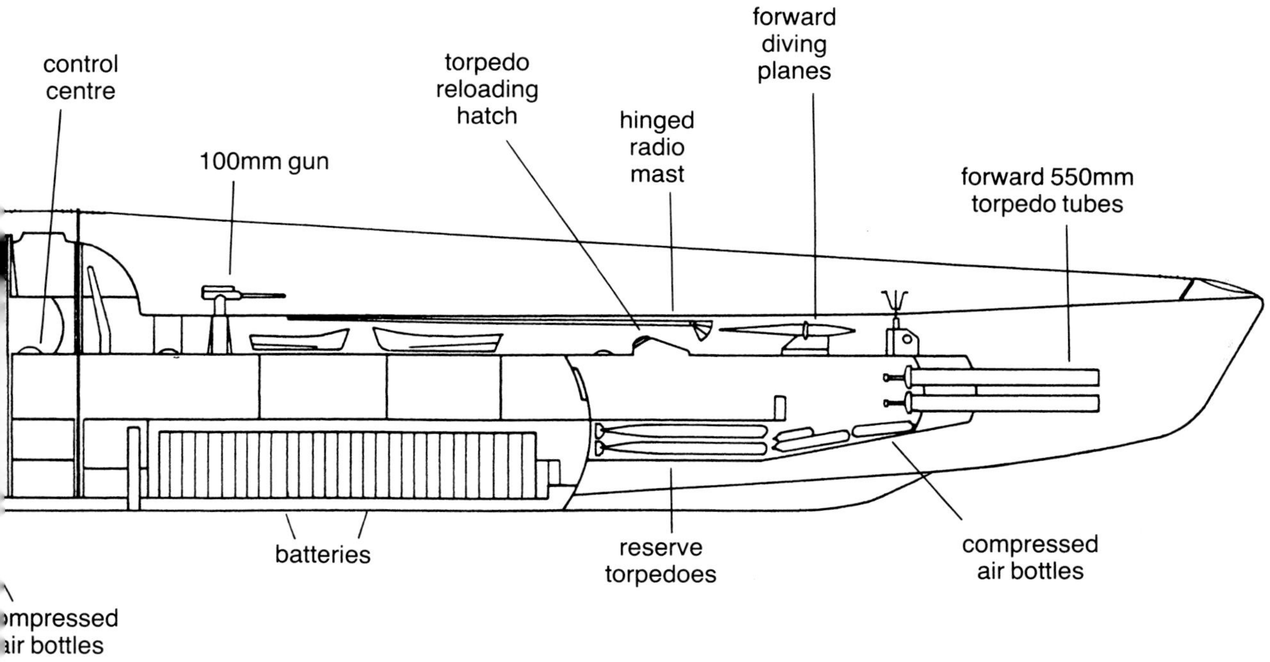


stowage was increased, thereby reducing the dependence on vulnerable external bunkerage and giving the submarines an endurance of 10,000nm at 10kts. The auxiliary machinery was located in a special compartment with improved access for maintenance. The hull was all-welded, and improvements were made in the location of the control surfaces. The forward diving planes, which were above the surfaced waterline, were fully retractable, and the after hydroplanes were forward of the propellers. Superior sea-keeping should have resulted, enabling the submarines to maintain high surfaced speed even in heavy seas

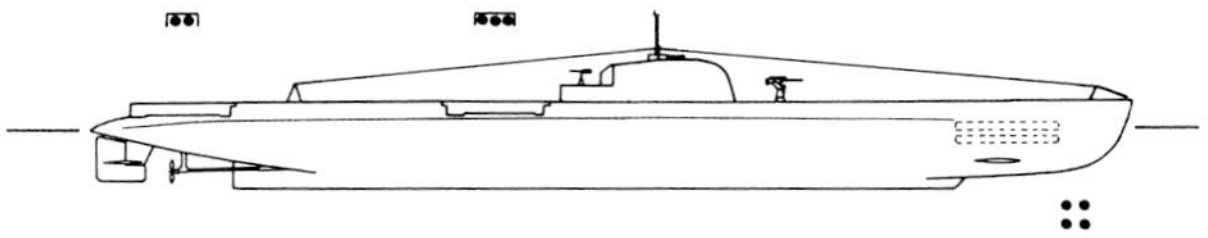

Aurore *class, general arrangement.* (Author)

## *Aurore Class*

| | | | |
|---|---|---|---|
| Auth 1934 | Q192 Aurore | Auth 1938 | Q200 L'Astrée |
| | | | Q201 L'Andromède |
| Auth 1937 | Q193 La Créole | | Q202 L'Antigone |
| | Q194 La Bayadère | | Q203 L'Andromaque |
| | Q195 La Favorite | | Q206 L'Artémis |
| | Q196 L'Africaine | | Q207 L'Armide |
| | | | Q211 L'Hermione |
| | | | Q212 La Gorgone |
| | | | Q213 La Clorinde |
| | | | Q214 La Cornélie |

| | |
|---|---|
| Displacement: | 893t surfaced; 1170t submerged |
| Dimensions: | 73.5m × 6.5m × 4.2m<br>241ft 2in × 21ft 4in × 13ft 9in |
| Propulsion: | 2 shafts, 2 Sulzer/Schneider diesels, 2 electric motors, 3000bhp/1400hp = 15.5kts/9kts |
| Oil Fuel: | 85t |
| Torpedo tubes: | 9–550mm: 4 bow, 1 trainable triple, 1 trainable double |
| Guns: | 1–100mm/40cal Mod 1936,<br>1–13.2mm AA |
| Complement: | 44 |

The smaller counterpart of the *Roland Morillot* was the *Aurore*, a larger, much-improved *Amirauté* type with a maximum diving depth of 100m (330ft), superior hydrodynamic features, and more powerful diesels, which gave it a designed surface speed of 15.5kts with 3/4 power. Operational radius was increased, and the armament was simplified, as in the *Roland Morillot*, by eliminating the 400mm torpedo tubes in favour of a triple trainable 550mm mounting abaft the conning tower and a twin trainable mounting above the stern.

The lead units of each of the new types were authorised in 1934, but budgetry pressures resulting from the rapid expansion of the surface fleet meant that there was to be a three-year gap in authorizations before the second *Roland Morillot* and four further units of the *Aurore* class were authorized, together with the lead-boat of an improved *Saphir* class minelayer, the *Emeraude*.

In 1935 a new system of classification was introduced: the *sous-marins de grande patrouille* became *sous-marins de première classe*, and the *sous-marins de moyenne patrouille* became *sous-marins de deuxième classe*. The reclassification was effectively a reaffirmation of the concept of the *sous-marin d'escadre*. The smaller French submarines were no longer regarded as a separate type intended for the less glamourous duties of coastal defence and blockade. They were now 'second-rank fleet submarines': smaller, less capable versions of 'first-rank' boats. The increases in size, diesel power and armament of the *Aurore* are indicative of this growing trend.

The pattern established during this period continued up to the outbreak of war, further units of the *Roland Morillot, Aurore* and *Emeraude* types being authorized in 1938. Of the twenty-five submarines on the stocks in September 1939 only *Aurore* was to be completed prior to the armistice of June 1940. Many, including the first three units of the *Roland Morillot* class, were to be sabotaged on the building ways; others were still incomplete at the end of the war, their construction being slowed or halted altogether for want of essential components. Thirteen submarines of an enlarged *Aurore* design (the *Phénix* class), intended for service in the tropics, were authorized 1939–40 but never laid down.

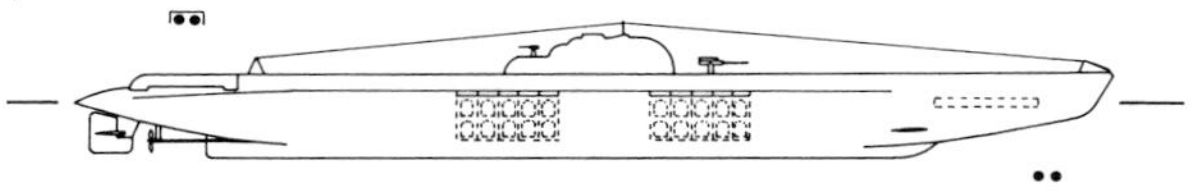

Emeraude *class, general arrangement.* (Author)

### *EMERAUDE CLASS*

| | |
|---|---|
| AUTH 1937 Q197 Emeraude | AUTH 1938 Q208 L'Agate<br>Q209 Le Corail<br>Q210 L'Escarboucle |
| Displacement: | 862t surfaced; 1119t submerged |
| Dimensions: | 72.7m × 7.4m × 4.1m<br>238ft 6in × 24ft 4in × 13ft 6in |
| Propulsion: | 2 shafts, 2 Schneider diesels, 2 electric motors, 2000bhp/1270hp = 15kts/9kts |
| Mines: | 40 HS 4 |
| Torpedo tubes: | 4–550mm (+2 reserve) 2 bow, 1 trainable twin |
| Guns: | 1–100mm/40cal Mod 1936, 2–13.2mm AA (1 × 2) |
| Complement: | 43 |

## *Conclusions*

In September 1939 the French submarine fleet numbered seventy-six active units, of which approximately half were large 'fleet' boats. All had been completed since 1926, and many of the older units had been extensively modernised in 1936–39. No other country in the world had completed more submarines in the interwar period.

Circumstances, however, were to conspire against this powerful element of the French Fleet. Switched hastily from the Mediterranean to the Atlantic, then back again to the Mediterranean to face the late entry of Italy into the war, the French submarine force found few worthwhile targets and experienced only frustration, together with the wear and tear which accompanied prolonged wartime patrols. Four of the *1500 tonnes* had to be hurriedly sabotaged at Brest in June 1940 while under extended refit in order to keep them out of German hands. A further seven were scuttled at Toulon in November 1942, and no fewer than ten submarines of this type were sunk while attempting to resist the Allied invasions of French North Africa and Madagascar. By this time there were only eighteen boats of all types in operational condition, and a number of these were fit only for training because of the difficulty of maintenance and repair.

The lack of success of the *1500 tonnes* was due to a number of factors. Flaws in their equipment, particularly the complex and fragile diesel engines and the vulnerability of batteries and electrics to shock damage, resulted in their being difficult to maintain under arduous wartime conditions. They proved to be on the large side for operations in the Mediterranean and were particularly noisy boats (in spite of the attention given to passive acoustic detection systems, which by 1939 were quite well developed). This appears to have made them easy targets for anti-submarine escorts and aircraft when they attempted to defend French colonial possessions against the Allied landings.

In mitigation it has to be said that the submarines which opposed the battle-hardened British and American forces had rarely ventured from their moorings over the previous two years, and many were short of key personnel. More importantly these boats, like their more famous surface counterparts, the *contre-torpilleurs*, were never employed in the way in which they were intended to operate. The defence of harbours was essentially a mission of the *sous-marins de défense côtière* of the *600 tonnes* and *630 tonnes* types. The latter performed reasonably well in the shallow waters of the North Sea and the Mediterranean, although their patrols were limited by their poor habitability and they were arguably too complex for their size.

The question which remains is whether the *1500 tonnes*, and their even more impressive successors of the *Roland Morillot* class, would have been successful in the mission for which they were designed, that of *sous-marin éclaireur d'escadre*. Of the major world naval powers only the French and the Japanese persisted with the idea of the 'fleet scouting submarine' right up to the Second World War. Britain and the United States had flirted with the concept into the early 1930s, but had finally abandoned it when it became clear that the advent of the fast battleship had made the concept unattainable. Ironically it was the construction of the 29.5kt French battleships of the *Dunkerque* class (the first was laid down in 1932) which sounded the death-knell for the British fleet boats, and was largely responsible for the cancellation of 20-strong *Thames* class after only three units had been laid down.

The French appear to have been undaunted by these developments. The *Roland Morillot* class is said to have

Cérès, *the last of the six 'second class' submarines of the* Amirauté *type. She and* Pallas *had the streamlined conning tower adopted for the* Aurora *class.* (Marius Bar)

Minerve, *the first of the six 'second class' submarines of the* Amirauté *type. These were built in private shipyards to a standard STCN design. The photo dates from 1939.* (Marius Bar)

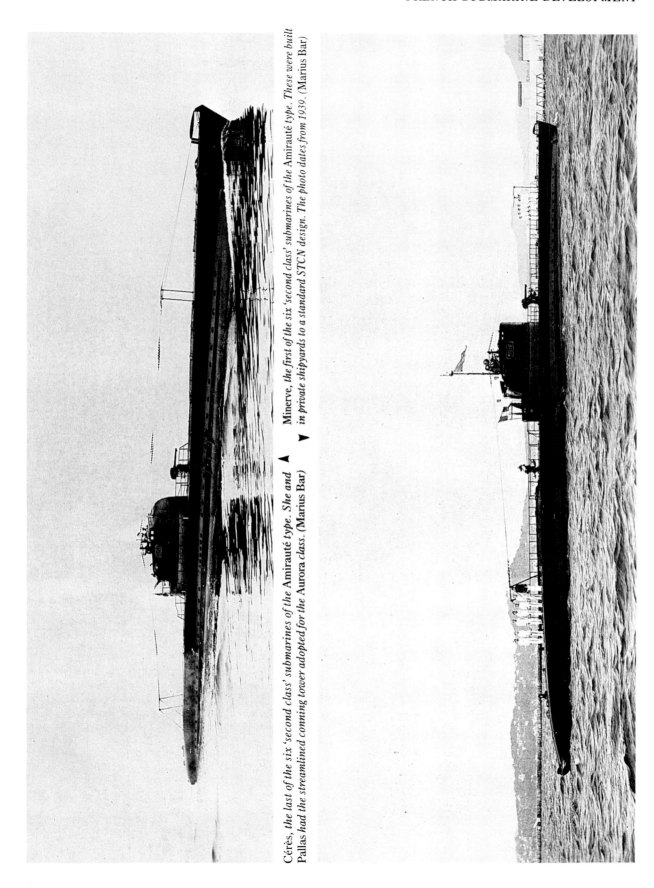

*The hull of* Créole *in July 1946. (*Jean Havet*).*

been requested personally from the *Conseil Supérieur* by the French C-in-C Admiral Laborde. Both he and Admiral Darlan fully endorsed the concept of using the *1500 tonnes* to scout for the battlefleet and to cooperate in fleet actions, and the necessary tactics were rehearsed in numerous prewar exercises in the Mediterranean. The *1500 tonnes*, grouped in tactical divisions of four, were well-equipped for surface radio transmission and reception, and were even fitted with a retractable signals mast to enable them to cooperate effectively with one another and with friendly surface ships.

It was not unreasonable to maintain this policy during the early 1930s, when both the French and the Italian battlefleets comprised elderly dreadnoughts capable of a maximum of 20–21kts. However, once the Italians embarked on the construction of 30kts battleships of the *Littorio* class in late 1934 the days of the diesel-powered fleet submarine were clearly numbered. Subsequent reconstruction of the older battleships of the *Cavour* and *Duilio* classes, which received new high-performance boilers and turbines giving them a maximum speed of 26–27kts, only served to hammer the final nail into the coffin. The *1500 tonnes* had been a laudable, if ultimately unsuccessful attempt to bring the 'fleet scout' concept to realization. Construction of the even larger, more unwieldly *Roland Morillot*, the lead boat of a projected class of at least thirteen submarines, serves only to reveal the extent to which French tactical thinking had become stuck in a time-warp.

**Sources**:

Henri Le Masson, *Les Sous-Marins Français* (Editions de la Cité, Brest 1980).

Alexandre Korganoff, 'Les Sous-Marins Français' in *Forces Sous-Marines*, Vol 1: 1920–1940 (Paris 1980).

# ANTI-AIRCRAFT GUNNERY IN THE IMPERIAL JAPANESE NAVY

Like most major navies, the IJN was quick to appreciate the threat from the air, but the provision of effective HA weapons and fire control systems took far longer. In this article Jiro Itani, Hans Lengerer and Tomoko Rehm-Takahara outline the history of Japanese shipboard armament and directors, concentrating on the famous type 89 12.7cm/40 (5in) gun.

THE high angle (HA) guns of the Imperial Japanese Navy according to the design concept, production requirements and kinds of ships which mounted them may be classified as follows:

1. Guns developed from low angle weapons
   a. 5cm (2in) HA
   b. Short 8cm (3in) HA[1]
   c. 40cal 3 year type 8cm HA
   d. 45cal 10 year type 12cm (4.7in) HA
2. Guns designed as HA weapons
   a. 40cal type 89 12.7cm (5in) HA
   b. 65cal type 98 10cm (3.9in) HA
   c. 60cal type 98 8cm HA
3. Guns designed for, or improved to meet the requirement for mass-production
   a. 45cal 10 year type 12cm gun in gun mounting type C
   b. short 20cm (7.9in) HA[2]
   c. Short 12cm HA[2]
4. Guns mounted aboard submarines
   a. Short 5cm HA
   b. Short 8cm HA
   c. 5 year type short 8cm HA
   d. 40cal type 88 8cm HA[3]
   e. 50cal type 88 10cm HA[3]
   f. 40cal type 88 12.7cm HA[3]

Besides the aforementioned guns, the IJN had a few dual-purpose (DP) guns: the 50cal 3 year type 20cm gun in type B turrets (carriers *Akagi* and *Kaga*) and type E (*Takao* class heavy cruisers); 50cal 3 year type 12.7cm (5in) gun (many classes of destroyer) which had several types and sub-types of turrets (A to D) capable of elevation angles from 55° to 75°; the 60cal 3 year type 15.5cm (6.1in) in triple turrets (*Mogami* class light cruisers) and 50cal 41 year type 15cm (5.9in) gun in twin turrets (*Agano* class light cruisers) allowed 55° elevation for limited AA fire. Generally speaking, neither of these last two so-called DP guns had the proper qualities of HA guns and will be omitted from this description together with their combined LA/HA fire control systems. Rocket launchers for AA defence have already been dealt with in *Warship* 34 by one of these authors and therefore readers interested in the subject are referred to this article.

The guns mentioned in (1) to (3) were for surface ships, and those listed in (4) were mostly experimentally produced. Because of the very special nature of the latter the production runs were very small, though even in the case of the standard HA gun (type 89 12.7cm) the output was surprisingly low.

For maximum effectiveness of HA fire, the fire control gear was the most important part of the system. This included the gun side equipment (computing sight, course and speed indicators etc) and the central fire control system placed high up on the ship and consisting at first of separate rangefinder and HA firing board (calculating elevation, bearing and deviation of the shell due to the rotation of the earth – the latter was called *Byoto* by the IJN) but later it became a HA gun director (*Hoiban* = bearing angle board) and computer (*Shagekiban* = firing board). The rangefinder was still separate but was later mounted in the director, while the computer which was combined first with the director was separated and placed inside a protected station. The real HA fire control systems (*Kosha sochi*) were the types 91 and 94. A thoroughly modified version of the type 94 system was designed for long-barrelled 10cm HA guns but before the production was begun Japan surrendered.

Since HA guns and fire control systems formed one unit, when the term 'HAG system' is used here it means

*A 40cal 3 year type 8cm with open breech.*

this combination. In this article emphasis is laid upon the guns designed as HA weapons and among them most space has been given to the 40cal type 89 12.7cm HA, being the standard heavy AA weapon of IJN warships in the Second World War. However, by far the most outstanding HA gun and mount in IJN service was the 65cal type 98 10cm HA which exceeded the 12.7cm HA not only in maximum horizontal and vertical range but also in the rate of fire.

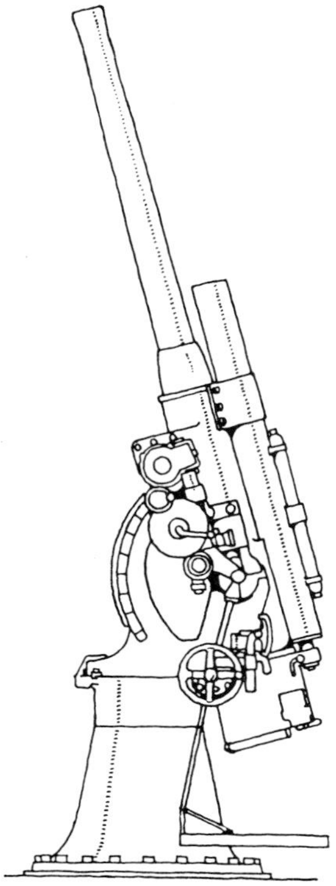

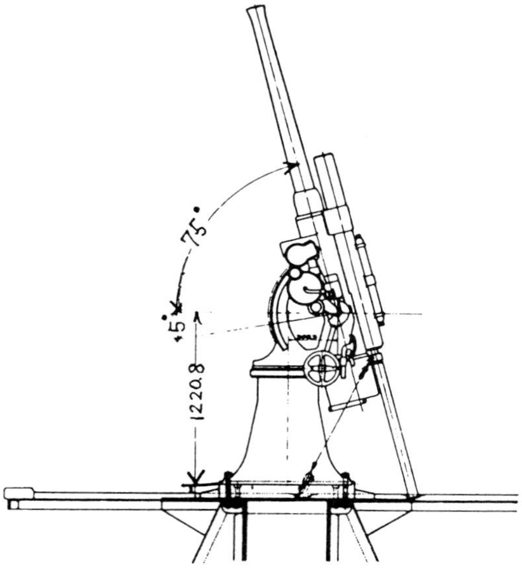


*The IJN's first 'converted' HA gun, the 40cal 3 year type 8cm.*

*Details of the 3 year type 8cm.*

## *Guns improved from low angle weapons*

Like other nations the early Japanese efforts at defence against aircraft involved attempts to modify ordinary gun mountings to increase elevation from the usual 15°–30° to 70°–75°. Therefore the original term for a HA gun was literally 'Large Elevation Gun' (*Dai Gyokaku Ho*).

**5cm HA.** This gun was the improvement of the 57mm heavy QF gun mounted on the torpedo-boats and destroyers of that time. An experimental mounting was carried on each side of the bridge of the seaplane carrier *Wakamiya Maru* when the ship was employed at the siege of Tsingtao at the beginning of the First World War. Among the three types of QF guns used by the IJN at that time, it is most likely that the Yamanouchi type was modified for this purpose.[4]

**40cal 3 year type 8cm HA.** The history of IJN AA gunnery properly begins with the 40cal 3 year type 8cm HA, which was improved from the 12pdr QF gun (later 8cm type 41) formally adopted on 5 February 1916 under the former name of 3in HA gun. When the basic design of *Ise* class battleships was developed from the *Fuso* class in 1914, not only were the dimensions, speed and general arrangement of the armament improved, but it was also decided to mount four 3in HA instead of the 3in LA guns in the former design. The first ship which actually mounted this HA gun was *Yamashiro* just after her completion and from this time onwards the 8cm gun was widely used as the HA weapon for major ships and sometimes also as the main gun for small vessels like submarine-chasers, coastal minelayers etc.

The single gun was fixed on a pedestal-type naval mount and operated manually. The barrel was of the built-up type and recoiled inside a sleeve-type cradle. The breech-block was set at an angle of about 45° from the vertical, being hand-operated and relatively large and massive in appearance.[5] On both sides of the barrel there was a targetting telescope and the firing was done individually. The differences between the 3in LA and 3in HA were principally the following:

1. To improve the elevation of the gun an extra weight was used at the breech to balance the gun on elevation and also a spring under compression, attached to the front of the cradle and to the base plate of the mount, was used for this purpose.
2. The movement of the barrel to return to the former plane freely was done without shock in the horizontal level.
3. Different aiming telescopes (a simple speed-ring sight was used for the first time).

*Front view of the 40cal 3 year type 8cm.*

From 1917 this gun was allocated to IJN warships by the principles decided in the same year for the ships of the '8-8-Fleet', namely for capital ships four guns (two per side) and cruisers two guns (one per side).

The 'History of Naval Gunnery' (*Kaigun Hojutsu Shi*) contains the records of exercise firing by two squadrons (*Nagato, Fuso, Ise, Yamashiro*; and *Kirishima* and *Hiei*) in 1926. The streamer target was towed by aircraft at 60kts, speed of the ships being 15kts, average distance 3000m, rate of fire 11.2rpm and hitting rate 4.57 per cent. This result was gained without using a gun director (at that time the ships were not equipped with the HA fire control system). The distance must have been measured by the rangefinder, changing rate of distance and corresponding fuse-setting time (scale) adjusted by the gunners and *Byoto* and the correction of the ship rolling and pitching decided by using pre-prepared calculation tables.

The mounting of the carrier *Hosho*'s two 8cm HA guns are of special interest because they were fitted on elevators situated below the flight deck. Each one of these disappearing guns was located at the sides very close to No 3 and No 4 14cm (5.5in) main guns one deck below. When planes took off or landed the guns disappeared into cylinders 1.6m (5¼ft) in diameter and 4.79m (15¾ft) high by means of hydraulic pressure and steel cables and the opening in the flight deck (2.5m, 8ft in diameter) was closed by a sliding cover.

The operation of these guns was very slow and after 1937 these weapons and those on light cruisers were replaced by 25mm MG in twin or triple mounts. The effective distance of the MG was almost equal to 8cm HA guns and the rate of fire, which apart from an efficient fire control system was the biggest problem in HA firing, was incomparably superior. Contrary to appearance, the change from HA gun to MG enhanced real fighting power. Incidentally, the only case of mounting both 8cm HA and LA gun aboard IJN small ships was in *No 1* class minesweepers.[6]

**45cal 10 year type 12cm HA.** In response to the development of aircraft performance, the comparatively poor qualities of the 40cal 3 year type 8cm HA and the trend in foreign navies to bigger calibres, the IJN adopted the 45cal 10 year type 12cm HA gun in 1922. The barrel was changed from 40cal 3 year type 12cm gun (commonly known as 12cm gun on type G gun mounting) to 10 year type with the same elevation angle as 8cm HA (75°) but the weight of the shell was 3.4 times heavier than that of 8cm HA (20.4kg to 5.99kg 45lbs to 13lbs) and the rate of fire was almost the same (11 to 13 rpm). When first adopted it was a single manually operated gun mounting carried on a conical steel pedestal of standard naval design like the 8cm HA (for example, mounted on *Aoba* class heavy cruisers as B1 type) but later it was improved to powered operation (electric oil pressure) (for example, mounted on *Myoko* class heavy cruisers as B2 type).

*A pair of 45cal 10 year type 12cm HA guns aboard the heavy cruiser* Nachi *in December 1928.*

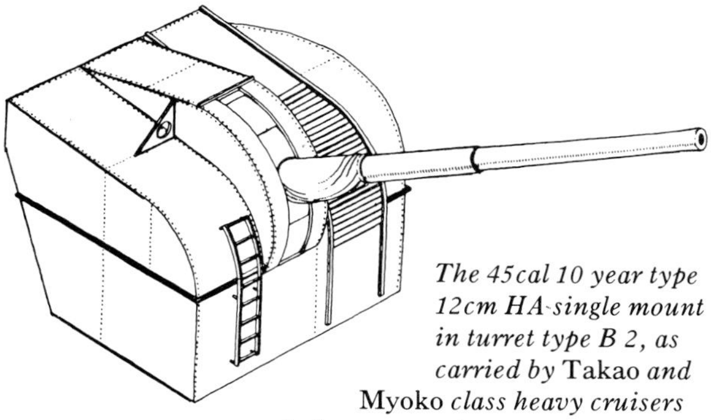

*The 45cal 10 year type 12cm HA single mount in turret type B 2, as carried by* Takao *and* Myoko *class heavy cruisers before conversion.*

This gun was applied to ships planned after the Washington Treaty by the programme of 1923 and was also scheduled for ships in succeeding supplementary programmes until the appearance of the first true HA gun.

The breech block was of semi-automatic horizontal sliding wedge type. One part of the rear portion of the barrel was machined to act as a bearing surface, which slid during the recoil within the sleeve mounted between the trunnions. There was no provision for automatic ramming of the projectile. On top of the barrel a recoil cylinder was mounted with one spring recuperator at each side.

The 12cm HA gun was produced in single and twin mounts. The most famous of the latter were the mechanically operated type A2 mounts aboard the carriers *Akagi* and *Kaga* but the gunboat *Hashidate* and survey ship *Tsukushi* were also equipped with twin mounts. After

*45cal 10 year type 12cm HA:*
*i) twin mount type A mod 1 (gunboat* Uji*);*
*ii) twin mount type A mod 3 (B type escorts);*
*iii) single mount type E mod 2 (*No 1 *class escorts)*

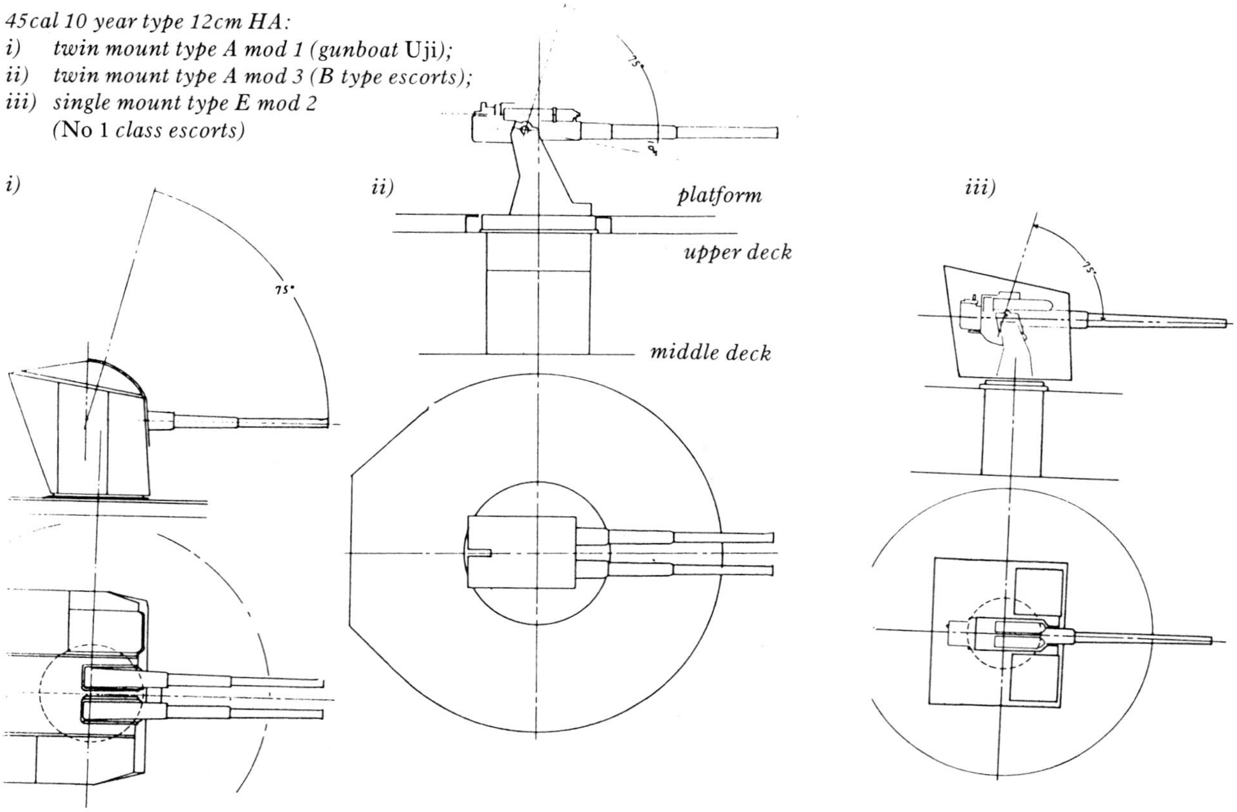

1933 the production of this gun was terminated but when the Pacific War began it was revived. Manually operated single u-type C mountings were manufactured and utilized for the land batteries along with the mechanically handled type D, which quite unlike type C, were only produced in small numbers. For the coast defence vessels (*Kaibokan*) types E, E1, and E2 were designed and built. They were used as DP guns with the sights for LA and HA firing.

The production figures from 1932 to 1944 (2152 guns compared to 190 8cm HA and 740 12.7cm HA) prove the realistic judgement of the Allied forces which pointed out that 'this weapon . . . was manufactured in large quantities by the Japanese Navy in 1944 [in fact the production was 1600 guns] . . . and there are strong indications that the Japanese are everywhere relying on this gun as the mainstay of their anti-aircraft defences . . .'[7] Of particular interest is the fact that in this gun as well as in the 8cm HA the fuse-setter was not a part of the gun mount. As in the case of the 8cm HA fuse was set manually at first but afterwards several similar type fuse-setters were developed and mounted on separate, small wheeled trollies.

*A 10 year type 12cm aboard the heavy cruiser* Chokai *in 1938.*

According to the 'History of Naval Gunnery' during the exercise firing of the four *Myoko* class heavy cruisers in 1931 the hitting rate was 2.2 per cent. The target was the same as in case of the 8cm HA, target speed 65kts, ship speed 18kts, average distance and altitude 3400m and 1500m respectively, and average firing speed 6.4rpm. The ships fired using type 89 Firing Board which was not the true computer but a comparatively primitive instrument which only calculated bearing and angle of roll while distance had to be measured by the HA rangefinder and fuse time adjusted manually corresponding to the distance.

## *Guns designed as HA weapons*

**40cal type 89 12.7cm HA.** The request for a better HA gun came from the fleet in response to improved aircraft performance and the design of the first true HA gun developed by the IJN was begun in 1928. Three years later No 1 gun completed successful AA firing tests and was finally adopted as the 40cal type 89 12.7cm HA gun in the following year. Together with the type 91 HA gun fire control system and type 91 time fuse, both adopted in the same year, these revolutionized the HAG system of the IJN and the way for the first step of modernization was

*Details of a 40cal type 89 12.7cm twin HA gun.*

paved. This gun became the standard Japanese HA weapon and up to the end of the Second World War 1306 examples were produced.

Before the adoption of this HAG system AA fire could be of little more than nuisance value against attacking aircraft because the converted HA guns were incapable of aimed shooting. Besides the great advances in aircraft performance, the direct impetus to the new design was the impending American adoption of the dive bomber. The following assumptions formed the basis of the design characteristics: an enemy dive bomber approaches the IJN warship with a speed of 320kph (200mph) or 88.88m per sec at 5500m altitude; before the bomber begins to dive the HA gun must be able to fire 60 rounds within 100 seconds (equating to an elapsed distance of 8800m)[8] and therefore two barrels would be necessary. When completed it was an excellent modern HA gun and even in 1945 members of the US Naval Technical Mission to Japan judged it 'in all respects as a good, sound DP mount[9] of about average performance'.[10] The main items strongly to be considered in the design were:

*1. Higher rate of fire*

The rate of fire of its predecessors, the 8cm and 12cm HA, was actually between 8 and 12rpm at low elevation angles and this speed decreased according to the rule that the higher the elevation angle the lower the firing speed. The target was to fire 14rpm at the highest elevation angle (90°). For this reason the following measures were taken:

a. Usage of fixed ammunition with total weight less than 35kg (77lb). The application of fixed ammunition was absolutely necessary to gain a high rate of fire. Considering the problems caused by the adoption of the 15cm shell (weight 45.36kg)[11] the round must not be heavier than 35kg. In accordance with this requirement, the calibre was fixed at 12.7cm.

b. Movable loader's platforms. The platforms for the loading tray operators were suspended from the rear end of the cradle and followed the elevation of the guns. Thus the loaders were always kept in the most convenient position for placing the shells on the loading trays and moving them to and from the breech.[12]

c. Ramming of ammunition by power. The fixed round was rammed by a heavy spring rammer situated below the gun and cocked by it during the automatic recoil operation. The stroke of the rammer was increased to twice the recoil length (451mm) by the use of a double rack and pinion gear. The rammer was automatically released by mechanical trip gear as the loading tray reached the ramming position. The ramming speed was controlled by means of an adjustable oil buffer. The setting of this buffer mounted in front of the rammer spring casing varied with the elevation of the gun. If a misfire occurred the next round to be loaded had to be rammed by hand, unless there was sufficient time to recock the rammer, which was connected to a simple wire whip secured to the baseplate of the mount and passed round a special

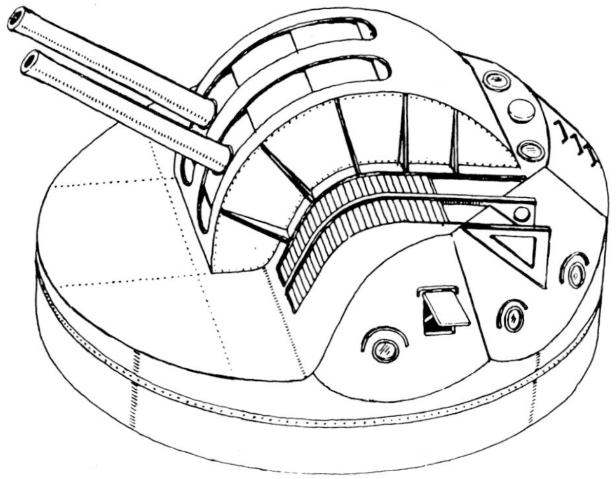

*40cal type 89 12.7cm HA, twin mount, with shield type A 1 mod, as mounted on* Shokaku *class carriers. (No 5 and No 7 guns for protection against funnel gases).*

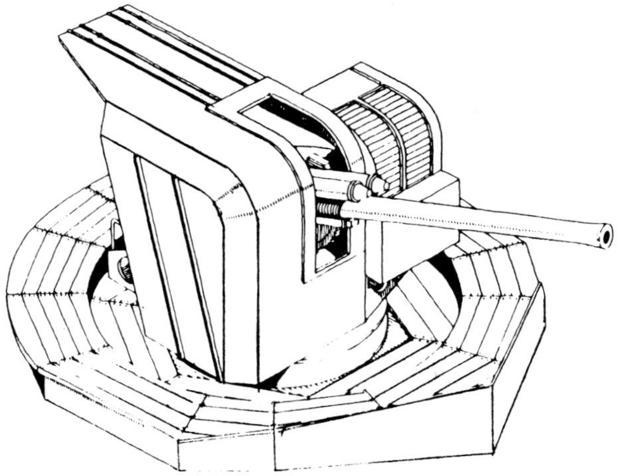

*40cal type 89 12.7cm HA single mount as carried by type D (*Matsu *class) destroyer escorts.*

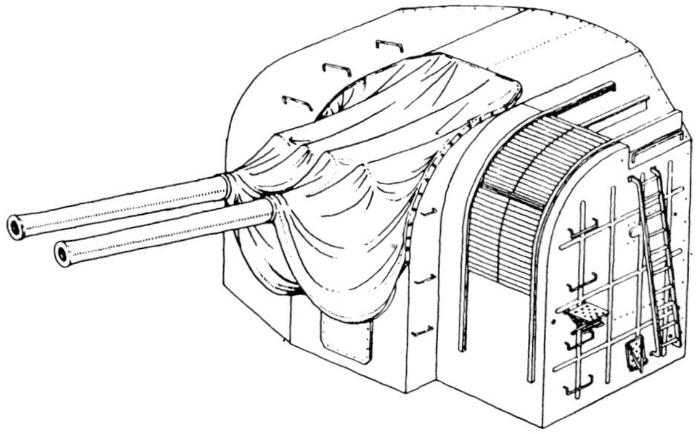

*40cal type 89 12.7cm HA twin mount with shield type A 1 mod 1, as mounted on* Myoko *class heavy cruisers after conversion.*

removable pulley at the rear end of the rammer casing and then hooked to an eyebolt of the gun by depressing the gun and thus hauling back and cocking the rammer.

d. Automatic fuse-setting machines. The fitting of automatic fuse-setters to the breech faces of the guns was necessary in order to shorten the time from fuse-setting to the ramming of the shell into the chamber and to improve the precision of the time set. By rod gearing passing through the trunnions, the fuse-setting machine was adjusted continuously to the fuse time to be set. The principle was as follows: when the loading tray was pushed over to the ramming position the fuse passed between the guides in the machine and while passing through the toothed fuse-setting ring on the fuse came into contact with a rack, which caused the fuse ring to rotate. The time delay set on the fuse depended on the length of time during which the fuse ring was in contact with the rack and was determined by the fuse-setter, matching his pointers in the fuse receiver.

*A twin type 89 12.7cm mount on the light cruiser* Mogami *in 1935.*

The design of the fuse-setting machine was begun in 1930. The development was very troublesome and it took nearly two years until a type which met most requirements was achieved. On 23 January 1932 10 rounds were fired with the right and left barrel elevated to 60°. In each case the fuse time was set to 15 seconds. The average time from firing until the detonation of the shell was 15.45 secs and 14.93 secs, the average deviation ±0.19 secs and ±0.09 secs. The biggest divergence was +0.55 and −0.35 secs in the right barrel, +0.12 and −0.18 secs in the left barrel.

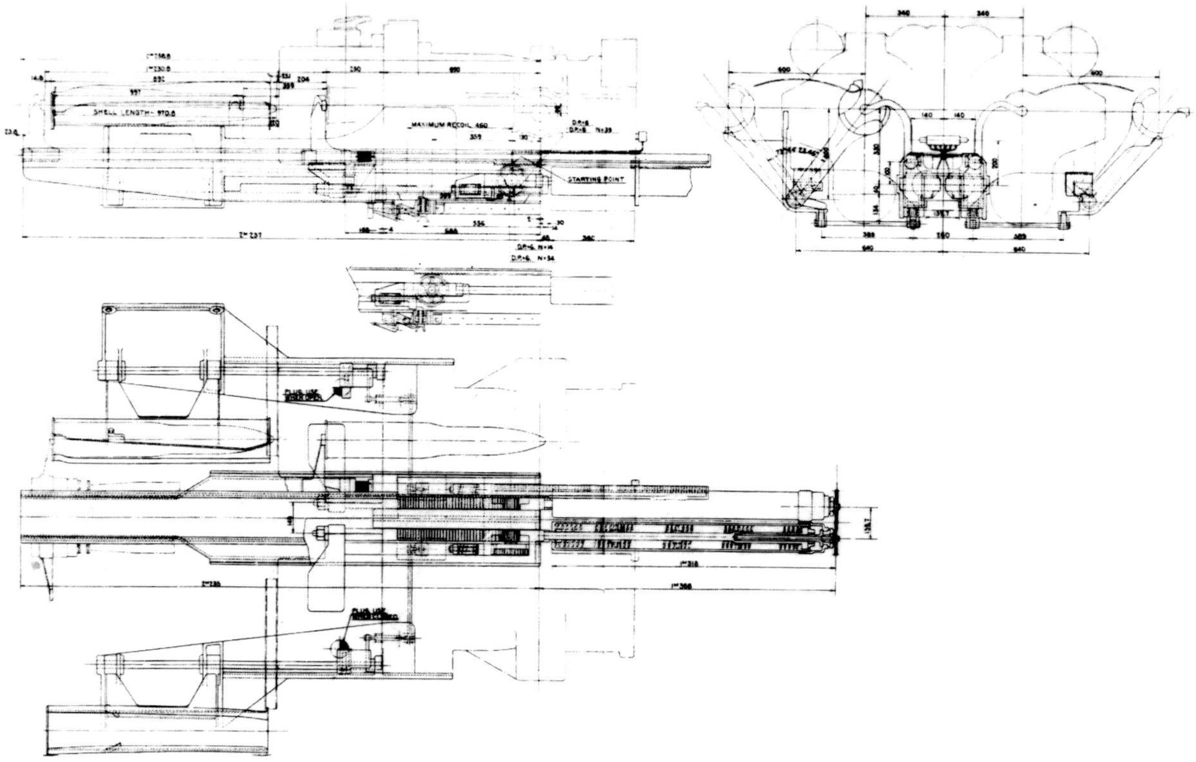

*General arrangement of power rammer of 40cal type 89* ▲ *12.7cm HA (twin mount).*

*General arrangement of 40cal Type 89 12.7cm HA (twin* ▼ *mount).*

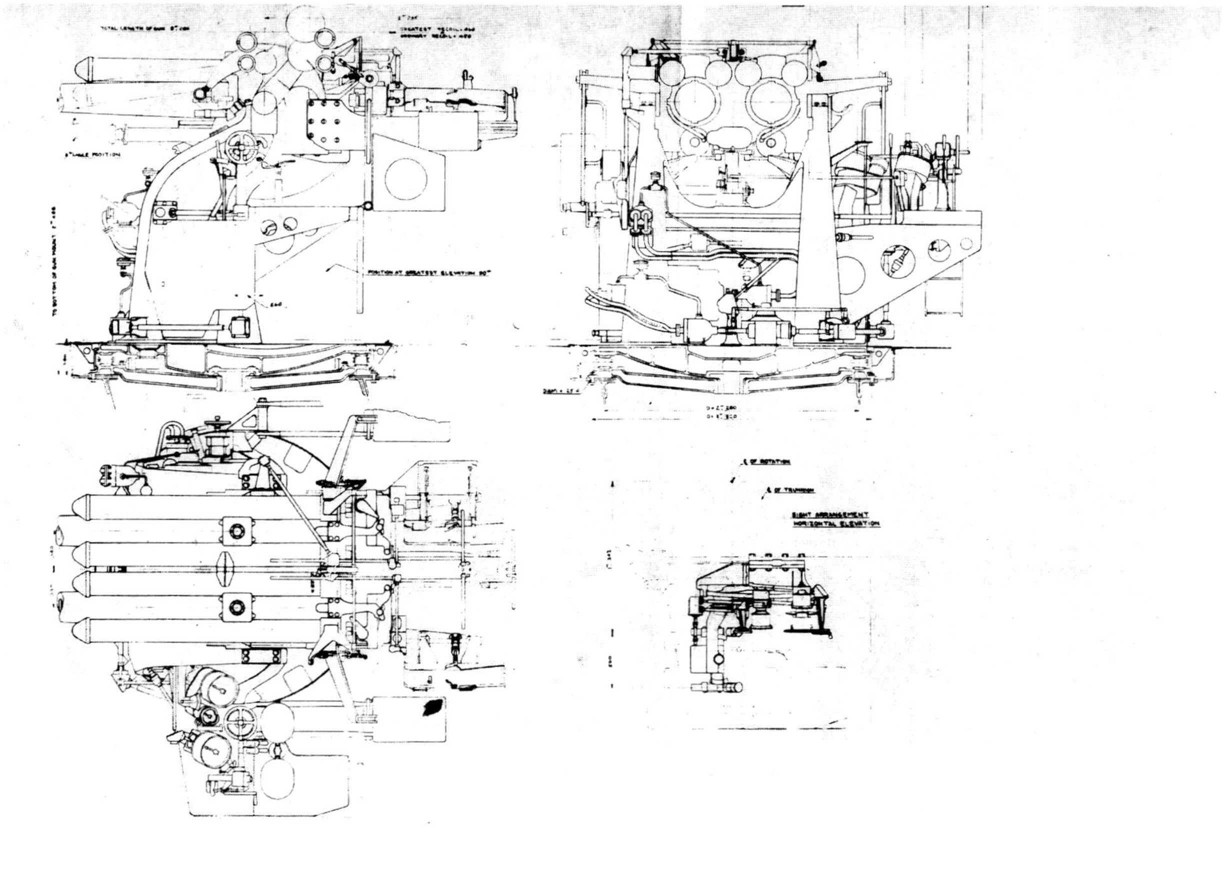

In this type of automatic fuse-setting machine the setting rack was cut and a drum revolved to vary the contact time. Therefore the moving teeth of the fuse ring, meeting the stationary teeth of the setting drum were frequently badly damaged and caused imprecise fuse-setting and failure of the machine. After improvement to the aforementioned type in which forward velocity component of the rack plate was equal to the ammunition causing the smooth meshing of the rack and fuse ring without any damage, the expected precision (±0.2 secs) was attained in January 1935.[13]

e. Empty cartridge case deflectors. Small empty cartridge case deflectors, fitted at the rear end of the rammer casing, were adjusted automatically by rod gearing during the elevation of the guns to deflect the case in the most convenient way (at low elevation the case was deflected downwards; at very high elevation it was deflected clear of the mounting).

*2. Higher destructive radius of the shell*

A comparison of the weight and effectiveness of the shells of the 45cal 12cm HA and the new 40cal 12.7cm HA shows the higher destructive radius of the 12.7cm shell.

| | *12cm* | *12.7cm*[14] |
|---|---|---|
| Weight of shell (kg) | 20.4 | 23 |
| Explosive charge (kg) | 1.536 | 1.778 |
| Effective volume ($m^3$) | 50,000 | 76,000 |
| Radius of destruction | | 60m (depth) |
| (by splinters) m | ? | 30m (width) |

*3. Mechanical operation*

Depending on the main target (dive bomber) the mount was elevated and trained by electric motors. For the same reason speed of elevation was emphasized (12° per sec) over training (6° per sec) but in the higher powered mounts both eventually became 16° per sec. When the electric motors failed, the cradle could be moved manually. In fact this HA gun was too heavy for manual operation and the 10hp electric motor used first was replaced by 15hp versions (*Matsu* class escorts), or even 25hp in the case of the gun with a heavy protective shield.

*4. Single cradle*

In order to reduce weight both barrels were fixed in one cradle, ie, each barrel could fire but not move independently.

This gun was produced in single (submarine) and twin (surface ships) mountings. Unlike the single mount, which had no variations, there were six different types of twin mounts ranging from A1 to B2, which differed in significant respects such as re-designing for mass production, changing of the computer sights and other targetting instruments, capable of LA/HA firing etc. As for the shields, five different kinds were used ranging from protection against small splinters to reinforcements against blast pressure and heavy seas.

The 40cal 12.7cm gun was called semi-automatic because after firing one round the breech was opened during the recoil of the barrel and the cartridge case ejected. Then one shell was loaded into the tray at the right side of the gun and by handling the contact lever the fuse-setting machine acted according to the data received from the computer and the shell was rammed into the chamber to fire the next round.

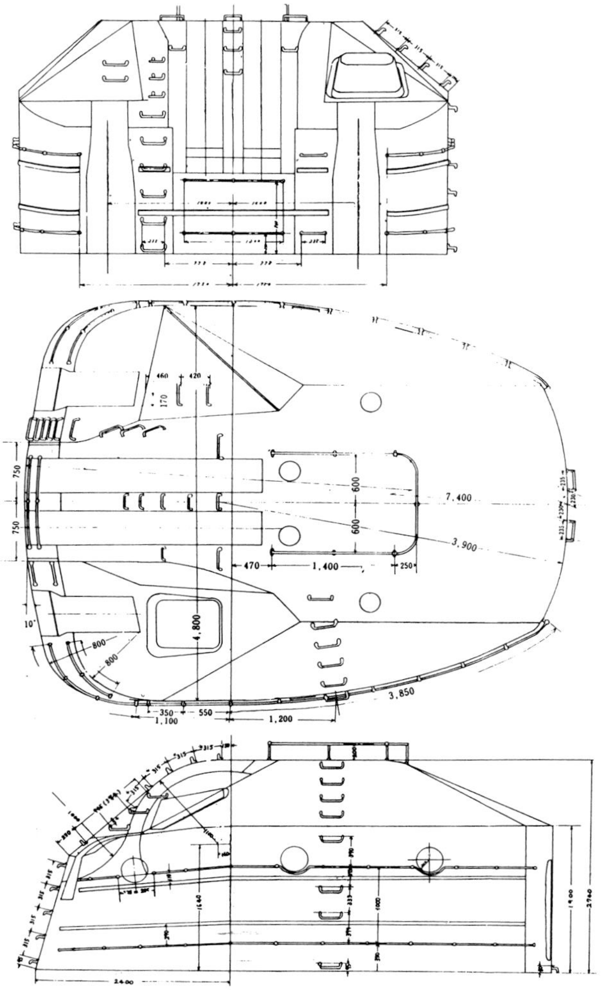

*Turret type A for 65cal type 98 10cm HAG used for DD* Akizuki *class (front view, top view, side view – from top to below).*

On 7 June 1932 the prototype was test-fired on Kamegakubi Naval Proving Ground. The result of the continuous firing was as follows:

| Elevation angle | No of rounds fired | Average time interval |
|---|---|---|
| 30° | 20 | 5.0 ± 0.7 secs |
| 60° | 30 | 5.0 ± 0.8 secs |
| 75° | 30 | 5.0 ± 0.8 secs |

Shortest interval between two rounds: 3.1 secs (19rpm)
Average interval between two rounds: 4.0 secs (15rpm)[15]

**65cal type 98 10cm HA.** The production of 40cal type 89 12.7cm twin HA guns went smoothly and when this weapon equipped all capital ships (replacing the old 40cal 8cm HA) fulfilling the decision to standardize the HAG arrangements on four mounts and two fire control systems, the design of a new long-barrelled high performance HA gun was begun. This was the result of further rapid progress in aircraft speed, which required improved effective firing distance, rate of fire, elevating and

traversing speed, and accuracy. This time the Japanese constructors chose a different route. Instead of increasing the calibre and reducing the length of the barrel[16] as in the past, the calibre was reduced and the length of the barrel increased. Several factors influenced the decision: the trial firing of an 80cal 14cm gun (improved from 55cal 14cm gun) in January 1933; the success of the 60cal 15.5cm gun which was popular because of its excellent properties; and the determination of new principles of designing HA guns in December 1935. At that time it was planned to adopt a 70cal 10cm HA but for reasons not known to the authors this was changed after the experiment to shorten the barrel to 65cal. By using this barrel length, a large charge of powder and a comparatively light shell, a muzzle velocity of 1000m per sec (1.39 times that of 12.7cm HA) was obtained. Comparing other important elements to the 12.7cm HA, maximum vertical range increased 1.6 times (14,700m), maximum horizontal range 1.4 times (19,500m), rate of fire 1.4 times (19rpm), traverse speed 2 times (12° per sec) and elevation speed 1.33 times (16° per sec). These data prove the very great advance on any previous HA weapon and this gun and the mount were undoubtedly the most outstanding IJN HA design.

The only defect was the rather short life of the barrel but this was compensated, at least to some degree, by using a removable liner in the radially expanded type I gun barrel which could be changed comparatively easily. The structure of the gun mount, loading trays, fuse-setting machines and rammers were very similar to those of the 12.7cm HA, but the rammers were mounted above the guns and embodied several improvements (principally in the tripper gear). Above each gun a recoil piston and cylinder (normal length of recoil was 490mm) was fitted and a run-out spring below. In addition, each had a run-out spring fitted between and to the rear of the guns.

*The destroyer* Haruzuki, *early in 1945. The main armament comprised four twin 65cal type 98 10cm guns. Note that only one type 94 director is fitted (above the bridge), the after mounting being omitted due to production shortages.*

As in the case of the 12.7cm HA the weight of these springs, loading trays and rammers was sufficient to balance the guns in elevation and it was not necessary to add special counter-weights as in the 8cm HA. Elevating and training worm gears were driven by 10hp electric motors; in case of failure of power not only the mounts but also the hoists (see later) could be operated manually. It may be added that the power supply for the gunloading pusher type hoists was independent of that for the remainder of the turret.

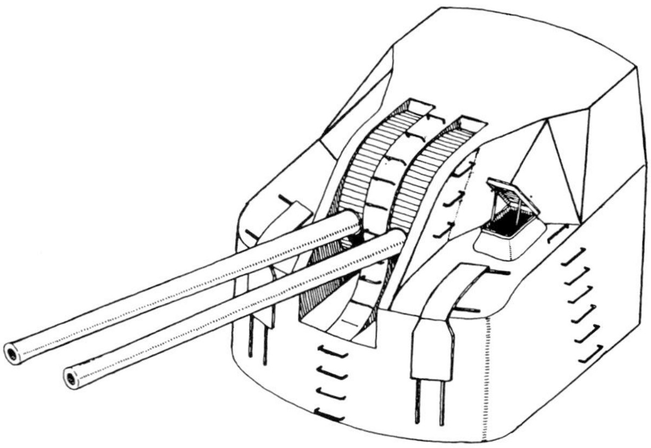

*65cal type 98 10cm HA twin mount in turret Type A mod 1, as carried by the light cruiser* Oyodo.

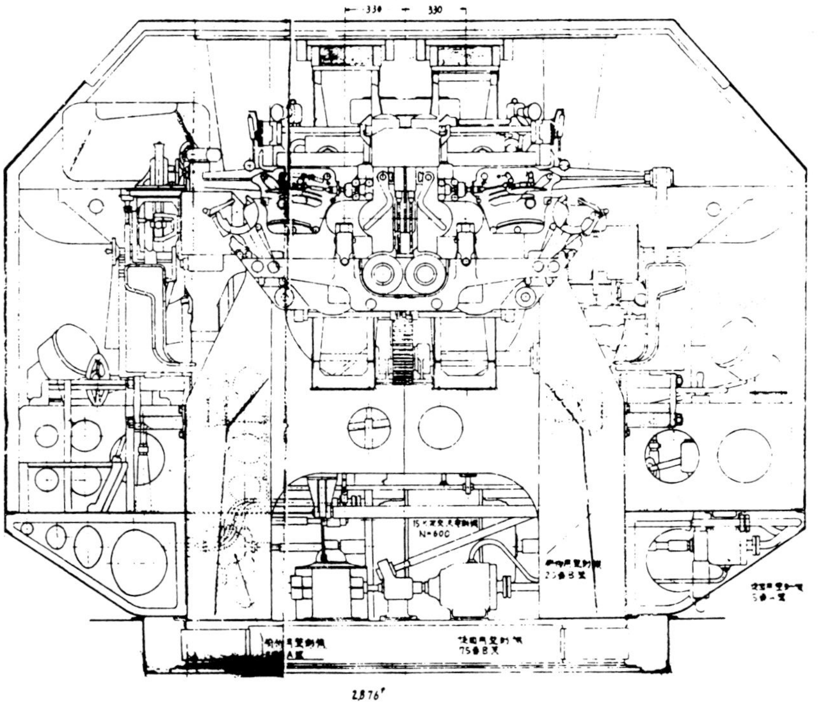

*65cal type 98 10cm HA in turret type A mod 1, as carried by the light cruiser* Oyodo *(*Official IJN drawing*).*

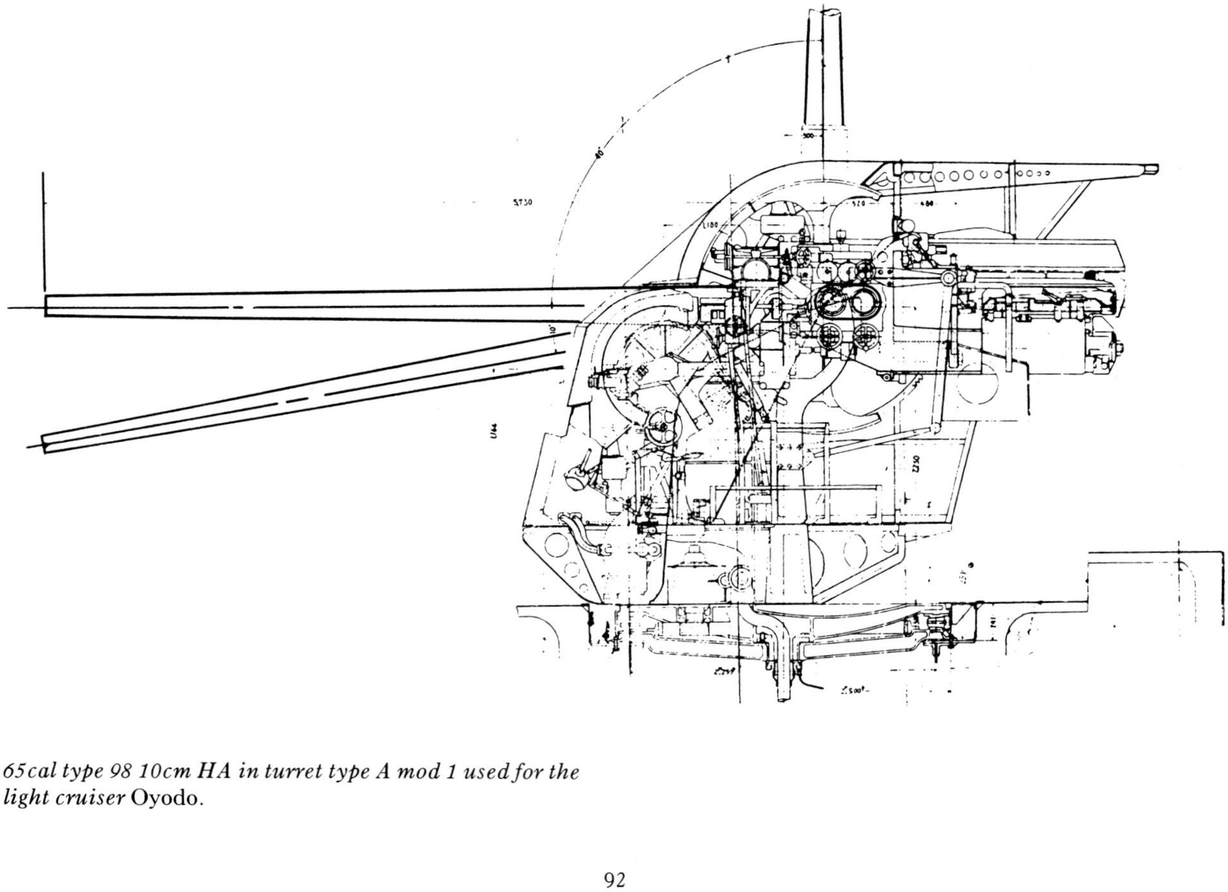

*65cal type 98 10cm HA in turret type A mod 1 used for the light cruiser* Oyodo.

This gun was produced as a twin mount and also as an enclosed turret. The latter equipped *Akizuki* class AA destroyers and the former were fitted in the carrier *Taiho*, cruiser *Oyodo* and also used as AA batteries on land. In contrast to the sometimes poor arrangement of the ammunition supply in the 12.7cm HA[17] two hoists were built as one unit in each turret. At first fixed ammunition was supplied from the magazines to the working chambers in the fixed structure below and at the rear end of the turret by two simple bucket-type hoists, at the rate of 20 to 22 rounds per minute per hoist. Then the ammunition was manhandled from the top of the hoists to awaiting positions at the entrances to the gunloading normal pusher-type hoists fitted in the shell supply room directly below the guns. These hoists were inter-connected and could not work independently of each other. The speed of ammunition supply (maximum rate was the same as in case of bucket-type hoists) could be varied at will by suitably positioning the control lever at the rear of the turret between the exit from the hoists. After leaving the top of the hoists, the rounds rolled automatically into the waiting positions and were passed to the loaders, who stood alongside the loading trays on the same type of loaders' platforms used in the 12.7cm HA (*ie* moving in elevation with the guns).

As with the 12.7cm HA the cartridge cases were ejected during recoil, striking a large fixed deflector, dropping down a chute below the gunwell and through a door into the fixed structure around the bottom of the hoists and then removed into spaces along the ship's side. Incidentally, the semi-automatic breech block was of the horizontal sliding wedge type and opened towards the outside of the left and right gun.

**60cal type 98 8cm HA.** This gun was fundamentally the 10cm HA on a smaller scale and was mainly designed as the AA gun for *Agano* class light cruisers. The barrels were produced in Kure Navy Yard and the turrets in Maizuru Navy Yard. Because of the smaller calibre compared to 10cm HA and 12.7cm HA the fragmentation effectiveness of the shell was of course inferior to that of the bigger guns and it was not adopted much. The decision to equip the *Agano* class with this weapon was mainly a matter of weight, being only 9.5 tons when compared to 10cm HA (20.5 tons and 33.4 tons for the two types of mounting) and 12.7cm HA (20.3 tons for the A1). The most outstanding characteristic was the high rate of fire of 26rpm[18] and thus, together with the 10cm HA, it really deserves to be called a rapid-fire gun.

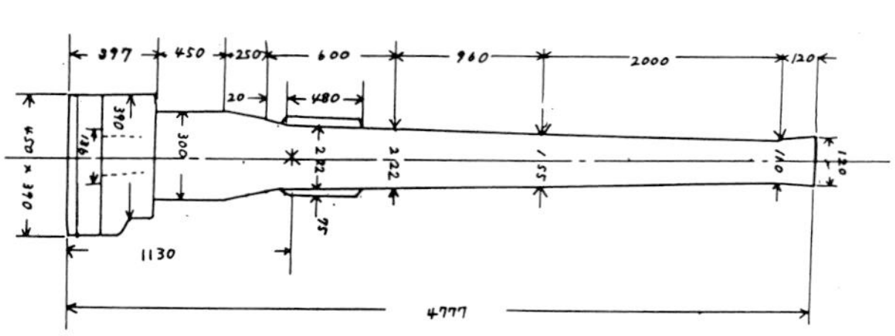


*General appearance and principal dimensions of 60cal type 98 8cm HA barrel and mount.* (Akira Endo, 'HAG and AA ships')

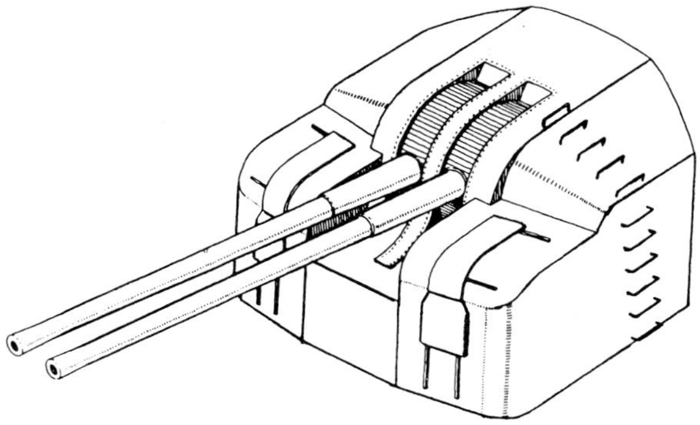

*60cal type 98 8cm HA twin mount, as carried by* Agano *class light cruisers.*

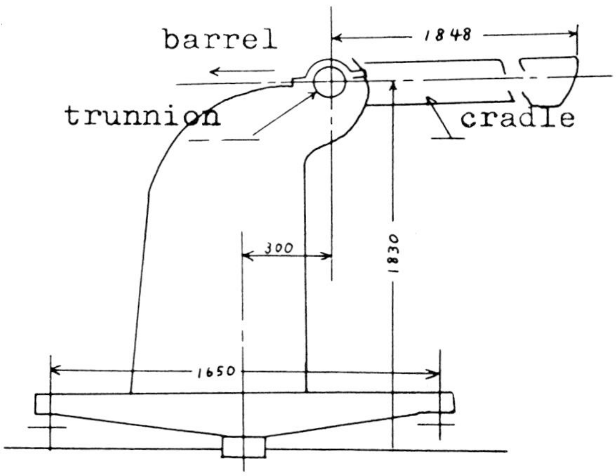


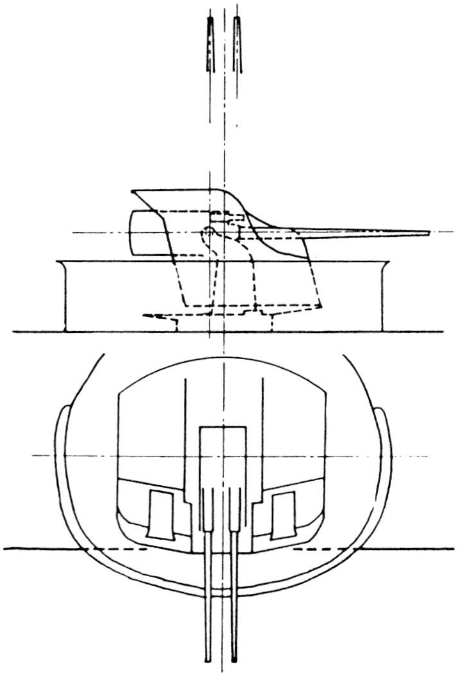

*60cal type 98 8cm HA in mount type A, as carried by* Agano *class light cruisers.*

## *Guns mounted aboard submarines*

**Short 5cm HA gun.** Analogous to the 5cm HA for surface ships the 25pdr HA was test-mounted on the submarine *No 14* (later *Ha-9*) which was built in Japan as a replacement for the same numbered boat ordered from Schneider Co in France but not delivered because of the outbreak of the First World War. This gun was based upon the Yamanouchi 47mm light QF gun and was later called the short 5cm HA gun.

**8cm HA gun.** Three types of 8cm HA were mounted on IJN 'Ro' type submarines. The short 8cm HA and 5 year type short 8cm HA were used on *Kaichu* (navy medium type) 'F' and 'L' classes, while 40cal type 88 8cm HA was utilized for AA defence aboard *Ro-33* and *Ro-34* as well as the wartime mass production *Ro-35* class. When the mounting of HA guns on submarines was abandoned after the ships of the Second Supplementary Programme of 1934, this class, exceptionally, was the only one fitted with a HA gun.

Among the earlier short 8cm HA guns there was the disappearing type (by means of oil pressure cylinders just below the centre of the gun mount). During submerging it was contained in a concaved recess in order to avoid increasing resistance.

**50cal type 88 10cm HA and 40cal type 88 12.7cm HA.** At the same time as the 8cm HA was mounted aboard medium sized submarines, large boats ('I' class) were equipped with the bigger calibre. Cruiser submarines *I-6* and *I-7* each received one 40cal type 88 12.7cm HA (even though the planning had been for two guns, but because of the decision to mount the seaplane one unit had to be omitted) while fleet type *I-65* to *I-73* (later *I-165* to *I-173*) had the smaller calibre guns.

It may be of some interest to add that the 50cal type 88 10cm HA had some influence upon the choice of calibre for the 10cm type 98 HA. This gun was test fired with the volume of the powder chamber increased (from 8 to 10 litres) to gain higher velocity (885 over 790m per sec) and maximum bore pressure (from 28.2 to 34kg/mm$^2$). As it showed no abnormality the maximum bore pressure for the new type HA gun was determined to be 30kg/mm$^2$.

Eventually, the air defence of submarines was left to the AA MG, whose performance was much improved by the adoption of Hotchkiss 13mm and 25mm MG, and the main guns were then changed to the LA weapons for greater destructive power against surface ships.

## *Fire control systems*

While the LA fire control system is fundamentally two-dimensional, with only range and bearing, a HA fire control system has one more dimension (height). The calculation of the firing data is very complicated and not only because of the requirement for three-dimensional cams but also because the high speed and manoeuvrability of the target demands very quick solutions to the problems; *ie* quick calculation of the firing data, speedy transmission to the gunhouses thus contributing to a high rate of fire.

The development of the fire control system was of course inseparably connected to the progress of the HA gun. The properties of the 8cm HA, the IJN's first such

*In this view of the bridge of the heavy cruiser* Ashigara *in May 1937, the type 91 director is at the rear of the bridge wing platform with its 4.5m stereoscopic rangefinder on the tall pedestal behind the navigation lights.*

weapon (1916 to 1922), were low and there was no especially elaborated firing method and no fire control system. On the other hand the development of the aircraft was still in its infancy but the rate of progress was very fast and the IJN was obliged to use the higher fire power of the 12cm HA from 1923. From this time onwards, research into firing methods based upon calculation was pursued seriously, which includes a quest for a fire control system which would answer the important requirements for AA defence: 1) discovery of the target; 2) measurement of the distance; and 3) calculation of the firing solution and control of fire.

Based upon a German rangefinder captured during the siege of Tsingtao, the IJN used a so-called 'stereo moving mark' in the earliest AA rangefinders. At the beginning of 1923, ten 3m rangefinders of the same type, bought in Germany two years earlier, were delivered and were tested in May of that year with favourable results. Following this it was decided to equip big ships with predictor gear and this was formulated in the new 'Proposal for Gunnery Battle Predictor Gears' (*Hosen Shiki Sochi*). According to this proposal, two control stations 5m$^2$ (54sq ft) in area were to be fitted in different positions in battleships and one in heavy cruisers; each should be equipped with one *Hoiban* (for bearing) and *Shojun sochi* (for aiming).

The controlled firing of HA artillery was first conducted in 1926 and in 1929 the value of the type 89 HA Firing Board (*Kosha Shagekiban*) was considered very high in the reports about battle firing. The development of this somewhat rudimentary fire control instrument resulted from a study in the Combined Fleet in 1927 of HA firing methods and the complete failure in fleet training in 1928 using smoke shells of various colours.

The requirements of the fleet became more and more demanding and the Navy Technical Department, which had begun the fundamental design of a complete HA fire control system about two years previously, was put to much trouble. In 1929 the basic design was completed and production was ordered at the Japan Optical Co in Odate. The company, which had no experience in the production of this kind of equipment, mobilized all its technical force and after great exertions completed the test production in June 1931. In 1932 the battleship *Yamashiro*, which was the training ship of the Gunnery School, began trial firing. Many problems were immediately manifest and it took until September 1933 before the modified version was available. This was the weapon adopted and before the appearance of the type 94 fire control system in May 1937, fifty units were produced by the Japan Optical Co.

The type 91 fire control system[19] consisted of the director (*Hoiban* =Bearing Angle Board) and the calculator (*Kosha Shagekiban* = HA computer) combined in one casing (*Koshaki* = HA firing instrument) and mounted on a pedestal. The separate HA rangefinder[20] was the Bu [Barr & Stroud] stereo type one with 4.5m base length and the measured range was delivered electrically to the director. The separation of the rangefinder and the fact that it had no level or cross-level assistance (*ie*, it was bi-axial), proved to be the handicap of this system since it was very difficult for the rangetaker to be on the same target as the pointer and trainer in the director. The ship's

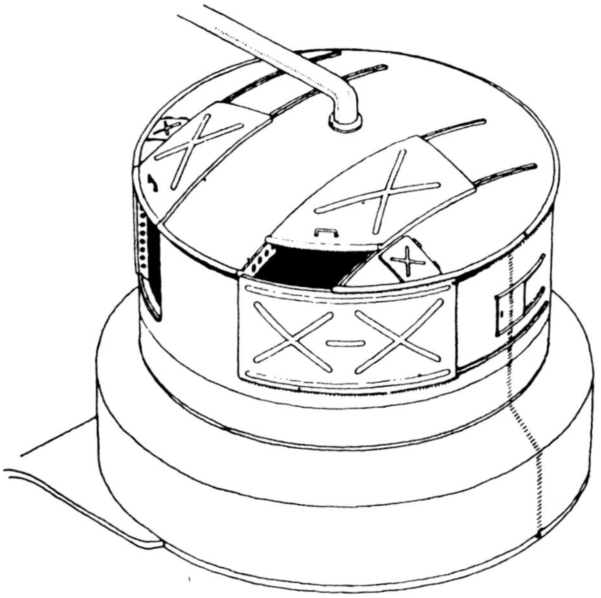

*The type 91 high angle director (with computer).*

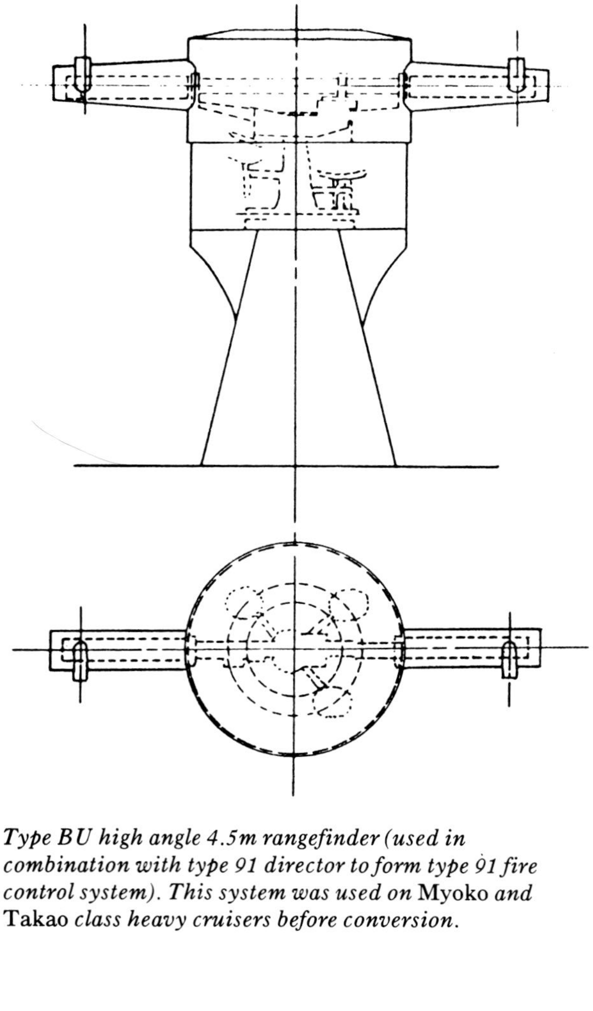

*Type BU high angle 4.5m rangefinder (used in combination with type 91 director to form type 91 fire control system). This system was used on* Myoko *and* Takao *class heavy cruisers before conversion.*

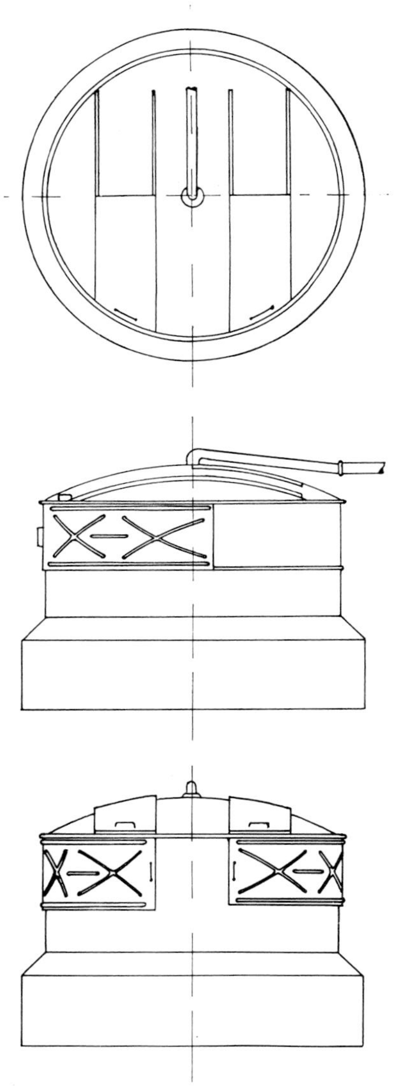

*The type 91 director.*

own course was continuously fed to the director by the compass.

The HA firing instrument was covered by a big hood and had no plotting room and no stable element. It was a full tachymetric system based on polar coordinate principles depending on accurate slant range and was therefore able to provide correct solutions for diving and climbing targets.[21] In this respect it was totally different from its model, the Army Vickers Predictor (based on height). On top of the director there were two binoculars for the pointer and trainer. These optics were levelled and cross-levelled by operators positioned at the front side of the instrument and thus the director was tri-axial. Other optics were for corrections due to deck tilt, *ie* correction for rolling and pitching by targetting the horizontal line to the perpendicular line. Corrections for the wind, own ship speed, parallax, daily corrections (barometric height etc) were put into the system in the same way as for surface firing.

The principle of the HA firing instrument was to calculate differentially the future positions of the target by means of the present values of range, elevation and bearing angles. From this the firing elements – vertical deflection (elevation angle), lateral deflection (training angle) and fuse time (a function of future range) – were calculated and automatically transmitted to the gunhouses. The training of this instrument was manual and there were no servos or follow-ups. Therefore it was cumbersome to operate, required ten operators and was difficult to maintain, even though maintenance was not very frequent since no electronics or power follow-ups were used.

Firing under battle conditions using the type 91 fire control system and type 89 12.7cm HA gun was first practised in 1933. Average distance of the target was 5800m (6900m), average altitude ? (3200m), target speed ? (85kts), ship speed ? (15.5kts), rate of fire 10.6rpm (same), hitting rate 0.4 per cent (0.9 per cent)[22]. Thus the achievement of the type 91 fire control system was not very impressive and most probably this was caused by the delicate mechanism and the mechanical nature of the calculation system which caused many errors.

In order to avoid these disadvantages, the type 94 HA fire control system was developed. Rangefinder and director were now unified and the computer was placed deep in the ship, so that the director and computer could not be put out of action by one hit, while the rangefinder and director personnel always aimed at the same target. The principal calculations were the same as in the type 91 system but instead of the two-step calculation it became a single-step process of greater simplicity. To minimize errors in mechanical calculation emphasis was placed on the better precision of the three-dimensional cams and gear-cutting.

In contrast to the type 91 training was hydraulic by using the tilting plate pump principle but was not automatic or rate-aided. The computer incorporated a spherical resolver for deck tilt, a so-called 'coordinate converter'[23], *ie* an optical model of coordinates was used for correcting rolling and pitching. Before transmission to the guns they were modified by correction devices (for converting tri-axial data to bi-axial). This optical follow-up system was replaced by a stable vertical based upon a

*Type 94 high angle director mounted aboard of an aircraft carrier (most probably* Ryuho*).*

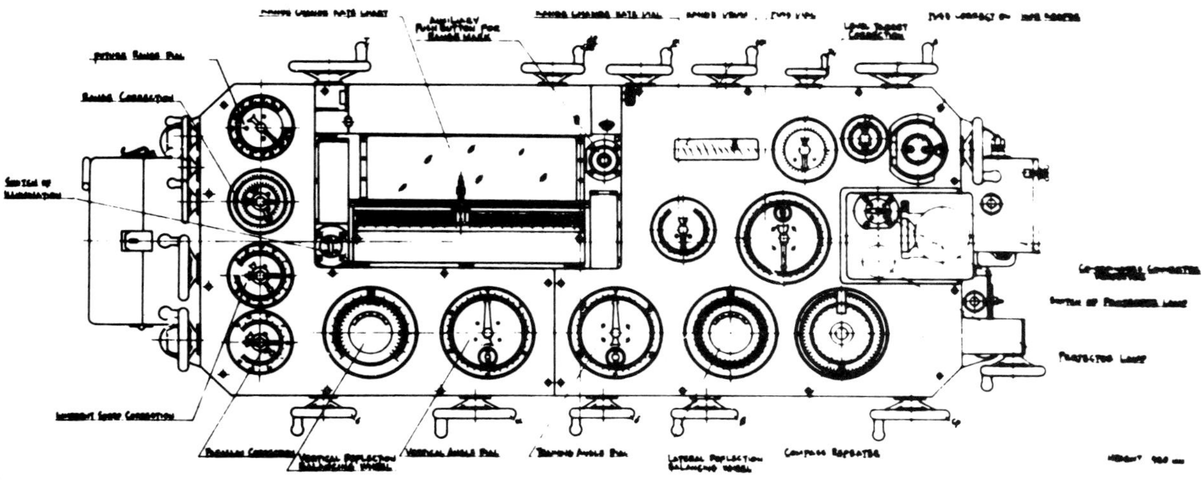

Type 94 computer – arrangement of controls and pointers.

pendulous gyro in the modification 1, fitted aboard warships from about the middle of the Pacific War.[24]

During fleet training in 1938 and 1939 the carriers *Hiryu* and *Soryu* using type 94 fire control system and 40cal type 89 12.7cm HA guns obtained the following results (values for 1940): average distance 5800m (6400m), average altitude 1500m (1300m), ship speed 24.7kts (25.5kts), target speed 85kts (83kts), rate of fire 8.36rpm (9.99rpm), hitting rate 6.58 per cent (3.12 per cent). These results show a big improvement over the type 91.

Members of the US Naval Technical Mission To Japan who examined the HA fire control systems pointed out that 'the most outstanding characteristics of Japanese anti-aircraft fire control were (1) optics, (2) the limited application of power follow-ups, and (3) the use of optical methods for hand follow-ups' and mentioned the best features of type 94 HA fire control system as '(1) careful design, (2) unity of thought, and (3) excellent layout'. An inspection of the carrier *Ryuho*'s type 94 confirmed these impressions. According to the description, 'the director both inside and out was spotlessly clean and tidy; the layout was excellent. There were no untidy cables, pipes, tubes or excresences. The inside of the director had polished linoleum on the false deck and was supplied with indirect lighting giving an impression of excellent cooperation between designers, manufacturers, and navy yards.'[25]

If the main fire control system failed, 65cal and 60cal type 98 10cm and 8cm HA guns were fitted with a combined local director sight and computer, developed from the French Le Prieur sight (called LPR in the IJN). It was fundamentally a simple course and speed sight in which target speed, course and range were resolved to receive flight time and vertical and lateral deflections. These elements were transmitted manually to the sights and fuse receivers by matching pointers and following-up time of flight curves on a drum. Vertical and lateral spotting corrections could be added differentially to the output drives of the sights. Thus the local sight was capable of controlling these guns with considerable accuracy. On the other hand this local director sight was complicated and proved to be a production bottleneck. It was therefore replaced by various simplified types of sights during the later part of the war.

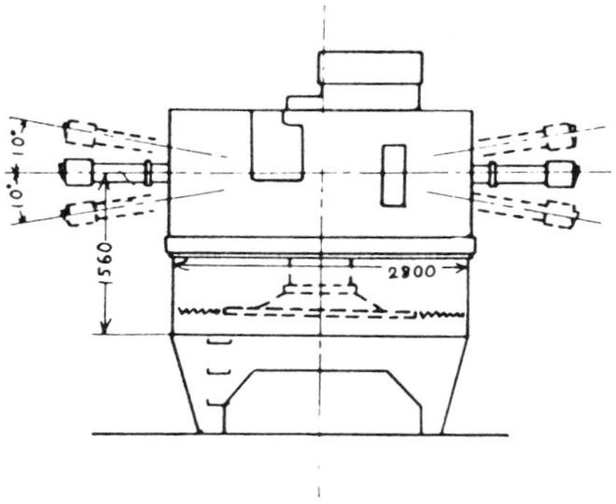


Type 94 HA director with 4.5m stereo rangefinder (general appearance and dimensions).

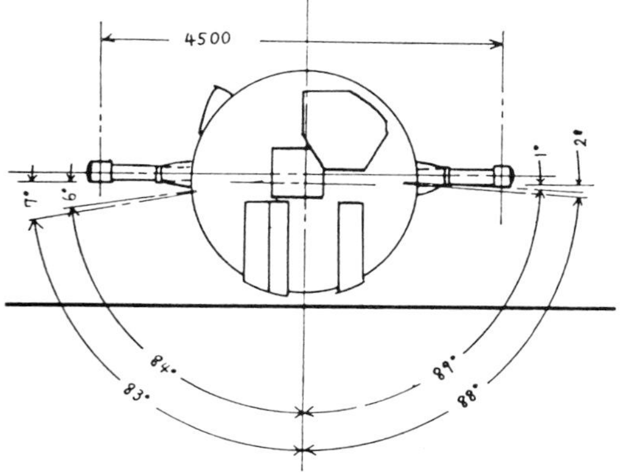


Type 94 director with 4.5m stereoscopic rangefinder (front view and top view – arrangement of handles, pointers, and position of the personnel).

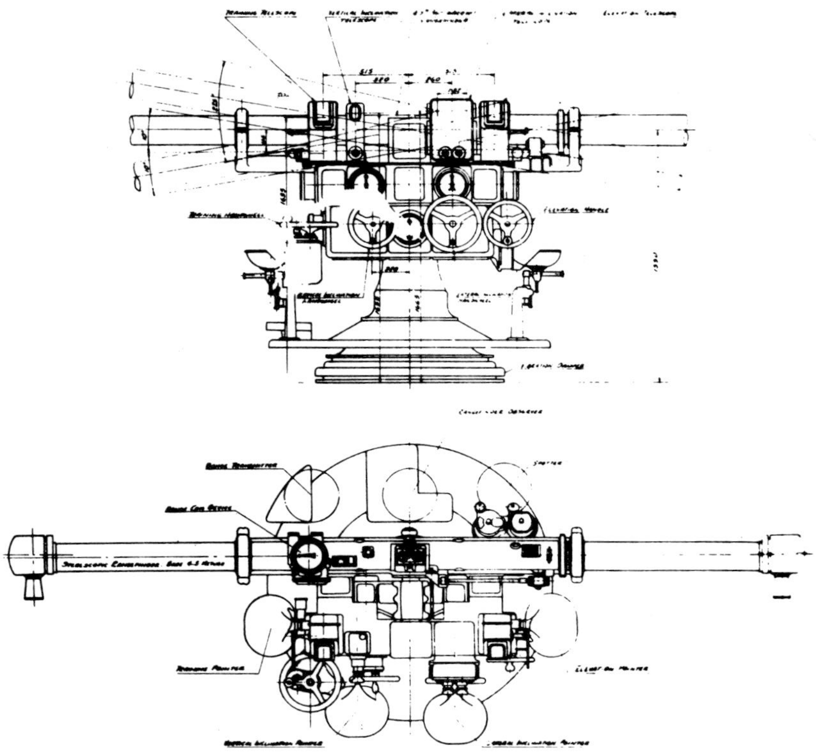

*Type 94 director with 4.5m stereoscopic rangefinder (front view and top view – arrangement of handles, pointers, and position of the personnel).*

**Notes**

1 Adopted for the river gunboats of the *Atami* class.

2 Designed especially for wartime standard merchant ships (TL and TM types) and not mounted in warships.

3 Ad hoc modifications of the weapons listed in (1) and (2).

4 According to Akira Endo 'HAG and AA Ships'. These test guns were apparently changed after some years because Shizuo Fukui in his voluminous series about the warships of IJN from 1868 to 1945 (Vol 3: *Aircraft Carriers*) gives the armament as 47mm gun (probably Hotchkiss).

5 War Department Technical Manual TM-E 30-480 (15 September 1945).

6 This was also a characteristic of the 12 destroyers built for the French Navy in the First World War.

7 As in 5.

8 In fact the IJN was unable to meet this target. One of the best results was an interval of 4 secs between two rounds, *ie* one barrel could fire 25 rounds within 100 secs at best.

9 This was due to the fact that *Matsu* class escorts were equipped with one twin (type B1 without shield but 15hp electric motor) and single (type B1 mod 4 with shield and 10hp electric motor) mounts as the main artillery and many guns were used as land based ones.

10 O–47 (N) 1 'Japanese Naval Guns and Mounts – Article 1, Mounts under 18in.'

11 This dates back to the building of the battlecruiser *Kongo* in Britain. The 15cm gun was adopted as secondary armament but the shell was too heavy for the average Japanese sailor and from the *Ise* class a 14cm gun was used instead.

12 In no case was power used for working loading trays.

13 This automatic fuse-setting machine was among the requests by the German Air Force to the IJN during technical exchange discussions.

14 Data for common projectile model 3 (in fact an incendiary shell) which was filled with 43 tubes containing an incendiary mixture with a piece of quickmatch in the centre. Shell burst was initiated by type 9 model 1 time mechanical fuse. The incendiary steel tubes ignited 0.5 secs later, burnt for 5 secs at 3000° C and gave a flame about 5m in length.

15 This must be described as a very good result.

16 In the case of the 40cal type 89 12.7cm HA the decision of the barrel length was to avoid the vibration of the muzzle and the corresponding inaccuracy of firing.

17 For example, in the carrier *Katsuragi* one electric operated dredger-type hoist per mount was fitted and the rate of supply was insufficient to keep up with the rate of fire of two guns.

18 There are reports that 30rpm could be achieved by a well trained crew.

19 At first it was called 'Special HA Firing Equipment Aiming Equipment' (*Tokushu Kosha Shageki Sochi Shojun Sochi*) but the designation changed to type 91 *Kosha sochi*.

20 Designated as 'Bu type HA Range Follower (with) Additional Communication Equipment'.

21 This advantage was nullified when there was a lot of roll and pitch because the task of the operator for lateral and vertical deflection became too difficult.

22 Values for 1940 are given in parentheses ( ).

23 Flat linkages were used in the case of the type 94 HA fire control system.

24 After the Battle of Midway in June 1942 it was found that the standard type 94 HA fire control system did not meet the requirements and the Kure Navy Yard was ordered to design and manufacture a more effective system, which was called type 3 (for ship use); but the war ended when production of the prototype was nearly completed. This system was up to date and included many features not seen in its predecessors.

25 Report O–30 'Japanese Anti-Aircraft Fire Control'.

**Table 1.** *Basic Data For IJN HA Guns*

| *Type* | *40cal 3 year type 8cm HA* | *45cal 10 year type 12cm HA* | *40cal type 89 12.7cm HA* | *65cal type 98 10cm HA* | *60cal type 8cm HA* |
|---|---|---|---|---|---|
| Designer | | | Engineer C Hada (all types) | | |
| Manufacturers | NY Kure and Hiroshima | NY Kure, Steel work Muroran | NY Kure and Hiroshima | NY Kure and Hiroshima | NY Kure |
| Responsible for manufacturing | Cdr M Oyamada | Cdr M Oyamada | Capt T Fukuda | Cdr M Oyamada | Cdr M Oyamada |
| Production number (1932–44) | 825 | 2125 | 1306 | 169 | 28 |
| Design completed | July 1914 | February 1918 | October 1928 | April 1937 | November 1938 |
| Construction | Monobloc (type VIII), radially expanded (older types: built up) | Built up (types IX, $IX_2$); Monobloc and radially expanded (type $IX_5$) | Monobloc, radially expanded (autofrettaged) | Type I: removable liner, radially expanded; Type $I_2$ monobloc, radially expanded | Type I: removable liner, radially expanded; Type $I_2$ monobloc, radially expanded |
| Barrel and Breech | | | | | |
| Bore (mm) | | | | | |
| Nominal | 80 (3in) | 120 (4.72in) | 127 (5in) | 100 (3.9in) | 80 (3in) |
| Actual | 76.2 | 120 | 127 | 100 | 76.2 |
| Length of the barrel (cal) | 40 | 45 | 40 | 65 | 60 |
| (breech face to muzzle in m) | 3.048 | 5.400 | 5.080 | 6.500 | 4.572 |
| overall | | 5.604 | 5.284 | 6.730 | |
| Number of grooves | 21 | 34 | 36 | 32 | 24 |
| Groove depth (mm) | 1.02 | 1.45 | 1.52 | 1.25 | 1.02 |
| Groove width (mm) | | 6.688 | 6.63 | 5.565 | 6.12 |
| Rifling twist | | | Uniform, 28 cal one turn | | |
| Length of rifling (m) | | 4.649 | 4.450 | 5.631 | 4.036 |
| Bore cross section (cm$^2$) | 47 | 116 | 130 | 81 | 47 |
| Chamber | | | | | |
| Length (cm) | 39 | 65.5 | 53.44 | 75 | 44 |
| Volume (litres) | 2.1 | 10.774 | 9 | 10.5 | 3.5 |
| Weight incl breech (tons) | 0.600 | 2.950 | 3.058 | 3.053 | 1.317 |
| Type of breech | Vertical sliding | Horizontal sliding | Horizontal sliding | Horizontal sliding | Horizontal sliding |
| Ballistics | | | | | |
| Firing speed (rpm) | 13 | 11 | 14 | 19 | 26 |
| Muzzle velocity (m/s) | 670 | 825 | 720 | 1000 (1010) | 900 |
| Maximum bore pressure (kg/mm$^2$) | 22.3–23 | 26.4–26.5 | 25.0–25.3 | 30–30.5 | 30 (29) |
| Muzzle pressure (kg/mm$^2$) | 4.1 | 5.3 | 3.4 | | |
| Muzzle energy (m.t.) | 137 | 709 | 608 | 663 | 259 |
| Weight of assembled round (kg) | 9.6 | 33.5 | 34.6 | 28.2 | 11.9 |
| Projectile weight (common) (kg) | 5.99 | 20.4 ($2M/d^3=0.86$) (16.4) ($2M/d^3=0.69$) | 23 ($2M/d^3=0.81$) 21 ($2M/d^3=0.74$) | 13 ($2M/d^3=0.94$) | 5.99 ($2M/d^3=0.98$) |
| Propellant weight (kg) | 0.93 | 5.2 | 4.0 | 5.83 | 1.96 |
| Ignition weight (primer) (kg) | 0.02 | 0.02 | 0.02 | | |
| Length of the projectile (cal) | 4.26 | 3.46 | 3.46 | 4.13 | 4.24 |
| Ratio of charge weight to projectile weight (%) | 7.00 | 7.52 | 7.73 | 7.30 | 6.30 |
| Fuse | Type 89, very sensitive | Type 91 timed, mod 1 | Type 91 timed, mod 1 with gear | Type 98 timed | Type 98 timed |
| Length of the assembled round (projectile with fixed case) mm (cal) | 711 (9.33) | 1.068 (8.9) | 971 (7.64) | 1.163 (11.63) | 769 (10.1) |
| Projectile travel (m) | 2.658 | 4.744 | 4.546 | 5.750 | 4.126 |
| Point of complete combustion | −10cal from muzzle | −8cal from muzzle | 19cal from muzzle | | |
| Maximum range (m) | 10,000 (10,800) | 15,600 | 14,600 | 18,700 | 13,600 |
| Maximum altitude (m) | 7000 (6000) | 10,400 | 9700 | 13,300 | 9100 |
| Approximate life of barrel (service rounds) | 1500 (1200 – 1500) | 900 (700 – 1000) | 1000 (800 – 1500) | 350 (350 – 400) | 600 |

| *Type* | *40cal 3 year type 8cm HA* | *45cal 10 year type 12cm HA* | | *40cal type 89 12.7cm HA* | *65cal type 98 10cm HA* | | *60cal type 8cm HA* |
|---|---|---|---|---|---|---|---|
| MOUNTINGS | | | | | | | |
| Designer | Eng C Hada | Eng C Hada | | Eng C Hada | Eng C Hada | | Eng C Hada |
| Manufacturer(s) | NY Maizuru | NY Kure, Sasebo, Yokosuka | | NY Kure, Sasebo, Yokosuka | NY Sasebo | | NY Sasebo |
| Responsible for manufacturing | Cdr Hisasue | Eng N Sawamura | | Eng N Sawamura | Capt S Yashiro | | Capt S Yashiro |
| Production number | 1400 | 2600 | | | 50 | 50 | 20 |
| Name of mount | Type C | Type A mod 1 | Type B 2 | Type A 1 | Type A mod 1 | Type A | Type A |
| Type of mount | Pedestal | Pedestal | | Pedestal | Turret | | Turret |
| No of barrels per mount | 1 | 2 | 1 | 2 | 2 | 2 | 2 |
| Weight of mount (t) | 2.6 | 18.5 | 8.4 | 20.5 | 20.5 | 33.4 | 9.5 |
| Total weight (tons) | 3.2 | 22.3 | 10 | 29 (24.5) | 34.5 | | 12.5 |
| Type of operation | Electro-hydraulic (universal transmission gears are used) | | | | | | |
| Motors | | | | | | | |
| Training | None | 3hp 830rpm | 5hp 800rpm | 10hp 700rpm | 8hp 700rpm | | 5hp/700rpm |
| Elevation and depression | None | 3hp/ 830rpm | 3hp/ 830rpm | | | | 5hp/700rpm |
| Training speed | | | | | | | |
| Manually | 4°54′ | 0°59′ | 3°01′ | 1°18′ | 1°34′ | 0°16′ | 3°05′ |
| Electric motor | | 7°11′ | 8°23′ | 12°06′ (6°) ? | 11°40′ | 12°03′ | 18°0′ |
| Elevating speed | | | | | | | |
| Manually | 1°29′ | 1°26′ | 1°28′ | 1°30′ | 1°30′ | 1°30′ | 1°30′ |
| Electric motor | | 14°54′ | 15°21′ | 12°06′ | 14°54′ | 15°54′ | 16°0′ |
| Elevation angles (°) | −5 to +75 | −10 to +73 | −10 to +75 | −8 to + 90 | −10 to +90 | −10 to +90 | −10 to +90 |
| Training adjustment | None | 1.25A 2.5B | 1.25A 2.5B | 2.5A 2.5B | 2.5A 2.5B | 2.5B | 1.25A 1.25B |
| Elevation and depression adjustment | None | 2.5A 3.5B | 1.25A 1.25B | 2.5A 2.5B | 2.5A 2.5B | 2.5A 2.5B | 1.25A 1.25B |
| Height from base plate to trunnion (mm) | 1400 | 1870 | 1642 | 2488 | 2536 | 2022 | 1830 |
| Maximum recoil (mm) | 381 | 510 | 510 | 460 | 500 | 500 | 400 |
| Recoil power (tons) | 6 | 44 | 22 | 30 | 36 | 36 | 14 |
| Recoil mechanism | One oil-pressure type at the top | Two oil at top | One oil at top | Two oil pressure types below the barrel | Two oil pressure types on the top of the barrel | | Two oil pressure types on the top of the barrel |
| Run-out mechanism | One spring type at the top | Two spring type at the top | | Four spring type at the top | Two spring type below the barrel | | Two spring type below the barrel |
| Training gear | Yes | | | | | | |
| Elevation gear | Yes | same | | same | same | | same |
| Type | Cylindrical | | | | | | |
| Ammunition hoist | None | Bucket chain hoist, one set for 1 gun, 1 to 2 guns about 10rpm | | Bucket chain hoist, one to two per mount about 10rpm | Bucket chain hoist, two per one mount about 20rpm | | Bucket chain hoist, two per one mount about 25rpm |
| Loading angle | At any angle | At any angle | | At any angle | At any angle | | At any angle |
| Ramming | Hand | Hand | | Semi-automatic mechanical rammer actuated by recoil force of gun | Semi-automatic mechanical rammer actuated by recoil force of gun | | Semi-automatic mechanical rammer actuated by recoil force of gun |
| Turntable structure | Cast | Cast | | Cast | Fabricated | | Fabricated |
| Rollers spaced in roller path | Equidistant | Equidistant | | Equidistant | Equidistant | | Equidistant |
| Fuse-setter type | Hand | Hand | | Automatic fuse-setter attached at breech end of gun | Automatic fuse-setter attached at breech end of gun | | Automatic fuse-setter attached at breech end of gun |
| Fuse set | Directly before loading | Directly before loading | | Directly before the ammunition is rammed | Directly before the ammunition is rammed | | Directly before the ammunition is rammed |
| Shield | No | Yes/No | | Yes | Turret | | Turret |

| *Type* | *40cal 3 year type 8cm HA* | *45cal 10 year type 12cm HA* | *40cal type 89 12.7cm HA* | *65cal type 98 10cm HA* | *60cal type 8cm HA* |
|---|---|---|---|---|---|
| FIRE CONTROL SYSTEMS | | | | | |
| Type | None | Types 91 and 94 fire control systems | Types 91 and 94 fire control systems | Type 94 fire control system | Type 94 fire control system |
| Training and elevation method | | Follow the pointer | Follow the pointer | Follow the pointer | Follow the pointer |
| Method of firing | Trigger | Electric (from director to gun) Trigger | Electric (from director to gun) Trigger | Electric (from director to gun) Trigger | Electric (from director to gun) Trigger |

## Table 2. *BASIC DATA FOR IJN HA FIRE CONTROL SYSTEMS*

### DIRECTOR

| | *Type 91* | *Type 94* |
|---|---|---|
| Present range | 2000 to 15,000m | 1500 to 20,000m |
| Present altitude | | 0 to 10,000m |
| Elevation angle[1] | 0° to 90° | −15° to 105° |
| Training angle | ±180° | ±220° |
| Cross roll (vertical inclination) | ±15° | ±10° |
| Roll (lateral inclination) | ±15° | ±15° |
| Elevation spotting correction[1] | ±100m | ±200m |
| Training spotting correction[1] | ±100m | ±200m |

All above data transmitted by Power Selsyn to Computer. 1. for gunhouses.

### HA RANGEFINDER AND TELESCOPES

| | *Magnification* | *Field* | *Pupil* | *Objective* |
|---|---|---|---|---|
| 4.5m HA RF | 12,24 | 3°, 1.5° | 4, 2mm | 48mm |
| Sighting telescope for elevation | 8 | 7.5° | 5mm | 40mm |
| Sighting telescope for training | All data as above | | | |
| Sighting telescope for cross roll | All data as above | | | |
| Sighting telescope for roll | All data as above | | | |

Computer (Data received from director are not repeated)

| *Input* | *Type 91* | *Type 94* |
|---|---|---|
| Compass | 0° to 360° | 0° to 360° |
| Future range | 1000m to 10,500m (45cal/12cm HA) | 850m to 12,500m (60cal/8cm HA) 750m to 15,000m (65cal/10cm HA) 700m to 12,500m (45cal/12cm HA and 40cal/12.7cm HA) |
| Range change rate | 90m/sec | ±500 kts |
| Range correction | ±1000m | ±3000m |
| Range spotting | ? | ±3000m |
| Correction for target on the level | 1 to 40 secs | 1 to 43 secs |
| Inherent speed corr | ? | ± 5° 30′ |
| Parallax correction | ? | ± 4° |
| Fuse correction | ± 10 secs | ± 10 secs |
| *(Output)* | | |
| Fuse time | 1 to 40 secs | 1 to 43 secs |
| Lateral deflection (total corr) | | ± 45° |
| Vertical Deflection (total corr) | | ± 30° |

Range correction included 'Correction of the day', namely weather latitude correction, $V_0$ correction (−20m/sec to 10m/sec) etc. (specific gravity of air was from 0.9 to 1.1; wind speed from 0 to 20m/sec, ship speed from 0 to 40kts).

Deviation due to the earth rotation (IJN called this *Byoto*) was ± 12° in case of Type 91.

Elevation and Training angle changing rates were 2.5°/sec and 5.5°/sec respectively in the case of Type 91.

Elevation and Training prediction was ± 20° and ± 60° in the case of Type 91.

### PRINCIPAL DIMENSIONS AND WEIGHT
(for Type 94)

| | |
|---|---|
| *Director* | |
| Working circle | 5m diameter |
| Pedestal | 1.8m diameter |
| Height | 1.6m (without hood) |
| Weight | 3.5 tons |
| *Computer* | |
| Length | 1.5m |
| Width | 0.58m |
| Height | 0.92m |
| Weight | 1.25 tons |

The training motor of the director was electric with 5hp at 100v or 220v DC or 4kw at 220v or 440v AC.

The hydraulic gear was of Jonney type (K 2.5)

For the sake of convenience in sighting, an oscillation damper was installed.

# THE RISE OF JAPANESE NAVAL AIR POWER

The co-author of an important new book on early Japanese aircraft, Robert C Mikesh here describes the political, strategic and economic factors which led the Japanese Navy to develop the most advanced carrier-borne force in the world by the time of the Pearl Harbor attack.

IN June 1924, five weary men, American and Japanese officers, drenched with rain and tired through straining their eyes against a grey pall of clouds, were waiting restlessly for the American 'round-the-world fliers'. Everything was in readiness for the planned arrival except the weather. The location was Kushimoto, the Army fliers' next stop after leaving Kasumigaura, the big naval air base north of Tokyo.

'They can't possibly fly today,' said one of the Japanese on the evidence that two aeroplanes which had been planning to come down from Osaka had been prevented by the treacherous weather. But the Americans did come, popping suddenly out of the leaden sky, the sound of their engines drowned by the storm. Unerringly they had hit the designated refuelling stop after a flight down an irregular coastline and open water, with poor visibility all the way and rain during the last hundred miles.

This visit by the American airmen did more to fan Japanese air consciousness into a fervour of enthusiasm than anything and everything that had happened before. The Japanese asked the question, what if these aircraft had come laden with bombs instead of in a spirit of friendliness; and what was the answer? The aeroplanes that could come out of the storms from thousands of miles away, might come from any direction, and might come with high explosives and poison gas more destructive than earthquakes and volcanoes. From that moment Japan worked feverishly towards greater refinement of its own aircraft.

That was one opinion about Japan's aggressive attitude to air power as expressed by a former military attaché to Japan Lt-Col W Jefferson Davis in 1927 when he tried to awaken Western minds to what was brewing.[1] Few would listen to his advice, his being but one theory as to what caused Japan to prepare for war, coupled with other circumstances outside the scope of this study. Suffice it to say that the creation of a powerful surface fleet with a strong air power element integral with it became the objective. This seeming paranoia did not become apparent however until brought out in actual combat, a period that began in 1931 and would prevail for the next fifteen years.

## The early years

However, serious interest in air power in the Imperial Japanese Navy (IJN) can be traced back to the Washington Treaty's restrictions on capital ships, which imposed the so-called 5:5:3 ratio on Japan. As well as restricting her battleships and battlecruisers to ⅗ths of US and British tonnage, the Treaty applied the same ratio to aircraft carriers, though not to naval aircraft.[2] Thus when Japan began to search for ways of offsetting the restrictions on its surface fleet, air power was recognised as a potential solution.

To begin its new programme of building strength through air power, Japan looked to other nations to provide guidance, equipment and training. In 1919 the Army had already called on French expertise, embracing the ground support doctrine of air operations worked out over the Western Front. During the First World War Britain, on the other hand, had demonstrated an ability to use naval aircraft for reconnaissance, interception and offensive operations, so it was logical that the IJN would turn for assistance to the Royal Navy, with whom it enjoyed long-standing links. In April 1921 thirty British naval officers under Colonel the Master of Sempill[3] arrived in Japan and began active training the following September at the newly constructed Kasumigaura airfield and seaplane base, the IJN's first.

Over the next eighteen months the Sempill Mission introduced the Japanese to the latest techniques in torpedo bombing, navigation, reconnaissance, aerial photography and other aspects, such as maintenance, so important to naval aviation. Perhaps the most significant concept taught to IJN planners was the use of land-based aircraft with sufficient range to support a fleet in combat. Thus a

*Japan's growing naval strength is depicted in this naval review, off Yokohama on 25 August 1933, in which 180 naval aircraft took part. In the upper foreground are two Navy Type 15-2 Flying Boats followed by formations of carrier-based bombers. (All uncredited photographs by the courtesy of the author).*

*The first seaplane tender used by the Japanese Navy was the* Wakamiya *which was commissioned in 1913. It is preparing to lower a Farman seaplane to the water. Farmans of this type were the mainstay of Japanese naval aviation in the formative years.*

fleet of limited size need not lose its surface mobility to the shipboard requirements of aircraft while retaining the advantages of aerial support. This doctrine became a major and important aspect in planning the design of the IJN's future aircraft.

The British mission also brought examples of more modern aircraft, some of which were to be manufactured in Japan, beginning a programme of expansion that was planned to increase IJN squadrons from three in 1921 to seventeen by the time the mission left Japan in March 1923. The six land-based, nine seaplane and two training squadrons were to comprise 284 aircraft, a total that exceeded the strength of the Fleet Air Arm nearly a decade later. This ambitious plan fell foul of a big-gun versus aircraft argument within the IJN, uncertainty surrounding the new post-Washington strategies, and the diversion of resources following the great earthquake of 1923. As a result there were only ten squadrons by 1923 and it was not until 1931 that the target of seventeen was achieved.

## *Aircraft on ships*

Early IJN efforts had concentrated on seaplanes and since it was obvious that tactical use would mean their moving with the fleet, a tramp steamer was quickly converted into a seaplane carrier. Commissioned in 1913, the *Wakamiya* saw action in the First World War at Tsingtao, but postwar was used for experiments with land planes. On 22 June 1920 a Sopwith Pup flown by Navy Lt Torao Kuwahara became the first IJN aircraft to take off from a ship. Flying-off platforms were also fitted to the light cruiser *Kiso* and then the battleship *Yamashiro*, later to be superseded by the newly invented catapult, but as yet there was no provision for landing-on.

This came at the end of 1922 with the completion of the *Hosho*, Japan's first purpose-built aircraft carrier. Designed with the assistance of the Sempill Mission, the ship reflected the latest practice, with a complete flush flight deck and was intended to carry seven fighters, ten attack bombers and four reconnaissance aircraft. In February 1923, William Jordan, a former lieutenant in the Royal Naval Air Service but then a Mitsubishi test pilot, took off and landed on this carrier for the first time, flying a Navy Type 10 Carrier Fighter. The following month Lt Shun-ichi Kira became the first IJN pilot to do the same.

*In 1921, a British aviation mission invited to Japan consisted of thirty naval officers to provide training and demonstrate aerial tactics for the Imperial Japanese Naval Air Force. Part of the doctrine was the importance of land-based aircraft being able to support operations of the fleet at sea.*

*Herbert Smith's Mitsubishi Navy Type 10 Carrier Fighter. This appears to be a prototype. Type 10 referred to the tenth year of Emperor Taisho (1921), the year of type acceptance.* (John Stroud)

By 1927 naval aviation was deemed important enough to warrant an Air Headquarters (*Koku Hombu*) to co-ordinate and promote expansion. The growing squadrons were organised into six new Naval Air Wings (*Kokutais*), one for each of the naval air stations at Yokosuka, Kasumigaura, Tateyama, Ohmura, Sasebo and Kure. Despite growing naval staff support for shipborne air power, the tactical employment of the carrier was not clear and it was not until 1928 that carriers were included in fleet manoeuvre plans, largely as a response to the perceived threat of the huge US carriers *Lexington* and *Saratoga*, completed in 1927. By this time the *Akagi* and *Kaga* (like the US carriers converted from cancelled capital ships) had joined the fleet, producing a prototype carrier task force. Efforts to counteract the superior battleship strength of the US Navy included every kind of tactical study, most notably a proposal by Admiral Yamamoto for aerial attack against capital ships. In trials against the ancient cruiser *Akashi* in August 1930, bombing failed to sink the target, which had to be dispatched by a destroyer's torpedo. This experience led to a renewed emphasis on air-launched torpedoes and aircraft to carry them, a policy that developed steadily until the attack on Pearl Harbor.

## *The aircraft industry*

Although there were many small organisations mostly devoted to sporting aviation, Japan lacked a genuine aircraft industry. The Navy had built licensed types in its arsenals, and even designed a few experimental aircraft, but it became apparent to some forward-thinking strategists that the IJN, like the Army, would have to promote a commercial manufacturing industry if it was to expand.

The Navy had turned to Mitsubishi for the three new types – a fighter, torpedo bomber and reconnaissance aircraft – needed for the *Hosho* and in the 1920s other contracts were awarded to Nakajima, Aichi and Kawanishi, the last two being well established industrial companies that turned to the manufacture of aircraft based on the assurance of IJN contracts and subsequently became closely associated with the Navy. Competitive design was introduced by both Army and Navy in 1926, but prototypes were funded irrespective of whether they were chosen for production or not, so companies were encouraged to enter the frequent competitions, and came to depend heavily on their military sponsors, whether Army or Navy.

In order to achieve international standards quickly, Japanese industry drew on foreign engineering skill and manufacturing knowledge, moving from licence production to foreign-assisted domestic design. European engineers from Britain, France and Germany played a large part: Herbert Smith from Sopwith (by then Hawker) assisted Mitsubishi; Nakajima worked closely with Breguet and Nieuport of France; Short Brothers' design staff helped Kawanishi; and German expertise was much employed by companies like Kawasaki associated with the Army.

Ambitions within the Services drove the development of large-scale capitalism, and the momentum of this military-industrial complex made it difficult for the government to alter the military's objectives, which from the late 1920s began to look increasingly aggressive. Despite the constraining effects of inter-service rivalry, the Army and the Navy agreed to a division of responsibility for the possible theatres, the Navy taking the lead in any Pacific war with the US, while the Army would

*A later generation of catapult-launched seaplanes to be used as the eyes of the fleet was the Yokosho Navy Type 90-3 Reconnaissance Seaplane (E5Y1). These, the first of the welded steel tube fuselage seaplanes, served in combat during the Shanghai incident aboard the seaplane tender* Notoro.

*The* Wakamiya *seaplane tender provided the naval air support that was used against German posts at Tsingtao, China, in 1914. It carried four Farman seaplanes used for reconnaissance duties and innovative bombing tactics.*

*Japan's first aircraft carrier* Hosho *was completed in 1922, adding a new dimension to Japanese naval aviation. The potential of the aircraft carrier was not initially recognized; nevertheless Japan excelled in the early use of this and other carriers for extending airpower as a key element in a major fighting force.*

*The Blackburn T 7B (3MR4) after delivery to Japan in 1930. It is seen with two 250lb bombs. The T 7B enabled Mitsubishi to gain the navy contract for a B1M1 Type 13 Carrier Attack Bomber. The type went into production as the Navy Type 89 Carrier Attack bomber (B2M1 and B2M2) and 205 were built.* (Blackburn Aircraft)

control a land war with China or the USSR. This pointed up the difference in air power doctrine between them since the Army concentrated on a narrow air-to-ground role in support of field forces, while the Navy developed a broader view, including long-range bombers that could intercept US carrier forces before they were in a position to attack the Japanese homeland.

## *The Manchurian and Shanghai Incidents*

It was the Japanese Army that first flexed its muscle through the use of air power, but the Navy was soon to follow. Since Japan's expansionism was focussed continually on mainland China, only war would provide occasion for increasing its influence upon this foreign soil. That opportunity came on 18 September 1931 when the railway giving Japan right of interest across Manchuria, was sabotaged bringing about open conflict. The real cause, however, was that the Japanese Army had themselves destroyed the railway line to provide a pretext for open aggression in Manchuria. This segment of the Army, called the Kanto Command, was relatively isolated from the Japanese government and frequently operated on its own. This unilateral military action thrust Japan into war, which the government did not want but was obliged to support.

The war in Manchuria was mainly ground war, the powerful Japanese Army being initially without air power, but soon after the conflict began, two squadrons of First World War vintage Nieuport 29-C-1s and Salmson 2-A2s based in Korea, were dispatched to the action. The Army then used these aeroplanes to support the ground forces in localized areas of combat. Newer aircraft followed, and before long, the few Chinese aeroplanes in the sky, mainly on reconnaissance, fell to the Japanese as did the airfields from which they operated.

These air victories not only won Japanese public support to the side of military involvement, but brought about a radical change of concept in the application of Japanese Army air power. With Manchuria providing a base of operations the Japanese Army air force's prime mission turned more toward air superiority, this being recognised as a prerequisite in the event of war with China or Russia. In such a manner was the long tradition of having air power tied solely to the ground operation and support of ground forces, taught to them by the French, broken. Army leaders now recognized that in the event of a major conflict, with either China or Russia, opposing air power would be a major factor in the outcome.

Four months later the Navy was to become involved in a similar conflict, beginning on 29 January 1932 in Shanghai and leading to an isolated battle that lasted for 34 days. The 'incident' began with a skirmish between Japanese marines and Chinese civilians in Shanghai who were protesting at the Manchurian intrusion. There was no desire on the part of the Japanese to escalate the matter as the Chinese had the military advantage; nevertheless open conflict did develop. In this, Japanese Naval air power played a noticeable role since the Chinese were able to offer more opposition in the air than had been the case in Manchuria. The resulting combat engagements proved to be a practical testing ground for the Navy's aircraft and tactics, experience better by far than classroom theories.

The Japanese seaplane tender *Notoro*, with eight reconnaissance craft consisting of Yokosho Navy Type 14 (E1Y) and 90-3 (E5Y3) reconnaissance seaplanes had been off Shanghai when the trouble began. These aircraft were called into action immediately, and on the opening day

*Entering service in 1930, the Nakajima Navy Type 3 Carrier Fighter was among the best in the world, in its class. Adaptations of the Gloster Gambet, built under licence, these aircraft represented Japan's fighter strength during the Shanghai Incident.*

flew ten sorties, dropping small bombs on the city and gaining impressive and supportive Japanese newspaper coverage for their heroic activities.

Two and three days later, aircraft from the carriers *Kaga* and *Hosho* arrived as backup to the *Notoro*'s seaplanes; a further catapult seaplane was available on the light cruiser *Yura*. With this armada, the Japanese Navy had been able to muster a total of 76 aircraft for operations over and around Shanghai. Altogether, the carriers were equipped with 26 Nakajima Navy Type 3 Carrier Fighters (A1N) Gloster Gamecocks, and 41 Mitsubishi Navy Type 13 Carrier Attack Bombers (B1M). In addition to daily attacks against Chinese military installations until mid-February, air operations were mainly that of supporting the ground forces.

By this time, the Chinese had positioned their aircraft to begin defensive operations over Shanghai and there have been many accounts of these classic air operations, of dog fights between Chinese Vought Corsairs and other imported aircraft, with those of the Japanese of the day. Most engagements were hit and run encounters, inflicting some damage, yet both sides preferring to keep their distance, not knowing who might have the advantage.

On 22 February, three weeks after the conflict began, the Japanese scored their first victory when three A1N fighters from the *Kaga*, which were now operating from a land base near Shanghai, shot down a Boeing Model 218 (sole prototype of the metal fuselage P-12E/F series) flown by American volunteer pilot Robert Short after two minutes of combat. During this brief engagement, the Japanese unit commander in the leading single engine bomber was also killed and his gunner injured, but the pilot was able to return the aircraft and its crew to its land base at Shanghai (air unit commanders were not necessarily the pilot on board). This encounter showed both sides that an air war would not be a one-sided affair.

Air operations continued over mainland China, but air engagements were relatively infrequent until 26 February when attacks were made on Hangchow airfield, eighteen Japanese aircraft engaging five Chinese fighters, and succeeding in shooting down three of them. These kills were credited to the nimble Navy fighters, making the A1N the classic fighter during the Shanghai Incident. Accounts of Japanese losses vary in that Chinese claims record two Japanese fighters shot down while the Japanese claim Chinese ground fire accounted for the shooting down of three Japanese naval aircraft and none through aerial combat during the brief and testing conflict.[4]

## *Japanese emphasis on air power*

These two limited conflicts in Manchuria for the Army, and at Shanghai for the Navy with some Army involvement, taught both services about air operations and how to deploy air power more effectively. Much study was given subsequently to air tactics using experience gained. In addition, these air operations with their inherent notoriety, provided an excellent opportunity for ambitious militarists to arouse the nation to perceive the need to create a powerful air force for both the Army and Navy. Military leaders were now gaining considerable influence within the working structure of government to the point where they had little difficulty in winning support for their expansionist plans, including demands that were not only large, but also pressing.

By the year 1937 the Japanese aimed to build a naval force, particularly with aircraft, that would excel all others. In addition to their seventeen squadrons already established, the IJN asked for an additional twenty-eight, although the government only authorized fourteen. Undaunted by this restriction, the Navy proceeded with plans to organize the authorised thirty-one squadrons into nine *Kokutais* (Air Wings) which were to be shore based at scattered Naval Air Stations throughout Japan. These squadrons, as planned, eventually consisted of four fighter, two carrier-based reconnaissance, eight and a half carrier attack bombers (torpedo capable), six seaplane reconnaissance, two small and four large flying-boat, three training and one and a half operational-test squadrons.[5]

While planning how best to meet their expansion needs, the Army as well as the Navy realized that the aircraft previously used in Manchria and Shanghai, and still in their inventories, were either foreign designs or heavily influenced by foreign engineers. Both services needed to become self-sufficient in creating their own aircraft if they were to come off best in future conflicts. The military would have to become more heavily involved in the development of their new aircraft.

During the mid-1930s, manufacturers were by now better trained with a backing of experience which freed them from copying foreign techniques. Japanese-designed combat aircraft now began to attain levels of performance that were comparable to contemporaries in the Western world; significantly these new types entered service in time to play a major role in the forthcoming Sino–Japanese War.

Following the Shanghai incident in 1932, Navy requirements for new aircraft brought about many new designs, most of which resulted in one or two of each being built and entered in fly-off competitions for selection of the best designs. There was not a great upsurge producing a multiplicity of designs, but instead, a more cautious approach directed at sound design without direct involvement with foreign technology.

## *Kusho a key*

It was now, 1 April 1932, that the *Kokusho* (Air Arsenal) was established at Yokosuka as a combined organization for aircraft research, development and flight test (evaluation) as well as the organization of technical co-ordination between operational Naval units and aircraft manufacturers. It was known more popularly as *Kusho* (acronym for *Kigun Kokusho*, Naval Air Arsenal). Such an advanced aeronautical engineering centre, was unique in the world at the time, recognising that new concepts in technology might provide the edge to win wars.

Perhaps the most significant concept was that of perfecting the land-based long-range attack bomber that was to be the Japanese Navy's means of supplementing the shortage of surface craft brought about by the 1922 Washington Naval Treaty. Some felt that aircraft of this type should be the responsibility of the Army rather than Navy, but at this period the Army showed no interest in long-range bombers.

Beginning in 1932, the Navy undertook two projects for long-range aircraft capable of observing the United States Fleet, particularly at home ports such as Pearl Harbor and in the Philippines. This need was so great that early

*This deck view of the* Kaga *in 1936 shows Mitsubishi Navy Type 89-2 Carrier Attack Aircraft (B2M1) warming up in the foreground, with most of those in the background being Aichi Navy type 94 Special Bombers (D1A1). This was the opposition the world expected in a war in the Pacific.*

*The Navy had to resort to this Heinkel design to achieve an initial dive-bombing capability. Shown here is an improved version of the Heinkel He 50 which was the Aichi Navy Type 96 Special Bomber (D1A2) of the mid 1930s.*

requirements were that such an aircraft must have a range of 4000nm. Should that not be possible, a range of 2000nm would be acceptable but with the understanding that on the return flight leg from gathering intelligence information, the aircraft must be ditched by the crew, the information being recovered by submarine.[6] Flying-boats were considered too slow and in any case were often restricted in their operations due to rough water.

To achieve this long-range requirement, the Hiro Arsenal was tasked with designing the Navy Experimental 7-Shi Attack Aircraft. Designed to meet the required 2000nm range with a bomb payload of 2 tons, it became a large aircraft, equal in wingspan to that of the four-engined Boeing B-17 Flying Fortress which then was just a design concept. Design problems limited production to eight of these massive aircraft but much was learned from them about long-range bombers. These aircraft became the Navy Type 95 Attack Bomber (G2H) of which Mitsubishi built the final two.

A companion effort for nearly the same long-range mission was the Experimental 8-Shi Special Reconnaissance (G1M1), a sleek, twin-engined aircraft with a slim fuselage and such advanced performance that no armament seemed necessary. It incorporated the first retractable undercarriage on a Japanese aeroplane. Performance was so outstanding that Vice-Admiral Isoroku Yamamoto personally thanked the staff of Mitsubishi for their achievement and flew in a demonstration flight of this prototype. Further refinements made the G1M1 into an effective attack bomber which later became the G3M (Allied code name Nell)[7], for a while the mainstay of the Japanese Navy land-based bomber force, exceeding the performance of all other nations' medium bombers.

The Japanese were concerned about dive-bombing techniques demonstrated by Curtiss Helldivers and other dive-bombers of the US Navy. Efforts by the Japanese to perfect designs of their own ended in failures, causing the *Koku Hombu* to countermand their policy of insisting upon the exclusive use of Japanese designs. The export version of the Heinkel He 50, superficially an obsolete-looking biplane, but a very effective weapon, was selected. Aichi produced 162 He 50 dive-bombers under licence as the Navy Type 94 Carrier Bomber (D1A1). So secret was this development kept, that the title dive-bomber was never used in Japanese naval terminology.

With continued experimentation, and production of the best to replace obsolete types, 895 aircraft filled the IJN inventory at completion of the 1937 expansion plan. Of this number, 332 were assigned to ships; aircraft carrier strength had grown to five by 1937, the *Hosho, Akagi, Kaga, Ryujo* and *Soryu*, with the *Hiryu* added in 1939. The IJN also relied heavily upon seaplane tenders and their associated reconnaissance aircraft to act as eyes for the fleet as well as having some attack capability. By 1937 the Navy possessed five seaplane tenders; *Chitose, Chiyoda, Kamui, Mizuho* and *Notoro*. Altogether these ships made up three Air Wings, each of which generally consisted of one to three aircraft carriers or seaplane tenders with several destroyers.

Japan put considerable development effort into creating submarine aircraft carriers, pursuing this objective much more aggressively than other navies. Practical development of this strategy had begun in 1920 and was accelerated during the 1930s to the point where, during the Pacific War, a Yokosho Navy Type O Reconnaissance Seaplane (E14Y1) made two night attacks upon the continental United States in 1942. Giant *I-400* class submarines were within a month of delivering Aichi M6A1 Seiran bombers to attack the locks of the Panama Canal when the Pacific War came to an end.

During the period 1931 to 1937 the Japanese Navy evaluated more than fifty types of aircraft fully establishing a mutual confidence between manufacturers and the Navy in each other's abilities. Although aircraft designs improved greatly at this time Japan continued to have relentless problems with aero-engine design and reliability, along with lagging progress in hydraulic and electrical/electronic systems. By and large, however, the years 1936 and 1937 was the period when Japanese aeroplane designs achieved, and in some cases surpassed, the levels of US and European military aircraft.

*This Yokosho Navy Type O Reconnaissance Seaplane (E1Y1) is poised for catapult launch from the deck of a submarine probably in 1940.*

## *Sino-Japanese War*

The IJN had expanded its naval air power for planned completion in 1937, seemingly to meet a predetermined date for being involved in war. This was not in fact the intent, but as it turned out 1937 *was* the year Japan entered a long and continuous war that did not finish until the end of the Pacific War in 1945.

On the night of 7 July 1937, a civil disturbance had developed between Chinese civilians and Japanese soldiers in the outskirts of Peking (Beijing). While the Japanese government did its utmost to calm matters, militant members of the Japanese Army and Kanto Command stationed in the area, looked for provocation that would justify an invasion of China. Pockets of local agitators added to the volatile situation. Fighting spread through the area occupied by the Japanese, bringing about Japanese troop landings at Shanghai on 11 August. The air forces of both the Japanese Army and Navy now became involved, creating another unplanned situation in which the latest aircraft of both countries would be tested under combat conditions.

The aircraft carriers *Hosho* and *Ryujo* of the *1st Koku Sentai* (Air Flotilla) with the larger carrier *Kaga* of the *2nd Koku Sentai* took part in these initial operations against the Chinese, all three ships arriving off the coast of China with a total complement of 264 aircraft in mid-August.[8] Shore based airfields were not available to the Navy until the war escalated into other areas.

The most spectacular event of the war took place just five weeks after the opening of hostilities when on 14 August 1938, formations of Mitsubishi Navy Type 96 Attack Bombers (Nell), from Kanoya Naval Base on southern Kyushu, crossed the China Sea and attacked Chinese air bases and military installations near Hangchow and Kwangtoh. This first attack was pressed home through violent storm-turbulence, helped by the strong tail winds of a typhoon but hindering the return flight. This bombing mission, a 1200nm round trip, was astounding news to the Japanese people, who knew little of their expanding air power, and nothing of this type of bomber which had such long range and heavy load carrying capability, much less its capability through such treacherous weather. These attacks made spectacular headlines throughout the world as well, but by occurring so far from European and American capitals, the signals of growing air strength went virtually unnoticed, while at the same time fanning Western anger towards Japanese aggression in China.

Air raids by these advanced Navy twin-engine bombers continued from mid-August to the end of September. For the most part, these long-range attacks might be construed more as psychological warfare than strategic bombing, for after the first few days of operations as few as 18 bombers were available. However, repeated attacks against cities and air bases, seemingly at will, had a major and positive impact upon Japan's war effort.

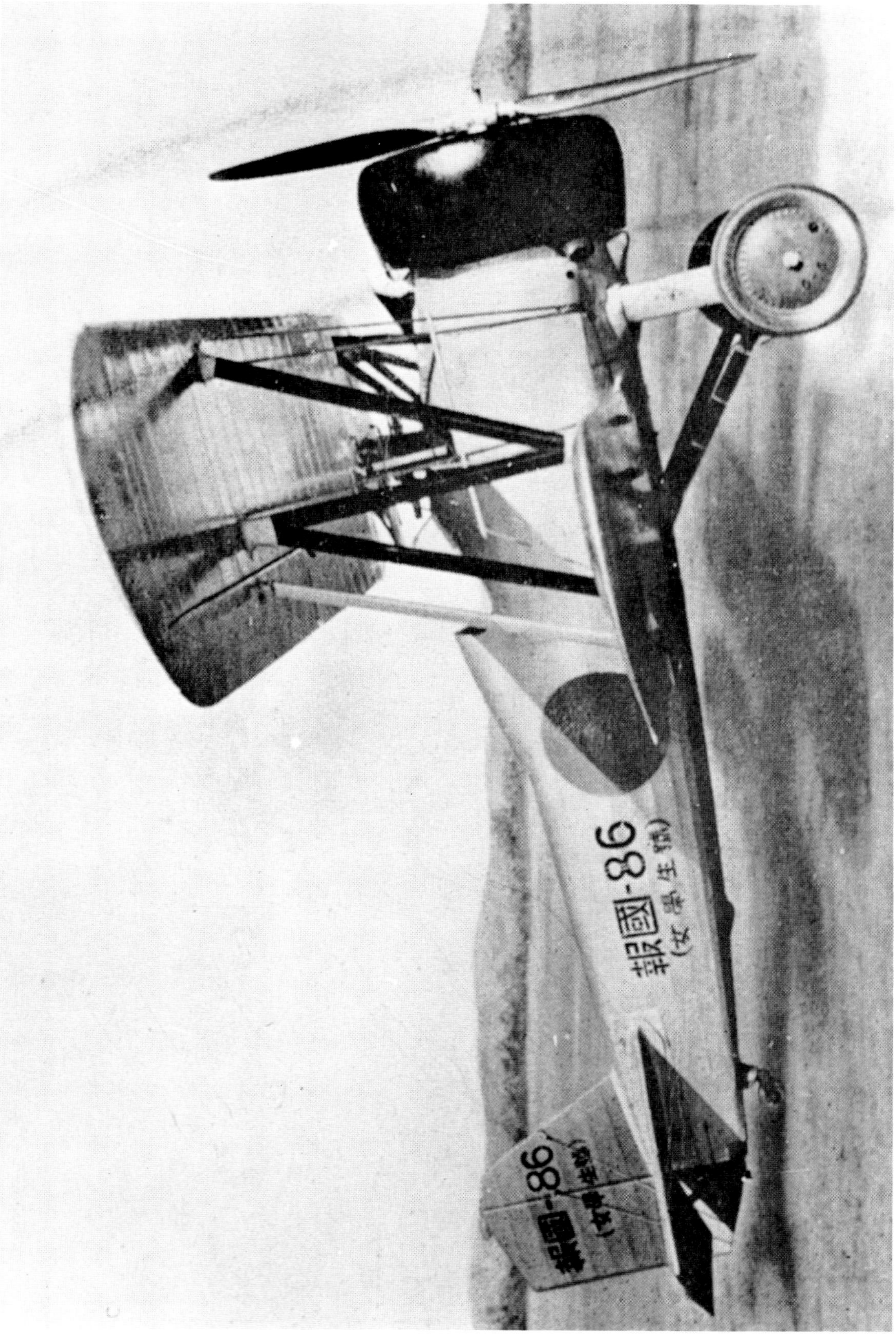


*Further improved over the A2N1, this Nakajima Navy Type 95 Carrier Fighter (A4N1), the Navy's last biplane fighter, was in time for service in the Sino-Japanese Conflict of 1937.*

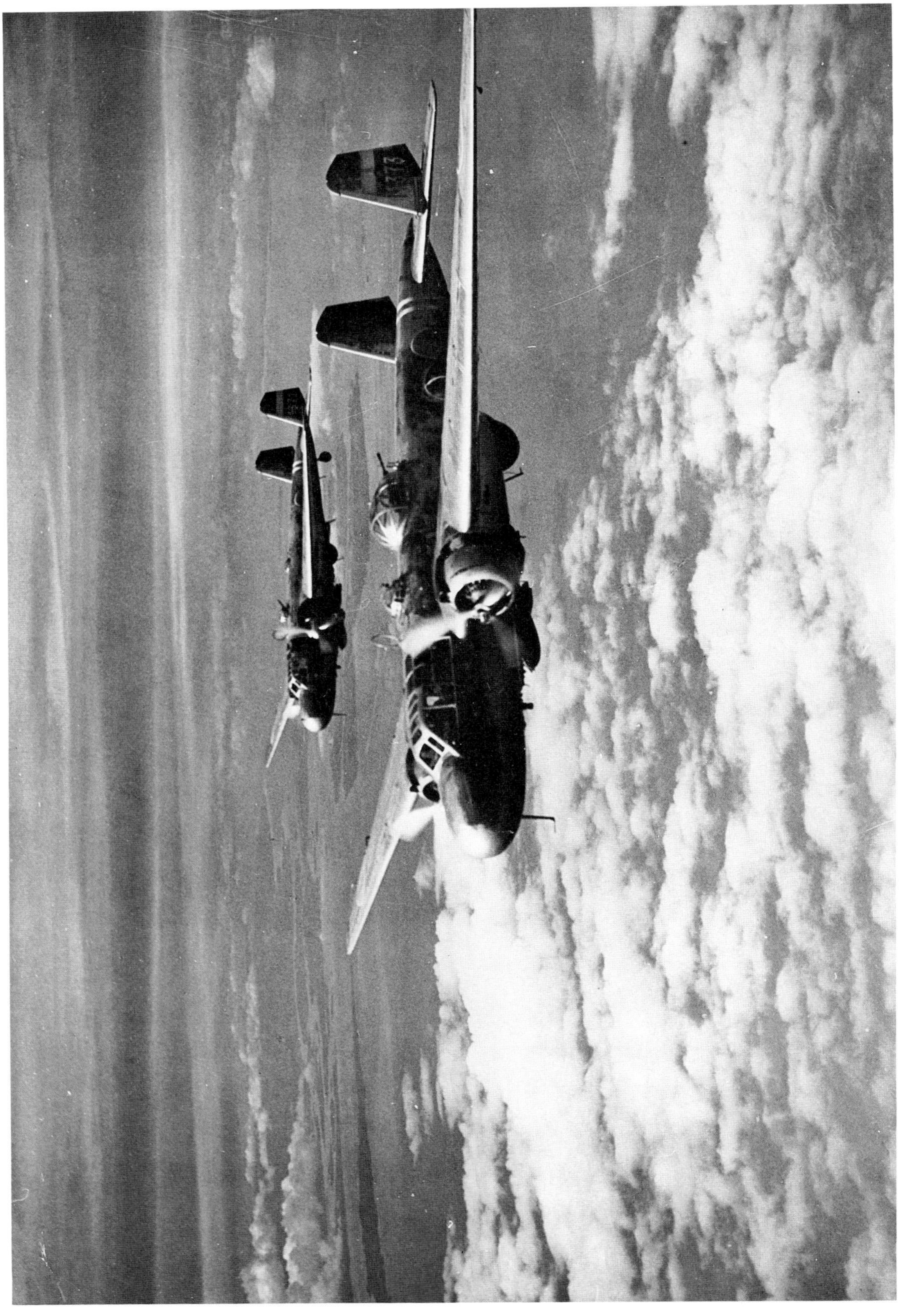

*Developed from a design intended for long range reconnaissance, these Mitsubishi Type 96 Land-based Attack Aircraft (G3M) were among the world's best in the late 1930s. They surprised the world when performing the first trans-oceanic bombing missions from bases in Japan to the Chinese mainland.*

Although Japan's aircraft had greatly improved over those used against the Chinese in the hostilities of 1931, the quality of China's aircraft and the training of its airmen had also improved. From the beginning of this conflict, and with the reservoir of additional resources, Japan held the upper hand in numbers of aircraft at their disposal, but not necessarily in the combat zone. The Japanese Army had 49 squadrons with 500 aircraft, while the Navy consisted of 29 squadrons and 400 aircraft.[9] At the beginning of hostilities, Japanese pilots were considered to be well trained, and backed by well organized maintenance and supply systems. This situation would continually improve as the war provided combat experience, making the Japanese even more potent when later meeting American and British forces in the Pacific War.

While Japan as the attacker was at a disadvantage in having to fight over Chinese territory, the defence also had an apparent advantage in numbers as well as the Chinese air forces had 31 squadrons, consisting of 650 to 700 aircraft and slightly more pilots. However, the numbers of aircraft in commission were inadequate, some squadrons achieving only 20 per cent of their on-paper strength. And overall, training was inferior for the combat ahead.

Adding to Chinese strength as the war flared were up-to-date Soviet-built fighters, later to be followed by four Russian fighter squadrons and two bomber squadrons flown by Russian pilots. Americans were soon involved as well, led by Claire L Chennault (later of Flying Tigers fame) who organized and trained Chinese pilots on US and British fighters.[10]

During the first three months of these air operations, Japanese Naval statistics recorded that 181 enemy aircraft were shot down and 143 destroyed on the ground. For their own losses, a total of 39 of their aircraft were admitted as destroyed or damaged; other sources claimed that Japanese Navy losses were 21 per cent for the 3000 sorties flown which equates to 630 aircraft. The truth may be somewhere in between.

Fighter engagements with the Chinese opposition were often a draw, emphasizing to the Japanese that better aircraft than their Type 90 (A2N) and 95 (A4N) Navy biplane fighters were needed. When losses continued to mount, the *Kaga* returned to Japan to take on a load of Mitsubishi's new all-metal fighter, the Navy Type 96 (A5M) Carrier Fighter (Claude), the world's first carrier-based monoplane fighter. Service trials were hardly completed when these open cockpit, fixed undercarriage fighters were sent into combat with the shore-based 12th and 13th *Kokutais*. Immediately the Japanese won air superiority with these fighters which could out-climb and out manoeuvre the Soviet-built Polikarpov I-16s flown by the Chinese. Only in maximum speed did the Russian fighter have a few knots advantage.[11]

By now, other Japanese aeroplanes were entering Navy squadron service in China. With further refinements, these would become the principal types that would open the war between Japan and the United States. Included was the introduction of the Aichi D3A1 carrier-based dive-bomber (Val) into the China conflict in October 1940. This looked obsolete by the standards of the day with its fixed, faired undercarriage, more cumbersome in appearance than the Junkers Ju 87. In fact the Val, with its innovative dive-brakes that did not jeopardize stability in the dive, proved to be an effective dive-bomber, a decided improvement over its antecedent, the Aichi D1A2 carrier-based dive-bomber biplane of Heinkel He 50 origin.

Replacing another outdated biplane was the Nakajima B5N1 carrier-based attack bomber (Kate). This three-crew low-wing monoplane was used as a level bomber as well as for torpedo attack purposes. Placed aboard aircraft carriers to replace the Yokosho Navy Type 92 Carrier Attack biplane bombers (B3Y1) and Kusho Type 96 Carrier Attack Bombers (B4Y1), Kates were shore-based in China and used for level bombing in support of ground operations, with fighter escorts as compensation for their lack of armour protection for crew and fuel tanks, coupled with light defensive armament.

*With the outbreak of the Sino-Japanese war, these newly produced Mitsubishi Navy Type 96 Carrier Fighters (A5M) were soon on charge to replace the A2N1s and A4N1 fighter biplanes.*

*The second prototype of the Aichi Navy Type 99 Carrier Bomber (D3A1) seen in late 1939. This was the Navy's last aircraft type to have a fixed undercarriage, a feature which proved no hindrance to its effectiveness during dive-bombing attacks at Pearl Harbor.*

## *The invincible Zero Fighter*

*The biggest surprise. The Mitsubishi Navy Type 0 Carrier Fighter (A6M2), better known as the Zero Fighter. Reports of its superior performance were made, but ignored because they seemed unbelievable.*

During the summer of 1940, new aircraft joining Japanese Navy squadrons included a pre-production group of A6M2 fighters. This was the most advanced carrier-based fighter of the time, and before long would become known the world over as the *Zero Fighter*, a name derived from its Navy designation of Navy Type 0 Carrier Fighter.

The Zero was a completely new design, making use of experience gained from Mitsubishi's previous A5M (Claude). The new model had a retractable undercarriage, was heavily armed with two 20mm cannon and two 7.7mm machine guns, was highly manoeuvrable, and had exceptional range. When first introduced into combat on 19 August 1940, these fighters were used to escort Navy bomber formations but encountered no enemy opposition. On 13 September, however, Japanese formations with Zero escorts encountered 27 enemy fighters over Chungking. Within 30 minutes all of the Chinese aircraft had been destroyed without the loss of a single Zero.[12]

From this and similar encounters that followed, the Chinese considered the Zero fighter to be invincible, and their pilots treated it with such caution that interceptions virtually came to an end. Thus, the Japanese gained air superiority over almost the entire Chinese theatre of war. This complete control of the air meant that bombers of all descriptions could be sent on operations deep into Chinese territory at will, protected by the awe-inspiring Zero. By the end of 1940 a total of 153 Zero sorties had been flown in 22 missions accounting for 59 Chinese aircraft being shot down and 101 destroyed on the ground without any losses in the Zero force.

The seeming invincibility of the Zero is said to have been responsible for some Japanese leaders pressing for war against the United States, convinced of its superior qualities. 'Despite the enemies awesome industrial might,' according to Jiro Horikoshi, designer of the Zero,

> the Navy had confidence in the ability of our Zero fighter planes to wrest air control from the enemy over any battle area. Our intelligence and our

> technical groups stated flatly that the excellent performance and technical superiority of the Zero fighter meant that, in battle, one Zero would be the equal of from two to five enemy fighter planes, depending upon the type. Because of this unshakeable faith in the Zero, the Navy felt extremely confident of victory in initial campaigns.[13]

The Zero fought in China for sixteen months before the Pacific War began with the attack on Pearl Harbor. Why, with all this time in service, did the Western Powers receive such a surprise about the advances that Japan had made with their aircraft? The information had been reported, but the *users* of the intelligence information failed to appreciate the significance of the Zero. As William M Leary, University of Georgia points out in his in-depth article 'Assessing the Japanese Threat: Air Intelligence Prior to Pearl Harbour,' that appeared in the winter 1987 issue of *The Airpower Historian*:

> Allied prewar intelligence of Japanese aviation was dismal. Blinded by complacency, chauvinism, and arrogance, Allied observers reached dubious conclusions about the state of Japanese air power. Pilots were myopic, could not fly at night, and suffered from a defective sense of balance; their aircraft were only poor imitations of superior western models.

*The Japanese Navy was unrelenting in its efforts to perfect torpedo attack aircraft. When the Pacific War began, Japan had the best aircraft of this type in the Nakajima Navy Type 97 Carrier Attack Aircraft (B5N2), later Allied code-named Kate.* (US Navy)

An examination of *Jane's All the World Aircraft* of 1941 bears out this latter point by aircraft descriptions. Of the seventeen Navy types described, only seven were operational and accurately described aircraft. And of those described and implying that these represented the current status of the Japanese Navy air force, only five were in front line service, the Nell, Claude, Dave, Mavis and Zero with the last including the entry: 'The Type 0 is the latest single-seat fighter monoplane known to be in service in the Far East. No publishable details of this type are available.'

## At war

At the threshold of the Pacific War on 7 December, 1941, the Japanese Army and Navy air forces possessed about 1500 first-line aircraft each. The Navy had about 3500 trained pilots, and the Army about 2500. On average, these first line pilots had more than 500 hours flying experience and most of them had had some combat service in China. The 600 pilots in the Navy aircraft carrier groups were probably the best trained and most skilful in the world. By December 1941, in order to build up these air forces and to replace losses, Japanese factories were turning out about 425 aircraft per month and new pilots were being trained at the rate of 2750 a year.[16]

At that moment, the largest concentration of American forces in the Pacific was based in Hawaii. Stationed there were 231 Army Air Force and about 170 land-based naval aircraft. Of these, however, only 162 of the Army aircraft were considered to be modern types. At sea at the time of the Japanese attack were about 180 first-line aircraft aboard two American aircraft carriers.

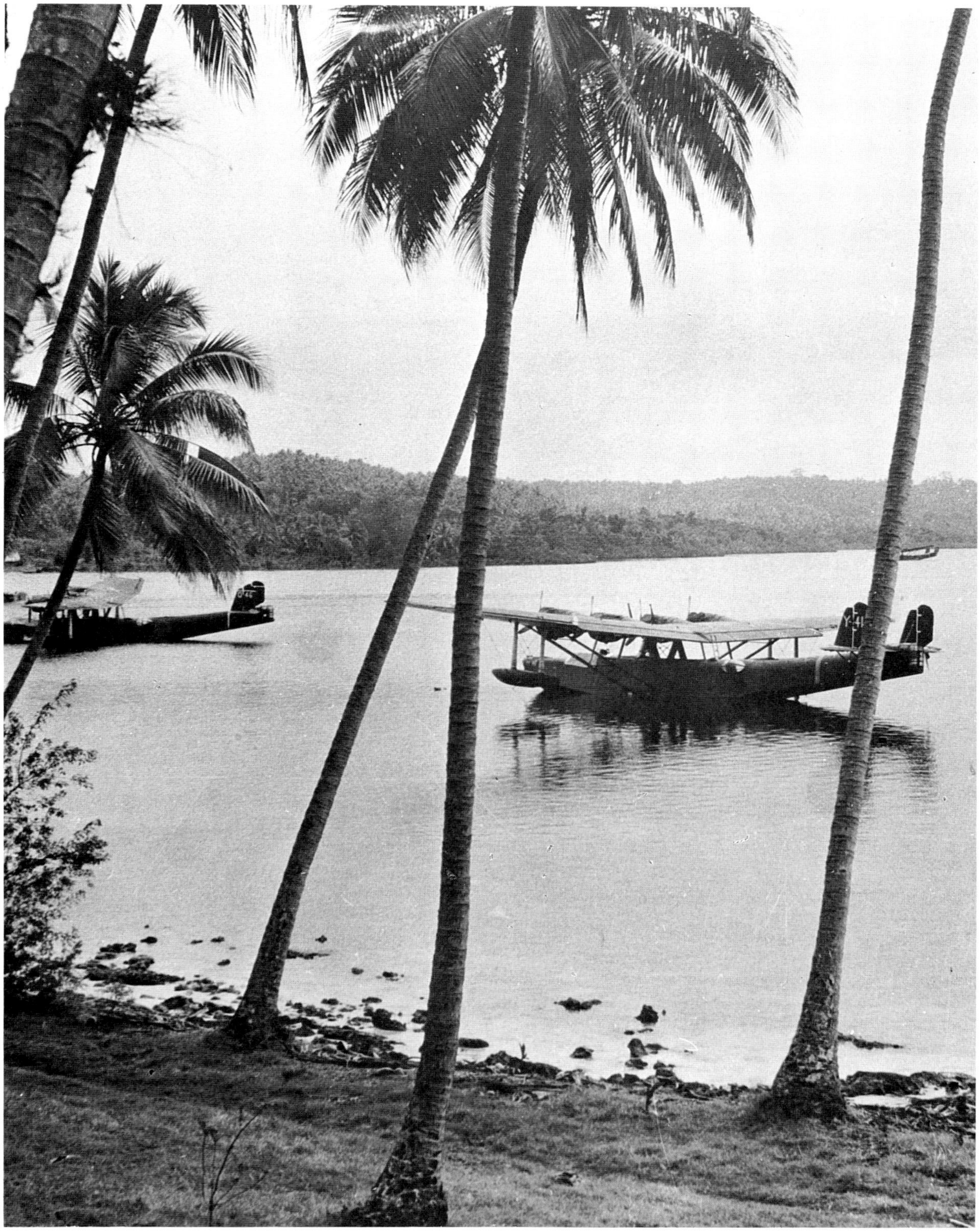

*Kawanishi Navy Type 97 Flying-boats (H6K1) in a Pacific lagoon.*

In other parts of the Pacific – at Midway, Wake Island, the Philippines, Netherlands East Indies, combined with those at Hawaii – the total aircraft count was 1426 of which 688 were considered first line equipment. Within this number, the British and Australians possessed 332 aircraft. RAF pilots had combat experience, and were probably as good as the Japanese, but their aircraft were old or no match for Japanese aircraft.

Comparing the respective operational aircraft with which the US Navy and Japanese Navy would confront each other, advantages varied. The Zero fighter was superior to the Grumman F4F Wildcat in speed and climb at all altitudes above 1000ft, and out-matched the Wildcat in service ceiling and range. There was no comparison between the two in manoeuvrability, for the Zero could out-turn the Wildcat mostly because of its light weight. That weight advantage, gained in part by not having protective armour plate or self-sealing tanks and a less durable structure, became a disadvantage when the Wildcat got into a firing position. Then the hard hitting 0.50in machine guns could give the Wildcat easy victory.[15]

The Kate was a more advanced carrier-based bomber than its counterpart, the Douglas TBD Devastator (soon to be replaced by the Grumman TBF Avenger). Like the Zero, the Kate was a lighter aircraft, giving it more agility, but due to its lack of armour plating for the crew and self sealing tanks, it was vulnerable to gunfire.

The dive-bomber, Val, was no match in performance to the Douglas SBD Dauntless, although it was a very effective dive-bomber in the opening months of the war. In addition to its obsolescence by having a fixed undercarriage as a weight saving measure, it too had the shortcomings of the Kate and the Zero in vulnerability.

Japan excelled in perfecting the long-range patrol bomber flying-boat Emily, which is regarded as the best aircraft for its mission of any in the world for that era. At the threshold of the war, the last and most successful seaplane-fighters produced were the Japanese A6M2-N Rufe and N1K1 Rex, causing the US Navy to consider developing similar opponents until such time that the need had passed.

Japan had other aircraft types which were equal to or perhaps surpassed Allied types, recognizing that crew proficiency played a vital role. It is rare that one war will build-up a nation's forces in preparation for yet another war, but this was evidently the case in the 1930s. Noted Japanese journalist, and respected aviation historian, Eiichiro Sekigawa sums up the circumstances:

> What, one may ask, did Japan gain from this four years of war against China? In short, it provided first-class training under battle conditions for . . . Army and Navy pilots [to have] the opportunity to practice their skills under combat conditions, so that by the beginning of the Pacific War they were as capable as any military pilots in the world. The numbers of aircraft available to them [in China] were insufficient for a major war, but their quality was high and operations throughout four years of war had given the pilots confidence in their weapons. Thus, the war in China had prepared the armed forces of Japan for war in the Pacific. Without this experience it is unlikely that Japan could have achieved such brilliant military success at the beginning of the new conflict.[16]

## *Acknowledgements*

The Author acknowledges with sincere thanks, the historical and technical assistance provided by Shorzoe Abe, a well known author and historian of Japanese aviation subjects and long time mentor of this author. Special thanks also go to Harold Andrews, noted US Naval aviation historian, and Alex Spencer, a specialist on naval treaties, for their observations and contributions.

**Notes**

1 W Jefferson Davis, *Japan, The Air Menace of the Pacific* (The Christopher Publishing House, Boston 1927), p53.

2 The United States and Britain agreed to limit their capital ships to 18 and 22 respectively each within their tonnage limits, and Japan would retain 10 ships. Stephen Roskill, *Naval Policy Between the Wars* (Walker and Company, 1968) p331.

3 Also Captain Sir William Francis Forbes-Sempill; the rank of Captain referring to the rank given by the Japanese, with lesser rank for the other participating British team members. 'Pioneer of Aviation in Britain', *The Aeroplane* 23 October 1942, p476.

4 Eiichiro Sekigawa, *Pictorial History of Japanese Military Aviation* (Ian Allan, London 1974), p39.

5 *Ibid*, p43.

6 Kunio Yanagida, *Zero Fighter*, (KK Bungei Shunji 1977), p138–140.

7 Code names assigned by Allied forces during the Pacific War to simplify Japanese aircraft identifiers employed male names for fighters and female names for bombers and reconnaissance aircraft.

8 Eiichiro Sekigawa, *op cit*, p60. This represented 65 per cent of all front-line carrier based aircraft in service with the Japanese Navy at that time.

9 *Ibid*, p60.

10 Chennault was about to retire from the USAAC as a Captain, noted as an expert on tactical warfare and fighter operations in particular. The Chinese Government invited him to become an Advisor on Aeronautical Affairs, with the rank of Colonel in the Chinese Air Force.

11 Rene J Francillon, *Japanese Aircraft of the Pacific War* (Putnam, London 1970), p345.

12 Robert C Mikesh, *Zero Fighter* (Zokeisha, Tokyo 1981), p4.

13 Masatake Okumiya and Jiro Horikoshi, Zero (Ballantine, New York 1956), p39.

14 Trevor Nevitt Dupuy, *Military History of World War II: Vol 13* (Franklin Watts, New York 1964), p14.

15 Robert C Mikesh, *op cit*, Zokeisha, Tokyo 1981), p27.

16 Eiichiro Sekigawa *op cit*, p72.

# JAPANESE OXYGEN TORPEDOES AND FIRE CONTROL SYSTEMS

One of the great Japanese successes of the Pacific War was the famous 'Long Lance' oxygen powered torpedo. An outline history of developments leading up to this weapon and a description of all related torpedoes is here combined with a brief survey of fire control equipment by Dr Jiro Itani, Hans Lengerer and Tomoko Rehm-Takahara

After the Meiji Restoration in 1868 the purchase of warships abroad was stopped for a few years but in 1875 the Imperial Japanese Navy (IJN) ordered the building of their most modern warships in British shipyards. When these ships were delivered in 1878 the armoured frigate *Fuso* carried spar torpedoes for the use of her boats. The first importation of the self-propelled or locomotive torpedo was not until 1884, but despite of the fact that there they were to be employed on British-built ships[1], the IJN purchased 200 35.6cm (14in) torpedoes from the German Schwartzkopf GmbH at Berlin which had purchased the patent from Whitehead. This torpedo was formally called type Shu model 84 but was popularly known (together with the type Shu model 88 of which 307 were bought in 1888) as *Akasuirai* (red torpedo) being the nickname for Schwartzkopf. The reason why the IJN did not adopt the Whitehead torpedoes from the start may have been the slightly superior speed of the German torpedo and the fact that the bronze air vessel did not rust. However, in 1893, when the IJN ordered the cruiser *Yoshino* in Britain, 100 torpedoes, called model 26, were ordered from the Whitehead Co at the same time, and thereafter the IJN enjoyed a close relationship with this British company.

Five years later, the IJN bought a torpedo with vertical rudders from Whitehead, called type 30 model A to distinguish it from type 30 model B bought from the same company but having four propellers instead of two in case of model A. Both of them were domestically produced by Kure Navy Arsenal Torpedo Department, first as pure copies but later some improvements with regard to the material were made. Later a type 30 with the new diameter of 45.7cm (18in), and types 32 and 34 each with the diameter of 35.6cm and 45.7cm were imported from Whitehead. Based upon the type 32, Kure, Yokosuka and Sasebo Navy Yards produced the type 37 45.7cm torpedo which increased the explosive charge to 100kg.

While the above-mentioned torpedoes had no combustion chamber – *ie*, they were so-called cold running torpedoes – the IJN's next torpedo, bought from Whitehead in 1905, was hot running and was equipped with the dry type heater. The Woolwich tail was also used for the first time. This torpedo was designated type 38 No 2 B to distinguish it from the cold running type 38 No 1 which was the IJN's first design (Kure Navy Yard). Both type 38 torpedoes were 45.7cm in diameter.

Successively type 42 and 43 torpedoes were bought from Whitehead; these belonged to the same type as type 38 No 2 B (dry type heater) and it is believed that the type 43 was imported in diameters of 53.3cm (21in) and 45.7cm (18in), the former being for capital ships. Generally speaking, the last group of these torpedoes were driven by the reaction of air, petroleum and water, had single-acting, 4-cylinder star engines, three- or four-bladed propellers (double converting) water pressure depth meters, air type gyros and steering mechanism and horn type body.

Utilizing fundamental research and experiments on the wet type heater in Kure Navy Yard Torpedo Department, the types 44 No 1 (53.3cm) and No 2 (45.7cm) were formally accepted in 1911. They were primarily domestic products (the air chamber was imported at first but after several years Nippon Steel Muroran Co and the Sumitomo Steel Production Factory manufactured the material for it, while other materials had been produced by Kure Navy Yard Steel Division from the beginning of the production). The defects of the type 44 torpedoes (occasional engine and heating system disorders, comparatively short range) were the direct inspiration for the development of the 6 year type torpedo, whose engine and heating system were completely re-designed, resulting in about 50 per cent increase in range. The design of this torpedo was begun in 1914 and it was accepted into service in 1916 after live ship trials in the Yokosuka Torpedo School one year before.

With this torpedo the Mitsubishi Nagasaki Weapon

*The light cruiser* Jintsu *launching torpedoes in 1927. They are probably 61cm 8 year type.* (Photographs by courtesy of Hans Lengerer).

Production Factory participated in the manufacture of torpedoes, which previously had been exclusively the work of Navy Yards. The designer of this torpedo, then Sub-Lt Matsushita, also designed the 8 year type torpedo of 60.9cm (24in) diameter, the world's largest torpedo then in use. It had the same system as the 6 year type and was accepted in 1921. Because the Washington Conference (begun in the same year) restricted the diameter of torpedoes to 53.3cm (21in), this torpedo was developed in strict secrecy. These two types were produced in substantial quantities and at the beginning of the Pacific War the 6 year type was mounted on 'Kaze' class destroyers, L type submarines and light cruisers up to the *Kuma* class, while 'Tsuki' class and early *Fubuki* class destroyers were equipped with the 8 year type.

After the conclusion of the Disarmament Treaty the torpedo was expected to be the most powerful weapon of fleet support forces and with this background the IJN made efforts to improve the 6 year and 8 year type torpedoes. However, since the torpedo was the main weapon of attack by flotilla craft on enemy capital ships, a strong demand was made for significantly upgraded performance, rather than the improvement of existing torpedoes. Therefore it was decided to buy the newly developed high speed (46kts) torpedo from Whitehead in 1926. This torpedo was propelled by a horizontal double-acting 2-cylinder engine instead of the 4-cylinder star engine of the past and compared to the 6 year and 8 year types was faster by 10kts and 8kts respectively. These torpedoes were produced between 1927 and 1929 and sent to Japan. Seven technicians working as superintendents were allowed to study the production process and this contributed much to the future development of the high speed torpedo.

Taking these torpedoes as reference, but also utilizing the experience of the superintendents, information gathered from abroad, its own researches under the control of the Navy Technical Department, and studies in the Torpedo Experiment Department (founded in Kure Navy Yard in 1922), the IJN was able to develop one 60.9cm (24in) and one 53.3cm (21in) high speed torpedo design. The former was called 'trial torpedo C' at first, to become type 90 torpedo in 1928 (accepted into service in 1932); while the latter was identified by the designation 'trial torpedo D' and later type 89. The 60.9cm torpedo was mounted on cruisers and later *Fubuki* class destroyers etc, the 53.3cm torpedo in 'Kaidai' type submarines etc. The high speed (46kts and 45kts respectively) was achieved by the direct imitation of the Whitehead engine, in place of the previous star engine. Being the main torpedoes for surface ships and submarines before the adoption of type 93 and type 95 oxygen torpedoes they can be called the intermediate products using the conventional air-petroleum-fresh water system before the invention of the still faster torpedoes with their new source of energy.[2]

## *Development of the oxygen torpedo*

Fundamentally the principle of the wet type heater torpedoes from type 44 to type 90 was to lead the air in the air vessel to the combustion chamber (generator) where the fuel (kerosene) was burnt to convert the latent energy of the compressed air into the active heat energy in order to increase speed and range. The only useful (active) element in this air (composed of 23 per cent oxygen and 77 per cent nitrogen in weight as well as some small amount of carbon dioxide and inert gases) is oxygen. The kerosene usually used as fuel was composed of 86 per cent carbon and 14 per cent hydrogen. The volume of air necessary for combustion was about 14.5 times as much as the weight of the fuel and the burning of the oxygen corresponding to the fuel caused too high a temperature in the generator resulting in main engine damage. Therefore fresh water was delivered into the generator to depress the temperature to about 1200° C to be capable of sending gas of about 900° C to the main engine.

From this description it becomes evident that the biggest ingredient of the air, nitrogen, contributed nothing to the heating. Therefore in order to produce more speed and range than type 89 and 90 torpedoes an entirely new energy source was necessary. After some studies it was concluded that replacing all nitrogen by oxygen would increase the heat energy by as much as four times, resulting in a nearly equivalent improvement in the running properties of the torpedo. On the other hand, the temperature in the generator would be very high so that the amount of water (this time sea water) sprayed into the combustion chamber had to be increased to limit the heat to about 3.5 times as much as in the compressed air heated torpedo. By the use of compressed pure oxygen the explosive charge could also be enlarged (by using the surplus space) and nearly wakeless running could be expected. In addition, this gas was easily obtained and already widely used as a technical product.

The above advantages were behind the decision to use highly compressed oxygen as the new energy source for propulsion. Thereafter, torpedo specialists were mobilized to develop and perfect the oxygen torpedo. It is not certain when the IJN first had the idea to mix the compressed air with oxygen, but by the order of the Navy Technical Department, Captain Tokushiro Ogura commenced the first land experimental work in 1916 using type 44 45.7cm torpedoes without special modifications. The proportion of oxygen was increased from 10 to 20 per cent and then to 30 per cent of the total air, but explosions occurred in the generator at the instant of ignition when 30 per cent oxygen was employed, and so the work was then stopped. The principal reason for the explosions was the fact that the fuel combustion chamber had not been increased in proportion to the greater oxygen content.

When the Whitehead Works, Weymouth, was producing the twenty high speed torpedoes ordered by the IJN, Lieutenant (later Tech Rear-Admiral) Shizuo Oyagi, then studying torpedo design as the superintendent, occasionally heard secretly that the Royal Navy's new *Nelson* class battleships were equipped with oxygen torpedoes and

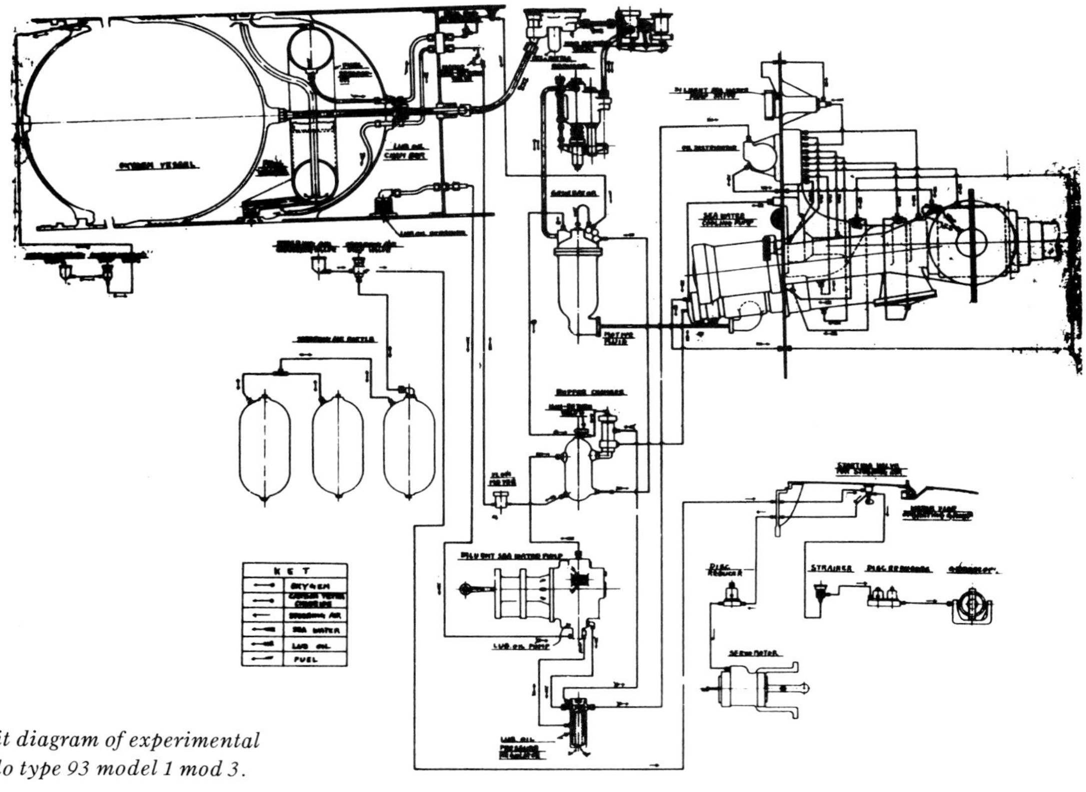

*Circuit diagram of experimental torpedo type 93 model 1 mod 3.*

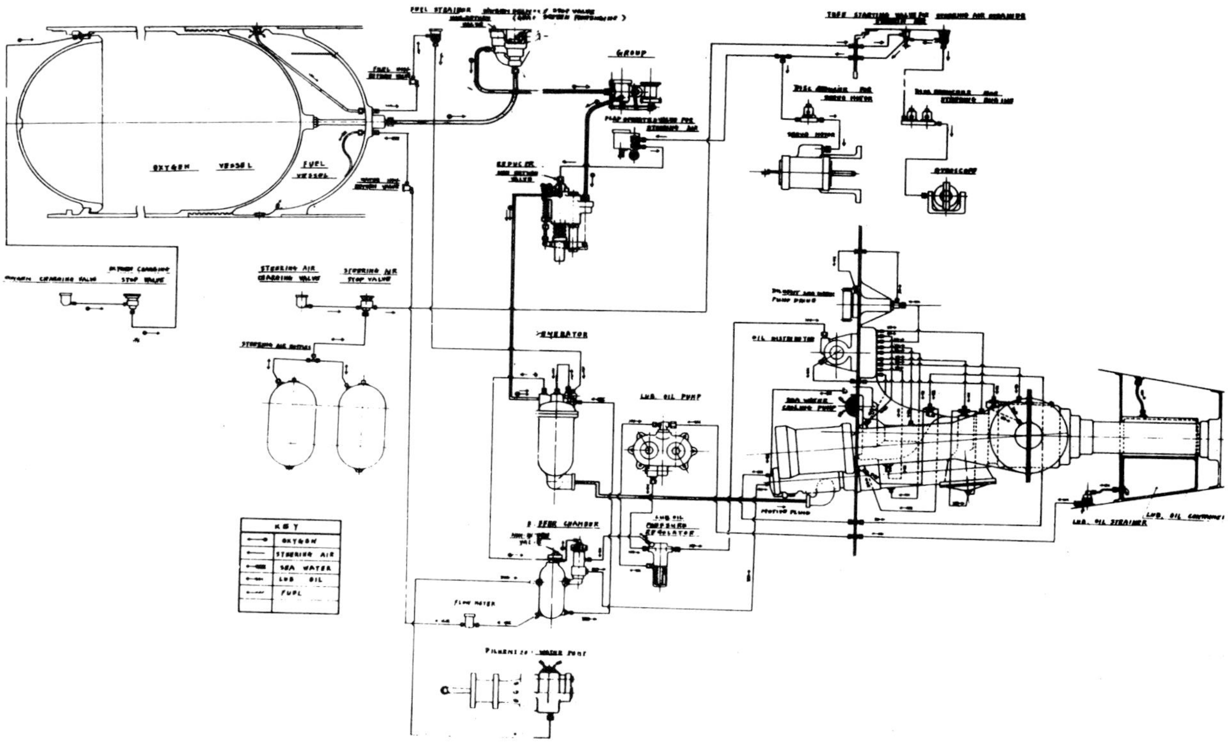


reported this to the Deputy Minister of the Navy, even though he was never able to ascertain the truth of this rumour (in fact no oxygen torpedoes were used in these ships). Stimulated by this report in 1928 the Navy Technical Department, 1st Division, 2nd Section (in charge of torpedoes) ordered the chief of Kure Navy Yard to re-open the research and experimentation on oxygen torpedoes. The Torpedo Experiment Division headed by Captain Kanemitsu Yamashita was put in charge and the chief member was Lt-Cdr Oyagi, who took this post after his return from Britain.

After their former experiences, the prevention of explosions at the instant of ignition was the highest priority and therefore the Navy Technical Department was ordered to make the experiments by gradually increasing the content of oxygen using two 8 year type torpedoes with modified air vessels, main engines and propellers. Lt-Cdr Oyagi planned to use a ratio of 50 per cent oxygen and 50 per cent air compressed at 195kg/cm$^2$ which roughly means 63.5 per cent oxygen and 35.5 per cent nitrogen by weight. This time the fuel vessel was increased to match the increase of oxygen. Since the larger volume of course occupied more space, it became impossible to install a fresh water vessel as in the past and Oyagi invented a method of suctioning sea water by a pump directly connected to the main engine and sending it directly to the generator and the lower part of the fuel vessel. This brought about a potential problem, namely the removal of the salt by the crystallization of the sea water, but since the temperature of the heated air was around 1200° C while the melting point of the salt was about two-thirds of this value the sea water did not produce any anxiety.[3]

*Circuit diagram of torpedo type 95 model 2. (*Reports of USNTMtJ*).*

The major problem of preventing explosions at the moment of ignition was overcome by the use of a small starting air chamber (volume about 50 litres) beside the oxygen vessel. The main engine was started therefore on natural air and then the sea water was drawn in by the pump; after passing the sea water buffer one part was led to the generator, the other to the lower part of the fuel vessel to push the fuel into the generator. The mixture of oxygen and air was then introduced and the rest of the air in the starting chamber was used for steering.

The use of natural air at the start of combustion (later it became known as the first air vessel) and sea water instead of fresh water became the keys to success of the

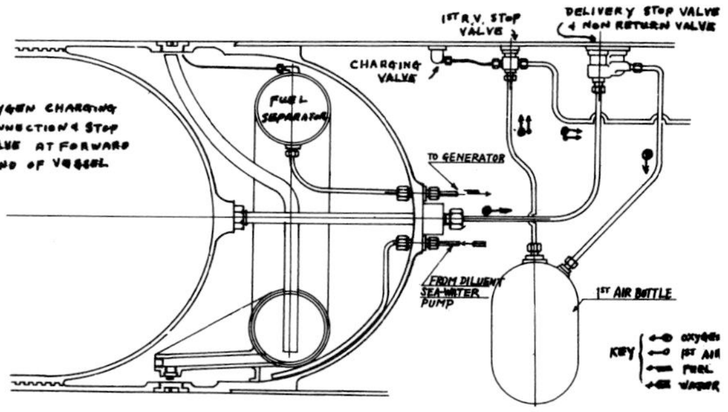


*Circuit diagram of torpedo type 95 model 1. (*Reports of USNTMtJ*).*

**Table 1.** *OXYGEN TORPEDOES OF IJN*

| | Surface ships | Submarines fleet | Submarines midget | Aircraft |
|---|---|---|---|---|
| IN SERVICE | | | | |
| *100 per cent oxygen* | Type 93 Model 1 mod 1 and 2 | Type 95 Model 1 | Type 97 | Type 94 Model 1 |
| | Type 93 Model 3 | Type 95 Model 2 | | Type 94 Model 2 |
| *38 per cent oxygen* | | Type 96 | Type 98 | |
| EXPERIMENTAL | Type 93 Model 2 | | | |
| | Type 93 Model 1 mod. 3 | | | |
| | Type $F_1$ to $F_3$ | | | |
| | Type 0 | | | |

pure oxygen torpedo. Known as 'special torpedo B', this was successfully tested in the summer of 1932 causing no explosion and running very well, but because of the small sized oxygen compressors at Kure Navy Yard (maximum 150kg/cm$^2$) speed and range were less than expected.

This 'special torpedo B' did not enter service but functioned merely as the preparatory experiment for the so-called 'trial torpedo A', which was the pure oxygen torpedo to be called later the type 93 torpedo model 1. The design of this torpedo was begun at the end of 1931 by Cdr Toshihide Asama based upon the 'special torpedo B'. The main differences were as follows:

1. different arrangement of circuitry;
2. oxygen vessel containing pure oxygen with the pressure of 225kg/cm$^2$;
3. separate starting air chamber (for first air vessel) with the volume of 13.5 litres, pressure of 235kg/cm$^2$;
4. start of the main engine by natural air and then gradually increasing the oxygen concentration to 100 per cent;
5. strengthening the structure of the main engine;
6. improvement of the sea water buffer.

The design was finished at the end of 1932 and two trial torpedoes were produced by Kure Navy Yard Torpedo Department; this was also responsible for the land tests using air, while the Torpedo Experiment Department was in charge of the experiments using pure oxygen. The latter were done in 1933 (2593 in Japanese calendar) and therefore this torpedo was called type 93 even though it did not enter service until 1935, after the Torpedo School test launching from the heavy cruiser *Chokai*.

The speed and distance tests (50kts/20,000m and 40kts/30,000m) were carried out very carefully and during the experiments the following problems were encountered:

1. damage to the generator because of inadequate control of the temperature;
2. breaking of the main engine piston rod;
3. inadequate speed;
4. deviation from course;
5. insufficient steering power.

These difficulties were overcome one by one and finally 50 ± 1kt/20,000m or 40kts/30,000m were obtained. Since this torpedo used the heat generated by the combustion of oxygen and kerosene no exhaust of nitrogen took place as in the air driven torpedo and therefore the wake was insignificant and very difficult to spot. Furthermore the weight of the explosive charge rose to 490kg from 295kg in type 89 and 400kg in type 90 torpedoes. Thus, all the advantages expected before the revival of oxygen propulsion research were obtained.

## *Adoption of oxygen torpedoes by surface ships, submarines and aircraft*

Following the success of 'trial torpedo A' (type 93 model 1) the almost identical type 93 model 1 modification 1 was designed in 1935 for actual service use. Successively a type 93 model 1 modification 2, experimental torpedo type 93 model 2, type 93 model 3 and finally type 93 model 1 modification 3 were designed and put into service (with the exception of the experimental model 2 and model 1 modification).

When the type 93 model 1 was almost proven (1934), the Navy Technical Department ordered the Nagasaki Weapon Production Factory to design and test produce for submarines two 53.3cm torpedoes with a propulsion system closely resembling that of the type 93. First called 'trial torpedo B' it became the type 95 model 1 which was developed into the type 95 model 2. In 1937 a 45.7cm torpedo was designed along the principles of the types 93 model 1 and 95 and called type 97 as special torpedo for the newly developed midget submarines (*Kohyoteki*).

In 1934 the IJN not only accepted the use of oxygen torpedoes in surface ships and submarines but also in aircraft and the Navy Technical Department attempted to develop an airborne oxygen torpedo as the successor of the type 91 air torpedo. This was a 53.3cm weapon named 'trial torpedo D', to become type 94 model 1 for type 97 flying boats in 1938. The very similar design of a 45.7cm torpedo was first called 'trial torpedo F' but became type 94 model 2 in 1939. After producing 95 examples of model 1 between 1938 and 1941 and 48 of model 2 (both by the Nagasaki Weapon Production Factory) from 1941 to 1942, production was stopped and the airborne torpedo was abandoned – mainly because of handling difficulties –

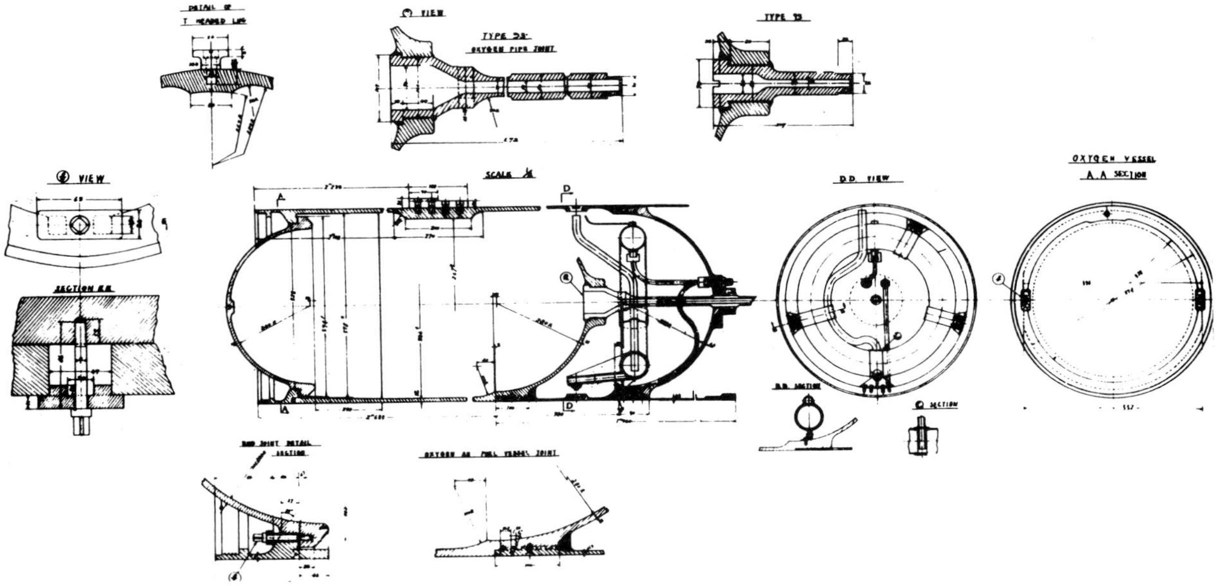

in favour of an improved conventional type 91 air torpedo.

In addition, the Yokosuka Navy Yard undertook the development of a turbine driven oxygen torpedo in 1934 to meet the requirements of the Navy General Staff for a high speed torpedo capable of 60kts for 8000m. Following the preliminary work the design was continued by Kure Navy Yard in 1936 to produce successively the 60.9cm 'trial torpedoes F1, F2 and F3'. The last obtained the required speed but was short in range. Since sea water was also used as diluent in the generator the deposition of salt in the nozzles and blades of the turbine (velocity compound, three-stage, Curtis type having two rows of moving blades in a single disc with a fixed row in between) was inhibited by the injection of zinc chloride solution. Despite achieving the required speed the de-

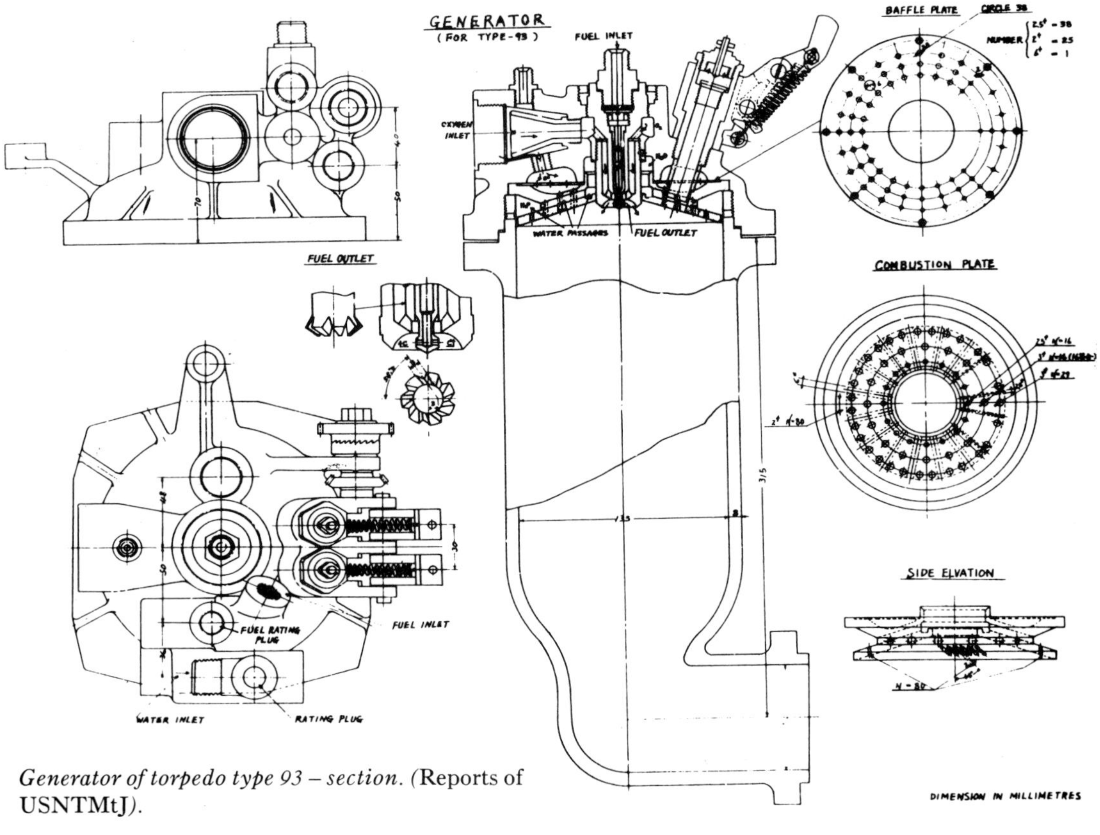


*Generator of torpedo type 93 – section. (*Reports of USNTMtJ*).*

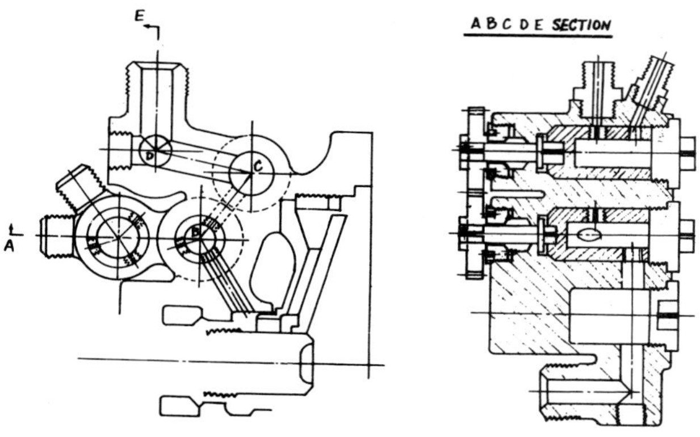


*Generator acting nozzles of torpedo type 93 – vertical and plan section.* (Reports of USNTMtJ).

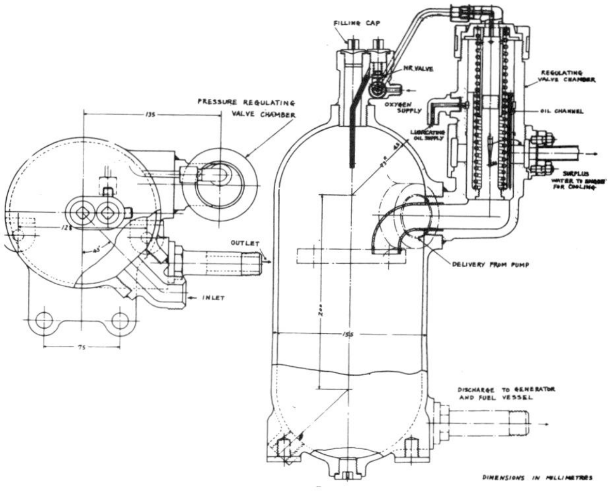


*Buffer chamber of torpedo type 93 – plan and section.* (Reports of USNTMtJ).

*Sea water and oil pump of torpedo type 93 – section.* (Reports of USNTMtJ).

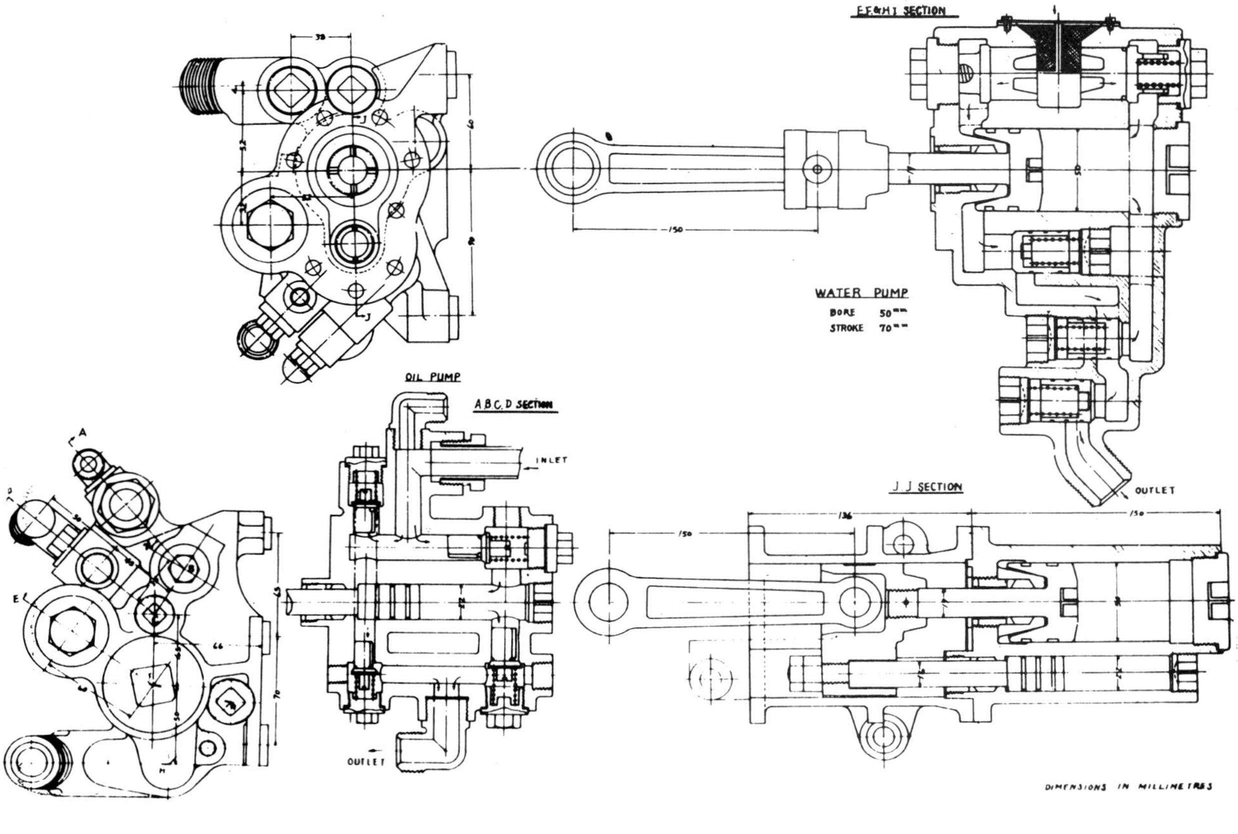

velopmant of the turbine was stopped since the Navy General Staff now demanded even more than 8000m range at 60kts and added a second speed setting (40kts/ more than 30,000m). On the other hand, little could be done to prevent the torpedo breaking surface and for these two reasons it was concluded that the tests ended in failure.

A gigantic 72cm (28.4in) torpedo for surface ships was designed in 1944 (total weight 5000kg, explosive charge 850kg, speed/range 40kts/54,000m or 55kts/27,000m). Before the end of the war some examples were produced but they were never actually used. Besides these torpedoes using 100 per cent oxygen there were two others using 38 per cent oxygen. These were the 53.3cm (21in) type 96 torpedo for submarines and the 45.7cm (18in) type 98 torpedo for midget submarines. Both were developed in 1942, the former as an interim measure before the development of the type 95 model 2 (which overcame the troubles experienced in the type 95 model 1 as already stated), the latter to replace the type 97 torpedo.

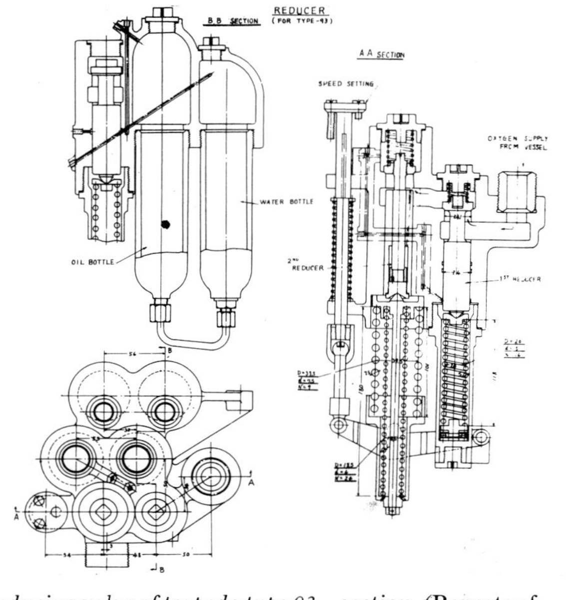


*Reducing valve of torpedo type 93 – section.* (Reports of USNTMtJ).

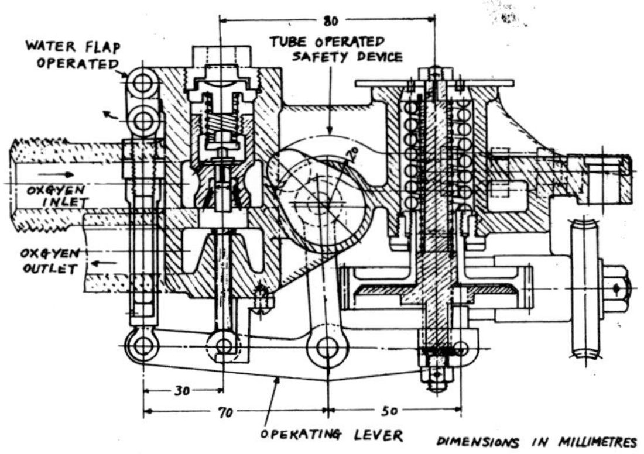


*Group valve of torpedo type 93 – section.* (Reports of USNTMtJ).

## *Torpedo Fire Control Systems*

Because of the steadily increasing importance of the torpedo in the tactical planning for the decisive battle against an enemy fleet crossing the Pacific and approaching the presupposed battlefield about 200 miles off Ogasawara Islands, considerable effort was spent on the design and manufacture of torpedo fire control equipment. Torpedo fire control system must be divided fundamentally into those designed for the use aboard of surface torpedo carriers and those produced for submarines. The support forces were to play a crucial part in the attrition phase of the decisive battle plan so emphasis was laid upon above water torpedo fire control equipment and the IJN's approach to problems of this kind was complete and comprehensive. The various units were well constructed and functioned accurately. Directors, target course and speed instruments and computers were the main equipment to be used in various combinations. Provisions were made for introducing into the computer almost every conceivable constant and variable pertaining to the torpedo problem. Unlike the high angle gunnery fire control systems, automatic inputs using electrical follow-up gears and slip ring follow-ups controlling a reversible motor through a magnetic type hunter switch were utilized. In contrast the submarine torpedo fire control systems were not so well developed and therefore were simpler and less accurate. This difference also existed in the target designation system and torpedo firing panels.

The difference in importance also becomes evident in studying the list of equipment produced by the Japan Optical Co published in the 'History of Japanese Navy Underwater Weapons' *(Kaigun Suirai Shi)*. According to this source torpedo fire control systems started with types 4, 8, and 14 directors for destroyers and cruisers followed by type 90 in 1930, type 91 model 3 in 1931, type 92 in 1932 and type 92 *Hasshashikiban* in the same year. All these instruments were for surface ships.[4] The first group of these instruments, constructed during Taisho era (1912–1926) – types 4, 8, and 14 – were very simple directors with 5cm binoculars, designed and produced by Navy Yards. From the beginning of the Showa era

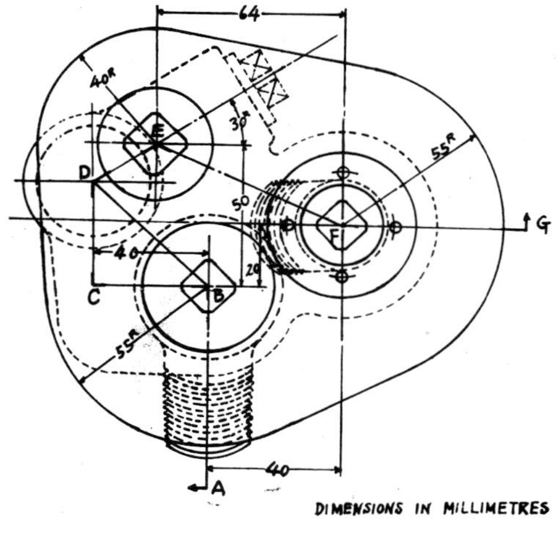


*Carbon tetrachloride ($CCl_4$) unit of torpedo type 93 model 3 – plan.* (Reports of USNTMtJ).

*Oxygen Torpedo Type 93*. (Photo: 1 Nov 1979 by Kunio Kitamura/Hans Lengerer Collection).

(1926–1989) the outline planning was the responsibility of the Navy Technical Department 2nd Division and detailed planning and production were mainly done by the Japan Optical Co. From 1929 Lt-Cdr Tamura and Eng Kazunori of the Navy Technical Department guided the Japan Optical Co and thereafter their precision increased gradually.

In 1933 there entered service the type 92 modification 1 director (as the successor of the type 90) and automatic chasing system for target angle by periscope for submarines, but according to the above-mentioned source it was not until 1938 that improved equipment for submarines was introduced (type 98 *Sensuikan Taiseiban*). The type 92 modification 1 director for submarines was based upon Vickers' torpedo fire director bought by the IJN in 1931 and lent to the Japan Optical Co to produce the prototype director for submarines. The test production was completed in November 1933, and after land and sea tests was accepted into service.

The appearance of this director stimulated the construction of torpedo fire control equipment, with new types and the production of newly modified versions following in quick succession. The director was much improved and a calculation panel and communication system were added as well as increasing the magnification of the binoculars (6, 8, 12, 15, and finally 18cm). This can be clearly observed in case of the instruments for surface ships when reviewing the years from 1934 to 1941. Type 93 target course and speed instrument was adopted in 1934 followed by type 93 model 1 and type 93 model 2 computers in 1934 and 1935 respectively as well as type 97 model 2 computer and type 97 model 1 and model 2 director in 1937. Before entering the war the type O director for destroyers (1940), type 1 submarine computer (1941) and type 1 computer as well as type 1 model 1 *Hasshashikiban* for cruisers appeared in 1941. The latter was an improved type 92 with 18cm binoculars and anti-vibration system.

Of those developed in wartime, the following are worth noting: type 3 (1943) and type 1 model 2 modification 2 (1944) target course and speed instrument for destroyers as well as type 92 model 2 submarine director (1944)[13] and type 5 model 3 director for midget submarines (1945). Beside these instruments which came into operation a certain number for surface ships and submarines were under development or in early planning stages by the end of the war.

Naturally, the ships equipped with oxygen torpedoes used the most modern fire control systems. As stated before, directors were used either alone or in combinations with other instruments. Typical combinations for cruisers, for example, were:

1. type 97 model 1 or model 2 director and type 1 (or type 97 model 2) computer;
2. type 97 model 1 or model 2 (or type 92 model 2) director, type 93 (or type 93 model 1) computer, and type 93 target course and speed instrument.

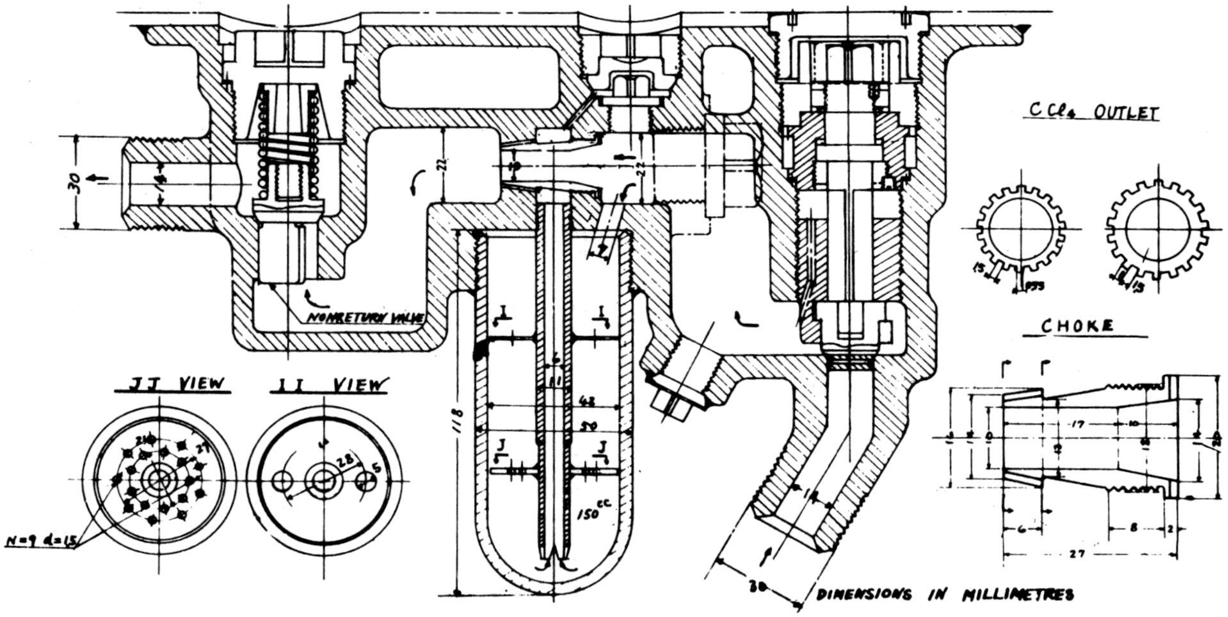


*Carbon tetrachloride (CC1$_4$) unit of torpedo type 93 model 3 – sectional elevation. (*Reports of USNTMtJ*).*

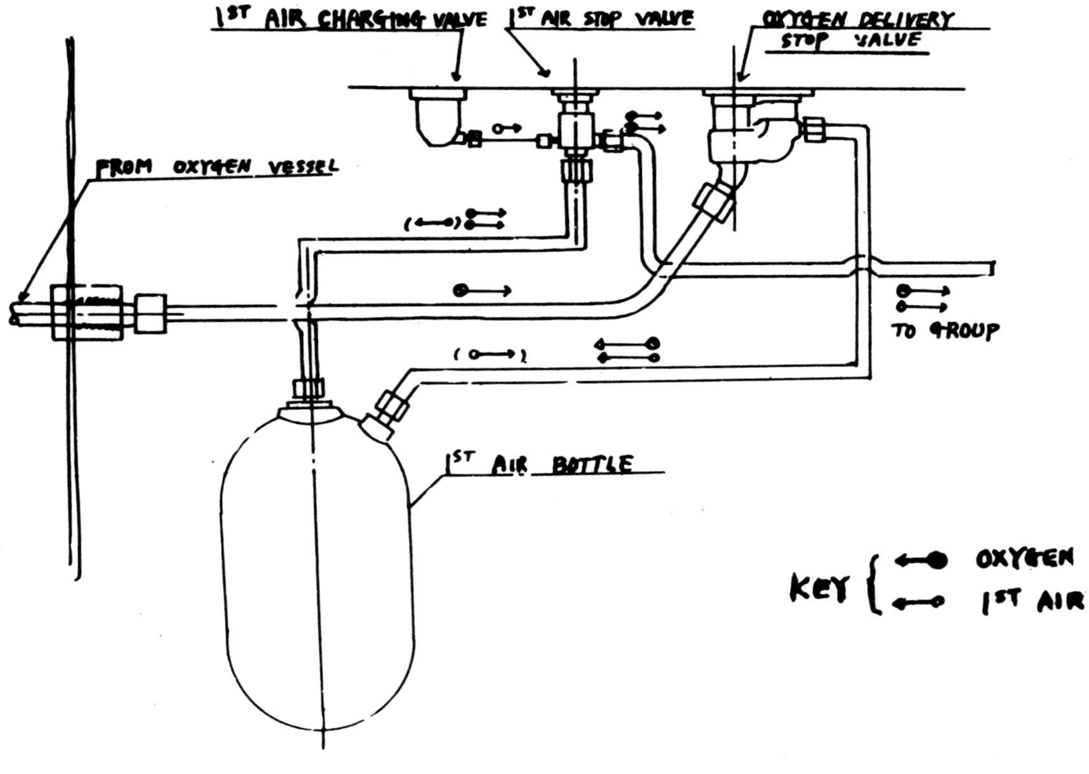


*Circuit diagram of torpedo type 93 model 1 mod 2. (*Reports of USNTMtJ*).*

For destroyers either the type 97 (or type O) director alone or combined with (1) type 3 model 2 target course and speed instrument or (2) type 3 model 2 target course and speed instrument and type 93 model 2 computer were used. Submarines used (besides the automatic chasing system for target angle by periscope etc):
1. mainly type 92 modification 1 director (of which 162 units were produced);
2. same director as in (1) and type 98 calculation system for target and own ship position;
3. type 92 model 2 submarine director (*eg*, two of each were mounted on *I-12* and *I-13*) and type 3 model 2 (or type 2 modification 1) target angle signalling system (*eg*, two of each were mounted aboard *I-12* and *I-13*).

As it is quite impossible to describe every system in detail one example for surface ships and submarines was chosen to provide some further data.

**Torpedo fire control system for surface ships**

*Type 97 director.* Type 97 model 1 and model 2 directors were improved types of type 91 director with anti-vibration system: 92 units were produced in total (of which 36 were type 1) by the Japan Optical Co with Engs Minaki, Komiya and Tatsuka in charge of the detailed planning and construction. This director mounted a 12cm binocular-type sight on the supporting column which was nested inside several annular rings. The sight column as well as the rings were free to be adjusted in rotation. These directors could be used in two modes: either as an independent instrument to provide all necessary firing data (by waiting until the relative movement of own and target ship caused the target to appear in the sight or to bring own ship to the proper position for earlier firing); or (principally) to transmit target bearing to computer and to target course and speed instrument.

*Type 93 target course and speed instrument.*[6] The output of this instrument was, as indicated by its designation, the target's course and speed, after setting own speed, present bearing and range. By the adoption of this equipment IJN warships became capable of blind firing[7] after the target was lost from view (*eg*, by smoke screen).[8]

*Type 93 computer model 1 and model 2.* Model 1 was designed to be used to calculate the launching parameters of the torpedo together with the type 93 target course and speed instrument. Model 2 did the same but in combination with a type 91 director. The former was designed specially for cruisers; the latter for destroyers. After the input of certain elements of data (mostly manually) both instruments calculated gyro angle and dispersion angle. The output of future range could be used to check the accuracy of calculated data.

**Torpedo fire control system for submarines**

Type 92 modification 1 submarine director with the automatic chasing system of the target angle (gyro angle) was designed to obtain the necessary firing data with no dead time by one operation. It was the director most widely used in IJN submarines and equipped the following ships: 'Kaidai' (Fleet) types 6a and 6b, new 'Kaidai' (*I-176* class), 'Junsen' (Cruiser) types 2 and 3, 'Ko' (A) class, 'Otsu' (B) class, 'Hei' (C) class, 'Ko' class (small type), and 'Chu' (medium) type (14 boats out of 18). The director was installed inside the conning tower. The inputs and outputs were as follows:
a. input data before engaging the target
1) torpedo speed, 2) own speed, and 3) time interval;
b. input data at the final observation of the target
1) target speed, 2) target course, (bearing angle), 3) range, and 4) targetting angle (? this might be turn angle);
c. output data
1) Gyro angle, 2) firing bearings, and 3) ratio of distance and speed.[9]

**Notes**

1 After the adoption of the torpedo *Fuso* was equipped with one trainable TT on each broadside and she made the first IJN launching of a torpedo in 1886. The first TBs (Nos 1 to 4), also imported from Britain, carried spar torpedoes, the later boats were fitted with locomotive torpedoes.

2 Around the same time 'tentative torpedoes A' (battery driven, later called type 92) and 'E' (predecessor of the type 91 air torpedo) were developed but they were special torpedoes.

3 In fact salt and sand were deposited in the engine inlet valves and cylinders to some extent but the trial torpedoes run without any accident.

4 Before the development of the type 4 director in 1915 torpedoes were fired by sighting devices mounted on the torpedo tubes or by visual estimation.

5 Fundamentally the type 92 modification 1 director which was improved for mass production.

6 Type 3, used aboard destroyers, was substantially the same but mechanical equations were different to provide target course and speed continuously.

7 Even so it was restricted to some degree because target speed and course were not available continuously.

8 The tactical use of smoke screens played a big part in IJN planning during the early 1930s.

9 There are two points of uncertainty in this description. One is (b) where targetting angle, *ie*, the function of this angle is not known and (c) where ratio of distance and speed are not evident as firing factor but given in *Nippon Kaigun Sensuikan Shi*. Furthermore, target speed in (b) could also mean torpedo speed. The authors would be glad to receive information from specialists about these uncertainties in order to be able to correct this article later. Please write to Hans Lengerer, c/o Conway Maritime Press, 101 Fleet Street, London EC4Y 1DE.

## Table 2. *Basic Data of IJN Oxygen Torpedoes*

| | *Type 93 model 1 mod 1 and 2* | *Type 93 model 3* | *Type 95 model 1* | *Type 95 model 2* | *Type 96* | *Type 97* | *Type 98* |
|---|---|---|---|---|---|---|---|
| **Development** | | | | | | | |
| First designed | 1933 | 1943 | 1935 | 1943 | 1942 | 1937 | 1938 |
| Production begun | 1936 | 1944 | 1938 | 1944 | 1942 | 1938 | 1939 |
| Used aboard | DD, CA, CL | DD | SS | SS | SS | Midget SS | Midget SS |
| Manufacturer(s) (No produced) | NY Kure and Sasebo (1150) | same (560) | NY Kure and Mitsubishi Weapon Factory (1450) | As mod 1 (500) | NY Kure (300) | As type 96 (100) | As type 96 (130) |
| **Particulars** | | | | | | | |
| Total weight (kg) | 2700 | 2800 | 1665 | 1730 | 1665 | 980 | 950 |
| Displacement (kg) | 2220 | 2220 | 1345 | 1345 | 1345 | 1345 | 729 |
| Negative buoyancy (kg) | 480 | 580 | 320 | 385 | 320 | 251 | 221 |
| Centre of gravity (from aft end) (mm) | 4966 | 5150 | 4003 | 4060 | 4000 | 3112 | 3116 |
| Centre of buoyancy (from aft end) (mm) | 5000 | 5000 | 3990 | 3990 | 3990 | 3145 | 3145 |
| Trim (mm) + up nose − down nose | +34 | −150 | −13 | −70 | −10 | −33 | −21 |
| Length (mm) | | | | | | | |
| Total | 9000 | 9000 | 7150 | 7150 | 7150 | 5600 | 5600 |
| Head | 1400 | 2275 | 1530 | 1750 | 1530 | 1800 | 1800 |
| Oxygen vessel | 3448 | 2595 | 1729 | 1729 | 1729 | 1590 | 1590 |
| Fuel vessel | 496 | 383 | 271 | 271 | 271 | | |
| Balance chamber and ER | 1580 | 1671 | 1540 | 2020 | 1540 | 850 | 850 |
| Buoyancy chamber | 1456 | 1456 | 1430 | 1430 | 1430 | 780 | 780 |
| Tail | 620 | 620 | 650 | 650 | 650 | 580 | 580 |
| **Performance** | | | | | | | |
| Speed and range (kts/m) (Direction wander at extreme range R or L) | 36 ± 2/40,000 (1500)<br>40 ± 2/32,000 (1000)<br>48 ± 2/20,000 (500) | 36 ± 2/30,000 (1000)<br>40 ± 2/25,000 (750)<br>48 ± 2/15,000 (350) | 45 ± 2/12,000 (250)<br>49 ± 2/9000 (170) | 45 ± 2/7500 (130)<br>49 ± 2/5500 (90) | 48 ± 2/4500 (70) | 45 ± 1/5500 (80 ± 15) | 41 ± 1/3200 (40 ± 10) |
| Depth (m) | 6 ± 0.5 | As model 1 | 5 ± 0.5 | As model 1 | 3 ± 0.5 | 5 ± 0.5 | 3 ± 0.5 |
| **Head** | | | | | | | |
| Total weight (kg) | 610 | 940 | 495 | 635 | 495 | 410 | 410 |
| Weight of explosive (kg) | 490 | 780 | 405 | 550 | 405 | 350 | 350 |
| Type of explosive | 97 | same | same | same | same | same | same |
| Type of pistol | Type 90, later replaced by type 02 | same | same | same | same | Type 90 | same |
| **Oxygen Vessel** | | | | | | | |
| Volume (litres) | 980 | 750 | 386 | 220 | 386 | 156 | 156 |
| Pressure (kg/mm²) | 225 | 200 | 215 | 200 | 215 | 200 | 175 |
| Weight of charge at 15°C (kg) | 299 | 204 | 113 | 60 | 106 | 41 | 37.8 |
| Composition | 100% oxygen | As type 93 | As type 93 | As type 93 | 38% oxygen | 100% oxygen | 38% oxygen |
| Thickness of wall (mm) | 12 | 12 | 10 | 10 | 10 | 7 | 7 |

| | *Type 93 model 1 mod 1 and 2* | *Type 93 model 3* | *Type 95 model 1* | *Type 95 model 2* | *Type 96* | *Type 97* | *Type 98* |
|---|---|---|---|---|---|---|---|
| AIR VESSEL | | | | | | | |
| Type | First air vessel | As model 1 | As type 93 | Steering air vessel | As type 95 model 2 | As type 95 model 2 | As type 95 model 2 |
| Volume (litres) | 13.5 | 13.5 | 7 | 7 | 15 | 4 | 4 |
| Pressure (kg/mm²) | 225 | 225 | 225 | 225 | 215 | 220 | 220 |
| Type | Steering air vessel (3 bottles) | As model 1 | Steering air vessel | As model 1 | As type 95 model 1 | As type 95 model 1 | As type 95 model 1 |
| Volume (litres) | 40.5 | 40.5 | 15 | 15 | | 7 | 7 |
| Pressure (kg/mm²) | 225 | 200 | 215 | 215 | | 230 | 230 |
| FUEL | | | | | | | |
| Volume (litres) | 128 | 95 | 50 | 50 | 50 | 20 | 20 |
| Composition | Kerosene | As type 93 | As type 93 | As type 93 | As type 93 | As type 93 | As type 93 |
| Displaced by | Sea water | As type 93 | As type 93 | As type 93 | As type 93 | As type 93 | As type 93 |
| LUBRICANT | | | | | | | |
| Volume (litres) | 67 | 67 | 50 | 50 | 22.8 | 5.0 | 5.0 |
| UNIT | | | | | | | |
| Type of reducer | Standard, two stage | As type 93 | As type 93 | As type 93 | As type 93 | As type 93 | As type 93 |
| Type of generator | Standard wet heater | As type 93 | As type 93 | As type 93 | As type 93 | As type 93 | As type 93 |
| No of ignitors | 2 | 2 | 2 | 2 | 2 | 2 | 2 |
| POWER | | | | | | | |
| Composition of filling | 58% nitro-glycerine; 5% mineral jelly; 37% gun cotton | As type 93 | As type 93 | As type 93 | As type 93 | As type 93 | As type 93 |
| Engine | Reciprocating, horizontal, 2 cylinders, double-acting | As type 93 | As type 93 | As type 93 | As type 93 | As type 93 | As type 93 |
| Cylinder bore (mm) | 142 | 142 | 130 | 130 | 130 | | |
| Cylinder stroke (mm) | 180 | 180 | 160 | 160 | 160 | | |
| Expansion ratio | 1.5 | 1.5 | 1.5 | 1.5 | 1.5 | | |
| Reducer pressure (kg/mm²/hp/rpm) | 20/200/860 24/300/950 38/590/1200 | As type 93 | 22/330/1150 37/430/1250 | As model 1 | 36/400/1220 | 36/205/1200 | 30/152/1200 |
| Oxygen/fuel ratio (by weight) | 2.8 | 2.8 | 2.8 | 2.8 | 9.0 | 3.0 | 7.5 |
| Water/fuel ratio (by volume) | 8.5 | 8.5 | 8.5 | 8.5 | 5.0 | 8.0 | 3.5 |
| Type of dilutent | Sea water | As type 93 | As type 93 | As type 93 | As type 93 | As type 93 | As type 93 |
| TAIL | | | | | | | |
| No of fins | 4 | 4 | 4 or 6 | 4 or 6 | 4 | 4 | 4 |
| No of blades | 4 | 4 | 4 | 4 | 4 | 4 | 4 |
| Forward propeller diam. (mm) | 568 | 568 | 482 | 482 | | | |
| After propeller diam. (mm) | 530 | 530 | 439 | 439 | | | |
| Wake | barely visible | As type 93 | As type 93 | As type 93 | visible | barely visible | visible |
| CONTROL | | | | | | | |
| Type of depth gear | Standard pendulum | As type 93 | As type 93 | As type 93 | As type 93 | As type 93 | As type 93 |
| Depth setting (m) | 2–16 | 2–16 | 2–16 | 2–16 | 2–16 | 5 | 3 |
| Type of gyro | Type 98 | As type 93 | As type 93 | As type 93 | As type 93 | As type 93 | As type 93 |
| Gyro angles | ± 180° | As type 93 | As type 93 | As type 93 | As type 93 | As type 93 | As type 93 |

Note: Type 93 Model 1 modification 3 was a combination of model 1 modification 1 with the propulsion system of model 3

# THE LENINGRAD CLASS AT WAR

By the standards of the Soviet surface fleet, the six big destroyer leaders of the *Leningrad* class had an active war that encompassed all theatres of Soviet naval operations. Their activities are chronicled by Pierre Hervieux.

When the Soviet Union entered the war with Germany, on 22 June 1941 at 0315hrs, the Soviet Fleet included six flotilla leader destroyers of the *Leningrad* class: *Leningrad* and *Minsk* in the Baltic, *Kharkov* and *Moskva* in the Black Sea, *Baku* and *Tbilisi* in the Pacific. Before that date, the *Minsk* had already taken part in a naval operation, during the short war against Finland. On 9 and 10 December 1939, the Finnish coastal batteries near Saarenpää on Koivisto fought a gun duel, without any result, with a bombarding Soviet naval force which, in addition to the *Minsk*, comprised the destroyers *Karl Marx* and *Volodarski*, the gunboats *Sestroretsk, Kronstadt* and *Krasnaya Gorka*.

## *Opening moves – the Baltic*

On 22 June 1941, at 1822, a Soviet naval force, under the command of 2nd class Captain I G Svyatov, with the heavy cruiser *Maksim Gorki*, the destroyers *Gnevny, Gordy* and *Steregushchi*, sailed from Ust-Dvinsk to cross the Irben Strait and take up a position off the western exit of the Gulf of Finland to cover minelaying operations. These were to be carried out by the following ships from

*The* Moskva *in the Black Sea, on 26 October 1939, during a naval review*

*The* Minsk *at Leningrad before the war.* (All photographs by courtesy of Jurg Meister)

Tallinn, under the command of Rear-Admiral D D Vdovichenko: the minelayers *Marti* and *Ural*, the flotilla leaders *Leningrad* and *Minsk*, the destroyers *Karl Marx, Artem* and *Engels*. Three 'Fugas' type minesweepers, some submarine-chasers and the destroyer *Smely* formed the anti-mine and anti-submarine escorts. On 23 June, at 0340, the covering force ran into the German 'Apolda' mine barrage, in the area of the Oleg Bank. The destroyer *Gnevny* (1936, 1722 tons) had her bow torn off by a mine and sank; the destroyer *Gordy* was damaged by mines which exploded against her bow paravanes; the heavy cruiser *Maksim Gorki*, as a result of hitting a mine, lost her bow up to frame 60. The destroyer *Steregushchi* detonated two mines with her bow paravanes and was slightly damaged, but she brought the disabled cruiser to Worms. From there minesweepers and motor torpedo-boats escorted her to Tallinn.

## The Black Sea – loss of the Moskva

In the Black Sea, on 22 June, in accordance with prewar plans, the Soviet Fleet began to lay out defensive mine barrages off its own bases of Sevastopol, Odessa, Kerch, Novorossisk, Tuapse and Batum. The heavy cruiser *Krasny Kavkaz*, the light cruiser *Chervona Ukraina*, the *Kharkov*, the destroyers *Boiki, Besposhchadny, Bezuprechny*, the minelayer *Ostrovski* and the training cruiser *Komintern* operated off Sevastopol and the destroyer *Dzerzhinski* off Batum. In all, 3453 mines and 509 barrage protection devices were laid off Sevastopol in 1941. On 23 June, following a report by the Danube Flotilla that six enemy destroyers and torpedo-boats had been sighted, the *Kharkov*, with the destroyers *Besposhchadny* and *Smyshleny*, proceeded to the area of Fodonisi Island but sighted no enemy ships and were back in port early on the 25th.

On the evening of the same day, a Soviet naval force sailed from Sevastopol, comprising the assault group (2nd class Captain M F Romanov), with the *Kharkov* and the *Moskva*, followed by a covering force (Rear-Admiral T A Novikov) with the heavy cruiser *Voroshilov*, the destroyers *Smyshleny* and *Soobrazitelny*. Their goal was to reconnoitre in strength the defensive system of the Romanian naval base of Constanţa, and to destroy the petrol and oil supplies which were stored there. Simultaneously, with a diversionary attack by aircraft of the Soviet Naval Air Force, the *Kharkov* and the *Moskva* opened fire with their 130mm (5.1in) guns on oil tanks and railway installations near Constanţa, in the early morning of 26 June. The shelling from the two ships was accurate and effective, although the distance was about 20km; 350 shells of 130mm were fired in 10 minutes. Fires started, an ammunition train blew up and considerable damage was

*The* Tbilisi *(TSL-50) in 1959, used as a target ship in the Pacific Fleet.*

inflicted. Nevertheless, the supplies of oil were not destroyed. Shortly after the shelling started, a railway battery and the 280mm (11in) German battery 'Tirpitz', respectively to the north and south of Constanţa (since March 1941 for the latter), opened fire and quickly bracketed the two flotilla leaders.

Opinions differ as to what happened next. It is generally admitted that, in avoiding the salvoes, the *Moskva* and the *Kharkov* sailed into a minefield, but

*The* Kharkov*, in the Black Sea, before the war.*

examination of the events on 26 June 1941 raise doubt that the *Moskva* was sunk as a result of striking a mine off Constanţa. At 0514, both *Moskva* and *Kharkov* began withdrawing from the bombardment and were zig-zagging at 30kts under shellfire. The *Moskva* was leading, laying a smokescreen and the *Kharkov* was following in her wake through the smoke. At 0520 the vessels had reached the outer edge of what was believed to be the possible mined area (11 to 12 miles from the coast) and the *Kharkov* signalled the *Moskva* to proceed at full speed on a direct course. A minute later the *Moskva* had acknowledged the *Kharkov*'s signal and had developed about 36kts or 37kts speed when a heavy explosion occurred beneath the vessel, blowing up a fuel tank, which caused the *Moskva* to break in two at the first boiler room and sink in four or five minutes.

Of the two possible causes, mine and gunfire, considered by the Germans at the time, the former was thought almost certain. However, a third possibility, a torpedo launched from a Soviet submarine fired through error, was not even considered as a cause. After the war, attempts were made to establish from German records the exact position of the German minefields off Constanţa, to discover if the *Moskva* was indeed outside the perimeter of the minefield at the time of the explosion. The Soviets say that it was later determined that four German minefields extended almost exactly as they had been estimated (11 to 12 miles from the Romanian coast). Five Soviet submarines departed for patrols off the Romanian coast on the first day of the war, 22 June 1941: *M-33, M-34, Shch-205, Shch-206* and *Shch-209*. They took up position between Capes Tuzla and Shabla on 23 June 1941. After having withdrawn, the *Kharkov*, which earlier had been damaged by near misses from aircraft bombs, and rendered unmanoeuvrable for a short time, was torpedo-attacked and missed by a submarine, at 0643 on 26 June 1941. That was followed, at 0700, by another attack against the latter vessel plus the destroyer *Soobrazitelny*. At this time the *Soobrazitelny* made an anti-submarine attack against the submarine, and it was reported that the stern of the submarine was seen briefly afterwards on the surface and that oil bubbles were also seen. Unfortunately, the only Axis submarine then in the Black Sea, the Romanian *Delfinul*, was in port and did not begin its first patrol until 10 July 1941.

Furthermore, there is something of a mystery relating to one of the Soviet submarines that was off the Romanian coast on 22/23 June 1941. For all submarines given the 'Red Banner' and 'Guardist' awards during the war, the Soviets have given the names of the commanding officers and political commissars or assistants from the very beginning of the war to the end. However, for the 'Guardist' *Shch-205*, the commanding officer, P D Sukhomlinov, is listed as taking command on 17 July 1941 (his predecessor is never mentioned). Moreover, the political commissar, V V Kolodenko, is stated to have been assigned on 26 June 1941, at which time the submarine was probably still at sea! Even stranger is that the 'Shch' type submarines either had a political commissar on the first day of the war, or one was assigned exactly one month later (22 July 1941), except in the case of *Shch-205*, where one was assigned on an odd day. Since the destroyer raid was planned on 24 June 1941, at which time the submarines were already at sea, it is possible the latter were not contacted by radio in order to be advised of the approaching surface vessels. It is therefore possible that the *Shch-205* attacked and mistakenly sank the *Moskva*. However, it must be admitted that during the action a mine was detonated by the bow paravanes of the destroyer *Soobrazitelny*, damaging temporarily the heavy cruiser *Voroshilov*, so the debate is still open. [See p151 for an alternative view of this action.]

On 12 July, the *Kharkov* was slightly damaged by a mine, dropped by the Luftwaffe. On 18 and 19 July, the Soviet Danube Flotilla evacuated the Kilia peninsula as part of the withdrawal of Soviet XIV Rifle Corps from the Danube and broke through the Romanian defensive positions near Periprava. Off the estuary, the monitors, armoured motor boats and minesweepers were met by a detachment coming from Odessa, consisting of the old light cruiser *Komintern*, the *Kharkov*, the destroyers *Bodry* and *Shaumyan*, the gunboats *Krasnaya Armeniya* and *Krasnaya Gruziya*, ten motor torpedo-boats and six motor launches. On 21 August, the Military Council of the Black Sea Fleet decided to keep the heavy cruiser *Krasny Kavkaz*, the light cruisers *Chervona Ukraina* and *Krasny Krym*, the auxiliary cruiser *Mikoyan*, the flotilla leaders *Kharkov* and *Tashkent*, the destroyers *Bodry, Bezuprechny, Besposhchadny, Sposobny, Smyshleny* and *Soobrazitelny* on the alert to support the coastal army in the Odessa area.

## *The evacuation of Tallinn*

In the Baltic, between 23 and 17 August, the heavy cruiser *Kirov*, the *Leningrad*, the *Minsk* and several destroyers, supported the defenders of Tallinn. It is worth digressing a little from the main subject, in order to outline the massive evacuation of Tallinn by the Soviet fleet. Foreseeing the big exodus of the Soviet ships from Tallinn, in face of the German ground troops' advance, the *Kriegsmarine* had decided to establish minefields off Cape Juminda. Between 11 July and 26 August, first the S-boats of the 5th Flotilla (Captain Dobberstein) laid 276 mines and 80 explosive floats. Then, between 8 and 26 August, it was the turn of the minelayers *Cobra* (Captain Brill), *Kaiser* (Captain Bohm) and *Königin Luise* (Captain Wünning), which laid 465 mines and 443 explosive floats, whilst the 1st S-Boat Flotilla (Captain Birnbacher) was laying 22 mines and 113 explosive floats. The Finnish Navy also participated in building up the barrage; as early as 29 June and until 22 August, its minelayers *Riilahti* (Captain Kivilinna) and *Ruotsinsalmi* (Captain Arho) laid 896 mines and 100 explosive floats. The Juminda barrage comprised a total of 1659 mines and 736 explosive floats.

The first casualty, on 3 August, was the Soviet minesweeper *T-201/Zaryad* (1936, 434 tons) which hit a mine and sank, near the Ristna lighthouse. On 11 August, off Suursaari, the transport *Vyacheslav Molotov* (1939, 7494 tons), with 3500 wounded aboard, was damaged by a mine after having sailed from Tallinn for Suursaari and Kronstadt, escorted by the destroyer *Steregushchi*, minesweepers and submarine-chasers. She did not sink, but was laid up for the rest of the war and was repaired only after the end of it, being then renamed *Baltika*. On 14 August, a Soviet convoy sailed from Tallinn for the same ports. The transport *Sibir* (3767 tons), with 2500 wounded on board, was sunk by an air attack. On 15 August, the minesweeper *T-202/Buy* (1936, 434 tons) was sunk near the Cape Juminda lighthouse, after hitting two mines. On the following day, a Soviet convoy sailing from Suursaari to Tallinn, with the icebreaker *Oktyabr* ahead of it, lost several ships in the Juminda barrage, a pattern repeated on the 21st.

On 24 August, a Soviet convoy with the icebreaker *Oktyabr* and nine transports, left Tallinn for Suursaari and Kronstadt. The destroyer *Engels* (1915, 1463 tons), the minesweepers *T-209/Knecht* (1938, 434 tons) at 59°47'N/25°19'E, *T-212/Shtag* (1938 434 tons), *T-213/Krambol* (1938, 434 tons) at 59°46'N/25°17'E and three transports were lost on the Juminda mine barrage. Two other transports were sunk the next day by air attacks, west of Suursaari. Among these five sunken ships were probably the transport *Daugava* (1891, 1430 tons), the transport *Lunacharski* (1922, 3618 tons), the tanker *Zheleznodorozhnik* (1898, 2029 tons), the tanker *No 11* (8000 tons) and perhaps the transport *Liisa* (1902, 782 tons).

After embarking the remainder of the 10th Rifle Corps units in the night of 27/28 August, the convoys and covering forces assembled in the course of the 28th in the Tallinn roadstead and sailed during the afternoon. These were organized as follows:

The 1st Convoy (Captain N G Bogdanov) comprised 6 transports, 1 icebreaker, 1 repair ship, 1 training ship, 3 submarines; the escort included the destroyer *Surovy*, 3 patrol boats, 5 old minesweepers, 2 submarine-chasers, 5 motor launches and 1 tug.

The 2nd Convoy (Captain N V Antonov) comprised 6 transports, 2 netlayers, 1 survey ship and 1 schooner; the escort included 1 gunboat, 1 patrol boat, 4 old minesweepers, 9 motor minesweepers and 2 submarine-chasers.

The 3rd Convoy (Captain Ya F Yanson) comprised 8 transports and 1 tanker; the escort included 1 gunboat, 2 patrol boats, 4 old minesweepers, 4 motor minesweepers and 2 submarine-chasers.

The 4th Convoy (Captain S A Gikhorovtsev) comprised 9 various small craft; the escort included 1 gunboat, 1 patrol boat, 9 motor minesweepers and 2 magnetic minesweepers.

The main force (Vice-Admiral V F Tributs) was made up of the heavy cruiser *Kirov*, the *Leningrad*, the destroyers *Gordy, Smetlivy* and *Yakov Sverdlov*, 4 submarines, 5 minesweepers, 5 motor torpedo-boats, 5 submarine-chasers, 1 tender and 1 icebreaker. There was also a covering detachment (Rear-Admiral Yu A Panteleev), which included the *Minsk*, the destroyers *Skory, Slavny*, 4 submarines, 5 minesweepers, 4 submarine-chasers, 4 motor torpedo-boats and 1 patrol boat.

The rearguard (Rear-Admiral Yu F Rall) comprised the destroyers *Kalinin, Artem, Volodarski*, 3 torpedo-boats, 2 motor torpedo-boats, 5 submarine-chasers and 1 minelayer.

*A* Leningrad *class flotilla leader destroyer before the war.*

After the departure of all the ships, the torpedo-boats *Burya, Sneg, Tsiklon* and the minelayer *Vaindlo*, all belonging to the rearguard, laid mine barrages in the harbour and in the approaches. The old minelayer *Amur* (1907, 3600 tons), the transport *Gamma* (1901, 696 tons) and three tugs were sunk as blockships. Shortly after having sailed from the port of Tallinn, west of the minefields, the Soviet naval forces were attacked by Junkers Ju 88 bombers of 2/KG 77 and of K Fl Gr 806. The icebreaker *Krisyanis Valdemars* (1925, 2250 tons), the transports *Skrunda* (2414 tons), *Lake Lucerne* (1909, 2317 tons) and *Artis Kronvalds* (1900, 1423 tons) were hit by bombs and sank, while the staff ship *Vironia* (1905, 2026 tons) was damaged.

During the night of 28/29 August, Soviet ships, having no other alternative, decided to break through the minefields off Cape Juminda. The losses were staggering: the destroyers *Y Sverdlov* (1911, 1291 tons), *Skory* (1939, 1712 tons), *Kalinin* (1915, 1375 tons) *Artem* (1916, 1436 tons), *Volodarski* (1914, 1463 tons), the staff ship *Vironia*, the torpedo-boats *Sneg* (1935, 457 tons), *Tsiklon* (1930, 457 tons), the patrol boat *Saturn*, the minesweepers

*The* Leningrad *after the war.*

*T-214/Bugel* (1939, 434 tons) at 59°46′N/25°17′E, *T-216* (1939, 434 tons) at 59°09′N/22°37′E, *Krab* (200 tons), the submarines *Shch-301* (1930, 578 tons), *S-5* (1937, 856 tons), *S-6* (1937, 856 tons), the submarine-chaser *MO-202* (1941, 61 tons), the gunboat *1-8*, the motor torpedo-boat *TKA-103* (1934, 14 tons), the transports *Alev* (1909, 1446 tons), *Tobol* (1911, 2758 tons), *Everita* (1917, 3251 tons), *Yarvamaa* (1894, 1363 tons), *Luga* (2329 tons), *Kumari* (1882, 237 tons), *Balkash* (1918, 2191 tons), *Yana* (1923, 2917 tons), *Naissaar* (1911, 1839 tons), *Ergonautis* (1902, 206 tons), *Ella* (1904, 1522 tons), *Ausma* (1889, 1791 tons) and the tanker *No 12* (1882, 1700 tons) were all sunk by mines. The *Minsk*, the *Leningrad*, the destroyers *Gordy* and *Slavny*, the minesweeper *T-205* and other transports were damaged.

On 29 August the remaining transports were again attacked, in the area of Suursaari, by the Junkers Ju 88s of 2/KG 77 and of K Fl Gr 806, after the fast warships had gone on to Kronstadt in accordance with orders. In this action the transports *Kalpaks* (1914, 2190 tons), *Vtoraya Pyatiletka* (1933, 3974 tons) and the training ship *Leningrad Soviet* (1895, 1270 tons) were hit by bombs and sank. The transports *Ivan Papanin* (1935, 3974 tons), *Saule* (1890, 1207 tons) and the repair ship *Serp I Molot* (1900, 5920 tons) were severely damaged and had to be beached near Suursaari. Only the transport *Kazakhstan* (1937, 3039 tons) succeeded in reaching Kronstadt, heavily damaged by bombs. Because of the damage, her Captain had been forced to disembark 2300 of her 5000 troops on the island of Seiskari, but despite being wounded when he was blown overboard by the explosion of a bomb, the Captain was later condemned to death for cowardice.

A special covering and salvage force (under Captain Svyatov) was sent out from Suursaari, consisting of 12 old minesweepers, one patrol boat division, six motor boats, two cutters and the rescue ship *Meteor*. In the following days this force rescued 12,160 troops in all, including some from the islands in the Gulf of Finland.

With thirty-one ships sunk by mines on 28 August alone, it was the biggest naval disaster occasioned by mine barrages to any fleet in one day. Yet the Soviets had taken adequate measures: by night they had swept channels, which explains why, by day, German army batteries positioned near Cape Juminda could not see any ship. But, to sail by night through an immense mine barrage of about 50km depth could only lead to heavy losses. Four other Soviet ships never reached their destination after leaving Tallinn in August 1941. These were the former Estonian schooners *Helga* (774 tons), *Orne, Paermumaa* (292 tons) and *Jaen Tear* (398 tons), which were carrying a great number of Estonians deported to Siberia, but at sea the prisoners succeeded in overpowering the Soviet guards and brought the ships back to Estonia. The first made the island of Saaremaa (ex-Oesel), the other two reached Tallinn (ex-Reval) and the last arrived at an unknown harbour after it had fallen to German troops.

On 30 August, ships of the Baltic Fleet were concentrated to form an artillery support force for the Leningrad Front under Rear-Admiral I I Gren. The first group was on the Neva, consisting of three destroyers and three gunboats. The second group was in the Leningrad area as far as the eastern part of the Sea Canal, with the heavy cruisers *Maksim Gorki* and *Petropavlovsk* (unfinished), the *Leningrad*, five destroyers and one minelayer. The third group was in the area Kronstadt-Oranienbaum with the battleships *Oktyabrskaya Revolutsiya* and *Marat*, the heavy cruiser *Kirov*, the *Minsk*, six destroyers and one gunboat.

*CONSTRUCTION AND TECHNICAL DATA OF THE LENINGRAD CLASS FLOTILLA LEADERS*

| | *Builder* | *Laid down* | *Launched* | *Commissioned* |
|---|---|---|---|---|
| *Leningrad* | Zhdanov Yard (Leningrad) | 5 November 1932 | 17 November 1933 | 5 December 1936 |
| *Minsk* | Zhdanov Yard (Leningrad) | 5 October 1934 | 6 November 1935 | 15 February 1939 |
| *Moskva* | Marti Yard (Nikolaiev) | 29 October 1932 | 1934 | 10 August 1938 |
| *Kharkov* | Marti Yard (Nikolaiev) | 19 October 1932 | 9 September 1934 | 19 November 1938 |
| *Baku* (ex-*Ordzhonikidze*) | Nikolaiev-Dalzavod (Vladivostok) | 15 January 1935 | 10 March 1936 | 25 July 1938 |
| *Tbilisi* (ex-*Tiflis*) | Amur Yard (Komsomolsk) | 15 January 1935 | 24 July 1939 | 11 December 1940 |

| | |
|---|---|
| *Standard displacement* | 2150 tons (*Leningrad, Moskva, Kharkov*); 2350 tons (*Minsk, Baku, Tbilisi*) |
| *Full load displacement* | 2582 tons (*Leningrad, Moskva, Kharkov*); 2680 tons (*Minsk, Baku, Tbilisi*) |
| *Length overall* | 418ft 3in (127.50m) |
| *Length between perpendiculars* | 400ft 3in (122.0m) |
| *Beam* | 38ft 6in (11.70m) |
| *Maximum draught fore* | 13ft 4in (4.06m) |
| *Maximum draught aft* | 12ft 3in (3.76m) |
| *Maximum speed* | 40kts |
| *Radius* | 2100nm at 20kts<br>873nm at 40kts |
| *Bunkers* | 210 tons (usually)<br>600 tons (maximum) |
| *Machinery* | 3 boilers, 3 shafts, 3 geared turbines 22,000shp × 3 = 66,000shp |
| *Complement* | 257 (peace) 311 (war) |
| *Armament* | 5–130mm (5.1in) singles (on some units, 4 in 1942/43)<br>2–76.2mm AA (3in) singles<br>2–45mm AA singles (removed in 1942/43)<br>(Added in 1942/43: 6 to 10–37mm AA and 6 to 8–12.7mm AA)<br>8–533mm torpedo tubes (2 × 4) with 16 torpedoes |
| Mines: | 68 Model 1931<br>or 84 Model 1926<br>or 115 Model 1912 |
| Depth charges: | 20 Model B-1 and<br>32 Model M-1 |

## *Late 1941 – loss of the Minsk*

In the Black Sea, on 7 September, the *Kharkov*, with the destroyers *Boiki* and *Sposobny*, brought the Commander-in-Chief of the Black Sea Fleet, Vice-Admiral F S Oktyabrski, to Odessa for inspections and conferences. During their stay the ships, together with the destroyer *Dzerzhinski*, shelled Romanian positions. The destroyer *Sposobny* was damaged by a near-miss bomb in the second engine room.

In the Baltic, during a Luftwaffe raid on 23 September, the flotilla leader *Minsk* received a direct hit from a Junkers Ju 87 Stuka and sank in shallow water off Kronstadt. On that same day, the heavy cruiser *Maksim Gorki* was also hit and damaged in Leningrad, whilst the heavy cruiser *Kirov* and the destroyer *Grozyashchi* suffered the same fate off Kronstadt. The submarine *P-3* was heavily damaged in drydock in Kronstadt and another submarine, the *Shch-302*, was also damaged.

In the Black Sea, between 1 and 9 November, the heavy cruiser *Krasny Kavkaz*, the light cruisers *Krasny Krym* and *Chervona Ukraina*, the *Kharkov* and seven destroyers evacuated 18,000 troops, which were cut off and dispersed, from the Tendra Peninsula and from the Crimean ports of Chernomorsk, Yalta, Evpatoria and Feodosia, transporting them to Sevastopol. In the Baltic, a third evacuation convoy to Hango left Kronstadt on 9 November under the command of Rear-Admiral M S Moskalenko, pausing at Suursaari until the next day. That naval force comprised the *Leningrad,* the destroyer *Stoiki*, the minelayer *Ural*, the transport *Andrei Zhdanov*, the minesweepers *T-201/Zaryad, T-211/Rym, T-215, T-217, T-218* and four submarine-chasers. On the way out, on the evening of 10 November, *T-217* and *T-218* collided in poor visibility and had to return. Because of the weather, the force turned back to Suursaari on the morning of 11 November, and set out again in the evening of the same day. In the night, the *Leningrad* (Captain G M Gorbachev) was brought to a standstill after two near-misses from mines and then returned with two mine-sweepers and the *Andrei Zhdanov* (1928, 3870 tons) which, however, ran on a mine and sank. On the morning of 12 November the remainder of the force turned round and went back to Suursaari.

In the Black Sea, between 7 and 13 December, the heavy cruiser *Krasny Kavkaz*, the light cruiser *Krasny Krym*, the *Kharkov*, two destroyers and five transports, carried the 388th Rifle Division – 10,582 men – from

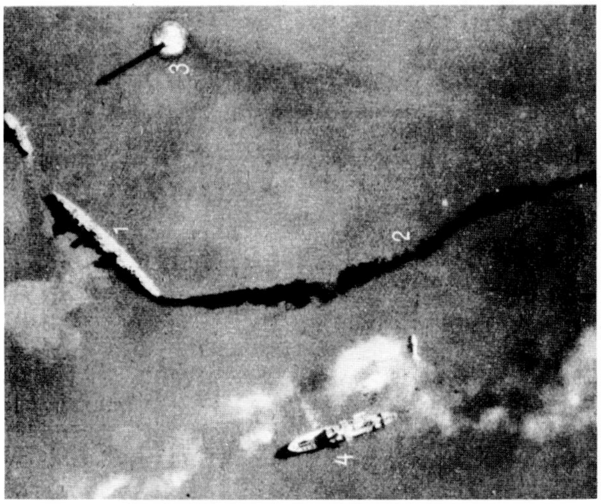


*The* Minsk *being towed, off Kronstadt, on 23 September 1941, after having been hit by a bomb from a Stuka. She capsized soon after, was then salvaged, but was only recommissioned in November 1942.*

Novorossisk and Tuapse to Sevastopol. On 19 and 20 December, the *Kharkov*, with the same cruisers and destroyers, transported the 79th Naval Infantry Brigade (3500 men) to Sevastopol. In operations to bring the 345th Rifle Division, comprising 10,600 men, and ammunition transports to Sevastopol, the following cruisers and destroyers shelled German positions and assembly areas on the Sevastopol front:

21 December, light cruiser *Krasny Krym*, flotilla leader *Kharkov*, destroyer *Bodry*;
22 December, heavy cruiser *Krasny Kavkaz*, light cruiser *Krasny Krym*, flotilla leaders *Kharkov, Tashkent*, destroyers *Bodry, Smyshleny* and *Nezamozhnik*. (On 21 and 22 December, 1938 rounds of 180mm, 130mm, 102mm and 100mm were fired);
23 December, flotilla leader *Tashkent*, destroyer *Smyshleny*;
24 December, flotilla leader *Tashkent*, destroyers *Boiki* and *Smyshleny*;
25 December, flotilla leader *Tashkent*, destroyers *Boiki, Bezuprechny* and *Smyshleny*;
26 December, destroyer *Bezuprechny*;
27 December, flotilla leader *Tashkent*, destroyer *Smyshleny*. (Between 23 and 27 December, 1299 rounds of 130mm were fired).

On 22 December, the heavy cruiser *Krasny Kavkaz*, the light cruiser *Krasny Krym*, the *Kharkov* and the destroyer *Bodry* were withdrawn in preparation for the Kerch-Feodosia landing which took place between 26 and 31 December 1941.

## 1942: Crimean operations

The flotilla leaders *Kharkov* and *Tashkent* transported supplies to Sevastopol from 31 Janaury to 2 February and from 3 to 4 February 1942 in cooperation with the destroyer *Bezuprechny*. Before returning, they repeatedly shelled land targets on the fronts near Sevastopol and, on 4 February, also near Feodosia. The *Kharkov* carried out a further operation from 7 to 9 February. On 27 February, the light cruiser *Krasny Krym*, the flotilla leaders *Kharkov, Tashkent* and three destroyers shelled the harbours on the South Coast of the Crimea as a diversionary move. The *Kharkov* and the destroyer *Svobodny* were involved in supply operations to Sevastopol (on 25 March, 2 April, and 10 April). On 1 May, the *Kharkov* brought more supplies to Sevastopol and shelled land targets. During the night of 4/5 May, German positions on the south-east coast of the Crimea were shelled by the *Kharkov* and three destroyers. From 10 to 16 May, the heavy cruiser *Voroshilov*, the flotilla leaders *Kharkov* and *Tashkent* and two destroyers intervened from the south in the fighting on the Kerch Peninsula, but with little success. On 19 May, the *Kharkov* brought further supplies to Sevastopol, and on 5/6 June, the *Kharkov* (Captain Melnikov), *Tashkent* and *Bezuprechny* succeeded in reaching Sevastopol again in spite of bomb and aerial torpedo attacks. On 18 June, en route once more to Sevastopol, the *Kharkov* was rendered unmanoeuvrable by near-misses from German bombers, but she was towed to safety by the *Tashkent* (Rear-Admiral Vladimirski).

The Commander of the Soviet Black Sea Cruiser Brigade (Rear-Admiral N E Basisty) went to sea on 2 August with the heavy cruiser *Molotov* and the *Kharkov* and shelled targets in the Bay of Feodosia, during the night of 2/3 August. On the return there were attacks by German torpedo aircraft and the Italian motor torpedo-boats *MAS-568* and *MAS-573*. The *Molotov* was hit by a torpedo launched by *MAS-568* which blew off 20m of her stern, but the crippled ship managed to return to port. The destroyed stern was replaced by a section from the incomplete cruiser *Frunze*, but the *Molotov* was not back in service until the end of 1944.

During the battle for Novorossisk, attacked by the German 5th Army Corps, the *Kharkov* and the destroyer *Soobrazitelny* supported Soviet troops with their 130mm guns. Their interventions took place on 1, 2 and 4 September, but German units succeeded, nevertheless, in entering the outskirts of Novorossisk on 5 September, capturing the centre of the city on the following day and occupying the harbour area on 9 September. Between 8 and 11 September, the light cruiser *Krasny Krym*, the *Kharkov* the destroyers *Soobrazitelny, Zheleznyakov*, and the torpedo-boat *Shtorm* brought troops and supplies from Poti to Tuapse and Gelendzhik. The heavy cruiser *Krasny Kavkaz*, the light cruiser *Krasny Krym*, the *Kharkov*, the destroyers *Besposhchadny* and *Soobrazitelny* transported 12,600 troops, 50 guns, 65 mortars and 100 tons of ammunition from Poti to Tuapse, between 20 and 23 October. In the night of 22/23 October, the ships were attacked unsuccessfully by four German S-boats.

## Reinforcements from the Pacific

In July 1942, in operation EON18, a Soviet destroyer force was transferred by the Northern Seaway from the Pacific to the Arctic. On the 15th, the flotilla leader *Baku*, the destroyers *Razumny, Razyarenny* and *Revnostny* left

Vladivostok. The last was involved in a collision on 18 July with the Soviet freighter *Terney* in the Tatar Sound and had to remain behind. The other ships went through the Kurile Passage on the 22nd and put into Petropavlovsk on 26 July for refuelling. They passed through the Bering Strait and reached the port of Tiksi, east of the delta of the River Lena, on 14 August, accompanied by the icebreaker *Mikoyan*. On 19 August the journey was continued but then they had to wait for nearly five weeks until ice conditions permitted them to pass Cape Chelyuskin. Constantly accompanied by an icebreaker, Dikson was reached on 24 September, the Yugor Strait on 9 October and, finally, the ships were met by the Northern Fleet off the Kola Inlet on 14 October.

In the Arctic, the *Baku* was first in action on 17 November, when the British convoy QP15 sailed from the Kola Inlet with twenty-eight merchant ships. The escort was provided by one anti-aircraft ship, five minesweepers, four corvettes, one armed trawler and, in addition to the *Baku*, the Soviet destroyer *Sokrushitelny*. Another Soviet destroyer, the *Razumny*, having engine trouble, had to turn back. In the Barents Sea, the convoy's escort was reinforced by five British destroyers and, further west, by the British heavy cruisers HMS *London*, HMS *Suffolk* and another five destroyers. Three British and one Soviet submarine took up positions off the North Norwegian fjords against German surface ships. On 20 November, the convoy was much dispersed in a heavy storm. At 2300, the *Baku* received a call for help from *Sokrushitelny* and turned back to close her, but could not find the ship. Parts of the *Baku*'s superstructure were simply blown away in the heavy seas, and with a major leak in her bows and boiler rooms, the ship only reached harbour with difficulty. For the destroyer *Sokrushitelny* (1936, 1722 tons) it was worse: she broke in two, and of 246 men on board, 187 were rescued in very heavy seas by the Soviet destroyers *Razumny* (which had rejoined), *Kuibyshev* and *Uritski*. The destroyer sank on 22 November after two attempts to take her in tow had failed. In the bad weather, German air reconnaissance did not locate the convoy. Nevertheless, two German submarines succeeded in torpedoing and sinking two cargo ships from the convoy:

the British *Goolistan* (1929, 5851 tons) by the *U-625* (Captain Benker), at 0056, on 23 November, at 75°50′N/16°45′E;

the Soviet *Kusnec Lesov* (1933, 3974 tons) at 0728 on the same day, at 75°30′N/08°00′E, by the *U-601* (Captain Grau).

In the Baltic, the flotilla leader *Minsk*, after having been salvaged and repaired, was recommissioned in November 1942, but neither she, nor the *Leningrad* – seriously damaged by mines in November 1941 – were ever again used operationally at sea, being only employed for supporting the Red Army with their artillery in the area of Leningrad. Returning to the Arctic, on 20 January 1943 the *Baku* and the destroyer *Razumny*, under the command of Captain Kolchin, made a sortie against the German traffic along the Polar Coast. Off Syltefjord, 60 miles west of Varangerfjord, they intercepted the German minelayer *Skagerrak* (two 105mm guns) which was on its way to lay a flanking mine barrage, escorted by the minesweepers *M 303*, *M 322* (two 105mm guns each) and the auxiliary submarine-chasers *UJ-1104* and *UJ-1105*. The speed of the German ships was, at best, half that of the Soviet destroyers; they were outgunned; the Soviets had torpedo tubes; and there was no shelter nearby. Nevertheless, the Soviet ships only fired some gun salvoes at extreme range, the *Baku* launched a salvo of torpedoes

*The* Baku, *in the Arctic, during the war, with American radar, and mainmast removed.*

and then they sheared off. No German ship was hit, but the Soviets claimed to have sunk one transport and damaged a second! They had identified the five German ships as being one destroyer, two transports, one motor minesweeper and one escort vessel.

## Black Sea operations 1943

In the Black Sea, between 29 November and 2 December, Soviet vessels operated against shipping on the Romanian–Bulgarian coast. The first group comprised the heavy cruiser *Voroshilov*, the *Kharkov* and the destroyer *Soobrazitelny*, and was detailed to shell the harbours of Sulina and Burgas and the radio station at Fidonisi. The second group included the destroyers *Besposhchadny* and *Boiki*, which was to attack shipping targets near Cape Kaliakra and Cape Shabla, and to shell Mangalia. On 1 December, the destroyers of the second group fired torpedoes at ships in the roads of Kalytch-Kiap, but they ran ashore. The *Voroshilov* and *Soobrazitelny* shelled Fidonisi, but the heavy cruiser was damaged by a mine detonation in the bow paravane of the destroyer and the force returned. The *Kharkov* did not find targets near Gibrioni.

Soviet landings were made west of Novorossisk early on 4 February. The covering force (Vice-Admiral Vladimirski) comprised the heavy cruiser *Krasny Kavkaz*, the light cruiser *Krasny Krym*, the *Kharkov*, the destroyers *Besposhchadny* and *Soobrazitelny*. It shelled the main landing area towards morning. The landing force (Rear-Admiral Basisty), consisting of the destroyers *Nezamozhnik* and *Zheleznyakov*, three gunboats, five minesweepers and a division of motor launches, lost two of the latter (*SKA-051, SKA-0141*, 50 tons each) on a mine barrage. In the face of heavy German defensive fire, only parts of three brigades were able to land and they were eliminated by 6 February. The other landing, carried out by motor launches at Cape Myschako, succeeded. The bulk of the forces was brought up by gunboats from 5 February and by 9 February there were 17,000 troops on shore. In operations by the German 1st S-Boat Flotilla (Captain Christiansen) against supplies, two Soviet warships were torpedoed and sunk on 28 February, near Cape Myschako: the minesweeper *T-403/Gruz* (1936, 434 tons) and the gunboat *Krasnaya Gruziya* (1920, 1100 tons), the latter by the *S-51*. In the night of 21/22 February, the *Kharkov* and the destroyer *Soobrazitelny* had shelled German positions off the Myschako bridgehead.

During the night of 13/14 May, the harbour of Auapa was shelled by the *Kharkov* and the destroyer *Boiki*. During this action there was an unsuccessful engagement with the German motor torpedo-boats *S-26, S-49* and *S-51*. In the night of 20/21 May, the *Kharkov* shelled Feodosia, and the *Besposhchadny* Alushta.

## Baku in action

In the Arctic, on 28 and 31 March, operations by the *Baku*, the destroyers *Grozny* and *Gromki* against the German supply traffic on the Norwegian Polar Coast met with no success.

Soviet icebreakers were moved from the White Sea into the Kara Sea between 17 June and 5 July. The operation began when the icebreakers *Mikoyan, Krassin* and *Fedor Litke* set out from Severodvinsk. They were under the orders of the Commander of the White Sea Flotilla, Rear-Admiral Kucherov, flying his flag in the destroyer *Uritski*, with the destroyer *Kuibyshev*, the patrol boats *SKR-28, SKR-30* and the British minesweepers *Britomart* and *Jason*. From 18 to 20 June cover was provided by the *Baku*, the destroyers *Gremyashchi* and *Grozny*. They returned on the 20th from the Kara Strait. The other escorts were on the edge of the ice in the Kara Sea, and the icebreakers reached Dikson on 22 June. A second convoy with the icebreakers *Admiral Lazarev* and *Montcalm*, escorted by Captain Kolchin with the *Baku*, and the destroyers *Gremyashchi, Gromki, Uritski*, the same patrol boats and the *Britomart*, sailed in the same way on 29 June to the Kara Strait in thick mist. The icebreakers arrived in Dikson on 5 July.

*The* Baku *in 1953.*

## Kharkov's last operation

In the Black Sea, during the night of 5/6 October, a group of Soviet destroyers went to sea to attack German evacuation transports off the Crimean coast. That group, under the command of Captain Negoda, consisted of the *Kharkov*, the destroyers *Besposhchadny* (1937, 1722 tons) and *Sposobny* (1939, 1712 tons). The *Kharkov* shelled Yalta and Alushta in the night, whilst the two destroyers, before joining her, had orders to fire on Feodosia. On their way, they encountered five German S-boats of the 1st Flotilla. They were the *S-28, S-42* and *S-45* of the first group, as well as the *S-51* and *S-52* of the second group. They were all under the command of *Korvettenkapitän* Büchting, aboard the *S-45*, and he decided to distract the attention of the Soviets as long as possible, while he was asking for aerial support from Stukas. The S-boats attacked the two Soviet destroyers, without any result, and they in turn pursued the German boats for a long

*The* Baku *in 1958, with the third 130mm gun removed and anti-aircraft armament reduced.*

time. It was a mistake, for it delayed their meeting with the *Kharkov* and, after they joined forces, the three Soviet ships found themselves dangerously near the coast, now in full daylight.

Soon after, a German reconnaissance aircraft saw them and called for the Stukas to attack. The Junkers Ju 87Ds belonged to *Stuka Geschwader 77*, temporarily based near Feodosia. Twelve of them flew over the S-boats shortly after 0600 and succeeding in hitting the *Kharkov* (Captain Shevchenko). The flotilla leader stopped, burning furiously and emitting a thick cloud of smoke. After the planes departed, the *Sposobny* took her in tow, but at 0930 the Stukas attacked again and the three destroyers were hit. The *Besposhchadny* was also immobilised and the *Sposobny* tried to tow in turn the two unfortunate ships. The Stukas attacked a third time, at 1145, hitting the *Kharkov* with three bombs and the *Besposhchadny* with two. At this point the crews abandoned the two ships. At 1630, the Stukas attacked for the fourth and last time; the *Besposhchadny* (Captain Parkhomenko) was hit three times and sank. Soon after, the *Kharkov* was hit again and sank too. The *Sposobny* (Captain Gorshenin) was hit in the after boiler room, as she was trying to rescue survivors. A cloud of steam rose up to 700m in the sky, above the disabled ship which had stopped, but her anti-aircraft fire was still intense. When the German planes withdrew, the *Sposobny* was listing heavily in a large area of spreading oil.

At twilight the German S-boats sailed from Ivan Baba to locate and sink the *Sposobny*. Despite the dark night, they found her easily, but the destroyer was surrounded by gunboats and motor torpedo-boats, so the S-boats were unable to get close to the destroyer, because of the murderous gunfire which met them. They therefore launched their torpedoes at the escorts and withdrew. The next day, when German reconnaissance planes flew over the zone they noticed small boats spreading over a wide area which was littered with floating wreckage, but no trace of the *Sposobny*. She had sunk. It was a real disaster for the Soviet Black Sea Fleet. The reasons were:
1) the initial success of the S-boats which held the attention of the superior Soviet force, without suffering any loss, till the arrival of the Stukas;
2) the Soviet Air Force's failure to send fighter cover, after the dangerous situation of the destroyers was known;
3) but the main cause of the Soviet losses rested with the senior officer who ordered far too long a pursuit of the S-boats.

When war broke out on 22 June 1941, the Soviet Black Sea Fleet had included three flotilla leaders (*Kharkov, Moskva, Tashkent*), nine modern destroyers and five old destroyers. Another destroyer, the *Sovershenny*, was put out of action by a mine in running her trials, whilst the *Svobodny* joined the fleet in Janaury 1942. Of the thirteen destroyers which had been commissioned, seven had been sunk before the tragic events of 6 October 1943. In addition, three of the five old destroyers had been sunk too, and the *Kharkov* was the only flotilla leader left. Such heavy losses explain Stalin's reasoning when he forbade the employment henceforth of big units and destroyers without his express permission.

## Arctic convoy battles

The Soviet icebreakers *Stalin* and *Fedor Litke* (*SKR-18*) set out from Tiksi on 22 October to return to the White Sea. On the 26th they were met in the Vilkitski Strait by the minelayer *Murman* and the icebreaker *Semen Dezhnev* (*SKR-19*) and brought, via Dikson, to the Kara Strait. There they were reinforced by a strong escort force (Rear-Admiral Kucherov) comprising the *Baku*, the destroyer *Grozny, Gromki, Kuibyshev, Razumny* and *Razyarenny*, as well as four ex-US minesweepers. On the way, in the Kara Strait on 15 November, north of the isle of Kolguev on 16 November and in the Gorlo Strait on the 17 November, the escorts made many depth charge attacks on suspected U-boats, and reported two U-boats sunk and three more seriously damaged. In fact, no U-boat was in the vicinity of the convoy AB55. The last boat, *U-636* (Captain Hildebrand) laid mines off the Yugor Strait on 14 November and then quickly returned

*The* Minsk *after the war.*

to base. The other U-boats at sea, *U-277, U-307, U-354, U-360* and *U-387*, were stationed in the passage between Spitzbergen and Bear Island as the 'Eisenbart' group. The convoy was continually located by the German 'B' Service and was sighted but not attacked by a Junkers Ju 88 carrying out armed reconnaissance north of Kolguev.

On the Murmansk front, in October 1944, German troops withdrew towards the south, whilst Soviet forces landed repeatedly in their rear. Kirkenes was occupied on 26 October, after having been evacuated by the Germans. To cover and support the landings, six destroyers and the air regiments of the Northern Fleet were deployed. As part of these operations, the *Baku*, the destroyers *Gremyashchi, Razumny* and *Razyarenny*, shelled Vardö and Vadsö, in the Varangerfjord on 26 October.

Before the return convoy RA62 set out with twenty-eight ships on 9 December, allied support groups and a Soviet destroyer force (Rear-Admiral Fokin), tried to drive off the U-boats from the entrance to the Kola Inlet. The Soviet ships were the *Baku*, the destroyers *Gremyashchi, Razumny, Derzki* (ex-HMS *Chelsea*, ex-USS *Crowinshield*), *Doblestny* (ex-HMS *Roxburgh*, ex-USS *Foote*) and *Zhivuchi* (ex-HMS *Richmond*, ex-USS *Fairfax*). In the process, the *U-997* (Captain Lehmann) missed the *Zhivuchi* and the *Razumny* with T5 acoustic torpedoes.

On 7 December, the *U-997* had used an acoustic torpedo to sink the Soviet submarine-chaser *BO-229* (ex-US *SC 1477*, 1943, 120 tons) near the island of Kildin. This boat belonged to a Soviet anti-submarine group (Captain Gritsyuk), comprising also *BO-150, BO-227* and *BO-228*. On 9 December, the *U-387* (Captain Büchler) was sunk by the British corvette *Bamborough Castle*, but the Soviets claim that she was rammed and sunk by their destroyer *Zhivuchi*. Only the *U-365* (Captain Todenhagen) was able to establish contact with the convoy. On 11 December, at 71°57′N/32°04′E, she damaged the British destroyer *Cassandra* (1943, 1737 tons) with an acoustic torpedo, after having missed a tanker of about 7000 tons the day before. On 13 December, as she was keeping contact with great determination, the *U-365* was sunk with all hands, by a plane (813 Squadron) from the British escort carrier *Campania*, at 70°43′N/08°07′E.

At the beginning of 1945, seven German submarines (*U-286, U-293, U-295, U-636, U-956, U-968* and *U-997*) were operating against Soviet coastal traffic off the Kola Coast. On 16 January, the Soviet convoy KB1, with six Allied freighters and four tankers, proceeded from the Kola Inlet to the White Sea. The escort (Captain Rumyantsev) consisted of the *Baku*, the destroyers *Deyatelny* (ex-HMS *Churchill*, ex-USS *Herndon*), *Derzki, Doblestny, Zhivuchi, Dostoiny* (ex-HMS *St Albans*, ex-USS *Thomas*), and three others as a covering group plus six Petlyakov Pe-3 as air escort. On 16 January, at 2030 (local time), the *Deyatelny* (1919, 1209 tons) was shaken by a strong explosion and sank, at 68°56′N/36°31′E. According to the Germans, the *U-286* (Captain Dietrich) claimed having sunk a destroyer belonging to convoy KB1, with an acoustic torpedo, but there is conclusive proof that the *U-286*'s attack did not occur. The destroyer could have been the victim of a mine.

## *The war against Japan*

On 9 August 1945, the second American atomic bomb was dropped on Nagasaki and, on that same day, the Soviet Union declared war on Japan. The Soviet Pacific Fleet comprised two heavy cruisers (*Kalinin* and *Kaganovich*), the flotilla leader *Tbilisi*, ten modern destroyers, two old destroyers and seventy-eight submarines. Commissioned on 11 December 1940, the *Tbilisi*'s first war operation did not take place until 12 August 1945, when naval troops landed on the east coast of Korea in support of the advancing 25th Soviet Army. Used as a headquarters ship, the *Tbilisi* was accompanied by the frigate *EK-5* (ex-USS *San Pedro*), two minesweepers, eight patrol boats and two motor torpedo-boats, as well as transports and one tanker. Soviet landing operations on the Kurile islands and their occupation took place between 18 August and 3 September 1945, the last Japanese capitulating on 20 August. The short Soviet–Japanese war was officially brought to an end on 2 September, with the signing of the Japanese surrender on board the American battleship *Missouri*, anchored in Sagami Bay.

*The* Tbilisi *(TSL-50) in 1959, used as a target ship in the Pacific Fleet.*

# ROMANIAN MINELAYING OPERATIONS IN THE SECOND WORLD WAR

One of the products of the loosening of political controls in Eastern Europe has been a trickle of new naval information based on hitherto inacessible sources. In this article Cristian Crăciunoiu, the leading Romanian naval historian, and Mark Axworthy reveal details with unpublished illustrations of the wartime Romanian minelaying effort against the Soviets. As editor of the magazine *Modelism* Cristian Crăciunoiu was able to acquire much information he has until recently been unable to publish.

ROMANIA had paid a particularly heavy human and material price for its contribution to Allied victory in the First World War but gained the predominantly Romanian populated territories of Transylvania from the Austro-Hungarian Empire and Bessarabia following the collapse of Czarist Russia. Romania consequently looked to its allies of the period, France and Britain, for the continued guarantee of its newly regained national integrity throughout the 1920s and 1930s. However, the diplomatic and military ineffectiveness of these two powers was finally confirmed by the fall of France in 1940. Left isolated in the Balkans, Romania was forced by Germany to cede much of Transylvania to its ally Hungary and Bessarabia to the Soviet Union. The rump of the country was obliged to rely on Germany to guarantee its survival. Thereafter Romania was inevitably drawn into the World War by the overriding need to recover both its lost territories. The first opportunity came with the German invasion of the Soviet Union on 22 June 1941.

## *Preparation for war*

The naval situation in the Black Sea overwhelmingly favoured the Soviet Black Sea Fleet which had a modernised battleship, 5 cruisers, 3 destroyer flotilla leaders, 14 destroyers, 44 submarines and numerous lesser craft. Against these the Royal Romanian Navy could oppose only 4 destroyers, 1 submarine and a few light vessels. The ratio in terms of tonnage was over 50 to 1 in the Soviet Union's favour. Initially the German naval and air force presence was minimal. War with the Soviet Union was the worst case scenario which Romanian naval planners had long contemplated. Although their 1937–39 building programme had included a cruiser and four destroyers, none was begun. This was partly because of budgetary constraints due to necessarily higher priority being placed on the rearmament of the air force and army.

With these financial constrictions and the desperate need to reinforce its fleet's defensive capabilities simply to enable it to survive at all, only the 1937–39 building plan's submarine, minelayer and motor torpedo-boat programmes were proceded with. The MTB order was placed with Vosper but the submarine and minelayer contracts were placed by the Ministry of the Air Force and Navy with the Romanian Reşiţa armaments company which was to build them to the designs and under the direction of the Dutch Ingenieurskantoor voor Scheepsbouw den Haag (IvS) company. The contract, for £1,430,755, was signed on 19 September 1937.

## *The minelayers*

The Romanian minelayers, which strongly resembled the Dutch minelayer *Jan van Brakel*, were to be the largest and most complex vessels yet built in Romania and £144,927 was spent on equipping the Santieri Galaţi dockyard for the task. In 1942 the Germans were to buy into the yard, increasing its capital tenfold, and it was to assemble or construct most of the naval vessels subsequently used by them and the Italians in the Black Sea. The two submarines, *Rechinul* and *Marsuinul*, began as part of the IvS contract, were to be long delayed and had to be completed under German supervision. They only became operational in 1944. The *Rechinul* was designed to carry 40 mines and could have presented a considerable threat to the Soviet Black Sea Fleet in even its most remote bases had she been completed earlier.

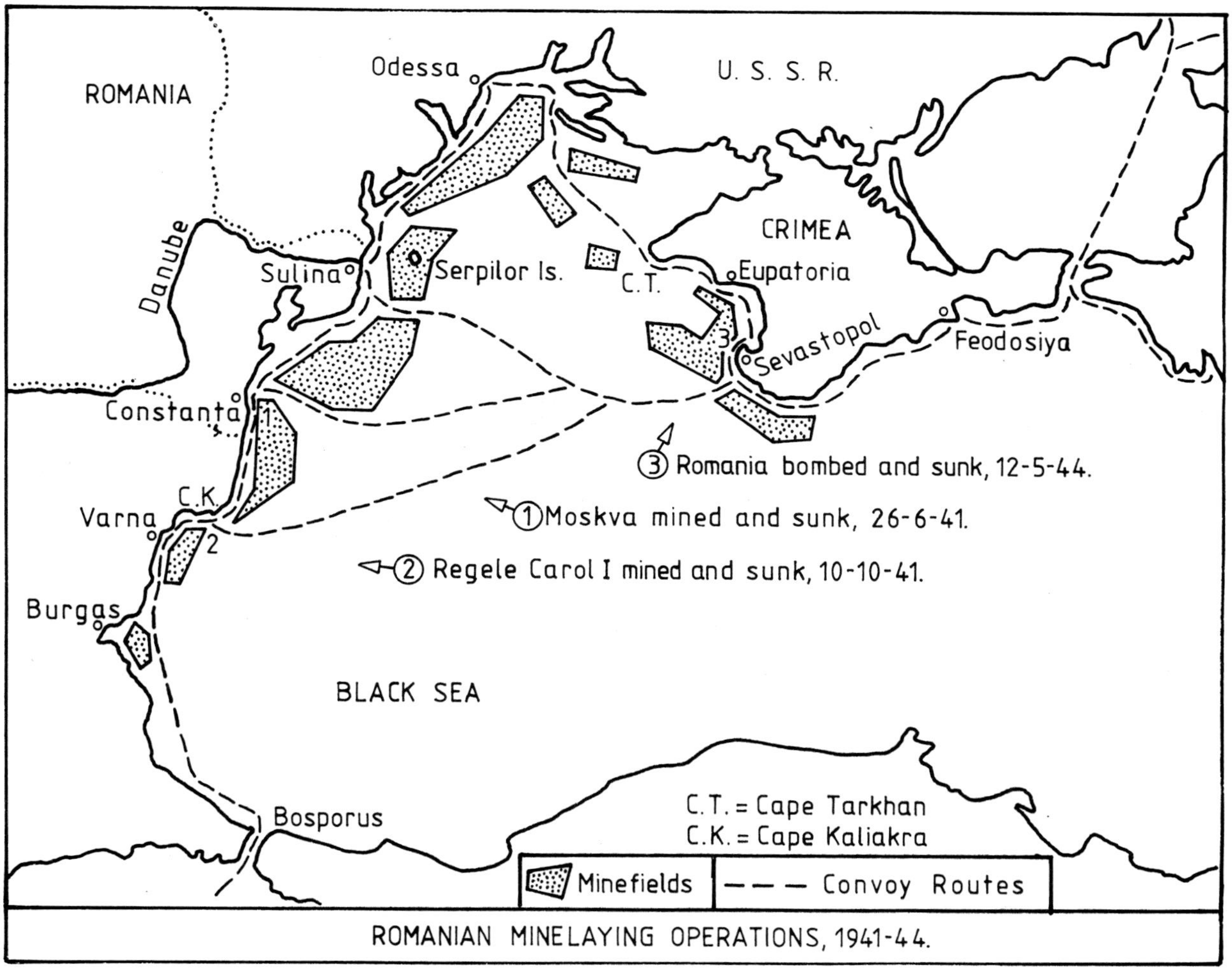


*Romanian minelaying operations 1941–44.*

The first minelayer was laid down on 1 August 1938, and launched on 14 June 1939. She was named *Amiral Murgescu* after Admiral Ion Murgescu who had distinguished himself in Romania's War of Independence in 1877–78 and commanded the navy from 1888 to 1901. Her completion was delayed by the general European crisis and the fall of the Netherlands to the Germans and she only became fully operational on 15 May 1941.

The minelayer programme called for four 812-ton vessels but only the *Amiral Murgescu* was completed. The second vessel, the *Cetetea Alba*, was laid down in 1939 but abandoned at an early stage. The *Amiral Murgescu* had a crew of 80 and was powered by two Krupp 1100 horsepower diesel engines and was capable of 16kts. Her radius of 3400 miles at 13kts was more than adequate for operations in the Black Sea. She could carry 135 mines and her anti-aircraft armament initially comprised two dual-purpose Bofors 102mm guns (4in), two Rheinmetall 37mm guns, two Oerlikon 20mm guns and two Lewis guns. She was also armed with two anti-submarine grenade launchers.

The *Amiral Murgescu* alone was clearly inadequate for the operational needs of the navy and the gunboat *Lepri* was fitted with mine rails to supplement her. The *Lepri*'s unsuitability led to her loss in an explosion during trials in January 1941, some six months before Romania's entry into the war, and put paid to any plans to convert the other three gunboats. The four 'M' and 'R' class destroyers, *Mărăşti, Mărăşeşti, Regele Ferdinand* and *Regina Maria*, each had a capacity of about 50 mines but they were more usually to be reserved for escort duties, leaving the minelaying to specialist vessels.

With no other naval vessels suitable the navy turned its attention to possible merchant conversions. The Romanian government had at its disposal its own merchant fleet, the *Serviciul Maritim Roman*, (SMR). The cargo vessel *Durostor* and passenger/cargo vessel *Regele Carol I* were accordingly taken up by the navy. The *Durostor* soon proved to have inadequate deck space and was returned to her merchant role. Her place was taken by a lighter vessel, the *Aurora*, which normally operated on the lower Danube.

The 2400-ton *Regele Carol I* had been launched in 1898 and had already served in the First World War as an auxiliary cruiser. In 1916 at Sevastopol she had been fitted with one 120mm (4.7in) gun forward and three aft and

Amiral Murgescu *with a full mine load.* (All photographs by courtesy of Cristian Crăciunoiu)

was used for coastal bombardment, troop transport and even as bait in an abortive attempt to lure the German *Goeben* onto the guns of the Russian Black Sea Fleet. She was now fitted with launch rails for up to 200 mines and received two 102mm (4in) guns as main armament and two 20mm anti-aircraft guns. Forty SMR crewmen, mostly engine room specialists, were kept aboard and a further 120 navy personnel were drafted aboard to handle the minelaying and gunnery. She was commanded by Locotenent-Comandor Ion Borcea.

In order to complement the minelayer building programme Romania's Reşiţa munitions works had obtained a licence to build Vickers mines, each filled with 250kg (550lb) of Trotyl explosive. *Regele Carol I*'s first load arrived in early June.

Because German troops were to attack from its territory, Romania was the only one of its allies that was informed well in advance of Germany's intention to assault the Soviet Union on 22 June 1941. This gave the Romanian naval staff, under the strategic direction of the German Black Sea naval command, a few days to make tactical preparations for the coming campaign. They correctly anticipated that the most likely initial move of the Soviet Black Sea Fleet would be to launch a raid on Romania's main port and naval base at Constanţa. Constanţa was of wider strategic significance as through it flowed much of the fuel that the Italian fleet needed to maintain an offensive potential in the Mediterranean.

On 14 June the newly converted *Regele Carol I* put to sea for successful trials in her new role. Then, in perfect conditions on 16, 17, 18 and 19 June, the *Amiral Murgescu, Regele Carol I* and *Aurora* laid a 1000-mine barrage five miles off the coast between Cape Midia and Tuzla. The mines were laid at a depth of 3m (10ft) in five double rows and covered the sea approaches to Constanţa. Every fifth mine was an explosive buoy designed to destroy any minesweeper's paravanes.

Amiral Murgescu *docked in Constanţa. Note the painted white rectangles bearing red diagonal crosses used for surface identification of Romanian vessels in the Second World War.*

Aurora *with a full mine load in June or July 1941.*

▲

Regele Carol I *in Serviciul Maritim Roman (SMR) livery at Constanța in 1906.*

Regele Carol I *as an armed merchant cruiser in the First World War.*

▼

Regele Carol I *loading Vickers mines in Constanţa in 1941.*

## *The Soviet raid on Constanţa, 26 June 1941*

Romania went to war with the Soviet Union on 22 June 1941, and Constanţa received a series of heavy Soviet air attacks over the succeeding days. After its initial surprise and a false call out in pursuit of non-existent Romanian destroyers, the Soviet Black Sea Fleet's raiding squadron attacked Constanţa on 26 June. The raid was intended to go in at dawn simultaneously with yet another air raid to split the defenders' attention. The night approach was to avoid detection from Romanian aerial reconaissance. The assault group consisted of the flotilla leaders *Moskva* and *Kharkov* which were to be supported by a covering force made up of the cruiser *Voroshilov* escorted by the destroyers *Soobrazitelny* and *Smyshleny*. The two flotilla leaders had been designed with just such an operation in mind (see p135).

At 0359 the silhouettes of the *Moskva* and *Kharkov* were spotted approaching Constanţa at high speed. Their anti-mine paravanes were out with the leader *Moskva*'s covering the *Kharkov*. At 0413 they opened an accurate fire against land targets, damaging oil storage tanks and blowing up an ammunition train. Due to the incessant air raids the Romanians had taken to dispersing their major vessels outside the port where they had some freedom of manoeuvre. At 0416 the two Soviet flotilla leaders came under the fire of not only the German 210mm coastal defence battery 'Bismarck' but also the Romanian 'R' class destroyer *Regina Maria* and the 'M' class destroyer *Mărăşti*.

During the first year of the war the Germans were reluctant to risk the Romanian destroyers in a surface engagement with Soviet vessels due to their poor mechanical condition and lack of adequate battle training. However, on this occasion the two Romanian destroyers were hidden against the high coast behind them and provided a difficult target for the two much larger and more modern Soviet vessels which were themselves clearly silhouetted against the dawn. This tactical advantage enabled the two Romanian destroyers to contribute significantly to the action.

In the lead, *Moskva* was soon bracketed by German and Romanian fire and shortly afterwards her rear mast was brought down by a hit. Soviet prisoners picked up by the Romanians after the action indicated they thought the damage was caused by a small calibre shell which would imply that it came from one of the Romanian destroyers. With their covering force still out of range and the supporting air raid late, the *Moskva* and *Kharkov* turned south under a smoke screen in order to cover their retirement to the east. Moments later *Moskva* struck a Romanian mine, blew up and sank.

As the Soviet covering force closed up the bow paravanes of the *Soobrazitelny* detonated a mine causing temporary damage to the nearby cruiser *Voroshilov*. The retiring *Kharkov* then came under Romanian air attack. She suffered a near-miss and control of her was temporarily lost. The other two destroyers had to cover her until control was regained. The whole force then retired on Sevastopol under cover of further destroyers sent out to reinforce them.

Sixty-three survivors of the *Moskva* were picked up by the Romanian MTBs *Viscolul* and *Viforul*. The belated air raid was broken up by Romanian Hurricanes and Me 109s and the surviving bombers lost so much height in the engagement that they became good targets for anti-aircraft fire. The *Amiral Murgescu* claimed two of them. The partially moored *Regele Carol I* was thrown against the quay by several near-misses but suffered no serious damage.

The defeat of this attack saved the Romanian navy and coastline from the further depredations of the Soviet surface fleet until it was driven from the western Black Sea by the arrival of German air power several months later.

*General arrangement of* Amiral Murgescu.

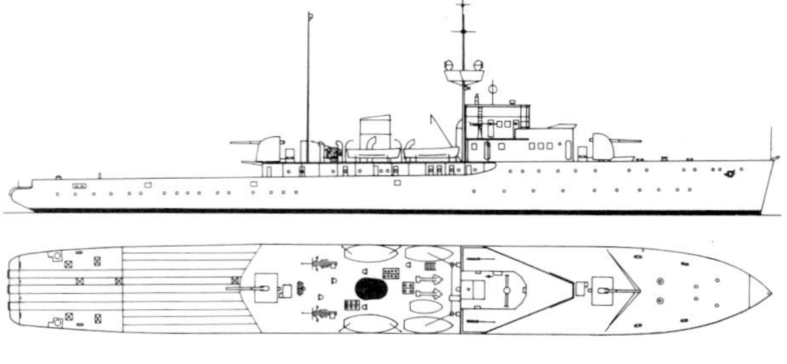

Regele Carol I *preparing to launch mines.*

## *AMIRAL MURGESCU TECHNICAL DATA*

| | |
|---|---|
| Displacement | 812 tons |
| Dimensions | 76.92m × 9.10m × 2.50m<br>252ft 4in × 29ft 10in × 8ft 2in |
| Machinery | 2 shafts, two Krupp 1100bhp diesels = 16 kts |
| Radius | 3400nm at 13kts |
| Armament | 2 – 102mm (4in) Bofors AA, 2 – 37mm Rheinmetall AA, 2 – 20mm Oerlikon AA, 2 Lewis guns, 2 depth-charge launchers, 135 mines |
| Complement | 80 |
| Design | IvS, The Netherlands |
| Builders | Santieri Galaţi, Galaţi, Romania |
| Laid Down<br>Launched<br>Operational | 1 August 1938<br>14 June 1939<br>15 May 1941 |
| Cost | £453,446 |

*Plan of the* Regele Carol I *as a minelayer.*

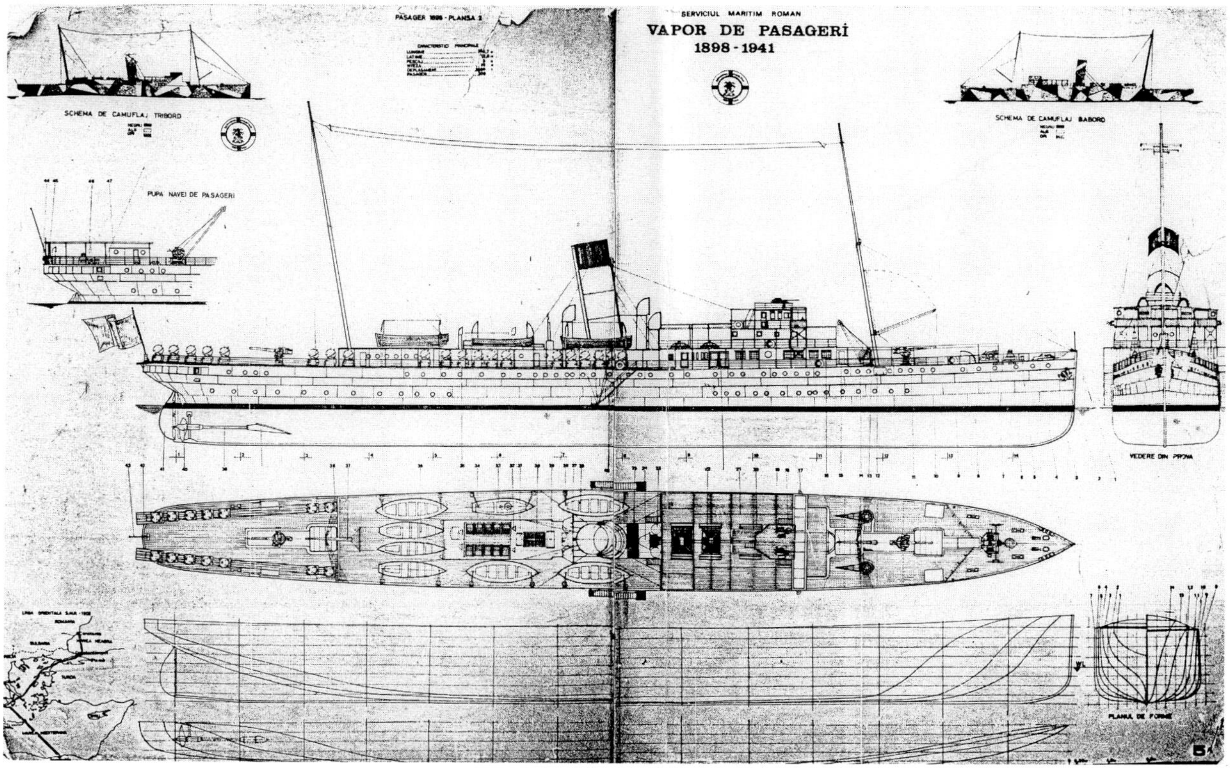

## *The loss of the Aurora and Regele Carol I*

The other major area to be defended was the mouth of the Danube where the Romanian river monitor fleet faced its Soviet equivalent. The shallow draught of the *Aurora* made her particularly suited to this task but when a Soviet air attack sank her in the harbour on 15 July operations had to be suspended until the Romanian army's land advance had driven the Soviets from their nearest air bases. However, she may have scored a posthumous success as the Soviet submarine *Shch-206* was probably mined off Sulina in September 1941. Later in the war six other light vessels, including tugs, were employed in laying inshore mine barrages.

During July and August Constanţa suffered several more air raids before the Soviet Air Force was obliged to concentrate its efforts on the defence of its bases around the port of Odessa which was besieged by the Romanian 4th Army. *Regele Carol I* suffered several wounded in air raids on 5 August but no structural damage, while *Amiral Murgescu* gained herself a reputation around the fleet by claiming three more attackers.

In the following months the whole fleet underwent degaussing and received dazzle camouflage. During the same period the 3418-ton *Dacia*, a passenger vessel launched in 1907 and of generally similar configuration to the *Regele Carol I*, was converted into an auxiliary cruiser with a minelaying capacity of up to 200 mines. Her armament included three 102mm guns.

After extending the Constanţa barrage the next major minelaying operation was to lay a similar barrage off the main Bulgarian port of Varna in order to protect the flank of coastal traffic to the Bosporus which was receiving increasing attention from Soviet submarines. *Amiral Murgescu, Regele Carol I* and *Dacia* left Constanţa on the evening of 8 October and at dawn the following day laid the first rows of newly received German anti-submarine mines south west of Cape Kaliakra.

The same day all three were reloaded in Varna and on the morning of 10 October left the port escorted by the Romanian gunboats *Smeul, Naluca* and *Sborul*, the torpedo-boats *Dumitrescu* and *Ghiculescu* and two Bulgarian torpedo-boats. The minelaying had barely started when, at 1204, the *Regele Carol I* herself struck a mine previously laid by the Soviet submarine *L-4*. The German and Bulgarian liaison staff and most of the Romanian crew were rescued but 21 Romanian crewmen went down with the ship when she sank thirteen minutes later. The Bulgarian freighter *Sipka* was another victim of *L-4*'s mines and when Romanian divers went down to blow up the wreck of the *Regele Carol I* they also cleared a further seven Soviet mines.

The surviving minelayers completed four and a half barrages off Varna and further south in the Bay of Burgas by 16 October. Only two days later the Soviet submarine *Shch-212* was reportedly damaged in the new minefields. On 12 November *S-34* was sunk in the Bay of Burgas and on the 16th *Shch-211* was also probably sunk off the Bulgarian coast. *M-34*, which disappeared in late 1941, may also have been a victim and *Shch-205* was believed damaged. The following year, in December 1942, *L-24* was also probably sunk on these barrages north of Varna. Just as German air cover came to make Soviet surface operations in the Black Sea prohibitively expensive, so Romanian mining operations began to make Soviet submarine operations on the convoy routes increasingly hazardous.

Dacia *in her inter-war SMR livery.*

The end of the Regele Carol I. *The torpedo-boat* Smeul *(left centre) initially assumed it was the result of a torpedo attack and dropped several depth charges.*

## *Minelaying Operations, 1942–43*

On 16 October 1941, the southern Soviet port of Odessa had finally fallen to the besieging Romanian 4th Army and for the next two and a half years was to be under Romanian administration. The Soviets had comprehensively demolished the port installations and the winter of 1941–42 was spent in restoring them. Odessa was an important way station for the increasing Axis coastal traffic between the mouth of the Danube and the advancing German–Romanian land forces in the Crimea and later the Caucasus. Responsibility for defensive convoy and minelaying operations in the western Black Sea largely fell to the Romanians in the years 1942 and 1943, their surface units not operating further east than Feodosia in the Crimea. German and Italian submarine and light surface forces carried the war to the Soviets in the eastern Black Sea.

From late February 1942, the *Amiral Murgescu* and the newly adapted *Romania* resumed laying defensive barrages off Sulina at the mouth of the Danube. The 3200-ton *Romania*, which had been built in 1904, was another Mediterranean passenger/cargo vessel similar to the *Regele Carol I* and had also served in the First World War as the country's first seaplane tender. She was now converted to carry up to 200 mines as a replacement for the lost *Regele Carol I*.

With the port of Odessa again functioning, the minelayers moved on to lay several flanking anti-submarine barrages off the Bay of Odessa in May. *Amiral Murgescu* and *Dacia* completed the operation in June 1942 by laying German UMA and UMB mines in two double lines on the night of 22/23 and the same on the night of 24/25 June. Two hundred mines were deployed on each night. The Soviet submarine *M-33* was lost on these barrages on 24 August and the *M-60* on 27 September. *Shch-208*, lost in the western Black Sea in August 1942, may have been a third victim and *M58*, which failed to return from operations in the late summer, was a possible fourth.

On 5 November, the *Amiral Murgescu* and *Dacia*, escorted by the two Romanian 'R' class destroyers and the 'M' class *Mărăşti*, laid a double pass of anti-submarine mines off the island of Serpilor. Serpilor lay off the main mouth of the Danube at Sulina from which emerged a continuous flow of light river and coastal traffic that hugged the coast en route to the front.

When not in use as minelayers, the *Amiral Murgescu* acted as a convoy escort and the *Dacia* as an armed merchant cruiser. During the winter of 1943–44 the well appointed *Romania* also acted as accommodation vessel for the German S-boat flotilla operating from Sevastopol and Odessa.

By late 1943 the German-Romanian armies on the northern Black Sea coast had been driven back to the Crimea which was then cut off in late October from the main German front to the north. The six German and seven Romanian divisions there were forced to rely on sea transport from Constanţa and Odessa to the port of Sevastopol for their supplies.

On the night of 13/14 September 1943, the *Amiral Murgescu*, escorted by the destroyers *Regele Ferdinand* and *Mărăşeşti*, began to reinforce the approaches to Sevastopol harbour by laying a single pass of mines off Cape Khersonesskiy. Follow up operations may have claimed *Shch-203* further north off Cape Tarkhankut, the western tip of the Crimea, the same month. The Sevastopol approaches were reinforced in another operation on the night of 9/10 November by *Amiral Murgescu* and *Romania*, escorted by the two 'R' class destroyers. A final extension of the field was made by the same two minelayers escorted by the *Regele Ferdinand* and *Marasesti* between 14 and 16 November. These barrages may have claimed the Soviet submarine *L-23* which was believed mined off Evpatoria on 17 January 1944.

*Dacia with a full load of Vickers mines. Note the decking with alternating red and white diagonal stripes painted at both bow and stern to aid aerial recognition.*

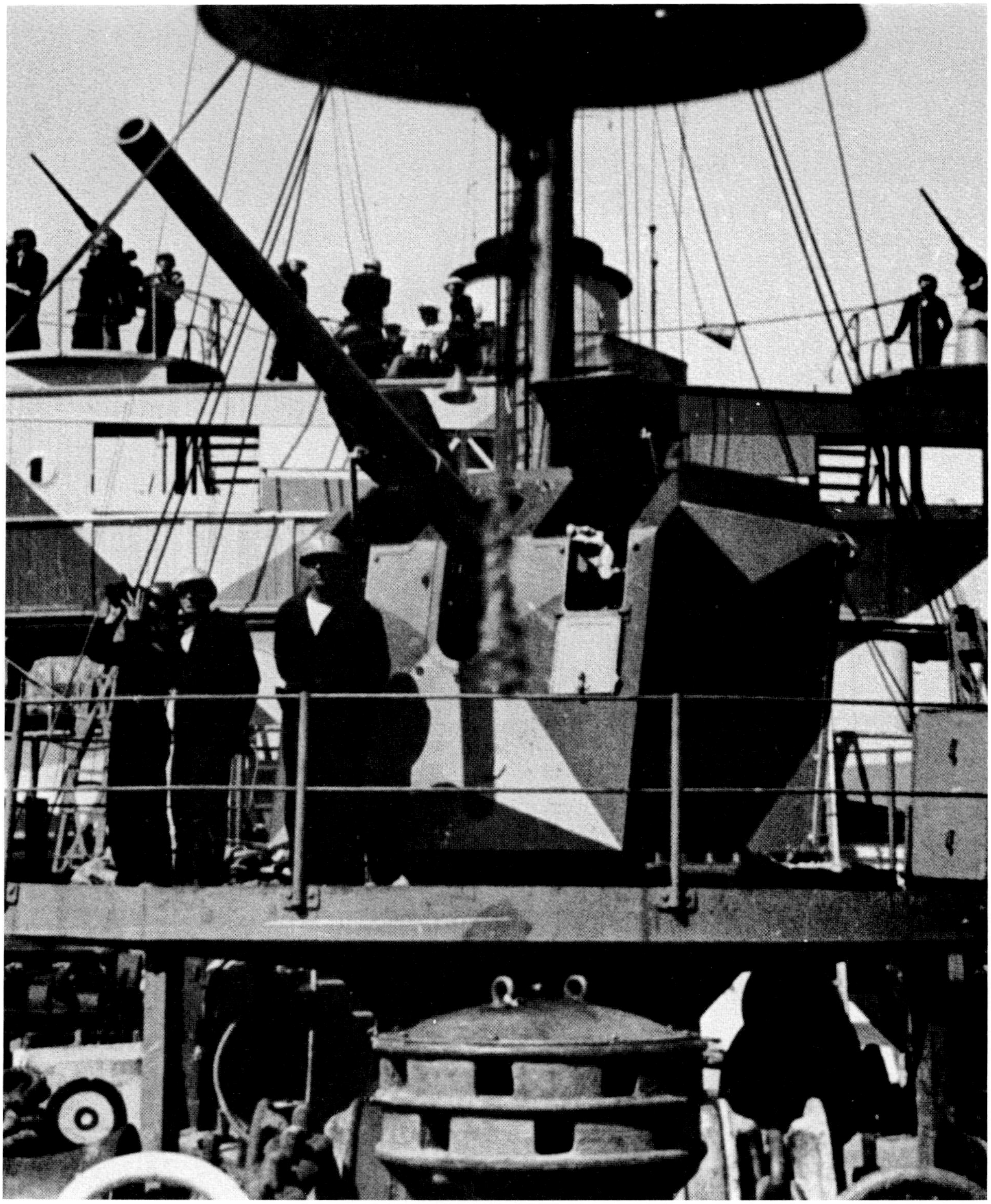

Dacia's *forward 102mm (4in) gun platform and 20mm AA positions.*

Romania *acting as a depot ship for German S- and R-boats, 1943–44.*

## *Final Operations, 1944*

The German-Romanian forces in the Crimea were successfully maintained by sea throughout the winter of 1943–44. The Romanians withdrew all non-essential troops but by early April, when the Red Army finally broke into the peninsula, there were some 64,000 Romanian and rather more German troops still cut off there and a desperate evacuation plan was put into effect. The Romanian withdrawal, codenamed 'Operation 60,000', involved using the entire surviving merchant fleet protected by the navy to evacuate its own troops to Constanţa. In the event only some 40,000 Romanian troops managed to reach the evacuation point at Sevastopol and the Royal Romanian Navy evacuated tens of thousands of Germans as well.

*Amiral Murgescu, Dacia* and *Romania* made several round trips between them, coming under increasingly accurate Soviet submarine, air and artillery fire as the Red Army closed in on Sevastopol. On 11 May, all three and the *Durostor*, which had proved unsuitable as a minelayer back in 1941, were amongst the last ships to evacuate troops from the Khersonesskiy peninsula, escorted by the two 'R' class destroyers and the gunboats *Stihi* and *Dumitrescu*. *Durostor* was torpedoed, bombed and sunk during the approach. *Romania* succeeded in loading with troops overnight but was bombed and sunk on the morning of 12 May with heavy loss of life. *Dacia* and *Amiral Murgescu* with 800 troops aboard fought their way out to sea through almost continuous artillery and air attack in the company of the destroyer *Regina Maria* and reached Constanţa safely. The Crimean evacuation in the face of overwhelming land, naval and air superiority was very much to the credit of the Romanian and German naval units involved.

In order to counter the renewed threat of Soviet surface raids on the Romanian coast the last minelaying mission of the war was carried out by the *Amiral Murgescu* and *Dacia* to the SSE of Sulina on the night of 25/26 May. The escorts were the destroyers *Regina Maria* and *Marasesti*, the torpedo-boats *Sborul* and *Smeul* and the MTBs *Viscolul* and *Vedenia*. This operation sealed the old convoy routes to Sevastopol and completed a line of mine barrages extending the entire length of the Romanian coast.

In April–May and June–July 1944 the newly commissioned submarine minelayer *Rechinul* made two unsuccessful cruises off the north Caucasus coast. She did not apparently lay mines on either mission. The Royal Romanian Navy retired behind its coastal flanking barrages in anticipation of renewed Soviet surface attacks. None materialised as Stalin had forbidden further surface raids after losing three destroyers to German Stukas off the Crimea in October 1943.

In the second half of August the Soviets began their land assault on Romania. On 22 August the *Amiral Murgescu* was heavily bombed in Constanţa harbour but escaped serious damage. The following day, with no further prospect of recovering Bessarabia from the Soviet Union, the Romanians defected to the Allies and began to drive the Germans and Hungarians from Transylvania in coordination with the Red Army. According to the Romanian interpretation of the terms of their collaboration with the Allies, they were to retain their navy for operations against the Axis. However, the Soviets unilaterally seized the Romanian fleet on 5 September 1944. Most of the fleet was returned several years later.

Romania's devotion of much of its limited naval budget to mine warfare was well conceived and rewarded with considerable operational success. It is difficult to confirm or attribute submarine minings with exactitude but it would appear that as many as ten or twelve Soviet submarines may have been lost on Romanian mines between 1941 and 1944. As *Amiral Murgescu* had laid up to half of them she was probably one of the most successful minelayers of the Second World War.

▲
Dacia*'s stern showing the rear gun platform and 102mm (4in) guns.*

Romania *on fire after bomb damage, 12 May 1944; she sank later that day.*
▼

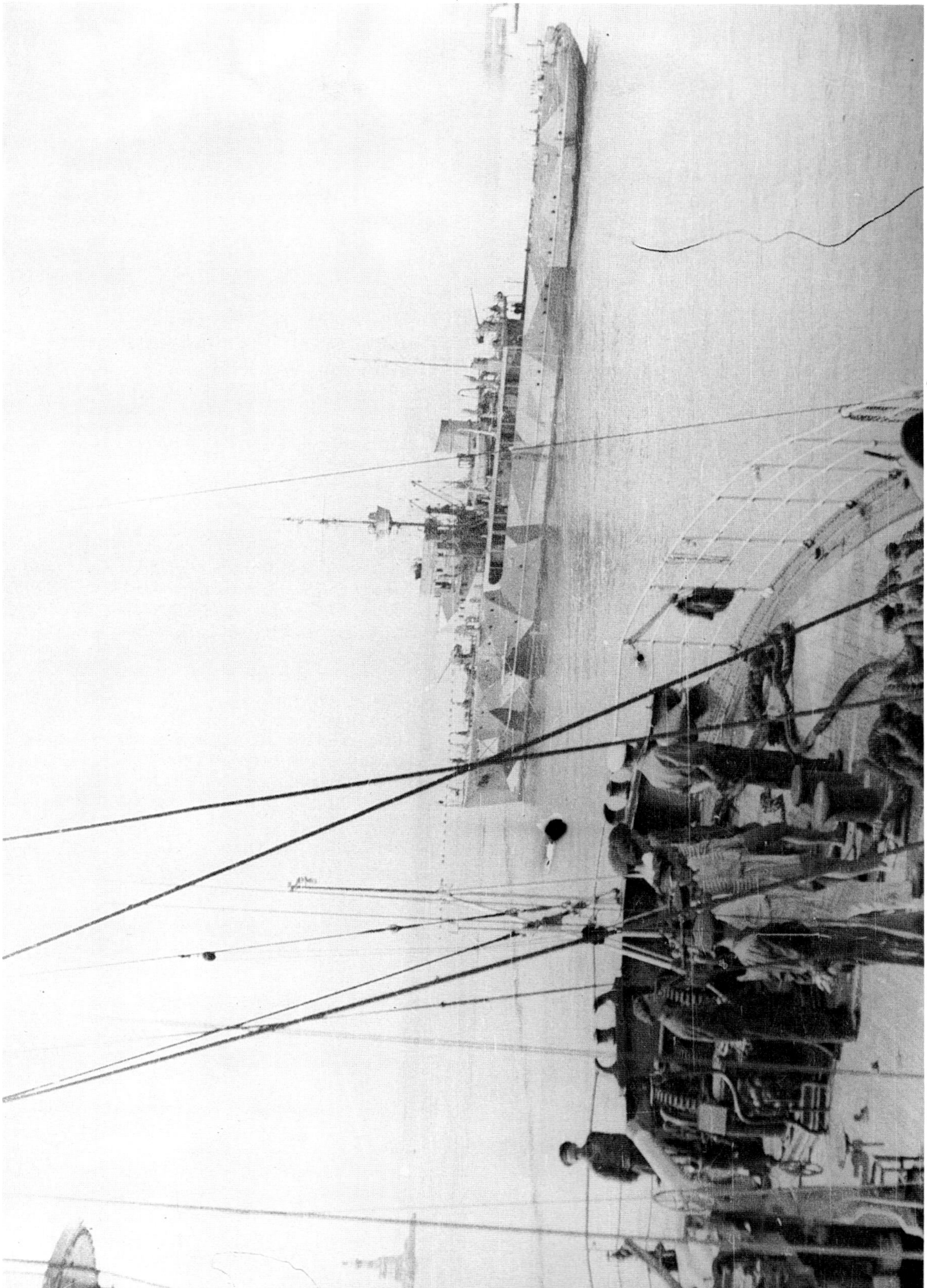

Amiral Murgescu at Constanţa. *The main armament did not carry gunshields during the war in order to improve their anti-aircraft capability.*

# SWEDISH TRE KRONOR CLASS CRUISERS

The cruiser is essentially a blue-water warship type so the *Tre Kronor* class has always seemed an uncharacteristic addition to a coast defence navy like Sweden's. In this revealing article Dan G Harris explains the political origins of these ships – as an attempt to avoid a potentially embarrassing problem of neutral protocol during the Second World War.

The German occupation of Austria in March 1938 shocked the Swedish government into beginning a rearmament programme which continued beyond 1945. Part of the programme was rebuilding of the navy, regarded as the first line of defence against invasion from Germany in the south, and Russia in the east. Two 8000-ton light cruisers, designed in Italy, became part of the new Swedish fleet in the late 1940s. The decision to build the two ships was a significant change in Swedish naval defence policies. Here is the story of the two cruisers *Göta Lejon* (Göta Lion) and *Tre Kronor* (Three Crowns).

## *Naval policies 1914–1942*

Because of Sweden's long coastline, the navy considered that its primary purpose was to prevent invasion of the Baltic coast, and to defend the Blekinge, Uppland and Stockholm skerries. In addition, in the event of conflicts between the major powers, it was to protect the neutrality essential to maintain overseas trade.

Between the two wars, the fleet's core was three 7500-ton *Sverige* class armoured ships. These ships, built between 1912 and 1920, were armed with four 28.3cm (11in), six 15.2cm (6in), and fourteen smaller guns. These vessels, strengthened for navigation in ice, had a maximum speed of 22½kts. The three ships' tactical purpose was to aid the light forces break through any enemy force attempting to bar passage outside the base areas. In addition, the *Sverige* class ships were to be support for light forces operating in Gotland's coastal areas, and to prevent landings on the mainland coast.

Between 1919 and 1937, the Board of Admiralty made various proposals for the replacement of the *Sverige* class vessels. Conflicts arose between the three defence forces; the Army and Air Force maintained that the armoured coastal defence ships could be easily destroyed by bombing, so construction of new coastal battleships would be a misuse of defence funds. The controversy continued throughout the 1920s and the early 1930s. The navy's only new construction during the period comprised six small destroyers, three 540-ton submarines, the seaplane carrying cruiser *Gotland* of about 4775 tons, and a few small craft such as minesweepers.

In the fall of 1938 the Swedish government directed the Chief of the Defence Staff, General Thornell, to present proposals for new armoured coastal defence ships. He directed the Naval Materiel Administration to design a vessel to have sufficient fire power and armour to be able to fight enemy cruisers and smaller craft not only within the Stockholm, Uppland and Blenkinge skerries, but also in the Åland Sea. The administration believed that the ship must have 25cm (10in) guns to be able to fight the German *Hipper* or Russian *Kirov* class cruisers, but its speed would be only 20kts, because the costs of increasing the proposed vessel's speed to 23kts would be too great for the 1938 defence budget. To deal with the German 'pocket battleships', the navy believed a 16,000-ton vessel armed with 28cm (11in) guns, capable of making 32kts would be necessary, but its costs were beyond the nation's resources. Early in 1939 parliament, on the recommendation of the Chief of the Defence Staff, approved funds appropriation to begin the construction of two armoured coastal defence vessels of 7500 tons armed with four 25.1cm (10in), six 12cm (4.7in) and eight 40mm anti-aircraft guns, and to have a speed of 22kts.

In June 1939 the Naval Materiel Administration asked the Götaverken, Eriksbergs, Kockums, Lindholmen and the Royal Dockyard Karlskrona yards to submit bids for the construction of two ships. The navy accepted the bids of Götaverken and the Royal Dockyard, although the latter had to construct a new slipway.

The outbreak of war in September 1939 caused a special session of parliament. The navy obtained additional funds for the construction of light craft, such as minesweepers. At the same time, Sweden tried to buy naval vessels, aircraft and light weapons from other neutral nations. In January 1940, Sweden bought two fourteen year old destroyers, two small six year old destroyers, four motor torpedo-boats, spare engines for the latter, mines, torpedoes, optical goods and aircraft from Italy.[1] Negotiations to acquire either a cruiser of the *Bartolomeo Colleoni* class of 5069 tons, or the American cruiser *Pensacola* failed.

Tre Kronor *at sea during full speed trials. As built 1949.* (All photographs by courtesy of Commodore (E) G Schoerner RSwN ret).

Work on the proposed armoured ships was cancelled early in 1940. The appropriated funds were used for the additional light craft. In July 1940, the Chief of the Naval Staff's policy was to postpone the acquisition of any coastal defence ships until the end of the World War, when new knowledge based on experience would be available.

## *New proposals*

In July 1940, the Naval Staff planned a new fleet to consist of four or five small cruisers possibly similar to the Netherlands *Tromp* class (4000 tons), armed with six 15cm (5.9in), four 75mm (3in), six 20mm guns, and six 53cm (21in) torpedo tubes. The proposed cruiser's speed was to be 34kts. The intentions were to have a force able to meet the Soviet's increased fleet of destroyers and light craft. The navy believed the *Tromp*'s plans, available from the Netherlands, would provide the basis for a Swedish cruiser design. The naval constructors believed changes to the *Tromp* type as a result of war experience, should be additional AA guns, and protection against splinters. These and other changes, necessary for service in the Baltic area, would raise the original tonnage from 4000 tons to 5000 tons. Alternatives were to build cruisers similar to either the Italian *Capitani Romani* of about 3500 tons and 41kts speed[2], the *Bartolomeo Colleoni* of 5100 tons, or vessels based on the lines of the seaplane-carrying cruiser *Gotland* built in 1934. The naval constructors proposed to invite Italian yards to prepare plans, since neither Swedish commercial shipbuilders, nor the navy had any experience in the series building of cruisers. Consequently, the Swedish Chief of the Naval Staff instructed the naval attaché in Rome to determine the feasibility of Italian shipbuilders designing cruisers for Sweden.

On 2 September 1940 Assistant Chief Constructor Captain (E) Ivor Hult submitted proposals to P Edwin Skiöld, Minister of Defence, to build four or five light cruisers of about 5000 tons displacement having a speed of at least 34kts, to be armed with six 15cm guns with 60° maximum elevation, ten or twenty 40mm and eight to ten 20mm AA guns on stabilized twin mountings. The

Industry Commission was ready to support the proposal if the number of ships was increased to six in order to relieve unemployment.

The next day, the Minister announced that he had no interest in the proposals to build four or five cruisers of between 3500 and 5000 tons. Cruisers were to be built but not the types proposed by Hult on 2 September.

In August 1940, Minister Skiöld had visited the Bofors armaments and steel plant. There, the company's president, S Sohlman, had shown the Minister two triple gun turrets for 15.2cm (6in) automatic guns under construction for the Royal Netherlands Navy's *Kijkduin* class cruisers[4]; in addition, four twin turrets of the same calibre had been ordered for Siamese cruisers to be built in Italy. Since Germany had occupied the Netherlands, it was doubtful if the Dutch cruisers would be built. Moreover a serious breach of neutrality would occur should the triple turrets and guns be delivered to Germany. Consequently, the Swedish cabinet ordered the turret's seizure. Since the Crown had to pay Bofors, the Minister ordered the navy to use the turrets in ships, and not in coastal batteries. He suggested low speed vessels for the turrets, but after discussions, he agreed that if the navy wanted cruisers then he would support the proposals. The navy had some reservations outlined in a memo of 2 September 1940 about the automatic 15.2cm guns. It considered the advantages to be high rate of fire (10 rounds per minute) and the 60° elevation; the disadvantages were complicated construction, combined shell and case, special machinery to feed the guns from the magazine, large magazines, space for the empty case storage and special ventilation. In addition as there was no stabilization, the guns could not be used against aircraft. Moreover, the high rate of fire could only be maintained for a few minutes at a time or the guns would overheat and the rifling get worn out, causing the rate and accuracy of fire to decline. These arguments and other alternative proposals made no impression on the Minister. He was adamant: his instructions were to build cruisers to fit the turrets, and to use the fire control systems available from Hazemeyer in Holland. Thus political expediency rather than the strategic needs, determined the size of the new cruisers.

Captain (E) Hult estimated vessels of 7500 tons would be required for the triple turrets with 15.2cm automatic guns. Since the navy's constructors were fully employed, and no Swedish shipyards had staff with sufficient experience to design cruisers, the Minister authorised negotiations to begin with the Italian authorities and shipbuilders. The Minister also consented to a contract with Ansaldo's Genoa yard to complete drawings for two 15,600-ton heavily armoured vessels with special underwater protection, six 28cm guns, the speed of one to be 20kts and the other 23kts.[3]

## The Italian connection

Sweden's naval connections with Italy began in the mid-eighteenth century when two officers, Lieutenants Rajalin and Kullenberg visited Genoa to study galleys. More recently, in 1909, the navy had one submarine, *Hvalen* (whale), built in Italy and acquired a licence to build similar craft in Sweden. In the inter-war years, one officer, Lieutenant Wetter, completed a course at the Livorno Naval School.

In 1937, the Swedish Admiralty appointed Lieutenant-Commander H O Hammargren as Naval Attaché to Italy. He became well acquainted with senior Italian naval officers, and the Italian shipbuilding industry. In December 1939, Hammargren was a member of the Swedish naval purchasing commission which acquired naval material from Italy. The Italian government required payment in American dollars which it used to buy raw materials in the United States. In addition, Sweden acquired licences to build the 'Baglietto' type motor torpedo-boats, and Isotta-Fraschini engines. The Swedish Kockums yard was later to build the motor torpedo-boat hulls of welded steel, using point welding techniques, instead of wood.

In the fall of 1940, the Naval Attaché obtained permission from the President of the Italian Board of Admiralty, Admiral Cavagnari, to negotiate with Italian shipbuilders for the construction drawings for the cruisers. A condition was that the Italian naval technical board was to examine the completed construction drawings, and authorize their release to Sweden.

Later, Captain (E) I Hult met with the Italian Admiral G Ducci and representatives of Cantieri Riuniti dell Adriatico, Trieste (CRDA) to negotiate prices for drawings of a cruiser to be armed with one triple 15.2cm turret forward, two twin 15.2cm turrets and two triple 53cm torpedo tubes aft. All the guns were to be fully automatic.

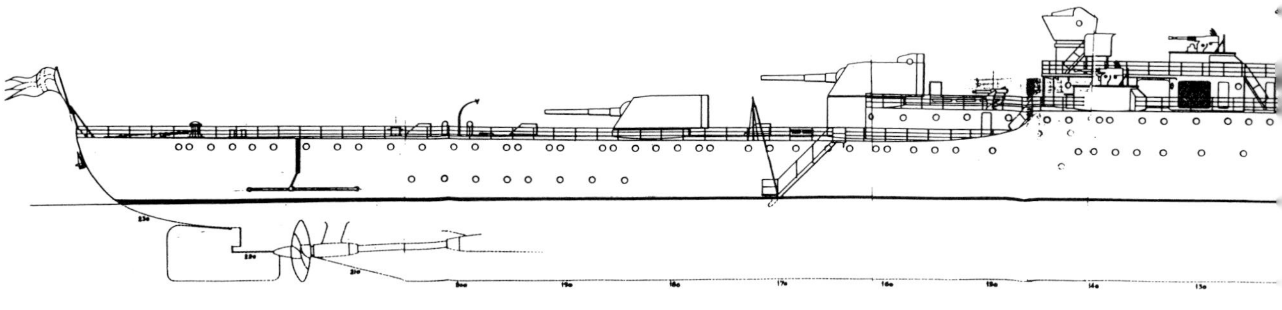

The vessel was to have both deck and side armour. The yard offered to complete and deliver a series of drawings for the preliminary project, including tank tests, originally for 105,000 US gold dollars. Bargaining seems to have reduced the price to 85,000 dollars. It planned to complete the work in six months from the date of the contract (24 October 1940), after it received particulars of the weights of guns and sizes of magazines required.

The work's start was delayed because it took time to translate the Swedish requirements into Italian. The first estimate of the cruiser's standard displacement tonnage with heavier armour was 7800 tons. To save weight, the constructors eliminated the proposed torpedo aiming tower. Review of the preliminary drawings brought about a greater separation of the two after turrets, the provision of greater spaces for magazines and used shell cases, and requirements for greater armour protection over the magazines. The result was that the cruisers were to have three armoured decks.

Early in 1941 the Swedish Naval Materiel Administration examined some of the CRDA drawings and criticised the proposed accommodation for the anti-aircraft guns' crews. The administration ordered changes so that the crews would be berthed closer to their guns. In addition, the Swedish Navy found the Italian proposals for the petty officers' and crew's accommodation were unacceptable. The Swedish high standards of space, and sanitary arrangements for petty officers and ratings came as a surprise to the Italian constructors. (Incidentally the Swedish Navy also had to refit the crew space in the destroyers acquired in 1940 to meet its standards.) In addition, the Italian constructors were to find that the Swedish standards for safety and reserves went beyond those used in the Italian Navy. The administration instructed CRDA to make the necessary changes, in addition to eliminate mine rails, and note that the conning tower was to have 60mm armour.

In February 1941, the Italian yard stated it could not complete the drawings within the specified contract time, arguing that the Swedish Navy's many changes to the plans caused delays, but it intended to complete drawings for tank tests and the results by the end of March, drawings for armour, weight and weight control, bottom and side valves by mid-May. A Swedish suggestion that the ships carry more torpedo tubes was rejected by CRDA – it would involve major changes to the hull design.

At the end of February, CRDA offered to complete drawings for the boilers; its price was US $4500; the Swedish Naval Administration Board accepted. CRDA then prepared and delivered thirty-two drawings, four material lists and strength calculations in mid-May for an additional fee of about US $2100. CRDA prepared drawings for the propellers, and offered to carry out tests on models, but no tests took place because more information on the dimensions of propeller and intermediate shafts were unavailable. Tank tests of models did take place to determine the final lines of the *Tre Kronor* class cruisers.

The CRDA yard proposed a certain type of steel for the hulls, but analysis by Swedish shipbuilders proved the Italian steel was unsuitable for welding. The Swedish constructors intended to use welding as much as possible in the new ships, but they discovered that the Italian shipyards did not employ welding in ship construction to the same extent as in Sweden. In addition, the analysis of the steel proposed for waterline belt armour by the Italians was not available in Sweden. In April 1941, the navy and the Götaverken shipyard, Göteborg, held discussions to determine if using different steel for the cruisers' hulls would necessitate changes to the construction drawings. The conclusions were that steel of familiar Swedish metallurgy would not require changes.

On 27 March 1941 Germany attacked Yugoslavia, which caused concern in Trieste, the arrival of refugees, and slowdowns in the CRDA yard. Nonetheless the manager assured Captain (E) I Hult that completion of the Swedish contract would have the highest priority, and all the drawings were completed and delivered on 16 September 1941.

Three days later, Hult had an interview with Colonnello G N A Mizzau of the Italian Admiralty's technical branch. He discussed the problems of protection against under-hull explosions since torpedoes were being developed for that purpose. Mizzau held that until the problem was solved, hulls would still have to be divided into many compartments.[6]

*Original profile drawing for Swedish cruisers, prepared by Cantieri Riuniti Dell Adriatico, Trieste, Italy 1940–41. The original drawing is annotated 'approved I Hult'.* (By courtesy of the Royal Military Records Office, Stockholm.)

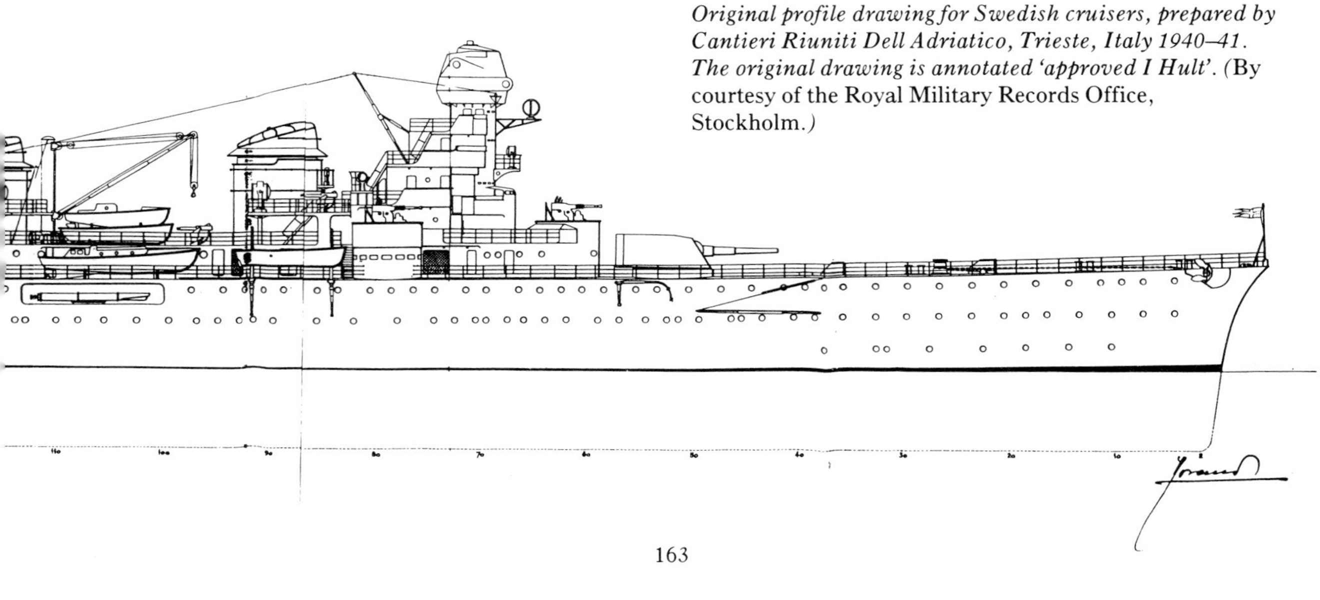

Tre Kronor *at sea escorted by destroyers* Halland *and* Småland, *after rebuilding of the bridge complex.*

## *Construction*

The naval adminstration placed a contract with the Götaverken yard at Göteborg to use the Italian plans to make working drawings and calculations. According to Captain Hult, the Swedish yard felt that it had been ignored in the cruisers' planning, and had difficulty in accepting the Italians' innovations. Götaverken changed the design on the funnels because wind tunnel tests proved the Italian vertical uptakes would cause problems to personnel and equipment on the bridge. Götaverken raked back the funnels to keep smoke away from the bridge. In addition, the revised design discarded plans to place searchlights on the funnels.

The navy now placed orders with Swedish industry for the turrets, electrical installations, engines, optical, and other equipment. However, there was another hurdle to overcome before the navy could make contracts for keel-laying.

In the fall of 1941, the Industry Commission which had earlier favoured the building of several cruisers, objected to any cruiser construction. It argued that more destroyers and small craft ought to be laid down; their construction would require less time. The commission maintained that the quantities of copper, chrome, and nickel required for the cruisers would strain Sweden's limited resources. A critical factor was the amounts of molybdenum required for the cruisers' armour plate.[5] The Commission got the navy's order for 2600 tons of armour plate postponed; it allocated the 21 tons of molybdenum to the production of steel for shells, bombs, and the army's armoured vehicles. The cruiser project was temporarily shelved, but in the spring of 1942, the cabinet decided to proceed with the construction. The navy called for tenders in June 1942, and received bids in September for building. Finally in February 1943, the naval administration contacted with the Götaverken and Eriksberg shipyards at Göteborg to build the two ships. The navy accepted Asea's bid for the fire control instruments for the after turrets, and ended discussions with Siemens Hazemeyer to build a factory to manufacture fire control instruments. It contracted with Swedish steelworks for the armour plate. Incidentally, the steelmakers were able to get 65 per cent of the nickel requirement from the armour plate of scrapped warships.

## The hull and armour

The hulls were to be partially welded, the longitudinal plating strakes being riveted at the ends; the transverse plating joints were welded. The upper strake below the main deck between the forward and after turrets, was of 20mm splinter-proof steel. A bolted belt of 70mm armour covered the waterline which did not affect the longitudinal stiffness.[7] The main deck between the fore and aft turrets was of 30mm armour plate. The lower deck was of 20mm armour, 30mm above magazines, 20mm above the fuel tanks, and 40mm above the steering gear. The conning towers had 60mm armour. The gun turrets fronts, roofs and barbettes were of 125mm, 50mm and 80mm armour respectively.

## Machinery

Two groups of main De Laval turbines were the ship's power units. Each group consisted of one high-pressure and two low-presure turbines. Each low-pressure turbine stood on its condensor. Each lower-pressure turbine had its reverse turbine in the same turbine house.

All three turbines operated on common simple gearing which was connected to a 520mm (20.5in) diameter propeller shaft. Each bronze propeller had three blades and a diameter of 4570mm (180in). The Avesta Steelworks made the reserve propellers of welded stainless steel. These were cast in three pieces – one blade and a third of the hub which were welded together, and the hub bored. In fact, these propellers were never used.[8] At the ships' maximum speed of 33kts, the propellers turned at 280 revolutions per minute.

The ships had no separate cruising turbines but the use of different sizes of steam nozzles gave similar results. Four water-tube oil-fired boilers at 32 kilo atmospheres, and 1700sq m of heating surface inclusive of superheaters, provided the steam. Steam was superheated to a temperature of 375°C. Fuel consumption at a speed of 33kts was 30 tons per hour. The feed water system was of the conventional type with a change over system to offset accidents, and other interruptions.

The auxiliary machinery comprised four steam turbo- and four diesel-powered generators. Two turbo generators were in each engine room; two diesel generators were in forward and after compartments. The generators provided 220v AC power.

The steering gear was the electric hydraulic type with four hydraulic cylinders operating the rudder. Steering was from either the conning tower, the operations centre, or the reserve steering position aft.

Tre Kronor *stern view after reconstruction 1951–52.*

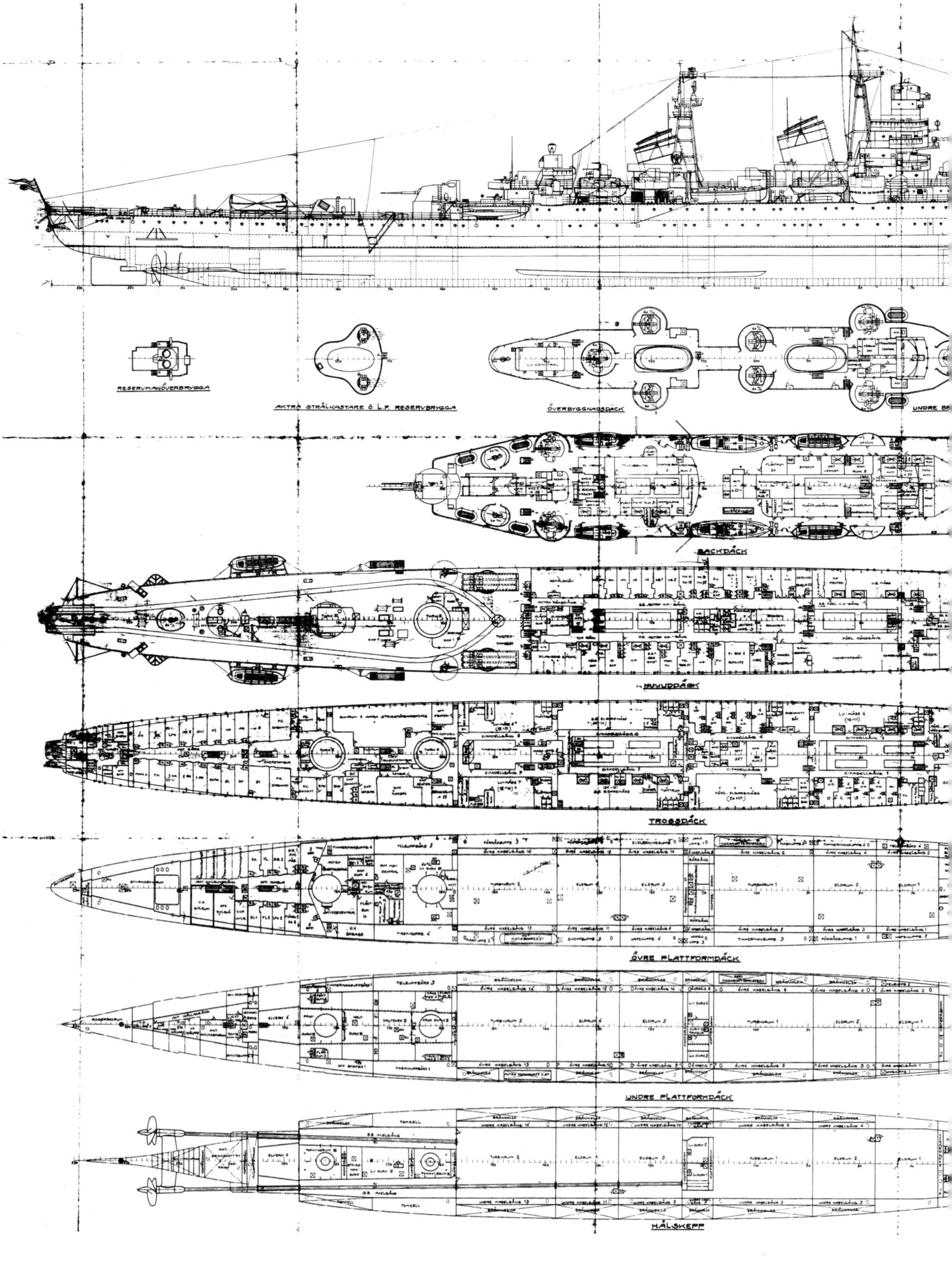
RESERVMANÖVERBRYGGA
AKTRA STRÅLKASTARE Ö L.F. RESERVBRYGGA
ÖVERBYGGNADSDÄCK
BACKDÄCK
HUVUDDÄCK
TROSSDÄCK
ÖVRE PLATTFORMDÄCK
UNDRE PLATTFORMDÄCK
HÅLSKEPP

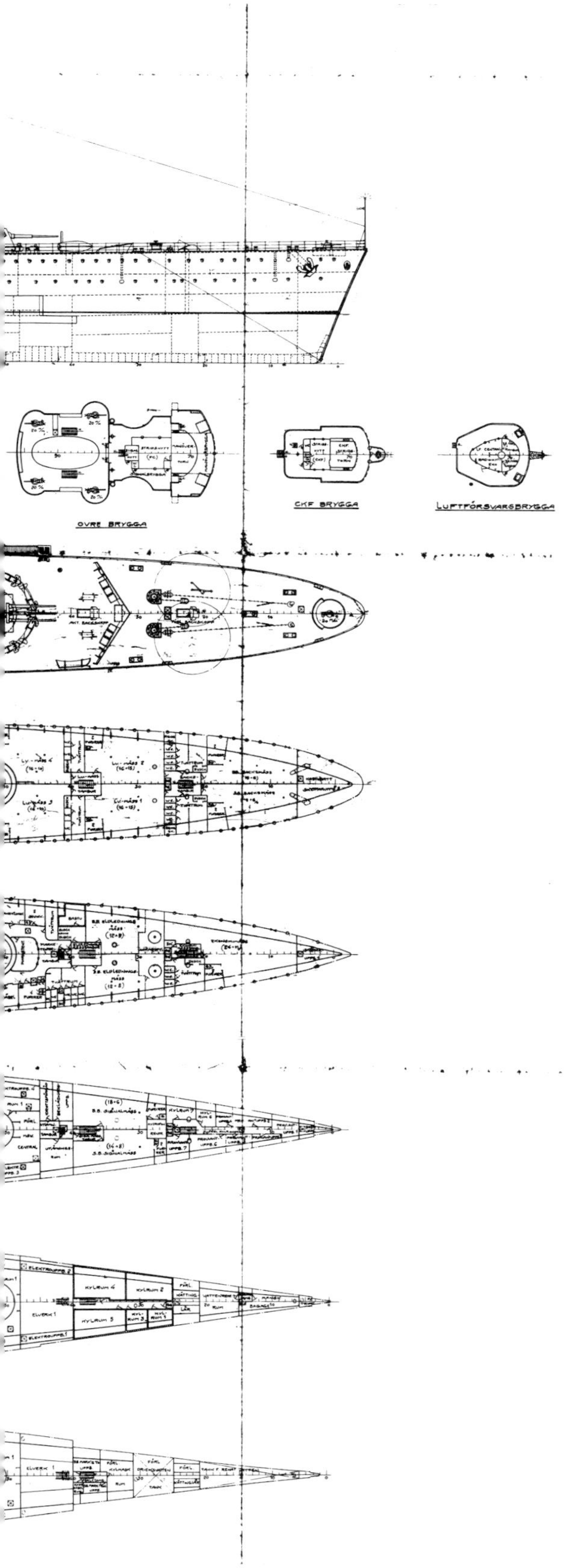


*Plan of cruisers* Tre Kronor *and* Göta Lejon, *as built, prepared by AB Götaverken, dated 20 June 1949 (prior to reconstruction of the bridge complex). (*By courtesy of Commodore (E) G Schoerner RSwN ret*).*

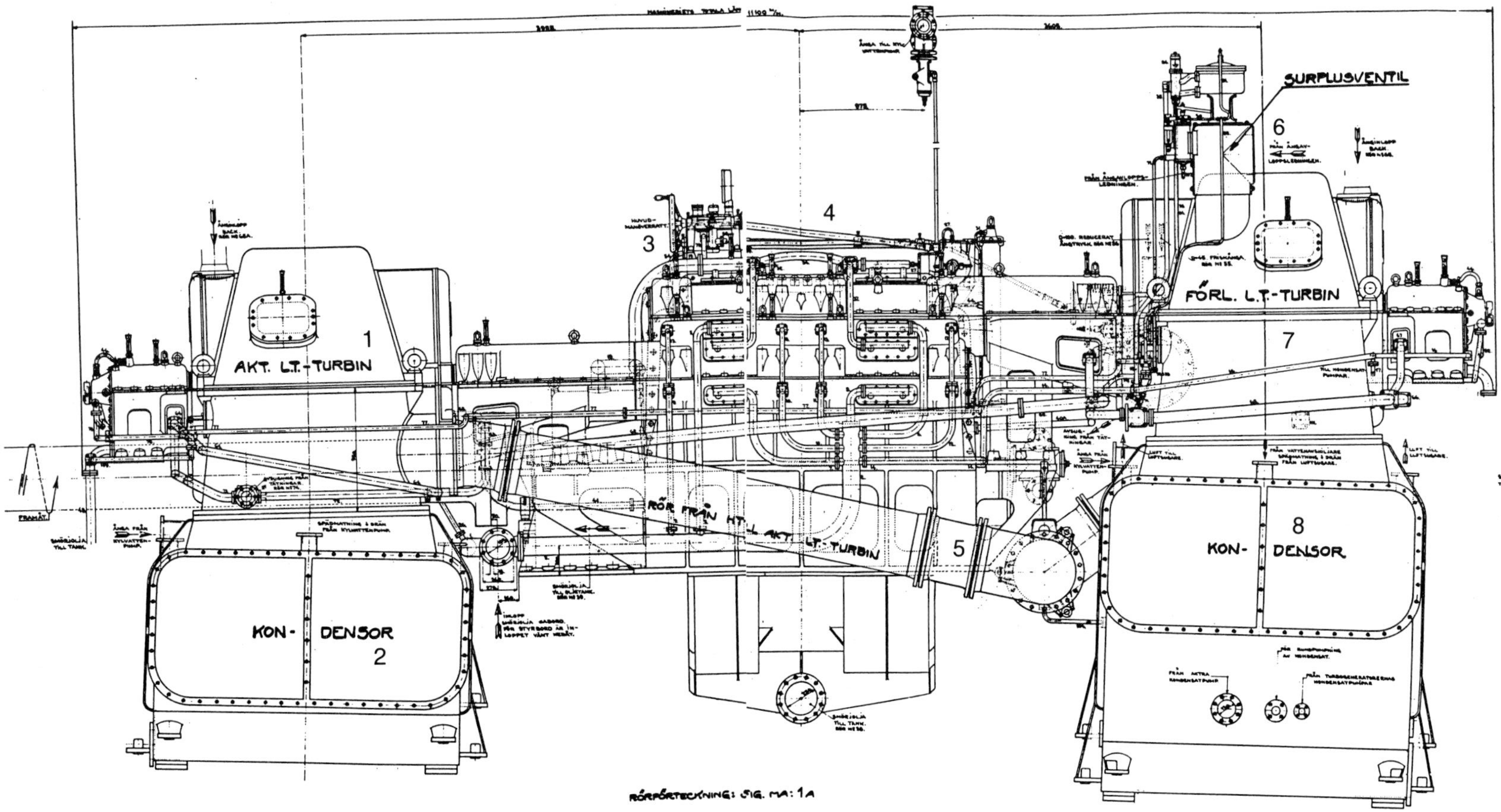


*Main turbine plan, side view, port side.*
**1.** *Aft low pressure turbine.*
**2.** *Condenser.*
**3.** *Main control valve.*
**4.** *High pressure turbine.*
**5.** *Steam pipe from high pressure to low pressure turbines.*
**6.** *Relief valve.*
**7.** *Forward low pressure turbine.*
**8.** *Condenser.*
(By courtesy of Commodore (E) G Schoerner RSwN ret).

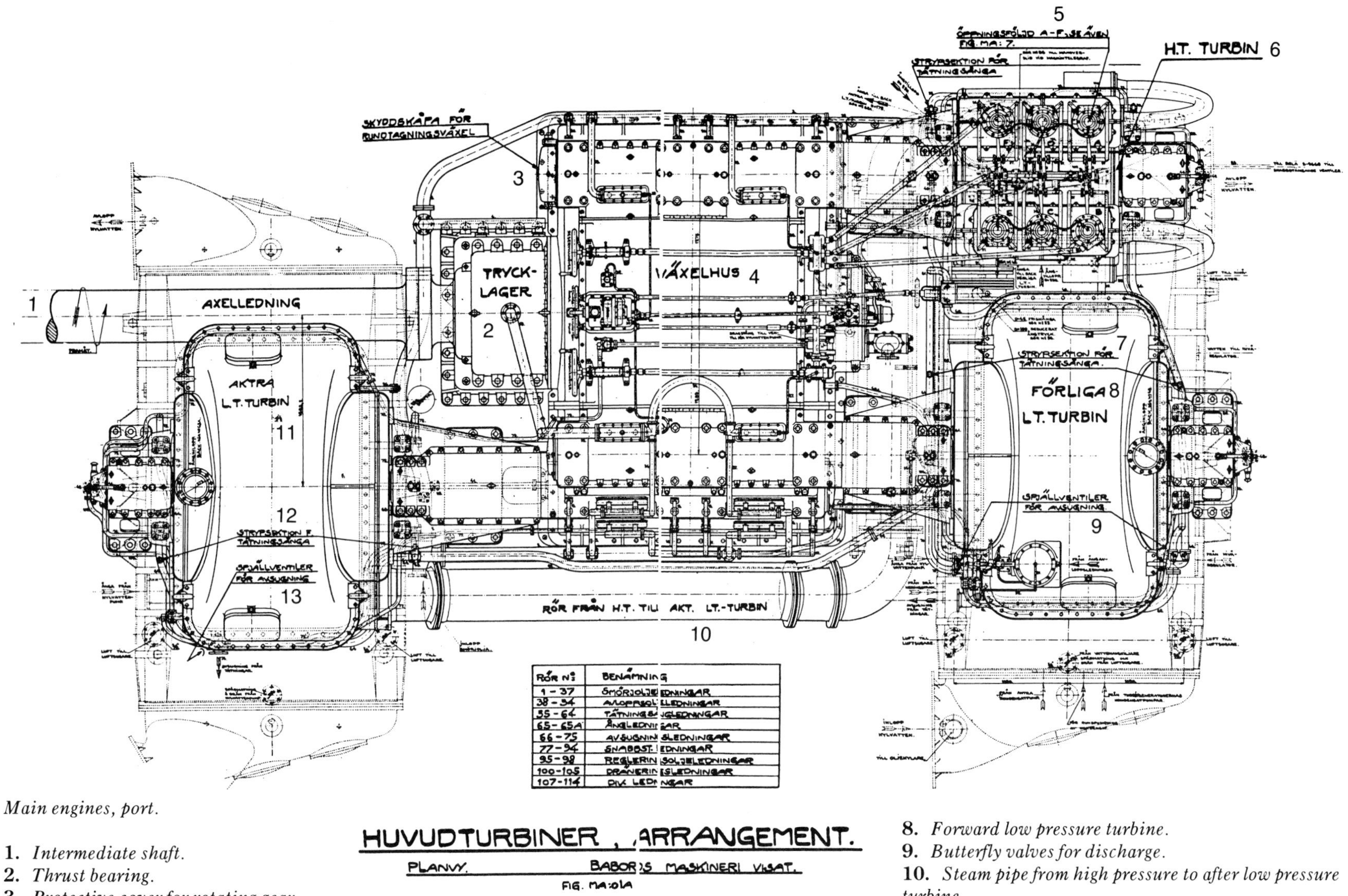


*Main engines, port.*

1. *Intermediate shaft.*
2. *Thrust bearing.*
3. *Protective cover for rotating gear.*
4. *Gearing.*
5. *Opening sequence.*
6. *High pressure turbine.*
7. *Choke section sealing steam.*
8. *Forward low pressure turbine.*
9. *Butterfly valves for discharge.*
10. *Steam pipe from high pressure to after low pressure turbine.*
11. *After low pressure turbine.*
12. *Choke section sealing steam.*
13. *Butterfly valve for discharge.*

(By courtesy of Commodore (E) G Schoerner RSwN ret).

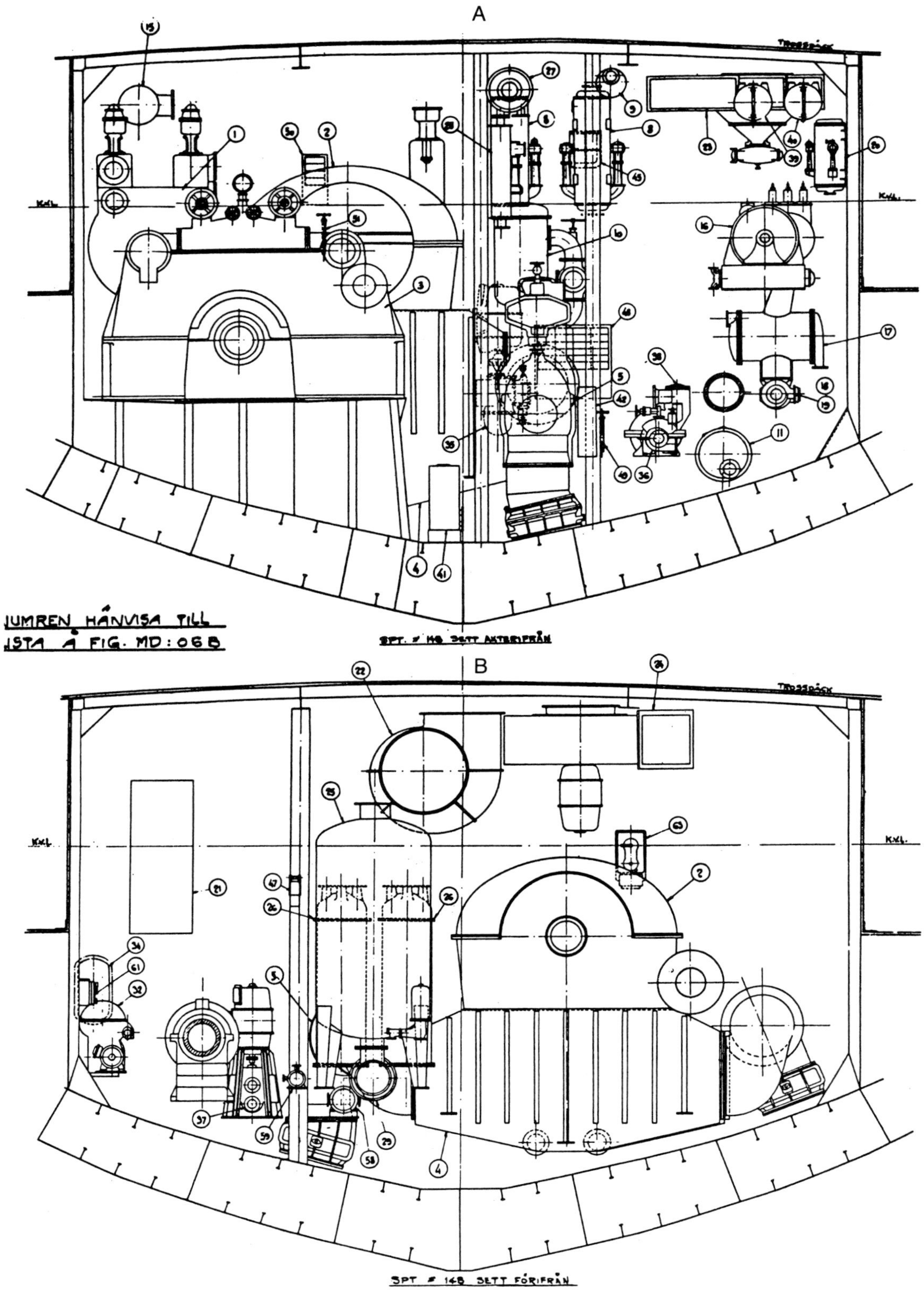


*Drawings showing engine room arrangements.*
*A. View aft.*
*B. View forward.*
*(*By courtesy of Commodore (E) G Schoerner RSwN ret*).*

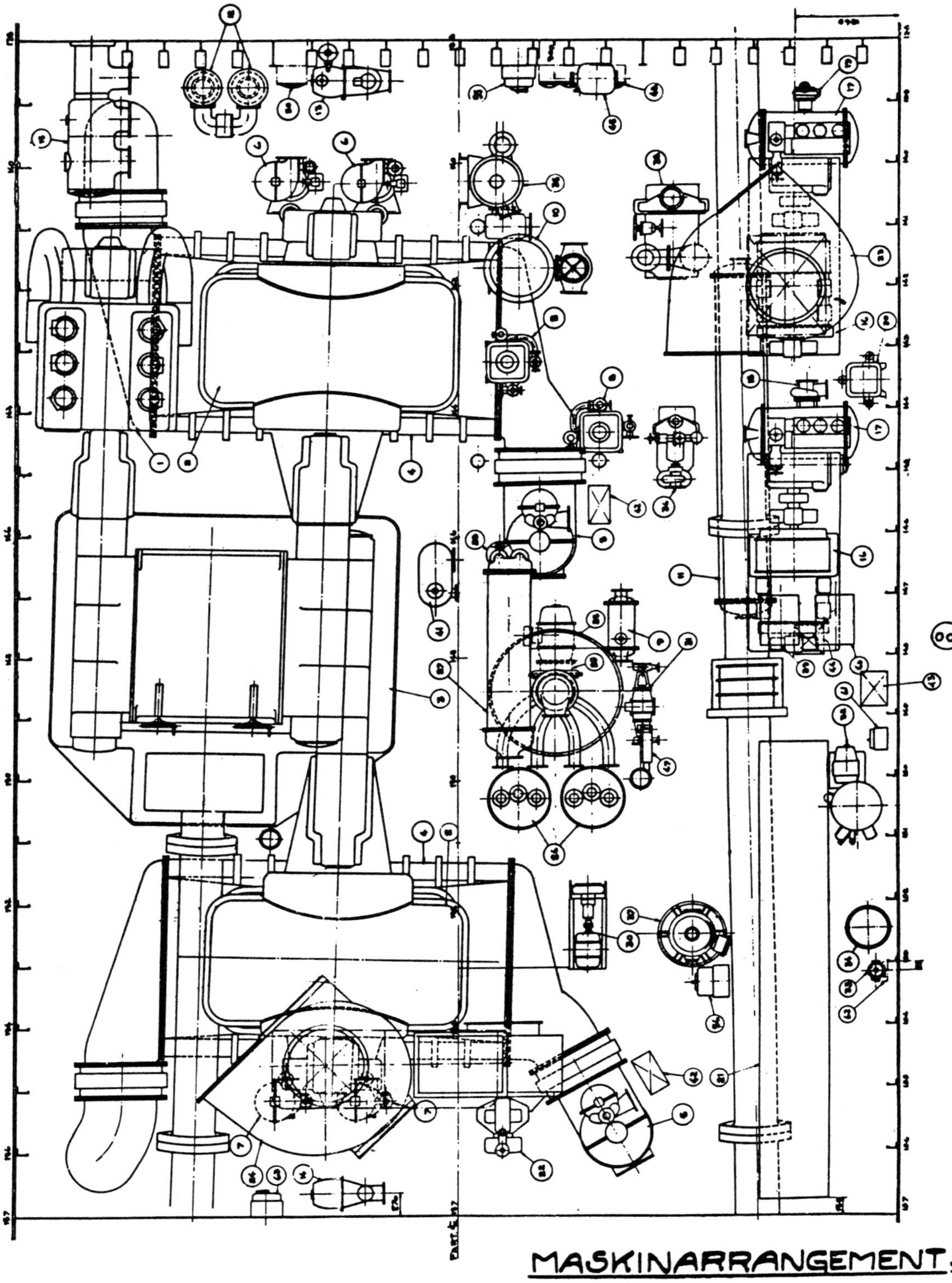


*Drawing showing arrangements of engine room No 2. (*By courtesy of Commodore (E) G Schoerner RSwN ret*).*

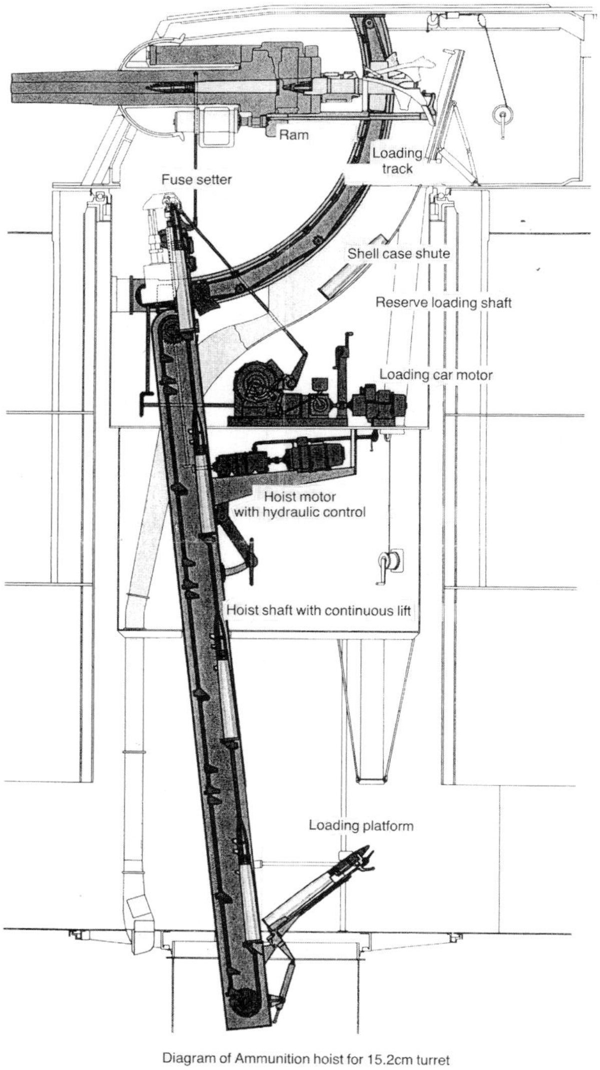


*Diagram of ammunition hoist for 15.2cm turret.* (By courtesy of the Royal Military Records Office, Stockholm).

## *The armament*

The new type of gun turrets for the 15.2cm automatic guns is shown in the accompanying drawing. The gunhouses were mounted on roller bearings on barbettes containing the machinery for training the turrets and for the operation of the shell hoists. The diagram shows the hoist in operation from the magazine loading platform to the gun's breach. The design was interesting enough to inspire a British delegation and the gunnery officer of HMS *Birmingham* to visit Bofors in the fall of 1945 to examine the turrets and guns.

The 53cm torpedo tubes were of the standard Swedish trainable type. During the 1950s 40mm AA guns replaced the 20mm weapons and both ships received rocket launchers and mining rails. The vessels could carry 120 mines.

Götaverken launched *Tre Kronor* on 16 December 1944; Crown Princess Louise (later Queen Louise) was the ship's godmother. The name ('Three Crowns') denotes the three Kingdoms, Skåne, Gotland and Svea, that make up Sweden. Eriksbergs launched *Göta Lejon* on 17 November 1945, with Crown Prince Gustaf Adolph (later King Gustaf VI) present at the ceremonies. Both ships were ready for sea trials in the second half of 1947.

Thus the Swedish Navy obtained two fine ships although not those it held to be ideal to meet its defence tasks. The politicians were successful in preventing any crisis with Germany over the ownership of the Bofors turrets and in strengthening Sweden's naval defences.

## *Tactical deployment*

The 1941 plans envisaged the naval forces operating in the dark hours. Destroyers and motor torpedo-boats were to be in the front line supported by the cruisers' guns. The navy held that the 15.2cm automatic guns were suitable for night actions, but the defence staff believed torpedoes and aircraft would replace heavy artillery as the principal weapons at sea. In addition, more resources including fighter aircraft would be needed for the protection of surface ships. The Chief of the Naval Staff's tactical review of 1941 maintained that the fleet should continue to have a 'main' force of armoured coastal defence ships, but proposed an aggressive advance task force. This task force was to comprise three groups, each consisting of one large cruiser, four destroyers and six large motor torpedo-boats. *Göta Lejon* and *Tre Kronor* were to head two groups; the proposal was for the construction of a third cruiser for the third group, but it was never realized. Incidentally, the head of the Naval Materiel Administration, Admiral S H Ericson, preferred the construction of large destroyers: he was convinced that the two cruisers were too large for operations in the Baltic, having regard to air power. Eventually the Crown ordered the construction of the two 2000-ton destroyers *Uppland* and *Öland* instead of a third cruiser.

## *Careers*

The Swedish Navy realised at the end of 1945 that it needed assistance from the American and British navies to enable it to meet the challenges of the electronic age. At the end of 1945, it approached the Royal Navy for radar equipment and arranged for Swedish naval personnel to undergo training in British naval establishments. In addition, in 1949, through Admiral Lord Mountbatten, Admiral Stig Ericson, head of the Naval Materiel Administration, and one or two other officers were able to join HMS *Liverpool* in the Mediterranean to see how the radar equipment bought in Britain could be used in operations.

During the years 1950–1960, only in 1951 were both cruisers in commission simultaneously. Both received radar equipment in 1947 and during the years 1951–52, both ships went into major refits at the Karlskrona royal dockyard for the rebuilding of the bridge complexes to reflect British experiences from the Second World War.

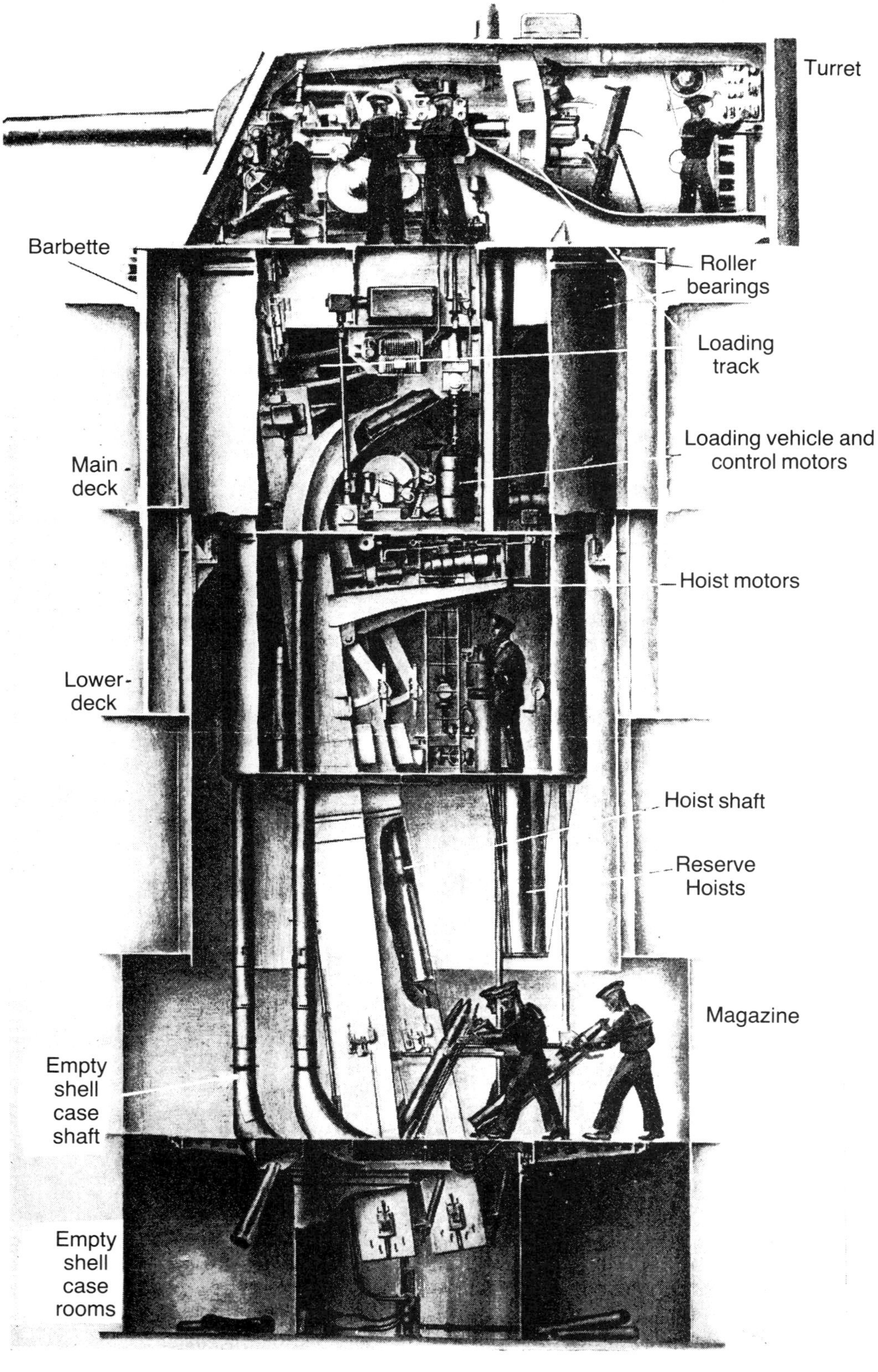


*Diagram of 15.2cm turret of cruisers* Tre Kronor *and* Göta Lejon.

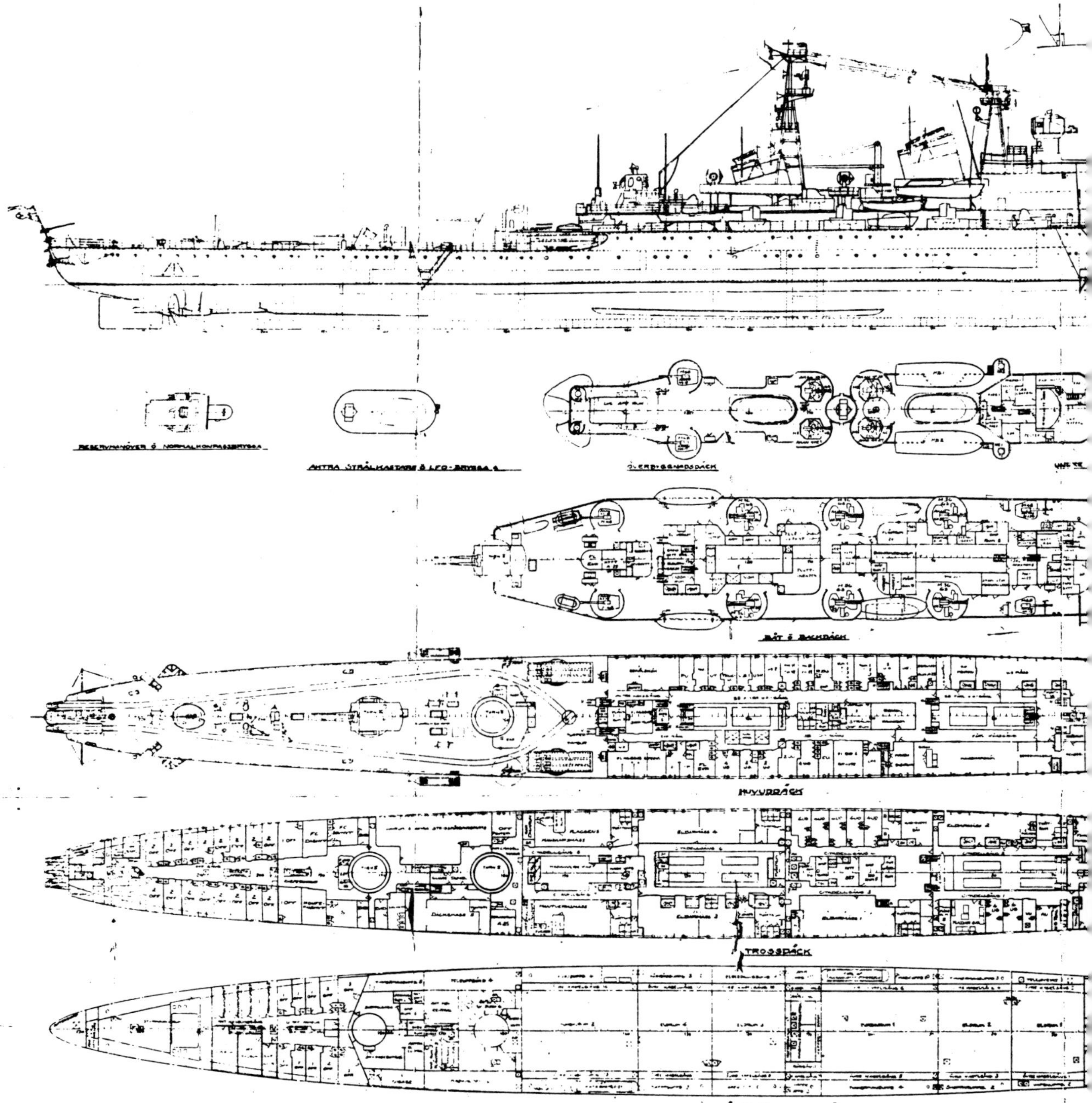
HUVUDDÄCK
TROSSDÄCK
ÖVRE PLATTFORMDÄCK
UNDRE PLATTFORMDÄCK

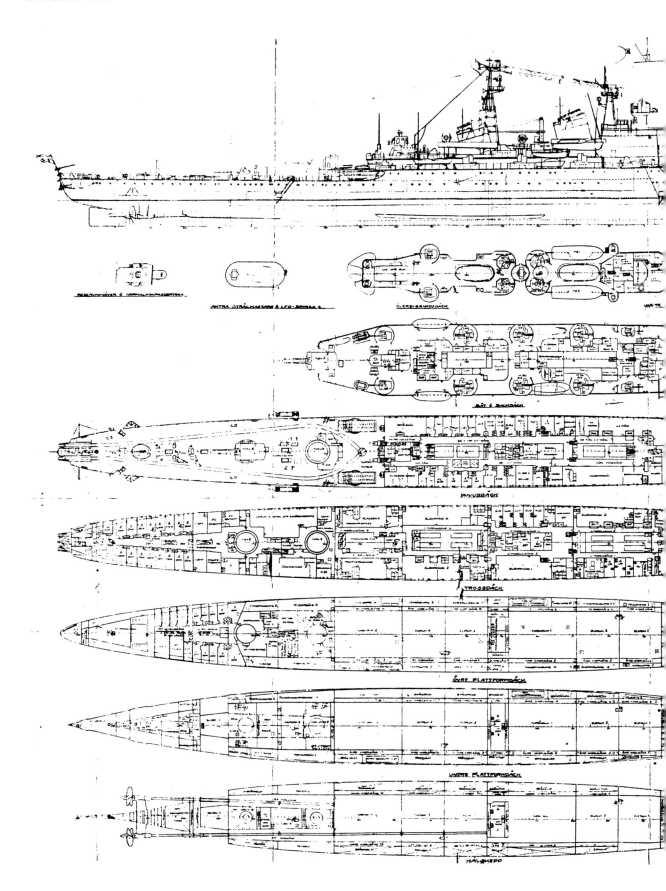

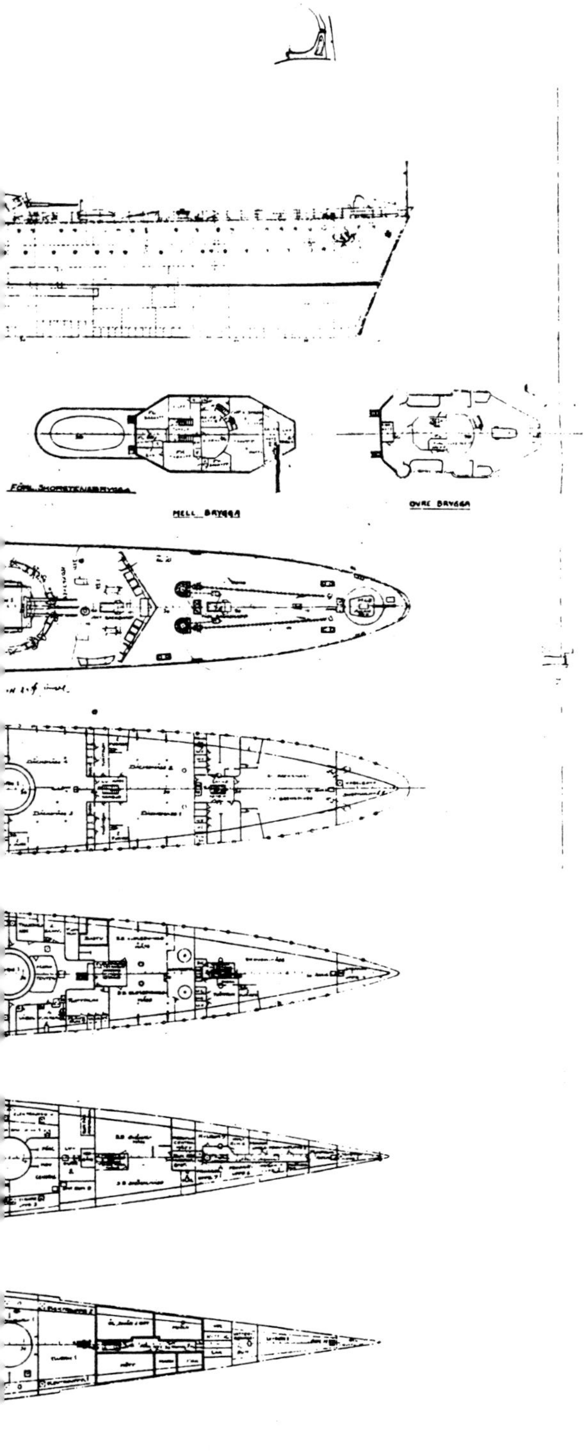

*Plan of cruiser* Göta Lejon *after reconstruction of bridge 1951–52, and installation of rocket flare launching equipment. (*By courtesy of the Sjöhistoriska Museet, Stockholm*).*

In 1950, *Tre Kronor* escorted by two destroyers made a voyage to Thorshavn, Faroe Islands, to take part in the opening ceremonies of the new legislature. She carried the Swedish parliament's gift of books, and the speakers of the Upper and Lower houses. In May 1951, both cruisers, now fitted with fire control equipment as a result of British assistance, together with four destroyers, six submarines and the depot ship *Patricia*, made an official visit, under Admiral Ericson's command, to the British Navy at Rosyth and London. The visit's purpose was to thank the Royal Navy for its cooperation in arranging for training of Swedish naval personnel in the use of radar and in anti-submarine warfare. In addition, Ericson was to deliver King Gustaf VI's letter to King George VI appointing him an honorary Admiral in the Swedish Navy.

The British Commander-in-Chief, Home Fleet, Admiral Vian, suggested that Ericson inspect HMS *Indomitable* and he inspect *Göta Lejon*. Vian was surprised to find the Swedish personnel so fluent in English.

In 1953 *Göta Lejon* took part in Queen Elizabeth II's coronation review at Spithead. At the review, the arrangements were for each nation's ship to leave in a planned order – the British first, followed by the USS *Baltimore, Göta Lejon* and the Soviet cruiser *Sverdlov*. The latter on reaching open waters increased speed to try to overtake *Göta Lejon*. The Swedish ship increased its speed to 28–30kts to maintain a separation of about 7000m. The Russian did not succeed in catching up with *Göta Lejon* during passage to the Kattegatt.

The ships were commissioned in the late 1950s and early 1960s but never after 1951, together in the same year. *Göta Lejon* made a visit to Riga during that period. The rumour was that she and her escorting destroyers were followed by a submerged Russian submarine across the Baltic.

Ericson became the Navy's Commander-in-Chief in 1954, a position he was to hold until the 1960s. He writes about the problems of the cruisers in his memoirs. The navy came to the conclusion that the Baltic was too small an area for 8000-ton cruisers, since the ships became prime targets for aircraft. There were three alternatives: keep them in materiel reserve; sell them to South American republics; or use them in the defence of Sweden's west coast. The last alternative was reasonable – the two ships could be held in reserve on the west coast, and be available not only locally, but also for the defence of Norway's west and north coasts in the event of Soviet attacks on Scandinavia. Both ships would require additional protection against guided missiles, additional AA guns, and heavier hull bottom protection. The costs of the latter were deemed too high and would absorb too much of the repair budget.

Early in the 1960s, it became clear that *Tre Kronor* would require new boilers. It seems that the navy was faced with the alternatives of reboilering *Tre Kronor*, or reducing expenditures on lighter craft more suitable for the Baltic. The result was that *Tre Kronor* was sold to Götaverken for scrap for a paltry sum in 1964; *Göta Lejon* was laid up in the Royal Dockyard, Karlskrona.

In the late 1960s various attempts to sell *Göta Lejon* failed. In 1971 Chile, which had lost the service of an

## Tre Kronor class
### *TECHNICAL SPECIFICATION*

#### *CONSTRUCTION*

| | |
|---|---|
| Builders – *Tre Kronor* | Götaverken, Göteborg |
| *Göta Lejon* | Eriksbergs, Göteborg |
| Final Authorization | May 1942 |
| Contracts signed | February 1943 |
| Laid Down | Fall of 1943 |
| Launched – *Tre Kronor* | 16 December 1944 |
| *Göta Lejon* | 17 November 1945 |

#### *DESIGN DATA*

| | |
|---|---|
| Displacement (standard) | 8200 tons |
| Length overall | 180.150m (590ft) |
| Max beam | 16.5m (54ft 2in) |
| Max draught | 5.7m (18ft 8in) |
| Design speed | 33kts |

#### *ARMAMENT*

Seven 15.2cm (6in) guns in one triple and two twin turrets
Twelve 40mm gyro stabilized automatic guns in six twin mountings
Eight 40mm manually stabilized automatic guns in four twin mountings
Nine 20mm automatic guns (replaced by seven 40mm guns)
Two depth charge throwers
Two depth charge releases
Six 53cm (21in) torpedo tubes in two triple mountings
Four rocket launchers
Mining rails – 120 mines.

#### *ARMOUR*

Main deck – upper strake 20mm
Main deck between fore and after turrets 30mm
Lower deck 20mm above magazines 30mm
20mm above fuel tanks
40mm above steering gear
Waterline 70mm
Conning tower 60mm

#### *ENGINES*

Boilers: 4 oil-fired water tube boilers
Engines: De Laval turbines = 70,000shp
Propellers: two, diameter 4570mm, weight 13 tons each

#### *COMPLEMENT*

Officers 37
Other ranks 563

#### *COST*

74,000,000 Kronor each

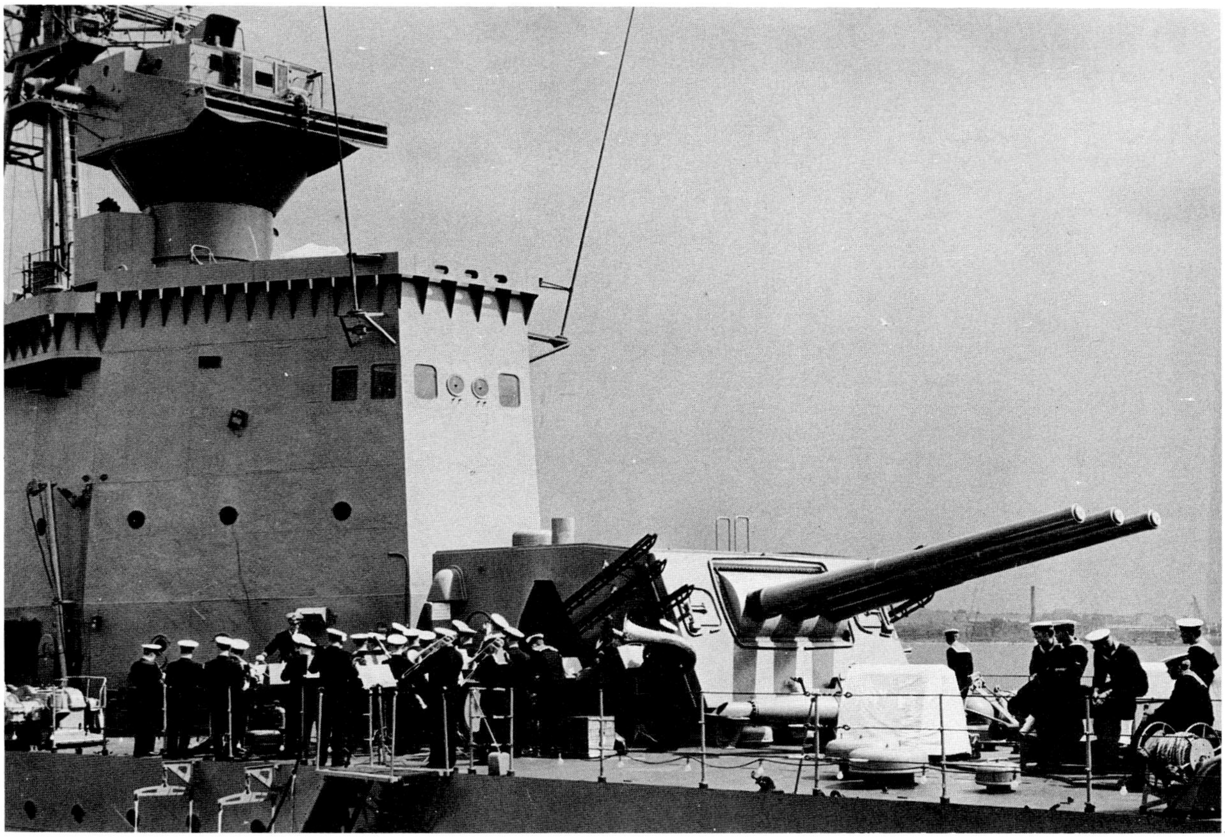

Tre Kronor *1958: view of new bridge complex completed 1951–52.*

ex-American cruiser, and was having some difficulties with the Argentine, began searching for a replacement. President Allende, then a social democrat, was interested in acquiring *Göta Lejon*. In March 1971, the Swedish government authorised the navy to begin negotiations with Chile's naval purchasing office in London. In April, a Chilean delegation examined the vessel, and on 15 July, President Allende issued a letter of intent to buy the ship, ammunition and spares for 45 million Kronor ($11 million). Both parties signed the sales contract. On 25 August, Captain Carlos Borrowman arrived to take comand of *Göta Lejon*, which was to be renamed *Almirante Latorre*.

Before taking over, the Chileans required extensions to be made to the ship's bakery because the crew expected to be supplied daily with fresh bread. The Chilean transport with 300 men arrived at Karlskrona in early September, and the flag transfer took place on 18 September. Some six Swedish officers were to train the crew, and accompany the ship to Valparaiso. The planned departure date was the beginning of December 1971, but as the Chilean authorities were slow in paying for supplies, the ship did not leave until 9 December 1971.

The ship passed through the Kiel canal on her way to the North Sea. The inexperienced Chilean engine room staff seemed to have had difficulties with firing, and successfully covered Kiel with vast volumes of heavy black smoke. Apparently, the Chilean officers of the watch called for the Swedish instructors' aid when the navigational radar screen showed some forty or so 'blips' in the English Channel – the Chileans were more accustomed to meeting a half dozen or so vessels in the Pacific. *Almirante Latorre* arrived at Valparaiso on 14 January 1972 after a passage through the Panama Canal to the Pacific.

In 1973, at the time of the revolt against President Allende, the insurgents tried to obtain the support of the cruiser's crew. They believed the Bofors automatic 15.2cm guns could reach Valparaiso, but since Chilean maintenance was poor, this was unlikely. Chile only made the final payment for *Göta Lejon* in July 1983. Two years later the hulk of the cruiser, according to the Canadian naval architects German and Milne of Ottawa, was still lying in the Valparaiso Naval Yard.

## Conclusion

*Tre Kronor* and *Göta Lejon* were the results of political expediency in 1940 and 1941 rather than the real needs of the Swedish Navy during the Second World War. The ships were well built, and their armament was revolutionary. They were no doubt useful to Sweden's defences from 1948 to the mid 1960s in the early years of the Cold War, but one is bound to wonder whether the money might not have been better spent elsewhere.

## Notes

[1] The acquisition of the two small Italian 'torpedo-boats' (destroyers) *Remus* and *Romulus* included the construction drawings. The Naval Materiel Administration examined the drawings and found the designs to be of no value. Northern climatic conditions, and accommodation acceptable to Swedish petty officers and rating would require major changes to this type of ship's interior.

The Swedish defence department purchased the following aircraft from Italy: 84 Caproni Ca 313 bombers; 72 Fiat CR 42 fighters; 60 Reggianne 2000 Falco fighters. The Italian aircraft were of poor quality, and killed many Swedish pilots. Some 200 railroad freight cars brought other war material including mines and torpedoes over the German/Danish railroads to Sweden.

[2] The Swedish constructors discovered that the Italian cruiser *Attilio Regolo* was able to attain the speed of 41kts when carrying no normal loads of ammunition, fuel, stores, and crew. Source: Captain (E) I Hult's papers.

[3] The Ansaldo drawings for the proposed armoured coastal defence ships are held at the Royal Military Records Office, Stockholm.

[4] Comparison of Dutch *Kijkduin* class with *Tre Kronor*

| | *Kijkduin class* (as planned) | *Tre Kronor class* (as planned) |
|---|---|---|
| *Standard displacement* | 8350 tons | 7500 tons |
| *Guns* | Ten 15cm | Six 15cm |
| | Twelve 40mm | Twelve 40mm |
| | Eight 12mm | Eight 20mm |
| *Torpedo tubes* | Six 53cm (triple) | Six 53cm (triple) |
| *Aircraft* | Two | — |
| *Armour, side* | ? | 60mm |
| | | 20mm |
| | Lower deck | 30mm |
| *Speed* | 32.5kts | 33kts |
| *Shp* | 78,000 | 70,000 |
| *Radius of action* | ? | 2500nm at 15kts |

Source: Hult's papers.

[5] In 1942 the Swedish Navy's Chief of Staff, Admiral Strömback requested the British naval attachés to support applications to the American Board of Economic Warfare and The British Ministry of Economic Warfare for the release of molybdenum for the armour plate. The Ministry and the Admiralty replied they would consider the request, in return for an analysis of the steel. Strömback replied he could not give away trade secrets so the matter was dropped. Sweden was able to get some molybdenum from Norway, and a small mine in northern Sweden. Source: D Harris.

[6] The Italians, led by Professor Bagianni and engineer Calossi, were developing a torpedo pistol that operated on the magnetic field of the target and exploded the torpedo under the ship's bottom. Early in 1942, the Swedish L M Ericsson Company discovered the activity in its Naples factory. It obtained details of the torpedo pistol, and gave these to the British Assistant Naval Attaché in Stockholm. After the fall of Italy, Calossi was spirited away from the Genoa area by an allied submarine and given employment by the American General Electric Company. Later, Bagianni was picked up by the American Army in Naples. Source: D Harris.

[7] A former employee of Götaverken believed the armour belt was 50mm and not 70mm as specified. Source: Captain (E) C Borgenstam RSwN (ret).

[8] Vessels operating in the Baltic and Baltic approaches because of ice, usually exchange bronze for steel propellers at the beginning of the winter season.

## Sources

*Naval Policies 1914–1942*

PUBLISHED

A Berge, *Forum Navale* 43 (Stockholm 1987).

G Hägglöt, *Samtida Vittne* (Stockholm 1972).

J Olofsson, *Forum Navale* 40 (Stockholm 1984).

S Ericson, *Knoppor på logglinan* (Stockholm 1966).

F Wedin, *Admiralitets Kollegiets Historia*, Vol V (Stockholm 1983).

*New Proposals*

UNPUBLISHED

I Hult, Captain (E) report to Admiral (E) Quistgaard (6 May 1942).

I Hult, Presentation to Minister of Defence (dated 2 September 1940).

I Hult, Memo (3 September 1940).

*The Italian Connection*

PUBLISHED

K Olsson, *Creation of a Modern Arms Industry* (Göteborg 1977).

F Wedin, *Admiralitets Kollegiets Historia*, Vol V (Stockholm 1983)

O Hammargren, *Vapen Köp i krig* (Stockholm 1960) covers the activities but is too concerned with self justification.

UNPUBLISHED

I Hult, Journals Series O II Vol 6a (cover period 1940–42./ Daily entries).

I Hult, Report to Admiral (E) Quistgaard (5 November 1942).

*Construction*

PUBLISHED

K Olsson, 'Forsvaret tillsjöss', *Forum Navale* 40 (Stockholm 1984).

K Olsson, *Creation of a Modern Arms Industry* (Göteborg 1977).

F Wedin, *Admiralitets Kollegiets Historia*, Vol V (Stockholm 1983).

UNPUBLISHED

C Borgenstam, *Svenska Kryssarer* (1990)

Commodore (E) G Schoerner RSwN (ret) supplied all the information concerning the ships' machinery, armour and hull construction.

*Tactical Use*

PUBLISHED

S Ericson, *Knoppar på logglinan* (Stockholm 1966).

J Olofsson, 'Forsvaret tillsjäss' *Forum Navale* 40 (Stockholm 1984).

F Wedin, *Admiralitets Kollegiets Historia* Vol V (Stockholm 1983).

*Careers*

PUBLISHED

S Ericson, *Knoppar på logglinan* (Stockholm 1966).

S Ericson, *Kuling längs Kusten* (Stockholm 1968).

*Aktuellt*, Marin Museum Karlskrona (1988)

T Olofsson, 'Forsvaret tillsjöss' *Forum Navale* 40 (Stockholm 1984).

# ALBACORE – THE SHAPE OF THE FUTURE

Neither nuclear powered nor offensively armed, USS *Albacore* is nevertheless one of the most important submarines of the postwar era. As the test-bed for virtually every important advance, except nuclear propulsion, she lived up to her motto *Praenuntius Futuri* – 'herald of the future' – and is the true prototype of today's nuclear submarine fleets. Her concept left its mark on submarine design worldwide, perhaps most strongly of all on the Soviet Navy. *Albacore*'s career is still shrouded in mystery, but the most important aspects have been pieced together by Robert P Largess and Harvey S Horwitz.

THE *Albacore* (AGSS-569) is well known as the first wholly streamlined submarine, with her 'teardrop' or 'body of revolution' hull. She was laid down at the Portsmouth Naval Shipyard (PNSY) on 5 March 1952, launched on 1 August 1953, commissioned on 5 December 1953 and began operations as a test vehicle on 5 February 1954. Decommissioned 1 September 1972 she joined the US Navy's mothball fleet at Philadelphia. Preserved today at Portsmouth, New Hampshire, she constitutes a ship memorial of great intrinsic interest. Mounted on concrete cradles in an excavated permanent 'drydock' near the Piscataqua River, her huge whale-shaped hull is completely and dramatically visible.

There, her smoothly curved, black bulk with its huge fins, evokes the image of some great sea creature rather than a ship. And most appropriately so, for she was the first submarine truly designed to use the waters of the sea not merely as a cloak of invisibility, but as her primary medium of operation. From her design stems the modern submarine's ability to manoeuvre like an aircraft in a three-dimensional envelope, a water envelope much more dangerous and less well known, even today, than that of the air.

The earliest American nuclear craft, *Nautilus, Seawolf,* and the *Skate* class, were relatively conservative in design: twin screwed, with extensive external 'casings', free-flooding superstructures and decks, giving them the relatively fine lines and ship-shape the traditional 'submersible' required for good surface performance. They were streamlined only by the removal of sources of turbulence and resistance such as external projections and angular lines.

The teardrop hull of the *Albacore* is streamlined however, in the proper sense that it conforms to the ideal lines of flow of water around a solid body; it offers the least resistance and turbulence of any shape in motion through a water medium. In addition, external projections to spoil this ideal body are eliminated as far as possible: even the small bridge on the sail is covered by a folding plastic fairing while submerged and all cleats and fittings for mooring lines are recessed or retractable. The free-flooding external casing is almost eliminated (the diesel *Albacore* requires a small casing aft of the sail to house mufflers and exhausts). Her original single large screw was mounted on the axis of the ship, at the point of the teardrop, for greatest efficiency. This design was adopted for nuclear submarines with the *Skipjack* class of 1958, upon which the first British nuclear submarine, the *Dreadnought* of 1960, was based.

*Albacore*'s hull was a total success from the moment she first put to sea. Her speed is still classified but often referred to by her operators as 30 or 35kts – double that of any contemporary submarine when she was built – even with her conventional propulsion system. *Albacore* provided the scientists at Washington's David Taylor Model Basin (DTMB) with basic data on the hydrodynamic forces which affect submarines at high speeds and in extreme manoeuvres, establishing the 'flight profiles' which enables the behaviour of subsequent craft to be predicted and controlled under such conditions.

In some respects she surpassed most later craft; one was manoeuvrability, especially the instant response at very low speeds provided by her first stern control surface configuration. Another was automated flexible control.

Albacore *under construction showing her 'Phase I' stern with control surfaces aft of the single large screw. This configuration gave her remarkable low speed manoeuvrability.* (Portsmouth Submarine Memorial Association)

For the first time motion in all three dimensions was placed in the hands of a single 'pilot' handling an aircraft-type wheel, yoke or 'stick'.

Another feature pioneered was the use of HY-80, a high-tensile, low carbon steel of 80,000psi yield strength. Her maximum depth remains classified: most operators refer to her test depth as 600ft (one CO, however, describes taking her to considerably greater depths). Greater diving depth is advantageous not only for eluding pursuit, but also for exploiting *Albacore*'s three dimensional manoeuvrability. HY-80 did present constructional difficulties: the *Skipjack*s and early British nuclear boats which used it next experienced numerous hairline cracks in hull welds, causing much worry.

Nevertheless, her limitations in depth were the chief sources of danger in operating *Albacore*. There was always the fear that some human error or material casualty, such as loss of hydraulic power to her controls while *Albacore* was in a high speed dive, could send her below her crush depth. As her seventh CO, Captain Bill St Lawrence, put it, it was like flying an aircraft at 600ft – very little room for error. Thus there was constant interest in various forms of 'dive brakes' to enable emergency recovery from an out-of-control dive. Also training in radical manoeuvres was conducted at 2kt increments and often in areas where the sea bottom lay between her test and crush depths, giving her crew a chance of survival should she go out of control.

During her nineteen years of service *Albacore* provided the basic scientific understanding of hydrodynamics necessary to control a submarine at high speed. She also was used to study underwater acoustics and the nature of the submarine's characteristic radiated noise over this entire period. She tested numerous design features incorporated into the nuclear fleet, including: the standard cruciform stern control surfaces; one-man 'single stick' control and its requisite instrumentation; sound-dampening measures such as 'raft' mountings for machinery and internal plastic ballast tank coatings; bow-mounted and towed sonars; advanced high pressure air and hydraulic systems; and an emergency ballast blow system operable at great depths. Many other features, some successful and some not, were tested but never adopted, including her initial cruciform stern with large control surfaces aft of the propeller, her X-shaped stern, a unique dorsal rudder, counter rotating props, a powerful silver-zinc battery based on advanced chemistry, viscous polymer fluid coatings to improve laminar flow, and various systems of dive brake including a drag parachute from a B-47 bomber and a circumferential ring of flaps. Never before or since has the US Navy possessed a pure test vehicle with a performance better than the most advanced attack submarines freed from restrictions on her use for wide-ranging research and experiment by her lack of combat capability – or of nuclear power, which removed her from the rigid and generally very conservative authority of Admiral Rickover.

Yet conversations with her operators reveal a deep sense of ambivalence. On the one hand, she represented a profound advance, yielded a tremendous body of scientific knowledge, and proved out many technical items of great value. On the other hand, there is the frequent complaint that 'no one was paying any attention to us', the sense that the true potential demonstrated by *Albacore* was wasted.

Albacore *under way early in her career. Note Phase I stern, bow planes and other early features.* (Authors' collection)

*Comparison of Phase I* Albacore *with contemporary US craft. The short, beamy AGSS-569 is very close in displacement to the finer-lined 'Guppies' and* Tangs. (PSMA)

Yet many have stated that service aboard her was the highest point of their careers. Many of her CO's were plainly ardent submariners fascinated by the unique potential of *Albacore*, stimulated by the challenge and independence of pure research into the nature of the submarine and her environment in co-operation with scientists, particularly those from DTMB, which initiated not only the research that led to her design but also many of her programmes of experiment and testing. They worked in close co-operation with the captain and crew whose task was to find ways to make the ship provide the desired information, with no one in the naval chain of command looking over their shoulders. As Captain St Lawrence put it: 'It was the closest thing to being John Paul Jones. They gave me a ship, gave me a crew, and told me to get the job done. It was a heady experience for a thirty-three year old man.'

## *Origins of the Albacore*

According to Captain Frank Andrews, submarine project officer at DTMB 1953–4, the concept of a submarine designed for maximum submerged performance was first proposed in 1948 by the Undersea Warfare Committee (UWC) of the National Academy of Science, a very influential body which initiated a number of crucial lines of research. The development of SOSUS, the oceanic system of sea bottom fixed sonar arrays able to detect submarines passively at great distances was first urged in 1949 by the UWC. Their 1948 recommendations included the 'body of revolution' hull, single screw and use of HY-80 steel. The 'Series 58' studies by DTMB took as their starting point the form of the British airship *R-101* of 1929 (itself the product of much original research). This provided the basis for the hull design, which was produced by the Stevens Institute in New Jersey and tested at length in DTMB towing tanks and Langley Air Force Base wind tunnel in 1949. Many individuals attribute a major role in convincing the Navy to proceed with *Albacore* to Vice-Admiral Charles B Momsen, inventor of the 'Momsen Lung' escape apparatus, appointed Assistant Chief of Naval Operations for Undersea Warfare in 1948.

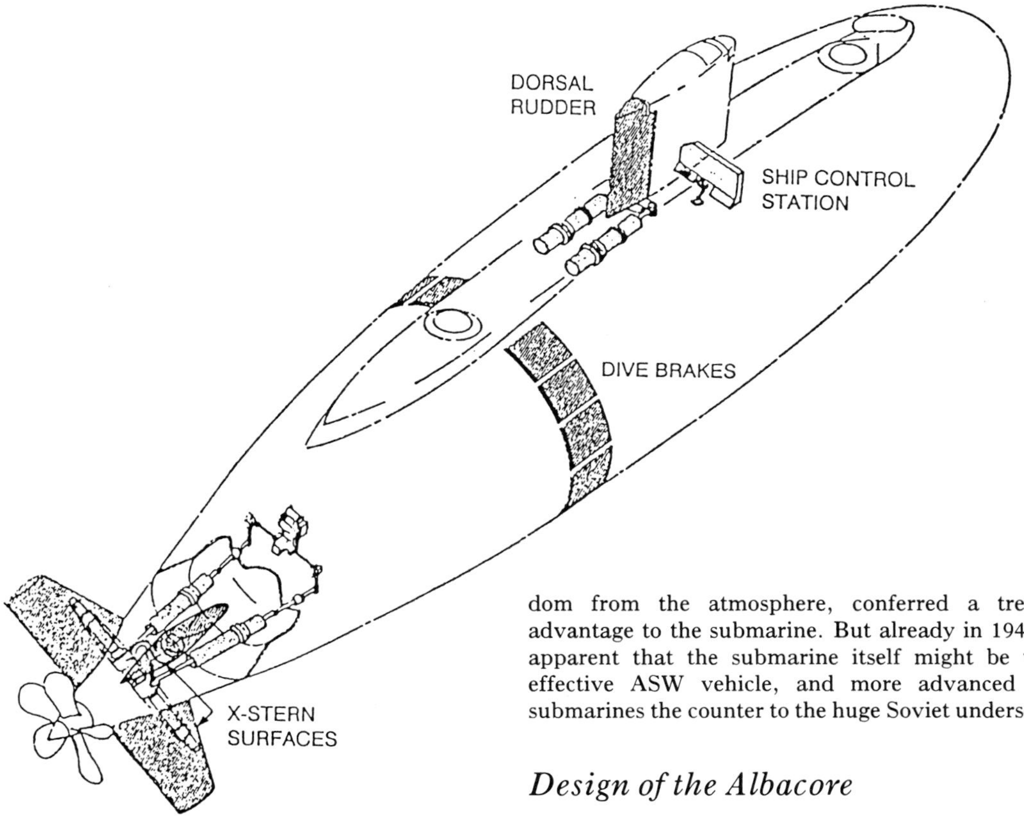


'Albacore *Design*'. (From Allmendinger and Jackson)

Resistance to the 'pure submarine' concept was substantial. It seemed in flat contradiction to the USN's experience in the Second World War, when US 'fleet' boats carried the conventional 'submersible' to a very effective level. They were large with a very high surface speed, powerful gun and torpedo armaments, along with radar and sonar far superior to the Japanese. Indeed, they were able to pursue on the surface major Japanese warships with strong escorts – such as the carrier *Shinano*. Resistance to the UWC's recommendations led to the compromise by which *Albacore* would be built as a test vehicle only, of reduced size. (This same conservative distrust of many of *Albacore*'s radical features persisted – for example the adoption of the single screw for nuclear submarines was strenuously opposed for reasons of safety, until *Albacore*'s superlative performance overrode all doubts.)

Meanwhile, the German Type XXI U-boat had indicated the potential of advanced underwater performance. With the snorkel, high battery capacity, and 17.5kts submerged speed, she wiped out at a stroke the laboriously achieved allied ASW superiority. Type XXIs were incorporated into the Soviet navy and copied in its numerous 'Whiskey' class. The submarine became the cornerstone of Soviet postwar naval strategy, initiating a technological 'cold war' between submarine and ASW which still continues. Certainly nuclear power, giving tremendous speed and endurance and almost total freedom from the atmosphere, conferred a tremendous advantage to the submarine. But already in 1948, it was apparent that the submarine itself might be the most effective ASW vehicle, and more advanced Western submarines the counter to the huge Soviet undersea fleet.

## *Design of the Albacore*

At 1692 tons, 205ft length, 27ft beam, *Albacore* is dwarfed by most nuclear submarines but quite moderate-sized for a conventional one. Originally she was intended to be a much smaller craft, leaving port daily with her cadre of scientists and a very small crew. She had to be enlarged when it was realized that the nearest waters sufficiently deep for submerged testing, the Wilkinson Deep, were far enough from PNSY to necessitate operating on a basis of weekly cruises, and thus adequate berthing and galley space for a crew of 5 officers, 52 men and 7 scientists had to be accommodated.

Her pressure hull is HY-80 low carbon high-tensile steel of 80,000psi yield stength. Her framing is conventional 50,000psi high tensile steel. Originally, double hulled throughout, the aftermost 20 per cent is single hulled, with internal framing. She received a new stern (and lost a ballast tank) along with her contra-rotating props and second electric motor in her 1962–5 'Phase IV' overhaul.

She is the first submarine to mount her sonar in bow tanks, the position usually occupied by torpedo tubes, which *Albacore* never carried. This feature was repeated in the *Tullibee*, then the *Thresher* class and all following US nuclear boats, which now carry their torpedo rooms behind the bow sonar, with tubes angled outwards to clear it.

Otherwise she is quite conventional internally. Externally she has been altered radically several times, with total replacement of her stern, bow, and control surfaces. The one feature never substantially altered was her hull form itself, a total success from the first moment she put to sea, the key not only to her speed but also her manoeuvra-

Albacore *surfacing at high speed early in her career; note JT sonar dome.* (Russell Van Billiard)

bility. As Captain Andrews has pointed out, this was dependent on her possession of inherent dynamic stability. She has a minimum of surfaces (essentially only her sail) creating unbalanced hydrodynamic effects tending to throw her out of control at high speeds. For example, the US 'Guppy' boats (streamlined conversions of Second World War craft) proved very difficult to control in high speed dives due to their large flat deck areas; the angle of the dive would continue to increase in spite of reversal of the diving planes, as the deck itself acted as a huge diving plane. Not only does *Albacore* lack such surfaces but her large stern fins act as feathers on an arrow, returning her to a stable course when placed in a neutral position.

The eternal weak spot of the *Albacore* was her surface performance. Because of the downward curvature of the bow she tended to push herself under at any speed. According to engineering officer Ronald Heinz, she could do no more than 139revs, 10–12kts, before her bow wave was up to her sail. Lacking any structures to damp rolling such as bilge keels, her crew suffered greatly, even in moderate sea states.

The great weak spot of her design was her novel lightweight General Motors radial or 'pancake' diesels: of 1000hp each, compared to her 7500hp electric motors. This relative lack of power posed its own problems: a full battery charge was good for 8–9 hours of submerged testing but recharging required 18–20 hours during which she could make, perhaps, 5kts. Surfacing with an exhausted battery in a hurricane on one occasion, she began rolling so badly in the heavy seas that she started taking on water through her main diesel air induction at the top of the sail. Unable to submerge or make headway, she came close to being lost. *And this was when the engines were working!*

Developed originally for landing craft, these engines were used in the *Tang* class as well as *Albacore* and plagued both with their breakdowns. Even the *Tang* with four engines often required to be towed in. Captain St Lawrence described *Albacore* losing both engines off Long Island; lacking any suitable padeye, the tow line had to be passed round the sail. Eventually the *Tangs* were re-engined; however, *Albacore* was too small for any other engine. The sixteen diesels from the *Tangs* were stored and provided *Albacore* with a reserve that lasted her entire career.

Her COs often have remarked on their unreliability in emphatic terms: '100 per cent headache'; 'not worth the powder to blow them to hell' – but frequently note the expertise of her engine room crews and their ability to keep them running. Certainly the potential value of such high power density, lightweight engines for small submarines is great. According to Chief Engineman Stan Zajechowski, their small size eased repairs, with only 2–3 men necessary for pulling a piston.

They possessed a major design flaw in that the generator was directly beneath the diesel, with its four banks of four cylinders each. Thus a defect in the seals allowed leaking oil to drop down into the generators and foul them. Zajechowski suggests that most engine crews were simply ignorant of the maintenance required; this was their first experience with a high speed diesel running at 1500rpm versus the 750rpm of the in-line 'Guppy' diesels. Vibration caused problems unless nuts were tightened to torque and lock wired. Maintained 'by the book' he found they performed quite well.

*Albacore* used a novel high pressure hydraulic system pioneered on the *Tang*. It used three pumps in parallel with two pressure mains, the 'main' and 'vital' systems running the length of the sub, with eight accumulators each able to be isolated from the system. According to Prof Eugene Allmendinger and Captain Harry Jackson, this and many other details were based on aircraft technology; 'Many of the concepts were originally developed for the *Spruce Goose* of World War II fame'.

## *Phase I: Speed, manoeuvrability and single-stick control*

After commissioning in December, 1953, her shakedown trials under Lt-Cdr Kenneth Gummerson established her speed in straight runs at a fixed depth. Her Phase I trials under Lt-Cdr Jon Boyes began in February 1955, and lasted until December 1955. During this brief period she revealed her incredible manoeuvrability. Probably no other submarine has possessed such sheer 'dogfighting' ability: diving, climbing and turning at top speed. Captain Ted Davis, her second XO and a skilled 'pilot' says, 'she could out-dive hedgehogs, outrun destroyers, and was a thrill to fly.' Manoeuvres such as diving at 30kts and 30°angles while simultaneously winding in 180° turns were commonplace. Sudden reversals of her controls or power at high speeds to explore the parameters of her behaviour produced heels of over 40° and down angles of 50°. The ship manoeuvred so swiftly that leather hand straps such as are used on buses had to be installed. These manoeuvres were still unnerving to some crew members. Captain Davis says the solution for some was to give them the opportunity to handle the controls, thus making the motions of the ship intelligible; but others never adjusted and had to be transferred.

Her initial stern configuration with very large control surfaces aft of the prop (used in the German Type XVIIB and early John Holland designs) gave her a unique, instant manoeuvrability at low speeds – the forces upon them were multiplied by the thrust of her 11ft propeller. Providing sufficient structural strength for these surfaces, mounted at the end of long, narrow fins, posed a problem. A second drawback was their great sensitivity and lack of stability at high speeds. To prevent over control, aircraft-type 'trim tabs' were added and used for steering control during high speed transits.

She also carried hull-mounted bow planes, unconventional only in that they used the same hydraulic cylinders for control and rigging-in. According to Captain Davis they were little used, valuable only for stability at shallow depths.

Her unique dorsal rudder was intended to counteract heel in high speed turns, and was controlled by the pilot through foot pedals. It imposed great loads on the sail structure and increased resistance as well as adding an additional complication to control and Captain Davis says the tendency was not to use it and accept the heel.

*Albacore*'s implications for ASW were revealed on 4 November 1955, when, with Admiral Arleigh Burke and Lord Mountbatten aboard (and each taking his turn at the controls) she operated off Key West, Florida against destroyers, patrol planes, and blimps. She was simply too fast for current short-ranged sonars to hold a contact on her; her miniscule turning circle meant her pursuing destroyers could never bring their primitive ahead-thrown or over-the-side weapons to bear. Instead she 'sank' her destroyer opponents, closing them at high speed and using her signal flare ejector to simulate vertically launched tactical missilies. Eluding their air support she escaped undetected.

This success depended on her operators and designers surmounting a crucial challenge. Her early trials showed how difficult it was to maintain a stable course at high speed and her behaviour in manoeuvre was not fully understood. Her single-stick control, replacing the traditional four-man diving team of diving officer, helmsman, bow- and stern-planesmen, with one 'pilot' allowed great speed and flexibility of response, but the danger of over control or pilot error was great. *Albacore*, however, was equipped with a fully automated control system, an analog servomechanism. As the craft's behaviour became better understood, this sytem could be programmed to anticipate her characteristic movements, yielding many advantages: less burden on the pilot, quicker reaction time, less control surface motion with consequently less noise and turbulence. This system was based on that newly provided for contemporary navy blimps; her first pilots trained aboard blimps before taking her controls.

At first, however, the system was unusable due to inadequate instrumentation. The first version of a combined instrument panel (CIP) was still flawed but gradually improved. Automatic depth and course control, rate of dive and turn indicators, and an aircraft-type artificial horizon were added.

According to Captain Davis, once it was perfected,

> We seldom used anything but single-stick control at max speed (30 plus kts); we would put about 10° dive on the stern planes for about five seconds and the ship would assume a 30° down angle. We did have rate-of-dive indicators which would tell us the rate at which we were headed down. That information wasn't really critical. What it provided that was *really* important was the increase or decrease in rate-of-dive. When in a 30kt, 30° down angle, changing depth at 30ft per second, it was nice to see the rate come off [decrease] when we pulled back on the stick. Sorta warm fuzzy feeling!

The huge control surfaces created some unusual behaviour: 'On a full rudder, high speed turn, the rudder at first acted like a sea anchor and radically slowed the ship. To prevent the bow from going up, large amounts of stern planes were required to hold it down.' However, the rudder provided an effective dive brake. 'Full rudder could be used in an emergency down angle to slow the ship and create an instantaneous "squat". Just don't leave it on!'

Captain Davis participated in the development of the even more advanced instrumentation used in later subs. However, he notes the tendency of the US submarine service in recent years to ignore single-stick control, automation, and advanced instrumentation in favour of the traditional four-man diving team. He attributes this to an emphasis on safety and tactical concepts which devalue low speed manoeuvrability and quick reaction, relying instead on superiority in quietness and sonar, a trend which began with *Albacore*'s next phase of testing.

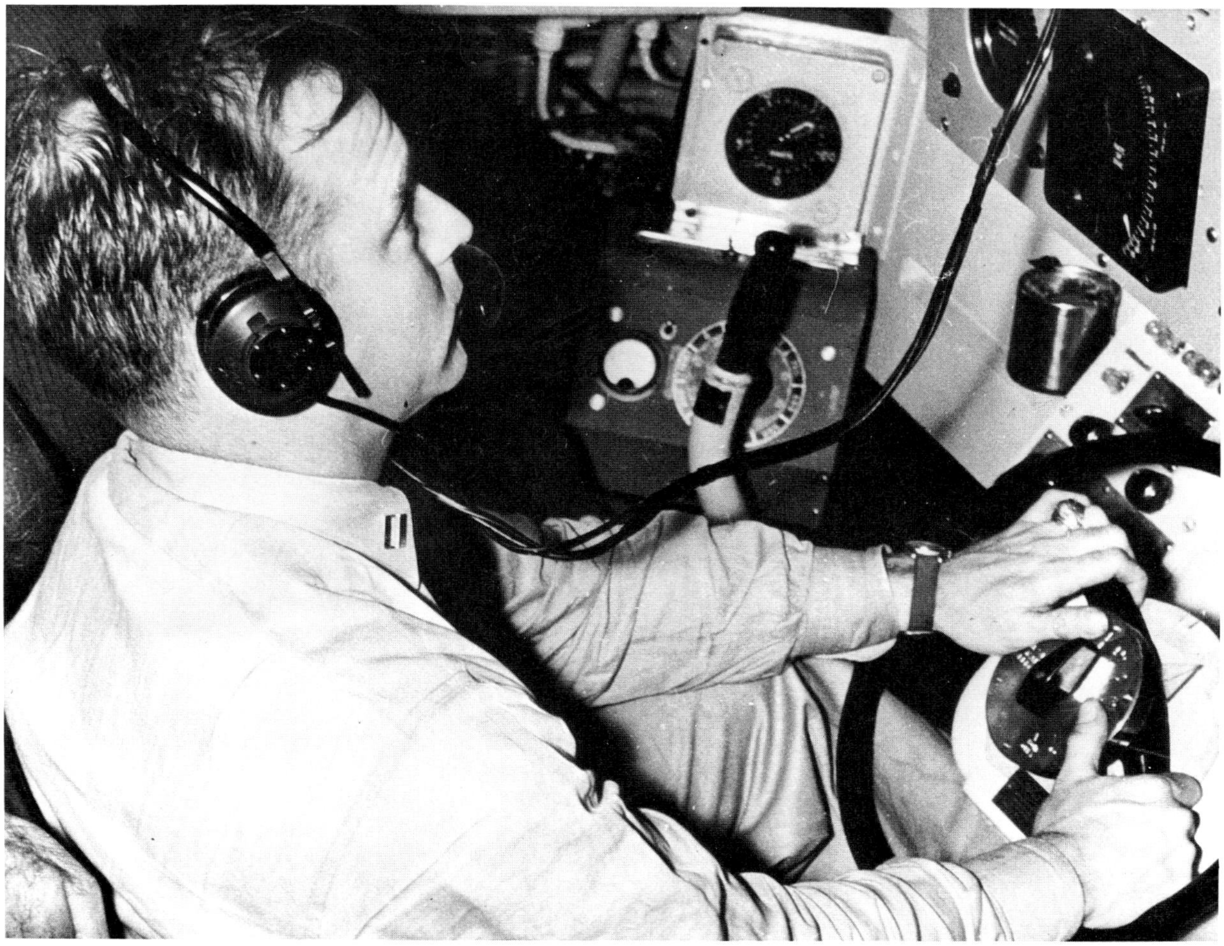

*Lt W J Herndon, XO under Lt-Cdr Kenneth Gummerson, piloting the* Albacore *with her novel one-man 'single-stick' controls during her intial period of trials.* (Authors' collection)

Albacore *during Phase I, showing her first sonar, a troublesome and primitive JT, mounted between her bow planes. Its purpose was to avoid collisions while surfacing.* (Authors' collection)

## *Phase II: Quietness and high speed stability*

*Albacore*'s Phase II conversion, December 1955 to March 1956, gave her the cruciform stern with large fixed areas and control surfaces forward of the screw which was adopted for the *Skipjack*s and practically all subsequent US and British nuclear boats, trading much low speed manoeuvrability for stability at high speed. The dorsal rudder was removed as were the bow planes in 1958.

On her sea trials in March 1959, the *Skipjack*, marrying the teardrop hull to nuclear power for the first time, took away *Albacore*'s record as the world's fastest submarine. According to his biographer, Francis Duncan, Admiral Rickover was initially reluctant to burden his ships with additional innovations and risks. But gradually he was convinced of the value of advanced performance in areas such as speed, depth, and quietness – if not manoeuvrability.

Speed came with the *Skipjack*s. But when Duncan says, 'Beneath the surface the *Skipjack* had behaved like an airplane, banking and rolling as she manoeuvred at high speed', it must be remembered that in this respect she was a step backward from *Albacore*, and within two years the *Thresher*, prototype of the next standard class of attack submarine, abandoned the teardrop hull and superlative speed of the *Skipjack*s for advances in other areas.

Helicopter and missile-carried weapons such as ASROC, and improved sonar ranges from powerful low frequency active sonars and variable depth medium frequency sonars reduced the tactical advantage of high submerged speed. Rather than avoiding attacks, the submarine must avoid detection. Also, not only does the submarine's radiated noise increase with speed but her ability to use her own sonar drops drastically. And the nuclear submarine with her noisy reduction gears for her steam turbines and water-circulation pumps for her reactor, is at a special disadvantage.

*Drawing of* Albacore *showing her cruciform Phase II stern, with control surfaces before the prop, which was adopted for the* Skipjack *and all subsequent US nuclear classes. This design sacrificed low-speed manoeuvrability for high-speed stability.* (PSMA)

The quiet but slow *Tullibee* of 1960 abandoned the teardrop hull; her bulky turbo-electric plant required greater volume towards the stern. The geared-turbine powered *Thresher* apparently required enlarged machinery spaces to accommodate the sound-dampening 'raft' machinery mounts which isolated sources of noise and vibration from the hull and prevented its radiation into the surrounding ocean. *Skipjack*'s bow torpedo tubes were replaced by a large spherical sonar at the bow, as far away as possible from her own machinery.

*Albacore* was the test-bed for these advances spending much of her Phase II testing until November 1960, on the study of submarine self-noise, quieting techniques, and sonar. Touring the *Albacore* today, numerous examples of rubber mountings isolating machinery and piping from the hull are immediately visible. According to Howell Russell, a DTMB scientist involved in these tests over many years, she was constructed without any concern for noise and in effect went from being the Navy's noisiest submarine to the quietest. In addition to resilient mountings, a water-based plastic 'Aquaplas' was used to coat the interior surfaces of all free-flooding areas such as ballast tanks, absorbing vibration and dampening water flow noises; ½in to ¾in thick, Aquaplas did not bond well to metal surfaces and has since been replaced by other substances. Hydrodynamic noise was reduced by recessing projections such as cleats or making hatches flush with the outer hull, and removing the bow planes. Possibly the 14ft screw fitted in 1959 was to reduce noise, requiring less revolutions to create the same thrust as her standard 11ft prop.

Typically, equipment in areas not under development was secondhand and inferior. Captain Davis says her original sonar was a JT from an old submarine, necessary to prevent collision when surfacing. 'More hours, hate, and discontent were devoted to that damn thing than all other troubles combined.'

During Phase I she was the first submarine to stream a towed hydrophone, from her sail. A simple affair, the first sounds it picked up were gunshots from a John Wayne movie being shown in the crew's quarters. According to radioman Ron Poloske, she towed a sonar alongside in 1959 to measure self-noise. It was streamed from a 20ft hinged outrigger mounted directly before the sail. From

Albacore *in drydock at PNSY undergoing her Phase III conversion. Her earlier cruciform stern has been removed and is about to be replaced with her single-hulled stern with its novel X-shaped control surfaces.* (Authors' collection)

January to November 1960 she tested an unusual concave bow sonar dome for DTMB. She was also the first sub to possess a conformal fibreglass bow sonar dome, the object being to place her sonar as far away from her own noise sources as possible. A cast was taken of her steel bow and used to create an exact duplicate. Then a 6ft section of the bow was cut off and replaced with the fibreglass copy, with an early model sonar placed in the storage tanks behind.

## *Phase III: The X-stern*

After Phase II, *Albacore* tested a number of features which, regardless of their potential, were not adopted for nuclear submarine design. One was the 'X' stern (which she still retains), which restored her fantastic manoeuvrability, especially at high speeds. It consists of four long narrow, completely moveable fins with no fixed surfaces.

With the cruciform stern, the lower vertical fin could not be longer than the radius of the hull, or it would contact the bottom before the keel, making drydocking very tricky. With the X pattern the two lower fins could be considerably longer. Also, all four fins could act as rudders, diving planes or both at the same time. It gave her a tremendously tight high-speed turning circle but according to Captain St Lawrence, created some serious control problems.

With the Phase I stern it was predicted that as she heeled, rudder angle would in effect become to some extent a diving plane angle, but this apparently was not a problem in service. But with the X-stern, this phenomenon had serious effects. High speed turns would create a sudden, sharp heel of up to 40°. As Captain St Lawrence describes it, left 10° rudder at 25kts would initiate this 'snap roll' to the left at which point the 10° 'rudder' angle would partially become a 'dive plane' angle, and an immediate adjustment was required to keep her at a stable depth.

Althought they possessed an analog system to compute these effects, her operators really had to learn them by experience and know them thoroughly to control her. This required extensive tests at every speed and rudder angle. One surprise was that there was absolutely no control going astern. When this was first tried submerged, depth control simply disappeared and was only restored by quickly going ahead flank.

Captain St Lawrence says there were many such incidents, 'and they were all hairy'. *Albacore* was repeatedly taken to the limits of control to learn her behaviour under such conditions. He describes backing her at 1/3 at 100ft, and when it appeared she was under control, ringing up 2/3, which suddenly caused her to rotate and assume a 45° up angle.

Even worse was her behaviour on the surface: 'It was impossible to dock the ship'. She had no control backing down – half of her control surfaces were out of the water – and the long thin fins made her very tender.

An enlarged dorsal rudder was restored to counter the 'snap roll'. Captain St Lawrence says it was very effective but notes it was quite large in relation to *Albacore*'s size and would have less effect on a larger boat.

The X-stern was considered for the high speed *Los Angeles* class but the decision was made for safety and stability over manoeuvrability and the Phase II cruciform was retained. It has since been adopted for the Dutch *Walrus* class and Swedish Kockums designs.

But more than ever the need for an emergency means to arrest an out-of-control dive was plain. A circumferential ring of 'dive brakes', ten hydraulically extended flaps, were sited just forward of her aft escape hatch. Lt-Cdr John McCarthy recalls that on their first test they sent the ship out of control in a shallow dive and she hit bottom at 300ft, off the Isle of Shoals, denting her bow. Later that day reports that she had 'sunk' originating with PNSY workers, caused a panic among *Albacore*'s wives and families.

Ronald Heinz, *Albacore*'s engineering officer, says the brakes were too far back on the hull, behind her point of maximum diameter, and thus did not extend beyond the boundary layer and so were ineffective for dive control. They were used mainly to create turbulence and thus noise for acoustic tests, but still caused problems. The last time they were used, they were cycled full open at high speed, when a hydraulic line ruptured under pressure. Outside sea water pressure caused the hydraulic fluid to back up and forced several hundred gallons out of the supply tank relief valve, producing the unique emergency report over the intercom, 'Flooding in the engine room! . . . with hydraulic oil?'

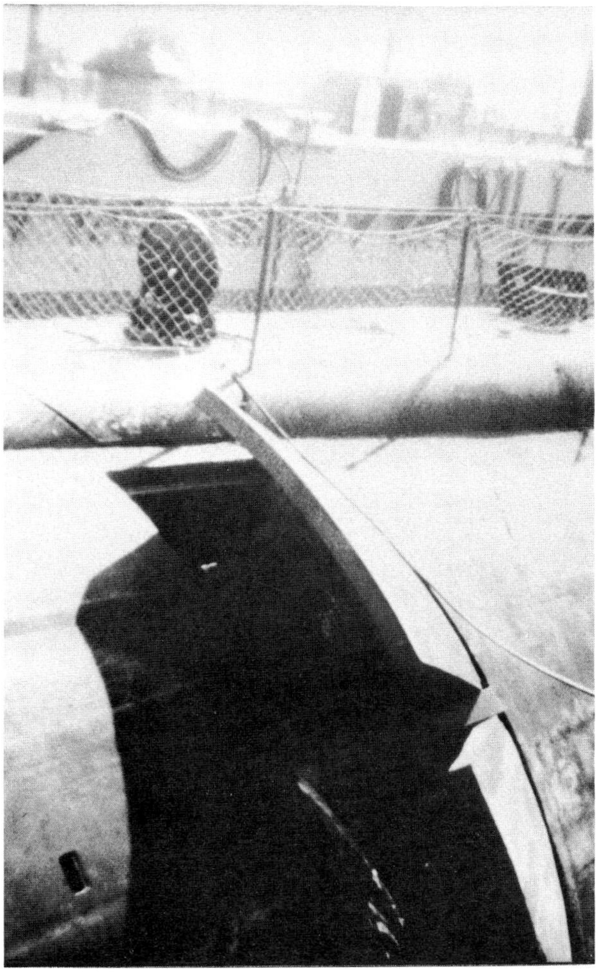

*View of the unique Phase III dive brakes, a circumferential ring of 10 hydraulically extended flaps intended to arrest out-of-control dives before* Albacore *went below crush depth.* (PSMA)

Another 'dive brake' was a landing parachute from a B-47 bomber which Captain St Lawrence saw in use at nearby Pease Air Force base. Mounted on a large canister on the sail, it was known as 'The Jolly Green Giant'; it ripped off on its third or fourth trial. In fact the most effective dive brake was to throw the dorsal rudder hard over, the way the stern rudders were used in Phase I.

During this period *Albacore* tested the prototypes of the two forms of advanced sonar on which the modern submarine's anti-submarine capability depends: the towed

Albacore *under way – note unusual wash created by X-stern.* (Authors' collection)

passive hydrophone array, and the bow mounted spherical array. Their ability to acquire low frequency sound at very long ranges coupled with advanced data processing, able to filter out the ever present oceanic background noises which otherwise masks the faint sounds of a distant submarine, provided the basis for the superiority of Western over Soviet craft through the 1970s and '80s.

*Albacore* tested TOWFLEX for DTMB in February 1962, and the bow-mounted DIMUS (Digital Multi-beam Steering) between April and December 1962. Captain Andrews attributes the concept of the towed array, which can be streamed clear of the submarine's self-noise, to scientist Marvin Lasski, who contributed to many aspects of *Albacore* including design, control, and quieting. He notes that what distinguished DIMUS from earlier bow-mounted sonars was its omnidirectional character and digital processing, twenty-four hydrophone 'searchlights', narrow beams covering all directions at once, capable of distinguishing the unique tonal of a submarine, revealed as a pattern built up over time. Interestingly, Captain Andrews says both concepts initially met with lack of interest or active opposition.

Captain St Lawrence also describes some of the secondhand equipment *Albacore* made do with, including her 'worst in the Navy' radio. She was required to send in a check report every six hours; failing this, her command would assume her lost and initiate search and rescue proceedings. But when passing through the Cape Cod Canal, the high sides of the cut would totally cut her off from radio contact. When *Albacore* dropped the pilot at the end of the canal Captain St Lawrence gave him a dollar and asked him to phone in and say they were all right.

*Note X-stern, closed bridge hatches.* (Courtesy Russell Van Billiard)

569

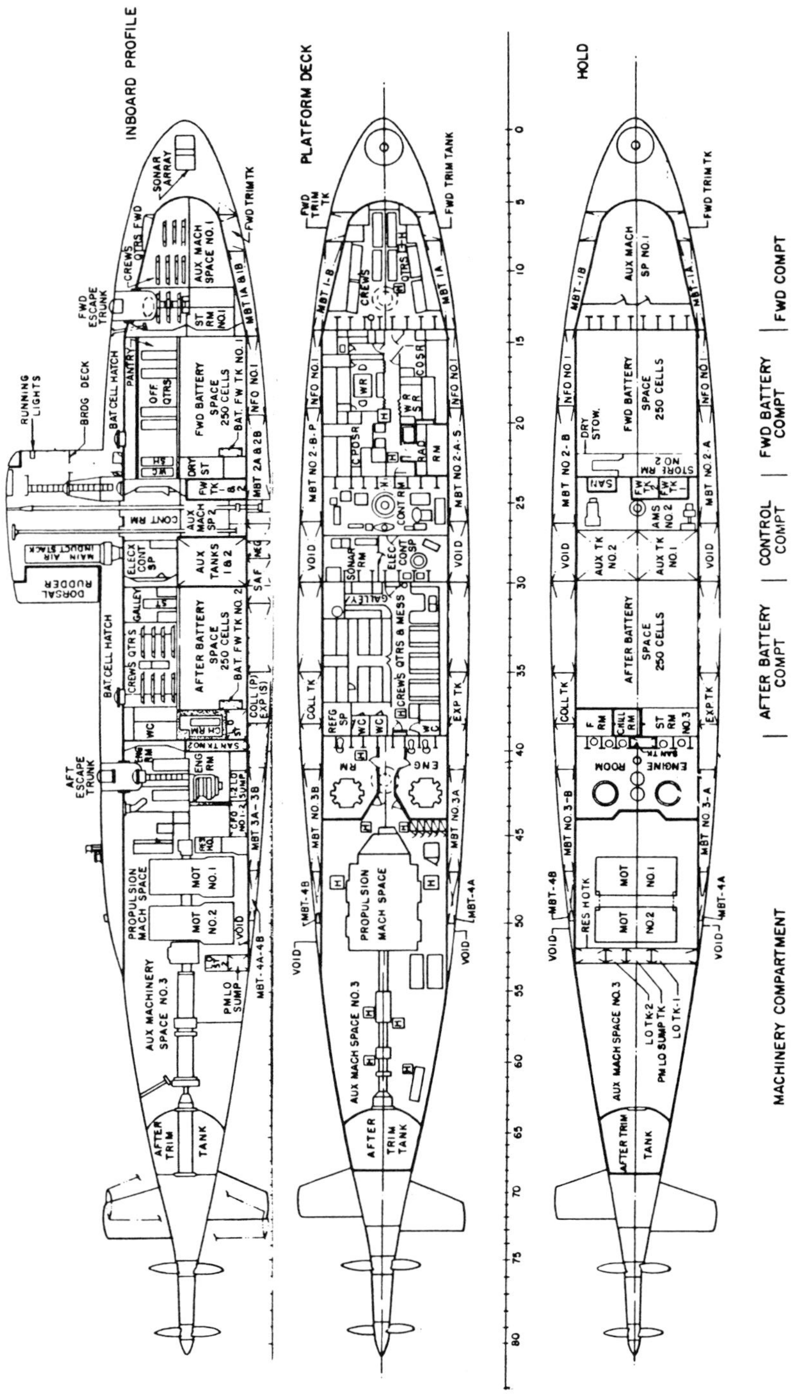


*Plan drawing of the* Albacore *taken from the Training Aid Booklet supplied to each member of her crew.* (PNSY)

## FACTS

| | |
|---|---|
| LENGTH | 205ft 4¾in |
| BREADTH | 27ft 3¾in |
| HEIGHT | 42ft 5¼in |
| WEIGHT | 1692 tons |
| MAX SPEED | over 20kts |
| MAX DEPTH | over 400ft |
| CREW | 50 men<br>5 officers |
| MAIN ENGINES | 2–1000hp diesel |
| MAIN MOTORS | 2–7500hp electric |
| BATTERIES | 500 cells (2 volts ea.)<br>weight 220 tons |
| LEAD BALLAST | 72 tons |
| FUEL OIL | 24,500 gallons |
| BALLAST TANK CAP | 228 tons |
| PROPELLERS FWD | 10.7ft diam, 8700lb |
| AFT | 8.8ft 6400lb |

## COMMANDING OFFICERS USS *Albacore* (AGSS-569)

LCDR Kenneth C Gummerson
1953–1955
LCDR Jon L Boyes
1955–1957
LCDR Lando W Zech, Jr
1957–1958
LCDR Robert O Thompson
1958–1959
LCDR William C Rae, Jr
1959–1960
LCDR Wallace A Greene
1960–1962
LCDR W P St Lawrence, Jr
1962–1963
CDR Roy M Springer
1963–1965
CDR J W Organ
1965–1967
CDR Roger H Kattman
1967–1969
CDR Thomas E Poole
1969–1971
CDR David A Kratch
1971–1972

Albacore *in extreme distress, caught in a hurricane in the late 1960s with an exhausted battery.* (Courtesy Norman Bower) ▲

*The combination of heavy seas and* Albacore*'s very poor surface characteristics left her taking water over her bridge and in through her main engine air induction at the top of her sail. Reportedly she came very close to being lost.*
▼ (Courtesy Norman Bower)

## *Phase IV: Silver-zinc battery and contra-rotating propellers*

Between December 1962 and March 1965, *Albacore* underwent her most extensive reconstruction receiving her single-hulled stern containing a second 7500hp electric motor, 60ft of concentric shafting, contra-rotating props, and a unique silver-zinc battery with twice her previous storage capacity. Initially 10ft apart, the screws were moved closer together (to 5ft apart where they remain today) to test their relative efficiency at these positions. Photographic equipment was mounted to observe their vibration and cavitation characteristics.

With this greatly increased power, *Albacore* set a new world's submerged speed record in February 1966, surpassing the nuclear *Skipjack*. Earlier operators referred to her as a '35kt sub'; Captain Roy Springer, her CO in 1963–65 notes that her top speed is still secret and declined to comment on how much she improved on her previous performance.

Captain Springer states that safety and controllability remained major concerns at her increased speeds. He describes a very tense moment the first time she went to maximum battery current – 'faster than any submarine had gone before' – when her main circuit breaker tripped with a tremendous bang cutting out the AC motor generators leaving *Albacore* without internal power and in total darkness. With her hydraulic pumps out she went into an emergency mode with high pressure fluid being supplied from reservoirs, so her controls remained operable. However, for about 8 seconds, until her dry cell emergency lighting came on, her instruments were totally invisible to the officer at the wheel – sufficient time for her to go out of control and below her crush depth. However, suddenly this officer noticed the sound of the hydraulic oil flowing through the circuits of his control stand, and realized that he could tell what he was doing with the controls by the changes in the sound, although he had never been consciously aware of it before. Thus, he was able to keep her on a stable course during the critical seconds.

The new battery with silver positive and zinc negative poles in a base (not acid) electrolyte gel of potassium hydroxide was a very promising technology but not without problems. Ronald Heinz and Russell Van Billiard note that each of 280 900lb cells had a potential of 1.8 volts, giving a total potential of 500 volts, and a rate of discharge of 16,000 amps for one hour, yielding 4355hp. This is compared to 4340 amps and 1375hp for one hour with her lead-acid battery. But battery charges at sea were more of a problem than ever; a few hours of test runs meant days of charging, easier in port where a charge from a tender or land power supply was available. Internal shorts were also a constant danger. A shorted cell would quickly heat up and burn unless it could be discharged. It was necessary for someone to go below and manually jump the burning cell out of the circuit. Under

*Testing the emergency ballast-blow system, developed after the loss of the* Thresher. *In case of engine powerfailure submerged, tanks would blow automatically at 3000lbs pressure.* (Courtesy Norman Bower)

Albacore *in a late configuration. R Van Billiard suggests the small tripod between sail and sonar dome is a television mounting for observing hydrodynamic phenomena.* (PSMA)

way it could be discharged through the motors but in port a huge carbon-pile resistor was kept handy on the dockside for this purpose. On the other hand it did not gas or require watering like a conventional lead acid battery. It was also very expensive – the silver was borrowed from, and eventually reclaimed by, the US Treasury.

The contra-rotating props offered greater transmitted power at lower rpm, with reduced noise and cavitation. But the main consideration was the potential for direct drive turbines on nuclear submarines, eliminating noisy reduction gears. It was tried in the nuclear *Jack* which suffered long standing serious engineering problems, primarily with shaft bearings and seals and a bowed turbine rotor, perhaps partly because it was a much larger and heavier installation than *Albacore*'s. Captain Springer says *Albacore*'s shaft with the larger bearings first refused to turn; all the voltage went to the shaft with the least resistance, like an automobile with one tyre on a patch of ice. The inner shaft had to be manually disconnected so the outer shaft would turn and would be operated this way until its bearings were run in – afterwards it performed well.

Many other advanced features were tested, including an emergency ballast blow system intended to prevent a loss like that of *Thresher* in 1963. Typically a submarine does not attempt to blow ballast at depth because of the great pressure; it rises on its planes and blows its tanks at periscope depth. *Thresher* seems to have been lost through a series of failures: a leak from a defective silver-brazed piping joint may have caused her reactor control board to short out, automatically shutting down her reactor and robbing her of motive power. Attempting to blow ballast at extreme pressure probably caused moisture in the compressed air to freeze and clog valves. *Albacore*'s historian, David Merriman, says that instead of using a manually operated air manifold she had 'a simple switch and indicator board that operated remote blow valves located near associated ballast tanks. These electro-magnetic valves blew ballast automatically if electrical power was lost . . .'

According to Ronald Heinz, maximum pressure was 3000lb. Stationary blows caused tremendous lists: her own air bubble was 'captured' beneath her, water did not drain quickly enough out of her superstructure, over-balancing her, and when she tipped the flat surface of her sail would push her over further.

Also tested were a semi-automatic propulsion control cubicle, combined radio antenna, the emergency hydraulic system, and a 'vernier control system' which reduced the signal to control surface servos at high speeds, reducing the danger of over control.

First tested in October 1967 was the 'Fly-around Body' (FAB), a towed sonar array deployed from the bow, incorporating a winged hydrofoil. Hydrodynamic lift was used to displace it, like a paravane or kite, 50ft to 100ft away on a parallel course to the submarine itself. Known to the crew as the 'Yellow Bird' it could be manoeuvred electronically from inside and was used to monitor the submarine's own 'near field' radiated noise. When it 'crashed' against the hull of the ship the crew memorialized it by hanging a rubber chicken from the sail and a sign saying 'Sighted Bird, Shot Same'.

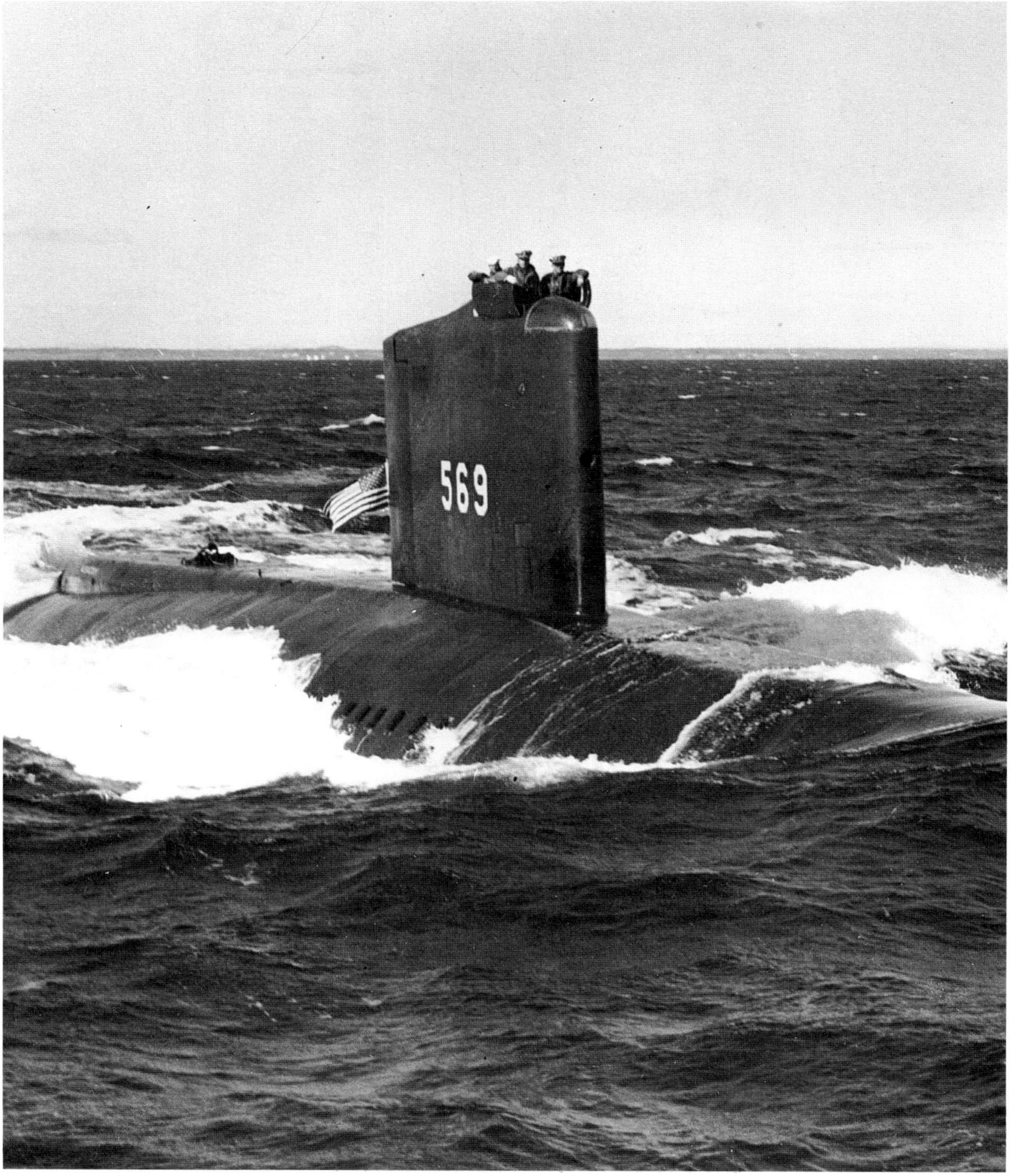


Albacore *making good speed on the surface.* (Authors' collection)

## *Phase V:*

*Albacore*'s last conversion was from August 1969 to August 1971, followed by Phase V testing from September 1971 to June 1972. No details seem to be available in print. Crew members have suggested that they are still classified, but part, at least, involved the use of viscous polymer liquids, expelled from jets at the forward part of

the hull to coat it and improve laminar flow. The effect is substantial (In *Warship 1989* D K Brown notes that up to 30 per cent reductions in frictional resistance have been demonstrated) but great quantities of fluid are required for even brief use. However, it would be most interesting to know if this technique enabled *Albacore* to once again improve her top speed. After all, many years earlier, Admiral Boyes tried the expedient of turning out the

Albacore *being moved into position for the first attempt to raise her to her permanent memorial site. Note the highway and to the left the railroad trestle breached to permit her passage.* (PSMA)

entire crew to *sandpaper* every inch of *Albacore*'s hull while she was in drydock, and obtained an extra 2kts.

## *Service aboard the Albacore*

The close rapport that existed between officers, crew and scientists has been mentioned. Her captains plainly respected the ability of the crew and the importance of the scientists' work. (Interestingly the only nickname she ever seemed to carry was under Lt-Cdr Wallace Green when the whole show – captain, ship, and crew – was known as 'Wally and His Little Red Wagon'.)

From the late 1950s she operated with a 'fixed crew' of highly trained and experienced men with up to 13 years service aboard. The reason was her many modifications; her behaviour in her new configuration could not be predicted with complete certainty. Ronald Heinz says: 'You could not ever tell when you flooded that drydock whether she was going to lean over 10° or what she was going to do. When we went to sea for that first dive we didn't know either.' She needed a resourceful crew who knew her thoroughly. Their abilities and interest in the technical challenges was much appreciated by the scientists, some of whom who worked aboard her over many years and were treated as shipmates by the crew.

Service aboard *Albacore* was good duty, especially for Portsmouth men, who often had fathers working at the shipyard. With relatively brief trips to sea, they got to see a lot of their families. Indeed, with her 2000-mile radius, she could not go further than Halifax, Bermuda, or Key West. Her main 'deployments' were to Fort Lauderdale, Florida, in the winter months as testing could continue in better weather conditions. On the other hand, young single sailors who 'joined the Navy to see the world' sometimes found this routine exquisitely boring.

## *Influence on other navies*

Many of *Albacore*'s contributions to the US and British nuclear boats have been pointed out. In addition, silver zinc battery chemistry has been adopted by several European navies for torpedo propulsion. Also, many advanced conventional submarines resemble *Albacore* greatly, for example the Japanese *Yuushio*, Dutch *Walrus*, and Soviet 'Kilo' classes.

One area where *Albacore*'s influence seems especially strong is Soviet submarine design. Where the USN abandoned the teardrop hull with the *Thresher*, emphasizing quietness over speed, and regained high speed by more that doubling engine power in the long, cigar-shaped *Los Angeles* class, the Soviets utilized the *Albacore* hull in all their latest attack boats: 'Victor', 'Alfa', 'Mike', 'Sierra', and 'Akula' classes. Bow planes are missing or retractable; some 'Victor III's have tandem contra-rotating props; and it has been suggested (and strongly disputed) that their hull coatings usually interpreted as anechoic, sonar absorbing, are actually compliant, to improve laminar flow. They go beyond *Albacore* in design for hydrodynamic qualities in eliminating her thin, high, angular sail, source of her worst control problems, using instead a low streamlined fairing for a bridge. The Soviets have also placed great emphasis on automation, reducing ship and crew size and 'hotel' facilities in favour of weapons and manoeuvrability, along the lines that Admiral Boyes and Captain Davis have strongly urged based on their experience with *Albacore*.

Today, the best Soviet boats seem to be considerably superior to the West's in speed, depth, and manoeuvrability, as well as resistance to torpedo hits gained from their tremendously strong, double hulled construction and multiple water-tight compartments. Cdr Roy Corlett, RN, suggests that the reason for this influence was *American* submarine development during the 1950s and 1960s, when the USN was achieving great advances in these areas and predicting even greater, such as 60kt speeds. But where the Soviets took on great technical risks and expense to excel in these areas, the US took a different direction, seeing sonar and quietness as paramount. For decades this seems to have been correct, but now that the Soviets are making great strides in quieting, their superiority in speed, toughness, weapons, diving depth, and 'dogfighting' manoeuvrability may give them the edge in submarine versus submarine combat.

**Sources**

This study is largely based on interviews, correspondence and published writings by individuals associated with *Albacore*. The authors would like to extend their thanks to Captain Theodore Davis, Vice-President PSMA Russell Van Billiard, Vice-Admiral Jon Boyes, Captain Frank Andrews, Captain William St Lawrence, Captain Roy Springer, Chief Engineman Stan Zajechowski, DTMB Scientist Howell Russell, NH State Senator John McCarthy, Engineering Officer Ronald Heinz, and Radioman Ron Poloske. Many took pains to find information, photos, or to direct us to new sources. We would like to thank in particular Captain Davis and Russell Van Billiard for their constant help and encouragement.

PRINTED

1. Professor Eugene Allmendinger and Captain Harry Jackson, '*Albacore*; Past – Present – Future', address to the New England Section of the Society of Naval Architects and Marine Engineers (6 May 1989).
2. Captain Frank A Andrews, 'Antisubmarine Warfare', *Encyclopedia of Physical Sciences and Technology*, Academic Press Inc.
3. Vice-Admiral Jon Boyes, 'Flying the *Albacore*', *The Submarine Review*.
4. Cdr Roy Corlett, RN, 'Soviet Submarine Propulsion: Signs of a Great Leap Forward?', *Jane's Naval Review* (1986).
5. Captain Theodore F Davis, 'Will Our Subs Have a Fighting Chance', *US Naval Institute Proceedings* (August 1988).
6. 'Decommissioning Ceremony – USS *Albacore* (AGSS-569), 1 September 1972', (Booklet, Courtesy PSMA).
7. Francis Duncan, *Rickover and the Nuclear Navy*, US Naval Institute, (Annapolis, MD, 1990).
8. David D Merriman, Jr, 'USS *Albacore*: Forerunner of Today's Submarines', *Sea Classics*.
9. Richard E Winslow III, *Portsmouth-Built: Submarines of the Portsmouth Naval Shipyard*, The Portsmouth Marine Society (Portsmouth, NH 1985).

# WARSHIP NOTES

This section comprises a number of short articles and notes, generally highlighting little-known aspects of warships history.

## MAINTAINING THE IMAGE

*In what amounts to a postscript to his new book on the sailing battlefleet, Andrew Lambert describes the thinking behind the names selected for British line of battle ships in the post-Waterloo era.*

Warship names have always been loaded with meaning. For the Royal Navy after 1815 the prime object was to sustain the image of invincibility. To this end the names selected for post-war battleships provide a guide to the Admiralty view of the navy's traditions and success, and an insight into the mind of a service at the peak of its' career rather than at 'the most unfruitful period in all our naval history', as one authority on the subject suggested.[1]

At the end of the Napoleonic War British warship naming policy emerged from a period of unprecedented demand, in which the huge forty-ship *Vengeur* class of 74s included the widest possible cross section of names, from the classical *Ajax* and *Hercules* to contemporary political and military figures, *Pitt* and *Cornwallis*. Third Rates were less significant than the larger classes, where politics and royalty made the selections particularly important. The Navy was always anxious to celebrate its victories and prize names such as *President, Chesapeake, Sans Pareil* were popular, along with those of important ships from past actions, and the Admirals they had borne. In the smaller classes these strands were used to build up a pattern of honours and credit that was a positive part of the Royal Navy's cult of superiority. The hero cult of Nelson was, perhaps, the single greatest element in this programme, but it was by no means confined to him. *Nelson, Trafalgar, Nile, Aboukir, Hero* and the frigate *Horatio* all carried his bust.

The last three-decked ships ordered in 1813–14, the *Prince Regent, Princess Charlotte* and *London* (later *Royal Adelaide*) reflected two important strains of nomenclature. The first pair were due recognition of the final collapse of the King's sanity; the Prince Regent was, by 1814, clearly established as the effective monarch, and it was common practice for the first new First Rate ordered after the accession of a monarch to carry his name. That of his daughter reflected the likelihood that she would eventually succeed to the throne. *London*, for many reasons, was an obvious choice, the last ship of that name having just been broken up.

After the War the naming of all new First Rates fitted into a clear policy. *Royal George*, ordered 1819, was named after the Prince Regent, while *St George* (ordered 1819), *Neptune* (1825), *Waterloo* (1823), and *Trafalgar* (1825), carried names intimately connected with the British conception of their place in the world order, their dominance of the seas, and the role of the two battles in establishing that position. The *Royal William* (1823) honoured the second in line to the throne, who was also a naval officer; while *Royal Frederick* (1827) honoured the recently deceased heir to the throne. Typically enough, she was renamed *Queen* on launching in 1839 to honour the newly enthroned Victoria. However, her sister ship, the *Royal Sovereign*, then took the original name. The *Victoria* of 1833 had honoured the then heir to the throne, while the *Algiers* celebrated the battle of 1816. This ship was never completed, effectively being renamed *Windsor Castle*, which had a more regal connection. The other sailing First Rates ordered, the *Royal Albert* and *Prince of Wales* of 1842, require little explanation. The first celebrated the marriage of the Queen, the second the birth of an heir. *Marlborough* symbolised British power in a way that the Government was anxious the French should understand, at a time of international tension. In a similar vein the *Windsor Castle* was renamed *Duke of Wellington* on the death of the great soldier in 1852. Conversely, in 1852 it was considered impolitic and insensitive to send the *Waterloo* as Mediterranean Flagship. As her replacement, the *Britannia*, spent more than a year as joint flagship of an Anglo-French fleet this turned out to have been a wise selection.

For two-deckers the available list of names was far longer, and the pressures of expectation that much lower. As a consequence, the selections made were more closely aligned with politics. The first post-war class, the *Formidable*s were dominated by three Indian-built ships with suitably Indian names. The remaining five were all time-honoured battleship names, the name ship of the class carrying that of Lord Rodney's flagship at the Saintes. On launching, the *Goliath* was renamed *Clarence*, in honour of the Lord High Admiral, but this was,

*The* Duke of Wellington *of 1852. Although the name was never used again, it was revived in the form of Wellington's nickname,* Iron Duke, *most recently for a new Type 23 frigate.* (CMP)

with the earlier Third Rate of the same name, an isolated and peculiar incidence of Royal names reaching down into the two-deckers, particularly as there was already a *Royal William* in progress. However, several two-deckers, *London, Superb* and *Majestic* among them, carried a bust of Queen Victoria. The battle honours of the *Formidable* class were impressive. *Goliath* had been at St Vincent and the Nile; *Powerful* at Camperdown; *Thunderer* had been present at both the First of June and Trafalgar; and *Vengeance* at Quiberon. This theme was to be continued in the succeeding class. The previous *Vanguard*, Nelson's flagship at the Nile, had a special place in the heart of the First Naval Lord of 1832, Sir Thomas Hardy, who became her captain after the battle. Her sister ship, *Collingwood*, reflected another tradition, that of keeping a talisman-like connection with the great commanders. Postwar ships were named after *Rodney, Exmouth* and *Hood*, while the greater part of the pantheon were already represented. It should be noted, however, that the 50-gun *Vernon* of 1831 did not fit this pattern, being named not after the admiral, but for the yachtsman and politician, patron of Symonds and friend of the Duke of Portland, as the figurehead demonstrated.

The larger *Albion* class included *Aboukir*, an alternative name for the Battle of the Nile; this was a piece of sharp practice to ensure that the Royal Navy had the maximum advantage from the greatest talisman of all, Nelson. Not only were there already a *Nile, Canopus* and *Vanguard* to celebrate this victory, but the bust of the Admiral aboard this latest ship was possibly the tenth in the fleet. *Exmouth* and *St Jean d'Acre* both reflected the power of the Royal Navy against coastal forts, while the latter heaped additional humiliation on the French who had been forced to stand back and watch their protégé Mehemet Ali being disciplined by the fleet in 1840. *Prince Albert,* later *Princess Royal,* reflected the rising status of the Consort, and the first child of his Queen.

The only politicians directly honoured in this period were Lord Melville and Sir James Graham, while the former ship, an Indian 74 may well have been a belated tribute to Henry Dundas, the driving force behind construction in India, the rationale for the latter would appear to have been vanity. Graham had his bust as the figurehead of the *Cumberland*, for which county he sat in the Commons. In addition, the frigate *Constance* was named for one of his daughters. One other First Lord had a direct personal impact on nomenclature: Lord Ellenborough, who renamed the three ships building at Bombay to convey a more immediate, imperial message. The *Madras* was altered to the *Meeanee*, in honour of the victory of his favourite general over the Sikhs. He also named the Fourth Rates *Sutlej* and *Nankin*, after victories during the Sikh and Opium Wars.

After 1840 the Admiralty, reflecting concern over poor relations with France, adopted a more overtly hostile series of names, notably the prize name *Sans Pareil*, re-used on a replica of the original ship. *Cressy* and *Orion* were after veterans of the First of June, Cape St Vincent, the Nile and Trafalgar. *Caesar* was another well honoured name after the First of June, the Gut of Gibraltar and Strachan's action. *Edgar* was a Copenhagen name, while *Agamemnon*, the Hayes-designed 80-gun ship, celebrated Nelson's first line of battle ship.

Fifty-gun ships also used talismanic names – *Raleigh, Arethusa* and *Leander*. In addition, the small Fourth Rate *President* was built to retain the prize name for the American ship, as well as her lines, and was sent to the North American Station for maximum effect.

The last generation of British sailing battleships carried a series of names which reflected the traditions, honours and loyalties of the Royal Navy.

Other navies adopted a similar approach, the United States keeping *Macedonian, Guerriere* and *Java* on their list, along with the names of their captors. The French naming policy reflected a lack of success at sea, having more to do with military victory and the touchstones of the particular regime of the day. Several ships had to be renamed on each change of system, something that is considered bad luck by sailors to this day. The Russian Navy had a few battle honours, *Hango, Tschesme, Navarin*; the other ships were perforce named after successes on land, including *City of Paris*, and royal and national figures. No other fleet had the tradition of the Royal Navy, and that provided an advantage which persisted through the succeeding decades.

[1] Manning, Cmdr T D & Walker, Cdr C F *British Warship Names*, London 1959, p33

## THE WHALER AND THE CORVETTE

*John Harland analyses the relationship between the 'Flower' class corvette design and its supposed prototype, the whaler* Southern Pride.

Early in 1939 Smith's Dock Ltd made a proposal to the Admiralty for the construction of a 'Patrol Vessel of Whaler Type', envisaged as an escort for coastal convoys. In a paper read before the Institution of Naval Architects in 1947, A W Watson, the Assistant Director of Naval Construction at the Admiralty mentioned that the proposal was based on the design of *Southern Pride*, a whaler built by the Middlesbrough yard in 1936. (*Selected Papers on British Warship Design in World War II*, London 1983, p85). This connection has been widely repeated since, and there is little doubt that *Southern Pride* formed the basis for the earliest pencilled concept. However, I would argue that by the time the final ideas were worked out, the corvette design, while strongly influenced by the steam whaleboat in general, owed little to *Southern Pride* in particular. For convenience I will refer to her simply as *Pride*; all the catchers of the Southern Whaling & Sealing Company were given *Southern* names, a tradition carried on by Christian Salvesen.

The essential whaler 'character' of the corvette was confirmed in the postwar period by the conversion of many corvettes to whaling purposes. By contrast, Smith's Dock had during the First World War built a class of anti-submarine patrol-craft, the 'Z-boats', the design of which was influenced by the pre-1914 steam whaler. Despite being given 'Whale' names, like *Arcticwhale*, they were ill fitted for whale hunting, and none was ever converted into a catcher-boat.

First of all, let me emphasize that the origin of the corvette engine is not in question. A machine almost identical to *Pride*'s engine, and initially built from the same patterns, was used to power not just the 'Flowers', but the 'Castle' class corvettes and many frigates besides. My thesis depends on the lack of correspondence between the bow and stern configurations of *Pride*, and those of the corvette.

The rather clumsy title 'Patrol Vessel of Whaler Type' underlines the project's whaler origins, and certainly the 205ft corvette shared some features with *Southern Pride*, so we must consider where this vessel stood in relation to the average whaleboat of the mid-1930s. Although the postwar whalecatchers were substantially bigger, reaching 216ft in the mid-1950s, the average prewar whaler was only about 140ft overall. In 1935, a small consortium of whaling companies ordered from Fredriksstad Mekaniske Verksted an 'Observation Catcher' of radically improved design, the *H J Bull* (Norwegian pronunciation sounds something like 'Ha Yott Bill'). She was bigger and faster than her contemporaries, and was designed to range out from the factory-ship, note where the best catching opportunities existed, and coordinate the activities of the expedition's other catcher-boats. Three more such 'Scout Catchers' were built in the run-up to the War: *Southern Pride* in Middlesbrough in 1936, and *Southern Gem* and *Unitas 1* by Bremer Vulkan in Germany the following year. All had an overall length of just over 170ft and carried twice as much fuel as the average whaleboat, or indeed of the early corvette.

I have been unable to track down an arrangement drawing for *Southern Pride*, but drawings of her stern frame, a pumping plan, and a shell expansion, suffice to establish the profile. I do have general arrangements for the other three boats. They differed from the average whaler of the day in having two boilers, and bunkering well over 400 tons of oil. In addition to the large thwartship bunker found under the bridge in all whalers, fuel tanks were installed abreast the boiler room. Rather than the typical three-cylinder triple expansion engine, all had four-cylinder engines, that in *H J Bull* being a double compound Frederiksstad Steam Motor, while the others had three-stage machines with two low pressure cylinders.

**Profile of the Stern.** Until the 1920s, whaleboats featured an elliptical stern, with a balanced rudder, and a stern frame designed so that much of the deadwood was unplated. A typical example was *Havørn 3* of 1924 (Fig 1). I am following Norwegian and German practice in referring to them as 'boats' (*Hvalbåt, Hvalfangboot*).

**Cruiser stern.** In 1925 Smith's Dock built *Southern Wave*, which had the profile shown – cruiser stern and spade rudder (Fig 2). She proved to be about a knot faster than similarly engined sister ships of the same dimensions, and by 1930 this arrangement had been adopted by all other whaleboat builders. In the interim, some boats were built (for instance by Nylands) with a cruiser stern, but retaining the 'old-fashioned' stern frame (Fig 3).

Although Norwegian whalers described their catchers as having a 'cruiser stern' (*krysser-hekk*), and I follow this practice for convenience, the purist might argue that the 'true' cruiser stern exhibits a definite 'knuckle' and 'tumblehome', a contour found in just two whalers, *Southern Gem* and the identical *Unitas 1* (Fig 4). Through the 1920s and 1930s, most Middlesbrough catchers continued to be given what we might call a 'canoe stern', and this generality includes *Southern Pride* (Fig 5). There was considerable variation in the actual profile of the stern between builders and between individual vessels. About 1930, Nylands favoured the rather ill-looking configuration shown in Fig 6. Smith's *Stora* (1929) had the rounded canoe shape somewhat squared off (Fig 7), while in the mid-1930s several builders began to design sterns with a definite knuckle: *H J Bull* (1935) built by Fredriksstad (Fig 8); *Unitas 2* (1937) from Bremer Vulkan (Fig 9); *Gos IX* (1937) from Kaldnes (Fig 10). Coming back to the Middlesbrough yard, the 'Lake' class Admiralty trawlers were a group of whalers which had been ordered by Anders Jahre, but in 1939 were taken over on the stocks and completed as anti-submarine patrol craft (Fig 11). In this case, the profile shows a knuckle, and closely resembles that of the corvette (Fig 12). It is possible that four boats of the *Sondra* class built for Salvesen in 1937, also had this type of stern.

Trawlers are about the same size as whalers, and trawler builders began to adopt the cruiser stern by the late 1930s. They continued, however, to favour the old type of rudder, as in the example shown, the minesweeping trawler *Sir Galahad* (Fig 13). The *Basset* class Admiralty minesweeping trawler (1937) offer an early exception, having the configuration shown in Fig 14. The large 'Isles' class minesweeping trawler (Fig 15), produced during the war, likewise had a stern very similar to the corvette.

In the profiles shown above, it will be noticed that there were differences in the line connecting the propeller

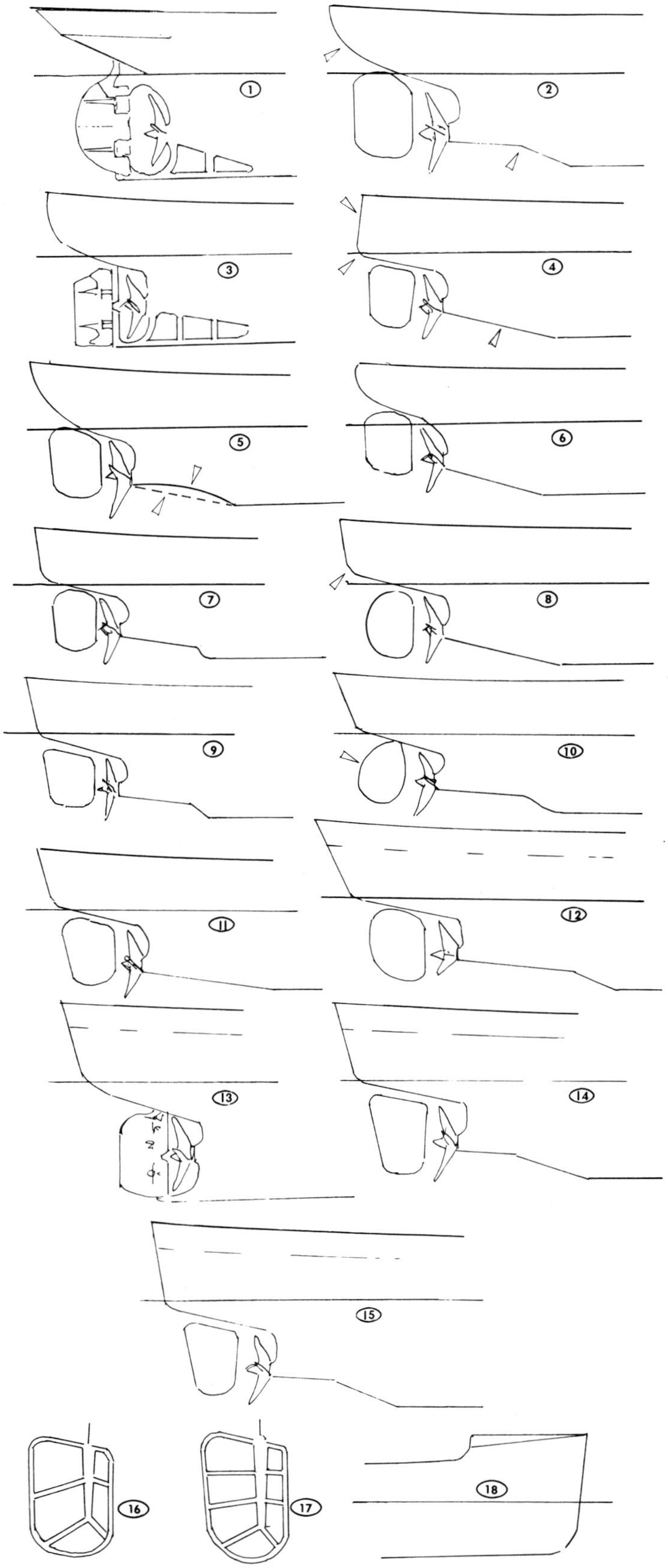

boss with the keel. Basically, this 'junction line' could be a straight as in the *H J Bull, Southern Gem,* 'Lake' class, or 'jogged' as in *Southern Wave* or *Unitas 2*. Most Middlesbrough boats continued to use this jogged contour through the 1930s, and it was used in the corvette. Whalers built by Kaldnes and Deschimag show the intersection of this line with the keel faired into a graceful curve, as in *Gos IX*. According to the drawing of the stern frame, and the pumping plan referred to above, *Southern Pride* was unique in having the line curved throughout its length, a contour unlike that of other whalers in general, and the corvette in particular. However, the shell expansion and a sectional drawing suggest that as built, the line joining propeller boss and keel was straight, as in *H J Bull* and *Southern Gem*, although the stern contour remained of the 'canoe' variety.

**Rudder.** From the early 1920s, whalers had used a streamlined, rather than a plate rudder, but each shipyard had their own ideas about the best profile to give it. In the boats built by Kaldnes in the 1930s and 1940s, it had a very distinctive 'cherry leaf' shape. The rudders of the corvette, 85.5sq ft (Fig 16) and the whalers produced by the Middlesbrough yard, including that in *Southern Pride*, 72sq ft (Fig 17), share a definite family resemblance. The sketches show the rudder-frame before plating up.

**Profile of the Bow.** The trawler bow until the late 1930s typically had an almost vertical stem, and a relatively deep forefoot as exemplified by the trawler *Vinur* (Fig 18). There were exceptions: the *'Northern'* trawlers (1936), built in Germany for British interests, had a very striking curved stem (Fig 19), and a standardised class of big trawler turned out by several German yards, just prior to the war, exhibited a Maierform 'icebreaker' bow, a contour also found in one British-built trawler, *Kingston Agate* (Fig 20).

Whalecatchers, from their earliest development in the 1860s, featured a raked stem and marked cut-up at the forefoot and after deadwood. This reflected the need for them to be very agile, manoeuvrability being more important than directional stability. In the 1930s, there was a good deal of variation between builders in the actual form of the bow, particularly as to the amount of rake given the stem. Smith's Dock boats – for instance *Stora* (1929) – were given a more vertical stem (Fig 21), than those in earlier boats, while catchers built by Kaldnes favoured a sharply inclined stem, for example *Gos IX* (Fig 22). In the late 1930s, the Middlesbrough boats were also given a well raked stem, that in *Southern Pride* (Fig 23) and the 'Lake' class (Fig 24) being inclined at 70° to the keel. For comparison, we give the bow profile for the other scout catchers *H J Bull* (Fig 25) and *Southern Gem/Unitas 1* (Fig 26).

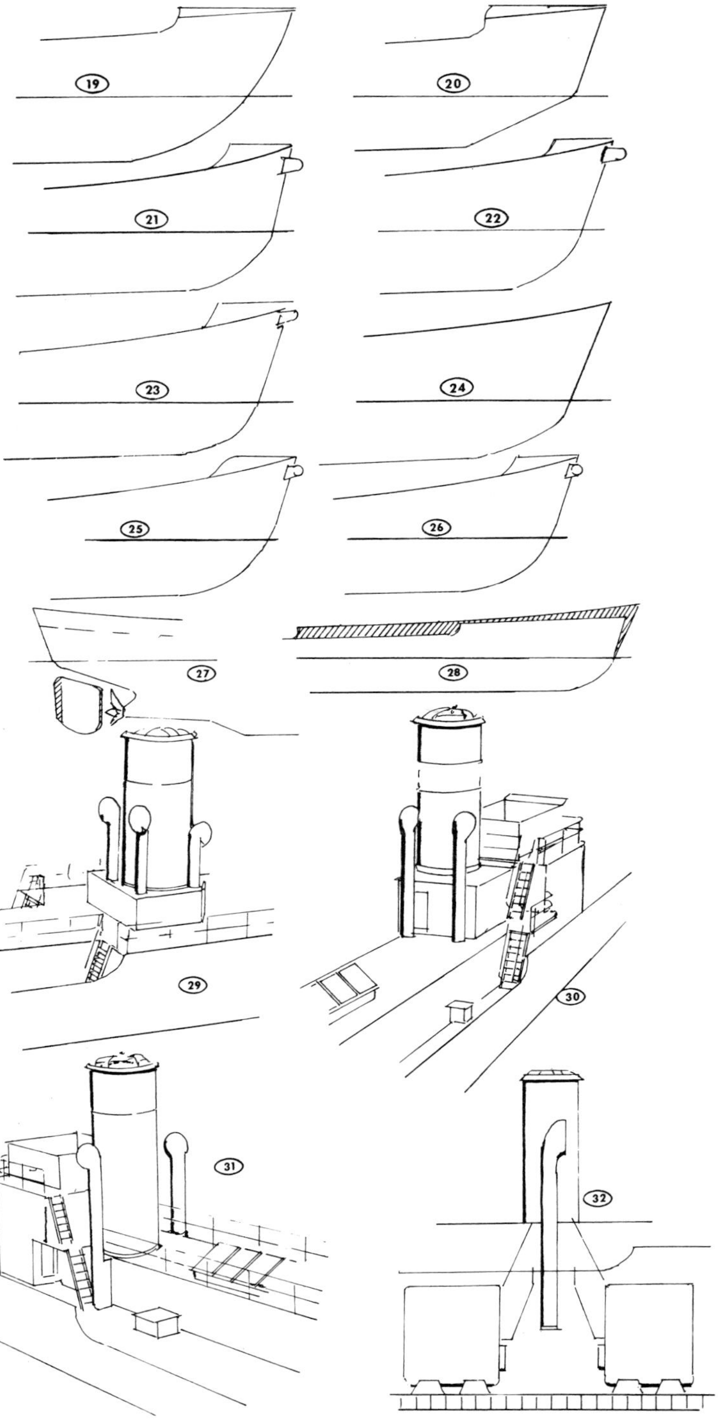

**Flare.** Whalers needed an adequately flared bow, because in the final stage of the hunt, the gunner had to stand on the gun-platform, right up in the eyes of the ship. He reached this station from the hunting bridge, via the gangway, which was such a characteristic feature of the catcher. Experience proved that the original corvette bow was given too little flare, and enhancing this was a major improvement in the 'Modified Flower' class corvette. The midship section of corvette and whaler were quite comparable, the rise of floor was about the same, and both had a generous radius at the turn of the bilge.

**The Modified Corvette**. The stern of the original corvette had the configuration shown in Fig 12, and the stern of the modified corvette, apart from having a somewhat larger rudder, was identical (Fig 27). The stem of the original corvette raked much less than that of *Southern Pride*, the corvette bow configuration resembled if anything, that in *Southern Gem*. The modified corvette was 3ft longer than the early corvette, and had a higher bow and greater sheer forward, features associated with greater rake of the stem. The two forms are compared in Fig 28.

**Bilge keels.** For the most part, whaleboats did not have bilge keels, because there was some danger of its cutting the whale-line while securing a harpooned whale. The first corvettes had 11in bilge keels, subsequently widened to 22in, to help alleviate the heavy rolling to which they were subject.

**Boilers**. Kaldnes and Smith's Dock had installed watertube boilers in a few whaleboats, in the late 1930s, but the majority of catchers operating at the outbreak of hostilities had the traditional Scotch boiler. The Scout Catchers had two Scotch boilers, but *Pride* was unique in having one Scotch and one three-drum watertube boiler. The later corvettes were fitted with watertube boilers, but the earlier versions had a pair of Scotch boilers.

*Southern Pride*'s profile is shown rather indistinctly on page 8 of Thomas Lynch's *Canada's Flowers* and might suggest that she had a 'funnel casing' or fiddley deck around the funnel, similar to that found in the corvette (Fig 29). On the basis of a couple of indifferent photos, this structure in *Pride* seems to have been about 8ft high, and may actually have been a 'drying room', for hanging wet clothing (Fig 30). We are uncertain about the internal arrangements of *Pride*'s boiler rooms, but the funnel would surely have been placed between the boilers as in the others. For some reason which is not clear to me, her ventilators were placed well abaft the funnel.

**Ventilators**. The corvette had four stokehold ventilators, which pierced the funnel casing. A double set was needed because the boiler rooms were separated by a bulkhead. In the Norwegian and German Scout Catchers, the cowl ventilators were placed exactly abreast the funnel. Fig 31 shows *Southern Gem* and Fig 32 shows the uptakes, funnel and ventilators in the *H J Bull*, in section.

**Comparison of Southern Pride and the corvette**. In summary, the features shared by *Southern Pride* and the corvette, and differentiate them from the average whaler of the day include the 4-cylinder triple expansion engine; having two boilers rather than one; having fuel tanks abreast the stokehold; a built-up funnel casing, atop the boiler room casing. The way the stern was constructed was similar in the two vessels, embodying a complicated steel casting which formed the stern frame and propeller boss.

The corvette differed in being 30ft longer; in the form of bow and stern; in having bilge keels; in not having a thwartship bunker; and in not having a watertube boiler. What looks like a small forecastle in the whaler is actually a fairly open structure supporting the platform on which the gunner stands. The closed in forecastle in the corvette, although a bit like that in a trawler, was something quite foreign to the whaler, which needed a relatively unencumbered foredeck to handle the whale-lines, and gear for securing the whale carcasses alongside. A couple of minor points: whalers always have a steering position on their 'hunting bridge', the helmsman being exposed to the weather, but in the corvette this was replaced with a trawler type closed wheelhouse. The gallery in whalers was invariably amidships, but in the first British corvettes, the gallery was at the after end of the casing, something which was characteristic of the trawler. In whalers, starting with the *H J Bull,* steering gear of the Wilson-Pirrie type was used, and this was installed at deck level, at the after end of the casing. In the corvette, the after deck was needed for depth-charge racks, and minesweeping equipment, and for this reason, although the steering engine was of the same type, it was installed below deck level, access being gained through a hatch. Whalers had no bulwarks from a point roughly abreast the funnel.

Sir William Reed, the designer of the corvette, in commenting on Mr Watson's paper, did not quarrel with the presenter's allusion to the role of *Southern Pride* in the corvette design, but neither does he himself mention this particular vessel. He explained that the First World War 'Z-boats' (also his brainchild) proved too small for effective anti-submarine work, and in 1917 the need was recognized for bigger vessels with a speed of 17–18kts and oil-fired watertube boilers. However, in the event, it was decided to substitute a class of coal-burning ships with Scotch boilers instead, the 'Kil' boats. He goes on to say, 'The corvettes built for the last war (ie 1939–45) were those proposed to be built at the end of the 1914–18 war, burning oil fuel and having watertube boilers'. This suggests that Reed had given sustained thought to the whole coastal escort matter, and that his ideas were not inspired by having built *Southern Pride*, but reflected a lifetime's experience of designing ships, particularly anti-submarine warships and whalers. My own feeling is that while *Southern Pride* may have figured prominently when the project was at the stage of drawing sketches on the backs of envelopes, its importance had been completely overshadowed by other considerations, notably ease of construction, by the time the drawings for the first corvette *Gladiolus* were finalized. It was the vast and sustained expertise developed while building all classes of vessels, particularly whalers, which the Middlesbrough yard brought to the task, that explain the success enjoyed by this very large class of warship.

# NAVAL BOOKS OF THE YEAR

The reviews are divided into three main sections: firstly, full reviews; then short notices and finally, a straightforward listing of books announced but not received. In all sections the order is alphabetical by author.

*R D Ballard,* The Discovery of the Bismarck, *published by Hodder & Stoughton, 1990. 232pp.*
*ISBN 0–340–52976–8. £19.95.*

This is best seen as a picture book and though some are magnificent many of those taken during the search are more suitable to the family album. The good ones include many interesting views of the *Bismarck* either while building or during her work up. Shots of the Royal Navy are poorly selected – one captioned as a North Sea patrol in the Second World War shows nine battleships, presumably exercising after a prewar review.

The important pictures are the 34 underwater shots of the wreck which are located on clear drawings and compared with photos of the same area taken before her last voyage. There are also half a dozen beautiful and accurate drawings by Ken Marschall of the ship as she now lies, which are keyed to the photos.

The text is chatty; some 40 pages describe the games played by the team while searching unsuccessfully in 1988 and successfully in 1989. There is a lengthy but superficial account of *Bismarck*'s last voyage.

Technical interest is slight; the ship lies in deep silt and the lower part of the armour cannot be seen. It is said that there are some 300–400 hits visible, the conning tower alone has 24 holes in the visible half of its 380mm armour. The thick armour of both B and D barbettes has been penetrated and there are many holes from smaller shells in the upper belt. Claims in several earlier books that *Bismarck*'s armour was so special that it was impenetrable are disproved; indeed test on plates removed from *Tirpitz* and tested soon after the Second World War had already made this clear. There was no significant difference between British and German armour though it seems that both were a good deal better than American material.

The number of rounds fired is recorded. (*Warship* 28, 1983, J Roberts)

| | | |
|---|---|---|
| *Rodney* | 16in | 375 |
| | 6in | 716 |
| *King George V* | 14in | 339 |
| | 5.25in | 660 |
| *Norfolk* | 8in | 527 |
| *Dorsetshire* | 8in | 234 |

*Rodney* claimed 40 hits from her 16in, mainly between 10,000 and 4000yds while *Dorsetshire* claimed 50 hits, which seem reasonably consistent with the visible damage.

The British battleships opened fire at 0847 at about 23,000yds and by 0908 *Bismarck*'s A and B turrets were out of action and her central fire control gone. C and D turrets fired occasionally under local control until 0931. From then until the cease fire at 1013, *Rodney* and *King George V* carried out unopposed practise at 4000yds or less.

Sometime after 1000 the order was given to scuttle the *Bismarck* and though it is unclear how effective this action was as it may not have reached all machinery spaces, her sinking was hastened by demolition charges. At 1025 *Dorsetshire* fired torpedoes and claimed two hits, one seen right aft by *Rodney*. This probably explains why the stern of *Bismarck* is missing.

In the last pages Ballard compares the state of *Bismarck*'s remains with the much older wreck of *Titanic*. The battleship's teak deck is sound while the liner's pine has all gone. It is of interest that Ballard has now accepted the hypothesis proposed by E Haig, RCNC, that implosion of air-filled compartments caused the severe damage to the stern of *Titanic* and led to her breaking in half. Though a draft article was sent to Ballard over a year ago it is not acknowledged.

**D K Brown, RCNC**

*Dick Cronin*, Royal Navy Shipboard Aircraft Developments 1912–1931, *published by Air-Britain (Historians) Ltd, 1990. 300 × 210mm, 384 pages, 500 illustrations.*
*ISBN 0–85130–165–7. £28.00*

The author's purpose is 'to highlight some of the lesser known aspects of the Royal Navy's early use of aircraft launched from ships in war and peace'. The text is based on unpublished sources and illustrated by 464 fascinating photographs as well as maps and diagrams. The layout takes a little getting used to. It is more the raw material of history than the processed summarised product, but none the worse for that to the inquiring general reader. He has purposely not dealt with 'mainstream' early naval aviation topics such as the fully converted seaplane carriers (with one

*One of the first British cruisers to take aircraft to sea was the* Undaunted *seen here in the delicate process of recovering a Sopwith floatplane. These early aero-naval efforts are well chronicled in Dick Cronin's new book, reviewed above.* (CMP)

exception, the operations of HMS *Ben-my-Chree* and *Empress* in the Levant, included for continuity); nor with the development of the aircraft carrier. The material aspects of both are already thoroughly described in Norman Friedman's *British Carrier Aviation* by Conway Maritime Press. This later book has an equally interesting field to cover.

About a third of the book deals with launching aircraft (usually wheeled) from ordinary warships, beginning with Samson's flight from HMS *Africa* in 1912 and continuing via cruiser fo'c'sle ramps, towed lighters and turret ramps as far as catapult trials and Flycatcher platforms in the 1920s. The other two thirds cover 'side-shows' from 1914 to 1919 which employed seaplanes hoisted out from crudely improvised vessels (apart from the exception noted above). Operations were mostly against the coastal flanks of the Turkish Empire, and some against German East Africa. In home waters anti-Zeppelin and anti-submarine patrols by seaplanes from paddle steamers and trawlers were seldom effective; but the other part of the book does describe the two successful interceptions of Zeppelins by wheeled fighters, one from a cruiser ramp and the other from a towed lighter. The 'side-show' chronicle ends with the British Caspian Sea campaign of 1919, during which seaplanes working from commandeered Russian tankers took a prominent role against the Bolsheviks.

Much of the text is straightforward operational narrative supported by many photographs and copious listings of the ships, aircraft, events and people involved. This mass of facts affords some intriguing insights, notably into the wide scope of the 'side-shows' and the creative improvisation with which they began. Outstripping even the *Königsberg* operations in that respect were the initial doings of an ex-German prize still, in early 1916, named SS *Aenne Rickmers*. She was commanded by a Captain in the Dublin Fusiliers (no doubt in the General-at-Sea mode; the ship was driven by a 23-stone British skipper) and manned chiefly by Greeks. The aircraft (two Nieuport seaplanes), pilots and air mechanics were French, and the Observers were British Army officers. After two months flying air reconnaissance over the Turkish Mediterranean shoreline and landing spies the ship was torpedoed by a Turkish torpedo boat (commanded by a German!). After repair she attained respectability at last as HMS *Anne* and ceased being run by the Egyptian Government Ports and Lights administration.

The inability of early seaplanes to take off from rough water, and sometimes from calm as well, encouraged the advent of launching ramps to be used by landplanes or by seaplanes taking off from trollies; but the former entailed ditching on return, and the latter demanded specialised ship conversions. Hence sideshows in good weather areas such as the Levant continued to use floatplanes hoisted out from merchant vessels which were only rudimentarily adapted for the job, with canvas awnings for hangars. As the book shows, better weather struck two ways. Take-off from water was more often possible, and damage on alighting was less likely, but high temperatures reduced power output and engines often overheated. Seaplanes lumbered with heavy high-drag floats needed all the power they could get. Hence they were frequently unable to climb high enough to fly inland and their engines often failed.

Despite these dangers and difficulties much vital reconnaissance and gunfire spotting was achieved. The book also chronicles many bombing sorties when conditions allowed some extra load to be lifted, but the bombloads were so small that the effect was to harrass rather than to destroy. The high point was a nine aircraft raid by Short 184, Schneider and Baby seaplanes led by the irrepressible Commander Samson against an inland railway junction in northern Palestine. The side-shows described were cheap, and most seem to have been worthwhile ventures. They helped the more conventional warships to exert continuous pressure against the long coastal flanks of the Turkish Empire and against German East Africa, where aircraft located the cruiser *Königsberg* and spotted for her destruction.

The French seaplane squadron provided aircraft for HMS *Anne* and *Raven II* until April 1916, otherwise the aircraft and crews embarked in HM ships came from the Royal Naval Air Service; but in the Levant the Observers were often Army officers, the first example of a happy partnership resumed in later years by Carrier Borne Army Liaison Officers.

The other section of the book shows many photographs of Grand Fleet and Harwich Force ships equipped with wheeled aircraft launched from turrets or fixed ramps. They would have to ditch on return from a sortie, unless in range of a friendly shore. The latter option presumably explains the retention of ordinary undercarriages, which unlike those of Second World War catapult fighters could not be retracted. If undercarriages had been dispensed with and the turret or ramp aircraft had launched from trollies like those used by ramp launched seaplanes the saving of weight and drag would have improved performance and the ditching characteristics would have been much milder.

As described, the ditching drill would have terrified later naval aviators. The safety harness was released before contact, so that when the aircraft pitched forward as the wheels hit the sea the pilot was hurled out of the cockpit to splash down several yards ahead. Evidently with ditching speeds around 40kts the impact was usually not hard enough to kill or maim, as would have happened with later generations of aircraft.

In hindsight it is obvious that these manifold operating deficiencies could only be overcome by creating the aircraft carrier, the only ship configuration to allow aircraft of high performance to be operated while a considerable sea was running, and without the hazard and expense of ditching on return. However the war was on and had to be fought with whatever means were already at hand. Behind the deadpan narrative one can sense that urgency, and the raw courage of the men who went to war in such flimsy and dangerous machines. This valuable book is a fitting tribute to them and to the ship's companies who supported them.

**David Stanley**

*Rene J Francillon*, Grumman Aircraft Since 1929, *published by Putnam Aeronautical Books, 1990.*
*138 × 216mm, 592 pages, 450 photographs, 58 line drawings. ISBN 0–85177–835–6. £30.00*

Yet another famous aircraft manufacturer is now covered in the celebrated Putnam series of company histories, with the appearance of this splendid volume by a recognised authority on American aircraft.

The Grumman Company was not founded until 1929, when three senior employees of the Loening Aeronautical Engineering Company set out on their own. It was a bold step – the US stockmarket had crashed only two months earlier – but before long the new company had won orders from the US Navy, and its aircraft have served continuously aboard the arm's carriers ever since.

Innovation was a Grumman watchword, and the SFF-1 prototype carrier-borne two-seat fighter of 1931 boasted a retractable undercarriage, an enclosed cockpit, and was powered by the new Wright R-1820 Cyclone nine-cylinder radial engine. Although many companies have found to their cost that it is wrong to put too many new ideas into a single airframe, Grumman got it right first time, and the chubby FF and SF biplanes gave the company a successful take-off.

Loening descendancy was evident in the JF and J2F Duck utility amphibians, with their boot-like main float blending with the hull and extending well forward of the propeller, but it was a last flourish before a whole succession of now-famous carrier fighters appeared: the F2F; the F4F Wildcat, first of the barrel-fuselaged monoplanes; and the F6F Hellcat, the F8F Bearcat.

Keeping them company were the TBF Avenger torpedo-bomber, twin-engined Skyrocket, Widgeon amphibian, and the sleek F7F Tigercat fighter. Hot on their tails came the jets: F9F Panther and Cougar, F11F Tiger A-6 Intruder, F111B and EF-111A, and F-14 Tomcat, again with a host of other types, most of them equally well-known – Guardian, Albatross, Tracker, Ag-Cat, Gulfstream, Mohawk, Hawkeye, Gulfstream II, and the intriguing X-29 with the sharply swept-forward wings.

This book maintains Putnam's high standards, both in the quality of text and the quality of production. The aircraft appear in chronological order, and there is an abundant supply of well reproduced monochrome pictures and the fine general-arrangement drawings to accompany the informative text. Appendices cover production, design numbers, projects, and the Lunar Module – not an aircraft, but certainly a product of which any aerospace manufacturer would be proud. Altogether this is excellent value for money, and should not be missed.

**Philip Jarrett**

*The cover illustration by Dugald Cameron for* Grumman Aircraft.

*Paul Kemp*, The T Class Submarine; the Classic British Design, *published by Arms & Armour Press, 1990.*
*160 pages, 204 illustrations.*
*ISBN 0–85368–958–X. £19.95*

This is one of the finest 'class' histories yet published. It describes the design, construction, operations and modernisation of the very successful 'T' class submarines accurately and comprehensively whilst remaining very readable. The story begins in early 1934 when it was realised that the new submarines would have to be smaller if sufficient numbers were to be built within the overall limits of the second London Treaty.

The Rear Admiral (Submarines), Laurence, an outstanding submarine CO of the First World War, believed that the improvements in ASW methods would mean firing at longer range and probably on acoustic data, hence a big salvo would be needed to ensure a hit. After debate, the early 'T's had ten forward firing tubes. There was the usual debate over double hulls versus saddle tanks but within the weight limit there was no real prospect of a double hull. The DNC, Sir Arthur Johns, a very experienced submarine designer did not accept Laurence's view that the double hull was more resistant to depth charge attack.

The structural design was conventional, completed just before von Mises' work on overall collapse of stiffened cylinders reached Britain and hence the hull was rather heavy. Vickers managed the fastest build in 11¾ months though they took 17 later in the war. The Dockyards were a good deal slower, due to interruption for other tasks. Various designs of diesels were fitted in the earlier boats but none were particularly reliable.

Surface operation was still very important and there were many problems with the shape of the bow and the bridge, all described with understanding. The book is more about the boats than their operations but these are given sufficient coverage to show both the merits of the 'T' class and the skill of their COs and crews. The excitement of gun action is brought out – the reviewer served in *Tabard* when she was champion gunnery boat. The operation of the heads and the dreadful fate of 'getting your own back' is described though the author does not mention the possibility of 'booby trapping' nor that different builders arranged the crucial valves and levers differently.

The introduction of welding enabled the diving depth to be increased from 300ft to 350ft as weight saving on flanges enabled thicker plates to be used. The author sees Vickers as welding enthusiasts, pressing welding on a reluctant DNC. The DNC, Goodall, tells the opposite in his diary and says that he had to exert very great pressure on Vickers to get them to weld. In any case, welding of the pressure hull was not possible until S quality steel was available in quantity.

The losses of *Thetis* and later *Truculent* are described with sympathy and lead to a discussion of escape methods during the long life of the class. Later chapters cover the 'T' conversions and streamlines. (Did *Totem* really go 3kts faster than the rest of the class? It would correspond to nearly 75 per cent more power.)

The author several times refers to the 'faults' of the earlier 'O', 'P' and 'R' classes and even suggests that they broke with the tradition and lessons of the First World War. In fact, they were designed as long range, 'Pacific', developments of the very successful 'L' class. Compared with other country's submarines of the 1920s they were quite good boats with an unusually great diving depth.

The illustrations are outstanding; well selected, relevant and mostly not over familiar. Older readers will enjoy their memories of this great class of submarines, the younger generation will read with amazement of the problems, hardship and fun of life in a 'T'. All will enjoy the book.

**D K Brown**

*The 'T' class submarine* Tally Ho *postwar; a detailed design history of these ships has been published recently.* (CMP)

## SHORT NOTICES

*'Anatomy of the Ship' series:*
*Peter Goodwin,* The Naval Cutter Alert 1777
*Ross Watton,* The Aircraft Carrier Victorious
*E Rossler & Fritz Kohl,* The Type XXI U-Boat
*all published by Conway Maritime Press, 1990–91.*
*Each: 240 × 254mm, 128* (Victorious *160) pages, approx 20 photographs and 300 line drawings.*
Alert *ISBN 0–85177–592–6. £20.00.*
Victorious *ISBN 0–85177–580–2. £20.00.*
Type XXI *ISBN 0–85177–570–5. £20.00.*

Both of the modern warship subjects in the past year's additions to this well known series are slightly out of the ordinary: the Type XXI because it was not commissioned for the series but was adapted from a German language work, so is lighter on drawings but includes a far larger number of photos than the norm; for *Victorious*, additional pages were required to do full justice to a ship that was so radically altered by her 1950s refit that the author is representing, in effect, two vessels. A perusal of the level of alterations to *Victorious* makes it abundantly clear why the ship's reconstruction took so long.

*Siegfried Breyer,* Battleship Tirpitz; Pocket Battleship Admiral Graf Spee; The German Aircraft Carrier Graf Zeppelin; The German Battleship Scharnhorst; The German Battleship Gneisenau; *all published by Schiffer Publishing, 1991.*
*Each: 300 × 210mm, 48 pages, approx 90 illustrations, paperback, £8.95.*
Tirpitz *ISBN 0–88740–184–8.*
Graf Spee *ISBN 0–88740–183 X.*
Graf Zeppelin *ISBN 0–88740–242–9.*
Scharnhorst *ISBN not quoted.*
Gneisenau *ISBN not quoted.*

A new series of monographs translated from the German; largely photographic and well produced. In the same format and approach, but 192-page hardback, there is also another series so far amounting to two volumes entitled *The German Navy at War 1935–1945;* the authors are Breyer and Gerhard Koop, and the first parts are subtitled *The Battleships* (ISBN 0–88740–220–8) and *The U-Boat* (0–88740–218–6). Each costs £34.95.

*David K Brown,* The Future Surface Fleet: Options for Medium Sized Navies, *published by Conway Maritime Press, 1991.*
*234 × 156mm, 224 pages, 50+ illustrations*
*ISBN 0–85177–557–8. £20.00.*

Recently retired after a prominent career with the Royal Corps of Naval Constructors, David Brown is well placed to set out the main problems facing the second division of maritime powers like Britain. He is at pains to stress that his views are personal and are not intended as covert criticism of his old masters, but he has distinctly different ideas about how the nation's money would be best spent in terms of the types of ship to be built. Believing that the number of helicopters available is essential to ASW, he develops his own version of the Hi-Lo mix, with more powerful destroyers and smaller corvettes than the Royal Navy's current surface combatants, paid for by giving the new designs enough range to eliminate the costly replenishment ships. As with all 'ships that never were', the proposed designs are intriguing – particularly so in this case since they are not the fanciful back-of-an-envelope sketches of the amateur.

*Don L Canney,* The Old Steam Navy, Vol 1: Frigates, Sloops and Gunboats, 1815–1885, *published by Naval Institute Press, 1990.*
*280 × 215mm, 288 pages, 80 photographs, 115 line drawings.*
*ISBN 0–87021–004–1. £32.95.*

Covering the principal unarmoured steam ships of the US Navy, this book fills a real gap. It is a straightforward design history of the kind that is now familiar, giving most of its attention to the characteristics of the ships themselves – nearly 150 vessels are covered and in substantial detail. The book is obviously the product of real research, and it is also well illustrated; the only slight disappointment is the absence of what one might call 'the Friedman touch', the ability to relate design to larger political, economic and strategic issues. Nevertheless, *The Old Steam Navy* is a fine piece of work and those interested in the period will avidly await the armoured ships volume.

*Richard Ellis and Lt Cdr Ben Warlow,* The Royal Navy at Malta, Vol 2: 1907–1939, *published by Maritime Books, 1990.*
*287 × 290mm, 144 pages, approx 100 photographs.*
*ISBN 0–907771–48–3. £27.00.*

This large format album of superb photos is a sequel to that devoted to the period 1865–1906 published two years ago. The photographs are mostly portraits of RN ships, all taken by various generations of the Ellis family of professional photographers at Malta; most types of ship are represented, and most are excellent examples of the photographer's art – technically first class, but exhibiting a real feeling for what makes warships exciting subjects. All have been printed large, and the designer has been careful to place the magnificent double-page spreads on natural folds. The only drawbacks are the quality of reproduction, which would be good enough for most books but is not quite adequate for these photos; and the captions, which are mostly potted biographies of the ships and do not direct the reader's attention towards actual details in the plates. Nevertheless, these are minor niggles, and by modern standards it is also very good value for money.

*Erich Groener,* German Warships 1815–1945, Vol 2: U-Boats and Mine Warfare Vessels, *published by Conway Maritime Press, 1991.*
*295 × 248mm, 256 pages, 450 line drawings.*
*ISBN 0–85177–593–4. £35.00.*

The second volume of this *magnum opus* [see Warship 1990, pp217–8 for a notice of the series] covers all German submarines, and mine warfare vessels – both sweepers and layers. The level of information is consistent with the previous volume, and to anyone familiar with the original that is recommendation enough.

*Eric Grove with Graham Thompson,* Battle for the Fiords: NATO's Forward Maritime Strategy in Action, *published by Ian Allan, 1991.*
*235 × 172mm, 128 pages, 155 illustrations.*
*ISBN 0–7110–1922–3. £15.95.*

Although of small compass, this is by no means the usual somewhat light weight picture album one expects of this imprint. Nor is it quite such an academic disquisition on strategy as its subtitle threatens. Instead it is a reasonably detailed and highly interesting account of the 1988 NATO exercise 'Teamwork' off Norway, which is a rehearsal for the implementation of the Forward Maritime Strategy. This book explains in layman's terms, why this came about and how it is supposed to work.

The ultimate goal of the strategy is to be able to reinforce Norway's vulnerable northern region if threatened by the Soviet Union, and involves an ASW force clearing a passage for a predominantly US Striking Fleet to approach the coast, followed by amphibious landings. Like all exercises, with friendly forces acting out the role of the enemy, it is never completely realistic, but the most entertaining part of the book is undoubtedly the 'factionalised' narrative of the sea battle between NATO and the simulated Warsaw Pact forces. Seeing this strategy in action certainly explains so many of the characteristics of Western warships, and on a more detailed level it is fascinating to get a glimpse of how well (or otherwise) certain equipment performs in combat conditions.

*Eric Grove,* Fleet to Fleet Encounters: Tsushima, Jutland, Philippine Sea, *published by Arms & Armour Press, 1991.*
*235 × 154mm, 160 pages, 57 photographs.*
*ISBN 1–85409–012–7. £16.95.*

Eric Grove has become established as one of the most intelligent commentators on naval strategy, and unlike most strategists he is entirely at home with the technology involved. Thus, in this book he is able to analyse three great naval clashes – each representative of a separate era of naval development – and draw strategic lessons from them, without ever losing sight of the technical details (the fatal role of British cordite at Jutland, for example). As descriptions of the battles, there is little new, but as ever the analysis provokes thought.

*Arnold Hague,* Destroyers for Great Britain: A History of the Fifty Town Class ships Transferred from the United States to Great Britain in 1940, *published by Greenhill Books, 1990.*
*244 × 185mm, 112 pages, 120 photographs.*
*ISBN 1–85367–075–8. £15.00.*

An expanded hardback edition of the World Ship Society publication reviewed in *Warship 1989*, with additional material and photos.

*Harry C Hutson,* Grimsby's Fighting Fleet: Trawlers and U-boats during the Second World War, *published by Hutton Press, 1990.*
*108 pages, 50 photographs.*
*No ISBN, £5.95.*

A high proportion of the Royal Navy's requisitioned trawlers came from Grimsby, and this anecdotal account describes those that were actively engaged against German submarines. It is far from a professional history, but so little is published on this subject that it is worth a mention.

*Derek James,* Westland Aircraft Since 1915, *published by Putnam Aeronautical Books, 1991.*
*216 × 138mm, 512 pages, 445 photographs, 62 line drawings.*
*ISBN 0–85177–847–X. £35.00.*

The last major British aircraft manufacturer to be covered in the Putnam series, Westland played a significant role in the development of postwar British naval aviation from the Wyvern to the current crop of helicopters (although the company can trace its naval associations back to the Walrus of the 1920s). The usual Putnam format is followed, with a brief history of the company preceding a chronological listing of all aircraft types, with design history, characteristics, and service careers. Not light reading but ideal and reliable reference.

*Andrew Lambert,* The Last Sailing Battlefleet: Maintaining Naval Mastery 1815–1850, *published by Conway Maritime Press, 1991.*
*295 × 248mm, 224 pages, 140 photographs.*
*ISBN 0–85177–591–8. £30.00.*

A major work on a long neglected period of naval history, this book is an unusual combination of academic concern for the political background to naval policy, with a study of the technical details of the ships themselves. While ministerial in-fighting may not be of much interest to ship enthusiasts, Lambert convincingly shows that there can be no real understanding of building programmes without reference to the politics of the period. The controversial appointment of Symonds as Surveyor was highly politicised, so even the design of ships was influenced by political factors in a way that was unprecedented. Too often the last decades of sail are ignored – only the coming of steam is seen as important – but much happened to the design, construction and arming of the sailing battlefleet that has long deserved a serious study like this one.

*Brian Lavery,* Building the Wooden Walls: The Design and Construction of the 74-gun Ship Valiant, *published by Conway Maritime Press, 1991.*
*270 × 200mm, 206 pages, 150 illustrations.*
*ISBN 0–85177–579–9. £25.00.*

Designed to accompany the excellent 'Wooden Walls' exhibit at Chatham Historic Dockyard (for which the author was historic advisor), this book charts the design, building and fitting out of a ship of the line, taking as his example the large '74' *Valiant*, launched at Chatham in 1759. While much of the material will be familiar to the real specialist, the requirement to follow the process from start to finish forces the author to address all sorts of questions that other studies conveniently ignore – the nature of launching ceremonies in the eighteenth century, for example.

▲ *The Type 25, an attempt at a cheap frigate. From David Brown's new book* The Future British Surface Fleet. *(MoD)*

*A typical illustration from Ross Watton's latest 'Anatomy', on* Victorious. ▼

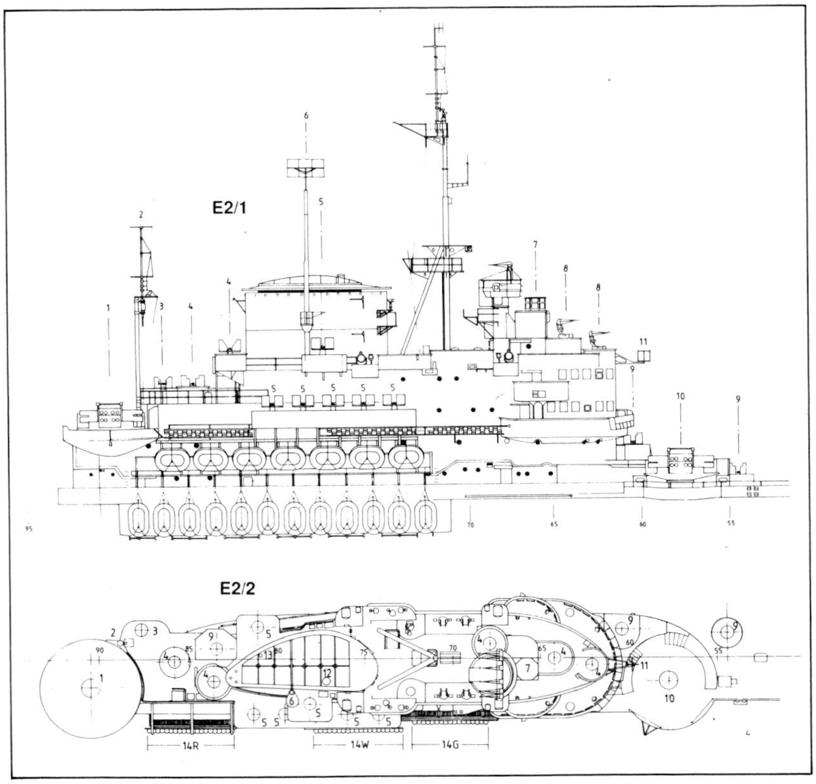

*R D Layman and Stephen McLaughlin,* The Hybrid Warship: The Amalgamation of Big Guns and Aircraft, *published by Conway Maritime Press, 1991.*
*270 × 200mm, 192 pages, 150 illustrations.*
*ISBN 0–85177–552–2. £25.00.*

A recurring *ignis fatuus* of twentieth century warship design has been the attempt to combine the characteristics of different types within a single hull, almost always with disappointing results. The battleship/aircraft carrier is the most spectacular example, and while history can point to few such ships completed, there were many more still-born. In this fascinating book, Dick Layman has unearthed a host of poorly documented or totally unknown examples, while the illustrative skill of his collaborator has provided the artist's impressions. They range from the frankly impossible dreams of total amateurs to fully worked out schemes by navy professionals (one of the most interesting chapters concerns the US Navy's official predictions of the layout of the *Nelson* and *Rodney* while they were still shrouded in secrecy). That the object was ultimately a waste of time does not detract from the seriousness of the pursuit, and there is no doubt that the authors are charting a real stream of naval development, even if it turned out in the end to be a backwater.

*Typical illustration from the latest volume of Groener.*

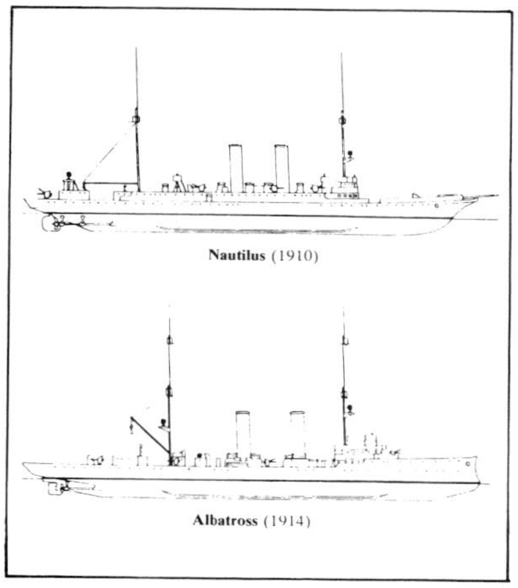


*Vice-Admiral Sir Louis Le Bailly,* The Man Around the Engine: Life Below the Waterline, *published by Kenneth Mason, 1991.*
*216 × 138mm, 192 pages, 25 illustrations.*
*ISBN 0–85937–354–1. £14.95.*

Although this book is nominally the first volume of Admiral Le Bailly's autobiography, it is far more than an old sailor's reminiscences. The author was a forceful, and ultimately successful, advocate of higher quality engineering for British warships, one of the weakest features of inter-war designs. After an eye-opening period operating with the US fleet in the Pacific in 1944–5, he exposed the cause of greater endurance for British ships, and was instrumental in numerous technical improvements. A good history of naval engineering is long overdue, but while this book has no such pretentions it goes a certain way towards that goal – personal account it may be, but it does provide some brilliant insights into the background. A further volume, *From Fisher to the Falklands*, is promised.

*A J Marder, Mark Jacobsen and John Horsfield,* Old Friends, New Enemies: The Royal Navy and the Imperial Japanese Navy; the Pacific War 1942–45, *published by Oxford University Press, 1990.*
*235 × 150mm, 640 pages.*
*ISBN 0–19–820150–8. £40.00.*

This is the long-delayed second volume of Marder's work on Anglo-Japanese naval relations, the first of which was published shortly after his death in 1981. Much of the research was already done and it has been completed and written up by two of his former students. As one would expect from its pedigree, it is a work of considerable scholarship and covers the larger issues of the naval war with Japan in great detail. There is some material on the technical problems for the British of operating alongside the Americans but on the whole it is not a book that has much to say about design or operational considerations.

*Official drawing of the famous* Kearsarge, *victor over the CSS* Alabama. *From* The Old Steam Navy.

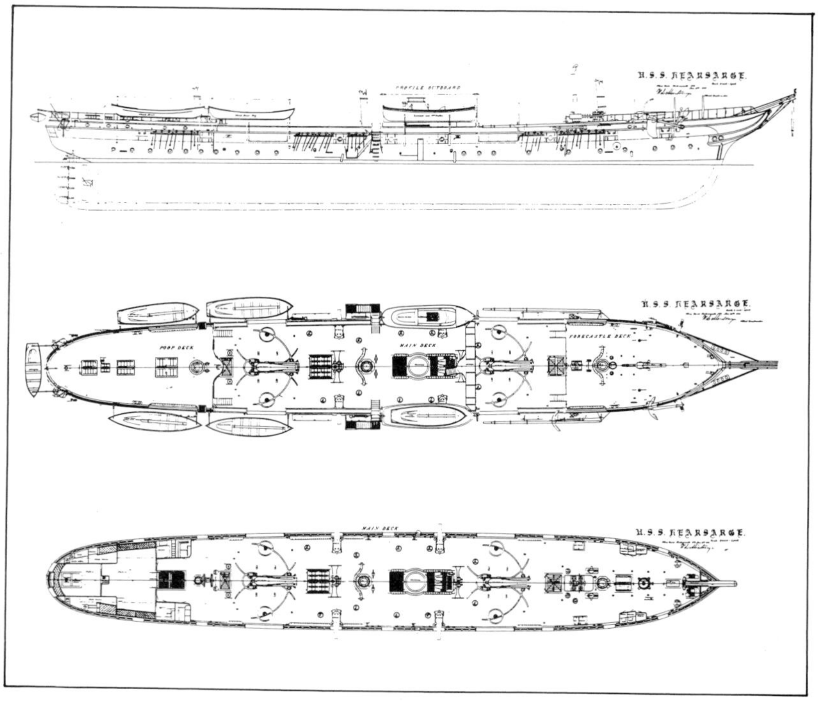

*Robert C Mikesh & Shorzoe Abe,* Japanese Aircraft 1910–1941, *published by Putnam Aeronautical Books, 1991.*
*270 × 200mm, 304 pages, 400 photographs, 15 line drawings.*
*ISBN 0–85177–840–2. £30.00.*

One of the most important additions to the impressive Putnam library of aircraft reference, this is the first Western publication to cover all the early products of the Japanese aircraft industry. Since the Imperial Japanese Navy was a major sponsor of so many designs, this book is worth bringing to the attention of *Warship* readers – if you need data on some obscure floatplane carried by Japanese cruisers in 1928–29, this is the place to look.

*Robert C Stern,* Type VII U-boats, *published by Arms & Armour Press, 1991.*
*245 × 185mm, 160 pages, 160 photographs, 10 line drawings.*
*ISBN 1–85409–011–9. £18.95.*

There seems to be no end to the fascination exerted by U-boats in general and the Type VII in particular. Leafing through this latest offering, most of the illustrations are familiar, and many – like the official plans – have been better reproduced elsewhere. However, the text is comprehensive and deals with the evolution of the design, its various systems, weapons and sensors, and incorporates material on the human aspects of U-boat service gleaned from interviews with numerous veterans. As a technical design history it is excellent, and since there is probably nothing new left to the said about Type VIIs, if you have to have one book on the subject, then this is the one to go for.

*V E Tarrant,* Battleship Warspite, *published by Arms & Armour Press, 1991.*
*254 × 204mm, 160 pages, 120 illustrations.*
*ISBN 0–85368–971–7. £18.50.*

Few ships have a better fighting record than *Warspite*, and consequently her career is well known, so the author has tried to give it some novelty by the use of private papers and interviews with those who served on the ship. The result is a concise and readable story, although anyone looking for new insights into the performance of the ship will be disappointed.

*Owen Thetford,* British Naval Aircraft Since 1912 (Sixth Edition), *published by Putnam Aeronautical Books, 1991.*
*216 × 138mm, 544 pages, 450 photographs, 120 line drawings.*
*ISBN 0–85177–849–6. £35.00.*

The new edition of this standard work – the first for nearly a decade – has taken the opportunity to completely revise the original, which was first published in 1958 and had received various ad hoc additions over the years. The Fleet Air Arm is no longer a large force so the number of entirely new aircraft entries is small; conversely, those in service have received many updates, so the extent of the revision is surprising. New and amended information has also come to light relating to earlier aircraft so the volume has benefited from a thorough overhaul.

*Spencer Tucker,* Arming the Fleet: US Navy Ordnance in the Muzzle-Loading Era, *published by Naval Institute Press, 1989.*
*254 × 178mm, 336 pages, 135 illustrations.*
*ISBN 0–87021–007–6. £27.95.*

This study of American guns down to the Civil War is largely based on contemporary manuals and published works. Little of any value has been written about gunnery in this period so the book is particularly welcome, but while it is good on characteristics of individual weapons, it would have given a better idea of development if it could have made some reference to policy and the rationale behind technical changes.

*US Naval Intelligence,* Uniforms & Insignia of the Navies of World War Two, *published by Greenhill Books, 1991.*
*194 × 261mm, 112 pages, 96 colour plates.*
*ISBN 1–85367–097–9. £25.00.*

A reprint of an official wartime booklet *Joint Army and Navy Publication 1,* this version includes all the combatants plus the neutral navies of Turkey, Sweden, Spain and Portugal. For all the interest in uniforms and regalia, navies are poorly represented among modern publications so this reprint fills a need.

*Bruce W Watson,* The Changing Face of the World's Navies: 1945 to the Present, *published by Arms & Armour Press, 1991.*
*233 × 154mm, 282 pages, 96 photographs.*
*ISBN 1–85409–017–8. £18.95.*

As a reasonably detailed chronology of naval events since the war, with short summaries of developments in the main navies every decade or so, this book is potentially very useful. It also contains numerous tables of fleet strengths during the periods under review, which give an instant appraisal of the way a navy is going. Unfortunately, although the quantity of information is impressive, the quality is less so: most of the sources so meticulously referenced are journalistic articles of no great authority, which raises doubts about the value of the analysis. On technical matters the book is also shaky – anyone who can claim that British Type 42 destroyers are primarily ASW ships and that *Sheffield*'s aluminium superstructure melted after the Argentinian Exocet attack, is not trusted to make qualitative judgements on warship design. Nevertheless, if the editorialising is treated with caution, or ignored, the bare facts add up to a usable reference.

*Anthony Watts,* The Imperial Russian Navy, *published by Arms & Armour Press, 1990. 245 × 245mm, 192 pages, 200 illustrations.*
*ISBN 1–85368–912–1. £35.00.*

This book seems to have been written around its photographs for there is little that is new in the data tables and text. The photos themselves are interesting, some unfamiliar, and mostly reproduced fairly large. They are not particularly well printed, however, which spoils the effect, and there are omissions in the sense that some of the smaller craft are not illustrated at all, despite the fact that photographs of these vessels have been used elsewhere. Bearing in mind that there is not much more in this book than in the two relevant *Conway's Fighting Ships* volumes, it seems a high price to pay for a collection of pictures.

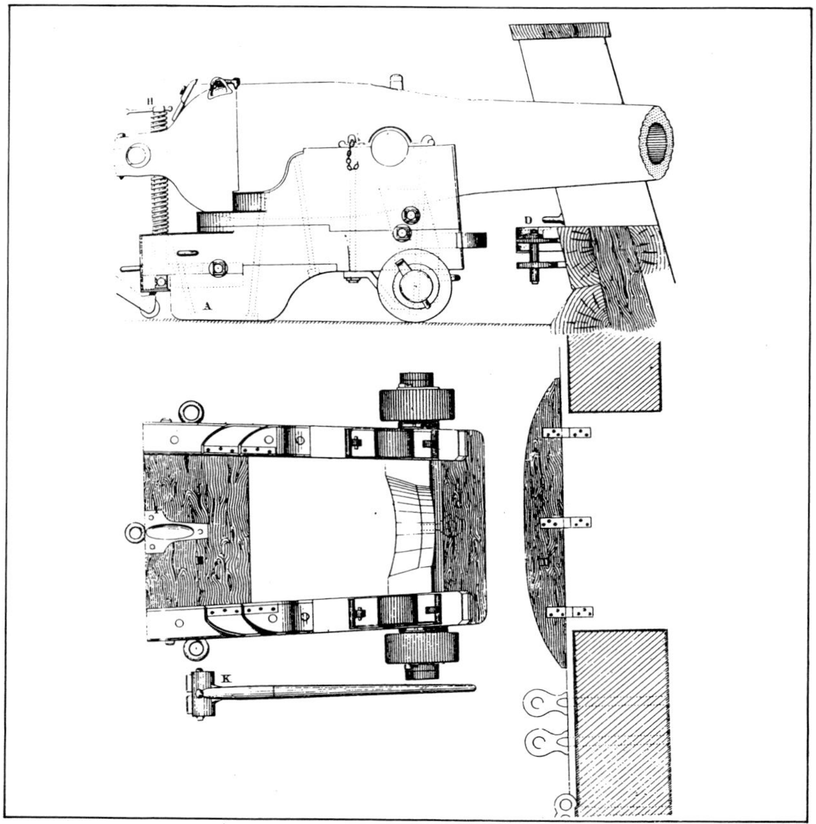

*One of the numerous line drawings from Spencer Tucker's new study of US ordnance in the muzzle loading era.*

*The Russian masted gun vessel* Korietz, *one of the more obscure vessels covered by Anthony Watts' new book on the Imperial Russian Navy. (*CMP*)*

## BOOKS ANNOUNCED

*Anon,* An illustrated History of Pearl Harbor and the War in the Pacific, *published by Salamander, £29.95.*

*Kenneth R Andrews,* Ships, Money and Politics: Seafaring and Naval Enterprise in the Reign of Charles I, *published by Cambridge University Press, £25.00.*

*Jim Allaway,* Lt Cdr Wanklyn VC, DSO: Hero of the Upholder, *published by Airlife, £14.95.*

*Fritz-Otto Busch,* The Drama of the Scharnhorst, *published by Robert Hale, paperback, £6.95.*

*Mike Critchley,* British Warships and Auxiliaries, *published by Maritime Books, £4.95.*
The latest edition of this useful little 'spotters' guide.

*John Daly,* Russian Seapower and the 'Eastern Question' 1827–41, *published by Macmillan, £40.00.*

*Norman Friedman,* The Naval Institute Guide to World Naval Weapons Systems, 1992–91, *published by Naval Institute Press, no price announced.*

*Frederick Grossmith,* The Laconia Order, *published by Hallmark Books, £11.95.*

*Gregory K Hartmann with Scott C Truver,* Weapons that Wait: Mine Warfare in the US Navy (Updated Edition), *published by Naval Institute Press, $29.95.*

*Sari R Hornstein,* The Restoration Navy and English Foreign Trade: A Study in the Peacetime Use of Sea Power, *published by Scolar Press, £35.00.*

*Richard Hough,* Bless Our Ship: Mountbatten and the Kelly, *published by John Curtis/Hodder, £19.95.*

*Paul Kemp,* Bismarck and Hood: Great Naval Rivals, *published by Arms & Armour Press, paperback, £6.95.*

*Paul Kennedy,* Rise and fall of British Naval Mastery, *published by Fontana, paperback, £6.99.*
Paperback edition of this somewhat controversial book.

*Alexander McKee,* Against the Odds: Battles at Sea 1591–1949, *published by Souvenir, £15.95.*

*Richard Ollard,* Fisher and Cunningham, *published by Constable, £16.95.*

*Oscar Parkes,* British Battleships 1866–1950, *published by Leo Cooper, £75.00.*
A new reprint of this classic work.

*Norman Polmar,* The Naval Institute Guide to the Soviet Navy (Fifth Edition), *published by Naval Institute Press, $49.95.*

*Norman Polmar and Jurrien Noot,* Submarines of the Russian and Soviet Navies, *published by Naval Institute Press, $58.95.*

*James Rusbridger,* Who Sank the Surcouf? *published by Century, £14.99.*

*Paul Silverstone,* The US Navy, 1945 to the Present, *published by Arms & Armour Press, paperback, £8.95.*

*Michael Simpson,* Anglo–American Naval Relations 1917–1919, *published by the Navy Records Society (Scolar Press), £37.50.*

*Paul Stillwell,* Battleship Arizona: An Illustrated History, *published by Naval Institute Press, no price announced.*

*Jack Sweetman,* American Naval History: An Illustrated Chronology of the US Navy and Marine Corps, 1775–Present (Second Edition), *published by Naval Institute Press, $36.95.*

*A model of the* Moray *class submarines (see 'Naval Year in Review', following) now being offered for export by the Netherlands.* (Rotterdamsche Drougdok Mij)

# THE NAVAL YEAR IN REVIEW

The events covered by this review stretch from approximately May 1990 to May 1991, with some reference before and after. Compiled by Ian Sturton.

## A. INTRODUCTION

The year was dominated by the Gulf crisis and subsequent war, but the underlying trends set in previous years remain. The Warsaw Pact's military structure was formally abolished, and Soviet troops will leave Poland by 1993 and the former GDR by 1994; a unified Germany with treaty-limited forces continues in NATO. The Soviet Union is still a superpower, but possibly heading for major unrest. The CFE Treaty was signed and, although implementation problems have jeopardised ratification, US and Soviet budget cuts will reduce future force sizes, regardless of treaties. The so-called 'peace dividend' already includes shipyard closures and mergers, bases shut down and the cancellation or postponement of new programmes; defence requirements are increasingly subordinate to financial constraints.

The East–West thaw has had no discernable effect on increased defence spending in the Asia–Pacific region, where China remains unstable, the Philippines have an uncertain future and fighting continues in Cambodia. One-third of Soviet nuclear and conventional forces are stationed in the Far East, and Japan is the world's third largest naval spender.

The strengths of the major naval powers are listed in Table 1.

## B(i). THE STRATEGIC BALANCE

Although the direct classical threat from the Warsaw Pact has evaporated, and some authorities consider that Moscow would need 18–24 months to prepare for a major war, a massive limited strike against specific objectives would need much less preparation – perhaps 45 days; ineffective political control of the military has brought a limited strike within the realm of possibility. Smaller, more mobile NATO land forces will require a full amphibious capability. New problem areas are likely to arise among the restless, heavily-armed

**Table 1.** *MAJOR WARSHIP TYPES OF PRINCIPAL NAVIES, 1 APRIL 1991*

| *Type* | *USA* | *USSR* | *UK* | *France* | *China* | *India* | *Japan* | *Italy* |
|---|---|---|---|---|---|---|---|---|
| CV (large) | 15 | 1 | – | – | – | – | – | – |
| CV (medium) | – | 4 | – | 2 | – | 1 | – | – |
| CV (small) | – | – | 3 | – | – | 1 | – | 1 |
| Battleship | 2 | – | – | – | – | – | – | – |
| Cruiser (helicopter) | – | 2 | – | 1 | – | – | – | 1 |
| Cruiser (missile) | 46 | 29 | – | 1 | – | – | – | 1 |
| Destroyer | 48 | 38 | 13 | 15 | 19 | 5 | 43 | 3 |
| Frigate (fleet) | 97 | 38 | 33 | 4 | 37 | 12 | 18 | 14 |
| (escort) | – | 121 | – | 17 | – | 9 | – | 7 |
| SSBN | 32 | 61 | 4 | 5 | 1 | – | – | – |
| SSGN | } 87 | 42 | – | – | – | – | – | – |
| SSN | | 64 | 14 | 4 | 4 | – | – | – |
| SS (all types) | – | 110 | 8 | 9 | c55 | 19 | 15 | 9 |
| MCMV (ocean and coastal) | 23 | 217 | 35 | 19 | c130 | 12 | 32 | ?15 |

*Note: The 15 US carriers include one in SLEP. Many Soviet escort frigates and diesel submarines are ineffective or unserviceable.*

*A striking photograph of the French TCD (LPD)* Foudre, *commissioned 8 December 1990. Orders for two sister ships have been postponed.* (DCN)

states to the south and east of the Mediterranean. NATO naval forces will continue to be needed 'in area' (its geographical coverage remains unaltered), and, as land forces are reduced, the importance of US reinforcements will increase. The response by NATO powers to the out-of-area Gulf crisis was disappointing, auguring badly for future western European military unity (ie NATO-without-America); whereas three NATO members (USA, Britain and France) sent ground troops to fight, and two more members (Canada, Italy) aircraft but no troops, other countries contributed only warships, not always very generously or wholeheartedly.

The long-standing but generally disregarded NATO rule of increasing defence expenditure by an annual 3 per cent above inflation was officially dropped. Current reductions in defence spending should be viewed in a wider context. According to figures published by SIPRI in Stockholm, defence spending in the USA rose by an average 6.7 per cent annually between 1980 and 1986 and in the USSR by an average 5.5 per cent between 1980 and 1987. American spending in 1990, although 6 per cent less than in 1989, was still nearly 30 per cent greater than in 1980. Similarly, Soviet spending in 1990 was 10 per cent less than in 1989, but nearly 38 per cent more than in 1980.

## B(ii). DISARMAMENT

Whereas the START II treaty framework binds Washington and Moscow not to deploy more than 880 nuclear-armed, 600km+ range, sea-launched cruise missiles (SLCM) each, general naval arms control remains off the CFE agenda; US naval power maintains regional stability, serving both US and Soviet interests, while Soviet START II strategic nuclear force totals, which rely heavily on naval protection, are as yet undetermined. The CFE Treaty was signed in Paris on 19 November; discrepancies subsequently discovered in its implementation by the USSR – the wholesale transfer and storage of modern weaponry across the Urals and a 'bizarre' switch of three army motorised rifle divisions to the navy – led to the postponement of ratification and of the 11 February summit in Moscow. The UK and France are not in the START negotiations.

▲ USNS Observation Island *(T-AGM 33) is fitted with a USAF phased-array radar for technical verification of foreign ballistic missile test flights, essential for START II.* (Raytheon)

*The interior of the Devonshire Dock Hall, VSEL, Barrow-in-Furness, showing Trident submarines under construction.* Vanguard *is due for floating out late 1991/early 1992.* (VSEL) ▼

# C. BUDGET PROPOSALS AND NEW PROGRAMMES

## C(i). USA, NATO and Allies

## *MAJOR NATO NAVIES*

**(a) United States** The defence spending (authorisation and appropriation) bill for FY91, beginning 1 October 1990, was finalised in November at $288.3b, a decline of 4.9 per cent over FY90 in real terms and a 20 per cent fall since 1985. The budget proposals for FY92 were $278.3b in budget authority, $283.0b in outlays, and for FY93, $277.9b in authority, $279.1b in outlays; present plans provide for the figures to remain between $278b and $283b until at least FY96; FY91 figures exclude a supplementary appropriation for Operation 'Desert Storm'.

By 1994, there should be 12 deployable carriers instead of 14, with 13 air wings instead of 15, and no battleships; 40 more *Knox* class frigates will go into reserve (28 in FY92), and new orders are being slowed (Table 2). The Trident II submarine programme will terminate at the 18th boat, approved in FY91, while the retrofitting of the Trident I boats with the Trident II missile has been deferred beyond FY97. The last 16 Poseidon boats will go during the 1990s, and the Poseidon base at Holy Loch will close in 1992. The A-12 Avenger, replacement for the A-6E Intruder, was cancelled, and the naval variant of the ATF deferred, probably indefinitely. The active fleet will number 451 ships by FY94; naval manpower will fall from 591,000 to 501,000, USMC manpower from 197,000 to 148,000. These proposals nominally depend on signature of both CFE and START treaties.

**(b) United Kingdom.** Actual defence spending for 1990–91, excluding the Gulf conflict, was estimated at £22.1b ($35.4b), some 4 per cent of GDP, rising to £22.8b in 1991–92, £23.3b in 1992–93 and £23.4b in 1993–94 (3.4 per cent of GDP), an estimated fall in real terms of 8.7 per cent. The 1990–91 provision for naval equipment, including the Trident programme, was £2.38b ($3.82b). The 'Options for Change' study – plans for reducing defence strength in 1990–95 – proposed the following changes in the RN (announced 25 July): all three carriers to be retained, total of destroyers and frigates reduced from 'about 50' to 'about 40', total of 28 submarines of all types to be reduced to 20 (4 SSBN, 7 *Trafal-*

USS Hue City *(CG-66), Ingall's 14th* Ticonderoga *class AEGIS cruiser, on first sea trials ('Trial Alpha'), March 1991; note the Mk41 Mod O VLS launcher. Vietnam War battles are no longer taboo as US ship names. (*Litton*)*

▲

*A 1990 view of* Fearless, *as refitted with a shorter mast and two 20mm Phalanx CIWS replacing after Seacat installations.* (DML)

*CPF-01,* Halifax *during builder's machinery trials off Halifax in October 1990. Despite unacceptable acoustic noise levels at speed, the ship will be turned over to the Canadian navy in July. However, with Saint John Shipbuilding Ltd, being responsible for correcting these during the up to 18-month naval trials period before the ship is finally accepted, these problems are expected to be identified and corrected within six months. Expected commissioning date is now tentatively given as mid-October 1991. Delivery of* Halifax *is now 18 months behind schedule.* (DND/LYNCAN Photo)

▼

**Table 2.** *USN SHIPBUILDING PROGRAMMES, 1989–1994*

| *New Construction* | *Approved (authorised and funded)* | | | *Proposed (subject to amendment)* | | |
|---|---|---|---|---|---|---|
| | *FY89* | *FY90* | *FY91* | *FY92* | *FY93* | *FY94* |
| SSBN *Ohio* | 1 | 1 | 1(1) | –(1) | –(1) | –(1) |
| SSN-688 *Los Angeles* | 2 | 1 | – | – | – | – |
| SSN-21 *Seawolf* | 1 | – | 1(2) | 1(3) | 1(3) | 1(3) |
| CVN | – | – | – | – | – | – |
| DDG-51 *Arleigh Burke* | 5 | 5 | 4(5) | 5(5) | 4(5) | 3(5) |
| MCM *Avenger* | – | 3 | – | – | – | – |
| MHC *Osprey* | – | 2 | 2(3) | 2(4) | 2(4) | 1(–) |
| LHD *Wasp* | 1 | – | 1(1) | –(1) | –(1) | – |
| LSD (cargo variant) | 1 | 1 | 1(1) | 1(1) | 1(1) | –(1) |

*Note: Proposals for FY92–FY94 according to FY1991–95 Shipbuilding Programme. Proposals according to the FY1990–94 Programme are in parentheses. Long-lead items for CVN-76 will be requested in FY93, the carrier funded in FY95.*

gars, 5 *Swiftsures*, 4 *Upholders*), MCMV total to remain at around 40, new amphibious ships programme to continue, personnel to be cut by 3000 to 60,000, Nimrod maritime patrol aircraft (MPA) down from 36 to 30. Other proposed changes include the closure of Rosyth and Portland naval bases. The third Polaris submarine was ordered, but as a result of increasing Treasury influence, other expected orders were frozen.

**(c) Canada.** The 1990–91 defence budget, set at $10.35b, was increased by 5 per cent in 1991–92. A Parliamentary Committee has recommended new diesel submarines and an acoustic sensor system in the Arctic, also reconsideration of the cancellations of the Polar 8 icebreaker and the extra six maritime patrol aircraft; the lives of the existing submarines may be extended from 1995 to 1999, pending a decision on new construction. The contract for the new maritime patrol vessels/MCMV should be signed in March 1991.

**(d) Germany.** The first defence budget for unified Germany was set at $35.4b, in real terms a reduction of 1.4 per cent for the West and up to 15.5 per cent for the previous West and East defence budgets combined. The backbone of the future navy will be 12 frigates for North Sea and Atlantic approaches. Three or four new Type 124 AAW frigates are to be procured, also Type 404 supply vessels and nine new maritime patrol aircraft. Twelve former *Volksmarine* warships, a representative selection of modern types, are being retained for one year and discarded when major refits become necessary.

**(e) Italy.** Amid continuing cuts – the 1990 budget fell by about $1.5b to $15.5b – the existing procurement programmes continue. A third *San Giorgio*, configured as a part-time training ship, has been ordered; four corvettes will be ordered to replace the *Albatros* class, when funds permit.

**(f) Netherlands.** Planned defence spending in 1991 is 1 per cent less than in 1990. According to the March 1991 Defence Review, naval personnel will be down 15 per cent over the next five years, 25 per cent over the decade. Two *Kortenaers* will be laid up in 1994, four more by 2000 while the new fast combat support ships will enter service in 1994 and 2000, the amphibious lift ship by 1996; six MCMV will be operational, the others laid up and only six of the planned ten Belgo-Dutch coastal MCMV will now be built. The active forces will constitute two large task groups, with one small in reserve.

**(g) The South–Eastern Flank. Greece's** defence spending in 1991 was budgeted at $2.12b, a cut in real terms of about 8 per cent. The eight-year Defence Cooperation Agreement (DCA) signed by Greece and USA in July included continuation of the US base at Suda Bay, and transfer of four *Charles F Adams* class DDG. **Turkey's** defence budget of $3.1b represents about 1.8 per cent of GNP; in addition to the submarine and frigate programmes, orders for new FAC and MCMV are expected.

*The German Type 122 frigate* Bremen; *note the reload magazines for the 8-cell NATO Sea Sparrow launcher forward of the bridge. Ships of this class were fitted with Goalkeeper as interim CIWS before deployment to the eastern Mediterranean during the Gulf crisis.* (Bremer Vulkan)

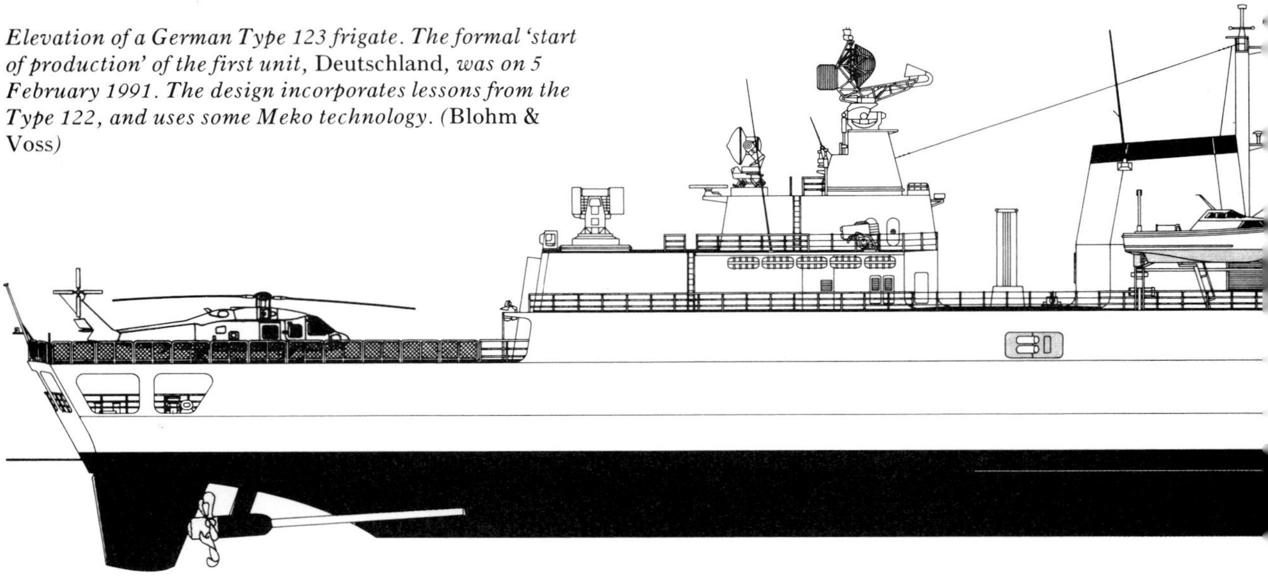


*Elevation of a German Type 123 frigate. The formal 'start of production' of the first unit,* Deutschland, *was on 5 February 1991. The design incorporates lessons from the Type 122, and uses some Meko technology. (*Blohm & Voss*)*

## *LESSER NATO NAVIES*

**Norway's** 1991 defence budget provided for zero real growth, curtailing the 2–3 per cent annual increases of the 1980s. New submarines and MCMV are in hand, but no decision has been announced on a new FAC class. **Denmark's** 1989–91 Defence Agreement froze the defence budget at $2.0b; Copenhagen naval dockyard to be closed, and the naval base reduced. Six more Stanflex 300 craft were ordered. **Belgium's** defence spending fell by 1.6 per cent, to $3.04b; four coastal and ten inshore MCMV will be decommissioned and the operational readiness of other ships reduced.

*The Portuguese frigate* Vasco da Gama *on trials, late 1990, is the lead-ship of the second Meko 200 class. Similar ships are built, building or on order for Turkey, Greece, Australia and New Zealand. (*Blohm & Voss*)* ►

*General arrangement drawing of the Danish patrol frigate* Thetis, *the first of four replacements for the* Hvidbjörnen *class. The new frigate, officially a Fishery Inspection and Surveying Vessel, is very lightly armed, but has 'space and weight' in plenty for a proper armament fit.* ▼

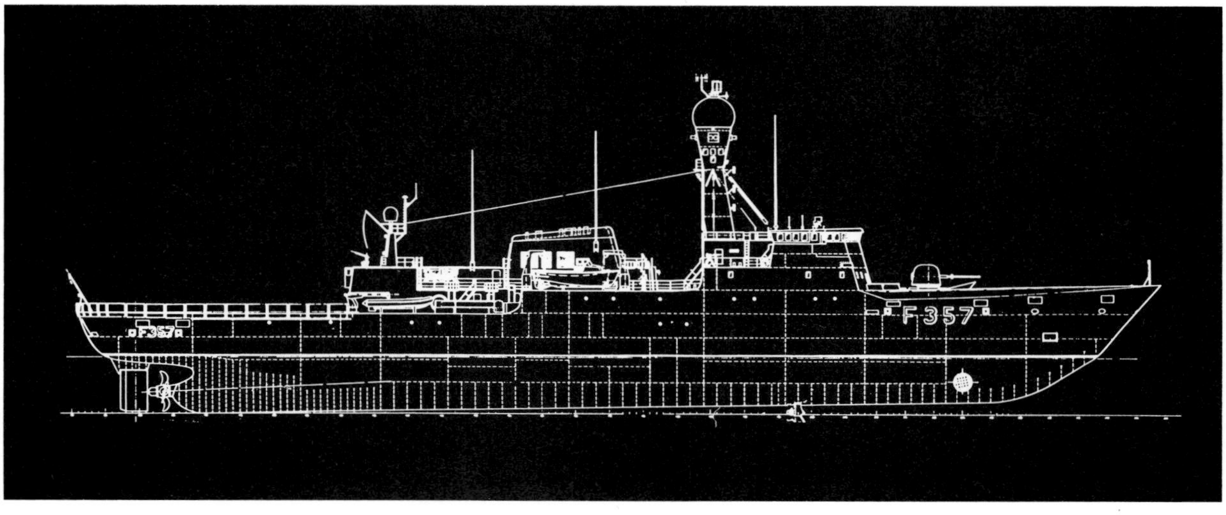

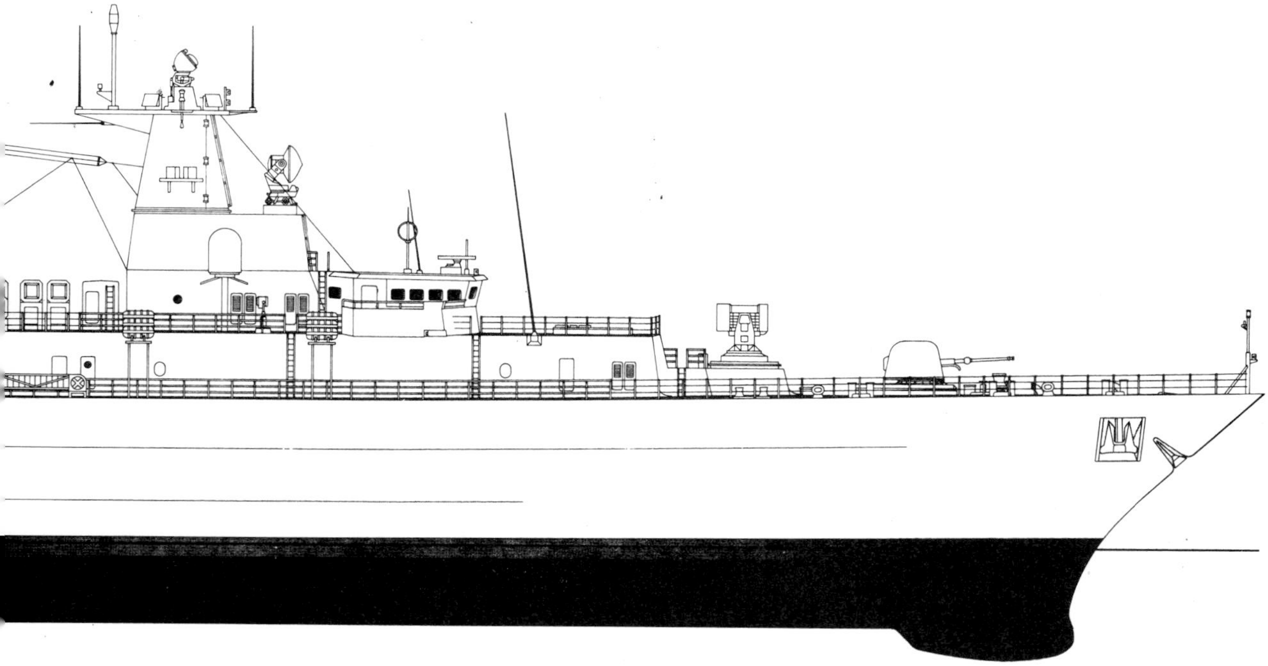

F330

*Model of French carrier* Charles de Gaulle; *launch is planned for 1995, first trials for early 1997.* (DCN) ▲

*The French SSN* Perle *fitting out in Cherbourg Naval Dockyard.* Perle *is the second of the* Amethyste *batch of the* Rubis *class;* Amethyste *is the name of the first of the batch, and also the French acronym for the improvements over the original* Rubis *quartet.* (DCN) ▼

## *FRANCE AND SPAIN*

**Cooperate with NATO but are not full military members.**

**France.** A 5.5 per cent rise in the 1991 defence budget, to $35.7b, was recommended; the draft defence budget for 1992 plans a 2.7 per cent increase. There is no official timescale for long-term procurement, but the following is expected: decision on the second nuclear-powered carrier in 1996/7, to be ready in eight years, new AAW missile system to be ready in 1999/2000, with frigates to fit ready in 2003/4. One SSBN will be completed every 2.5 years, and the pre-definition phase for the next generation of SSN is under way. France will cooperate with her partners on new frigates and diesel submarines, but not on the new generation SSBN (SNLE-NG).

**Spain.** The 1990 defence budget was $7.98b, 4.7 per cent of GDP, but cuts of 7.9 per cent imposed will delay some parts of the Alta Mar construction programme: the fifth and sixth FFG-7 frigates will begin in 1991, the MCMV will be one year late. Procurement is to fall by a real 20 per cent in 1991. The first F-100 frigate should be ordered in 1993.

## *MAJOR US ALLIES*

**Japan.** The FY91 Defence Budget was set at $29.3b, an increase of 5.8 per cent; annual increases in defence spending for the next 5 years will be limited to a real 2.93 per cent, half the average figure over the past 15 years, and less than the 3.75 per cent estimated economic growth rate. Requests in FY91 include the third AEGIS destroyer and extra P-3C ASW aircraft; a fourth AEGIS destroyer will come later in the five-year programme. Money for war aid to US will probably come from the JMSDF budget; one 50-ton FAC(M) and the new training ship were postponed. In spite of intense pressure on Japan to adopt a more prominent international military profile, Parliament failed to approve even a token non-combatant force for the Gulf; several MCMV were sent well after hostilities ended. The Kurile Islands question continues to bedevil relations with the USSR.

**Australia.** Defence spending in 1991/92 is to be increased by 5.5 per cent to $7.2b, around 2.3 per cent of GDP, with major naval outlays the *Collins* (Kockums Type 471) class submarines, the ANZAC frigates and the last FFG-7 frigates. The option on submarines 7 and 8 was not exercised; the RAN is looking at possible helicopter carriers, but *Jervis Bay* will not now undergo interim conversion. Larger, longer range patrol boats to replace the *Fremantle* class are under consideration.

## C(ii). Neutral European Nations

**(a) Finland.** The defence limitation clauses of the 1947 Paris Peace Treaty and the defence agreement with the USSR were abrogated, permitting submarine construction and the equipping of FAC with torpedoes.

**(b) Sweden.** Kockums won the $405m contract for three A19 submarines, subject to government approval, with options on two more and for inclusion of the Stirling AIP system. A five-year defence plan is to be adopted in 1991; if expenditure is not increased, defence objectives will have to be further scaled down.

*A photograph of a model of the ANZAC frigate; the ships will be built with the FMC 5in/54 Mk 45 gun, not the OTO Melara 3in/62 shown. 'Space and weight' is reserved for extra equipment, including a second VLS Sea Sparrow launcher, Harpoon and Phalanx. (*Blohm & Voss*)*

*The Japanese destroyers* Shirane *(143) and* Kurama *will be Japan's largest warships until* Yukikaze *completes in 1993. Two 20mm Phalanx CIWS were added in both, 1990. (*Ships of the World*)*

*The Japanese destroyer* Hamayuki, *fifth of twelve Hatsuyuki class. Since 1982, 22 destroyers have been completed for the JMSDF. (*Ships of the World*)*

*The Yugoslav frigate* Kotor, *completed in 1988, is a local design, dimensionally similar to the Soviet 'Koni' class but with a different sheer line. The SS-2-NC 'Styx' missiles face forwards in* Kotor, *aft in the 'Koni' class* Split *and* Kopar. *(Official)*

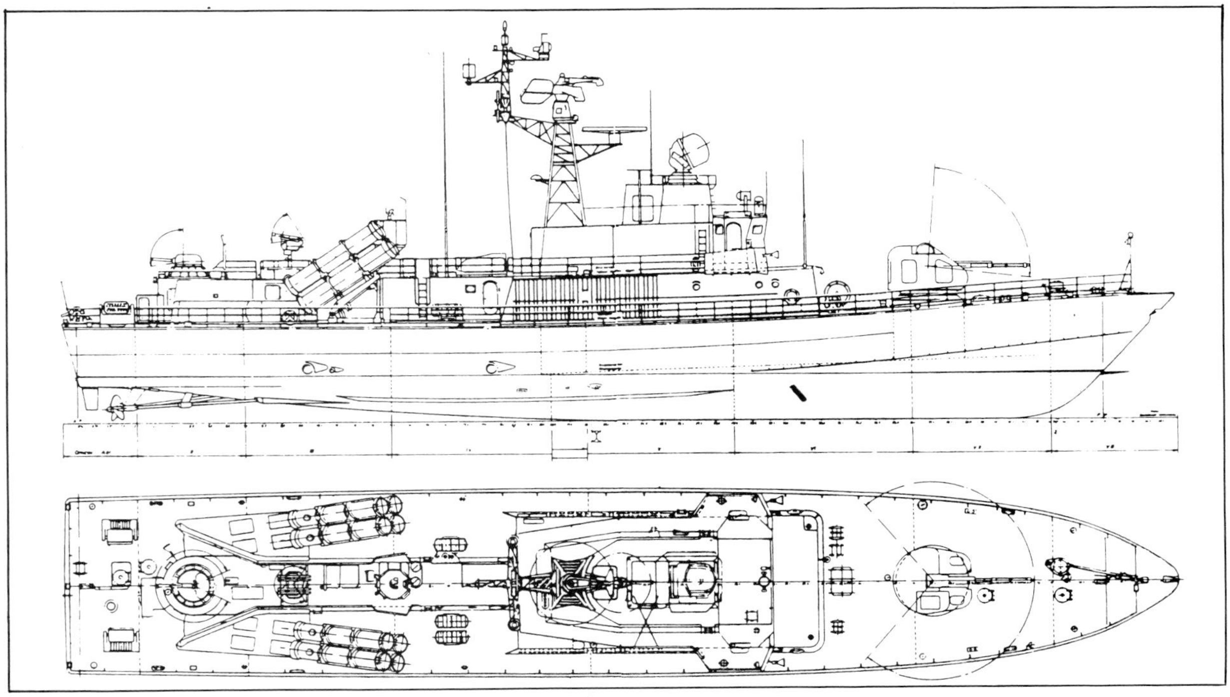

*Drawings of the GDR Type 151 missile corvette* Sassnitz *(NATO 'Balcom 10'), first of at least ten planned. Only one will be retained by Germany, two others may be sold to Poland. The SS-N-25 missile tubes were removed to the USSR before German reunification. (*Bremer Vulkan*)*

*A Soviet 'Kynda' class missile cruiser, first warships in the world with a main armament of anti-ship missiles (1962). For political reasons, the carrier* Riga *was renamed* Varyag *in 1990, suggesting withdrawal of the 'Kynda' unit of that name. (*USN*)*

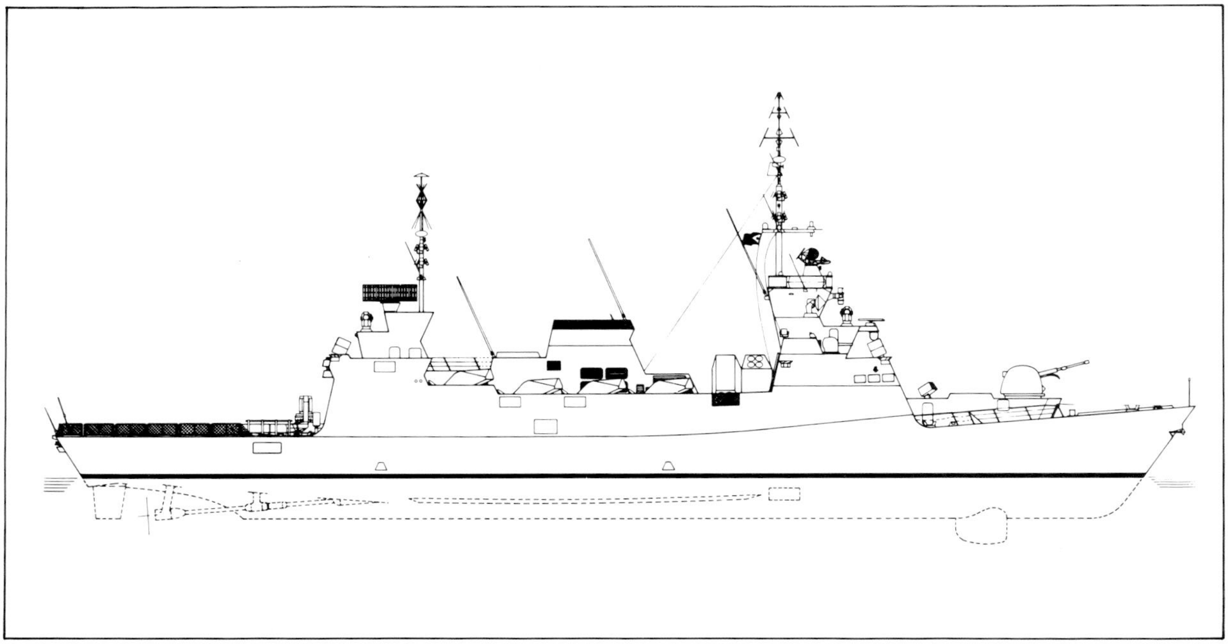

▲

*Outboard profile of the Sa'ar 5 missile corvette; three will be built for Israel by Ingalls, Pascagoula, under FMS. The heavy anti-ship armament includes 8 Harpoon and 8 Gabriel II SSM.*

*Amidships detail of the Indian frigate* Godavari*; note mix of Soviet and Western equipment on an enlarged* Leander *hull. The second batch of three, Project 16A, will be of modified type.*

▼

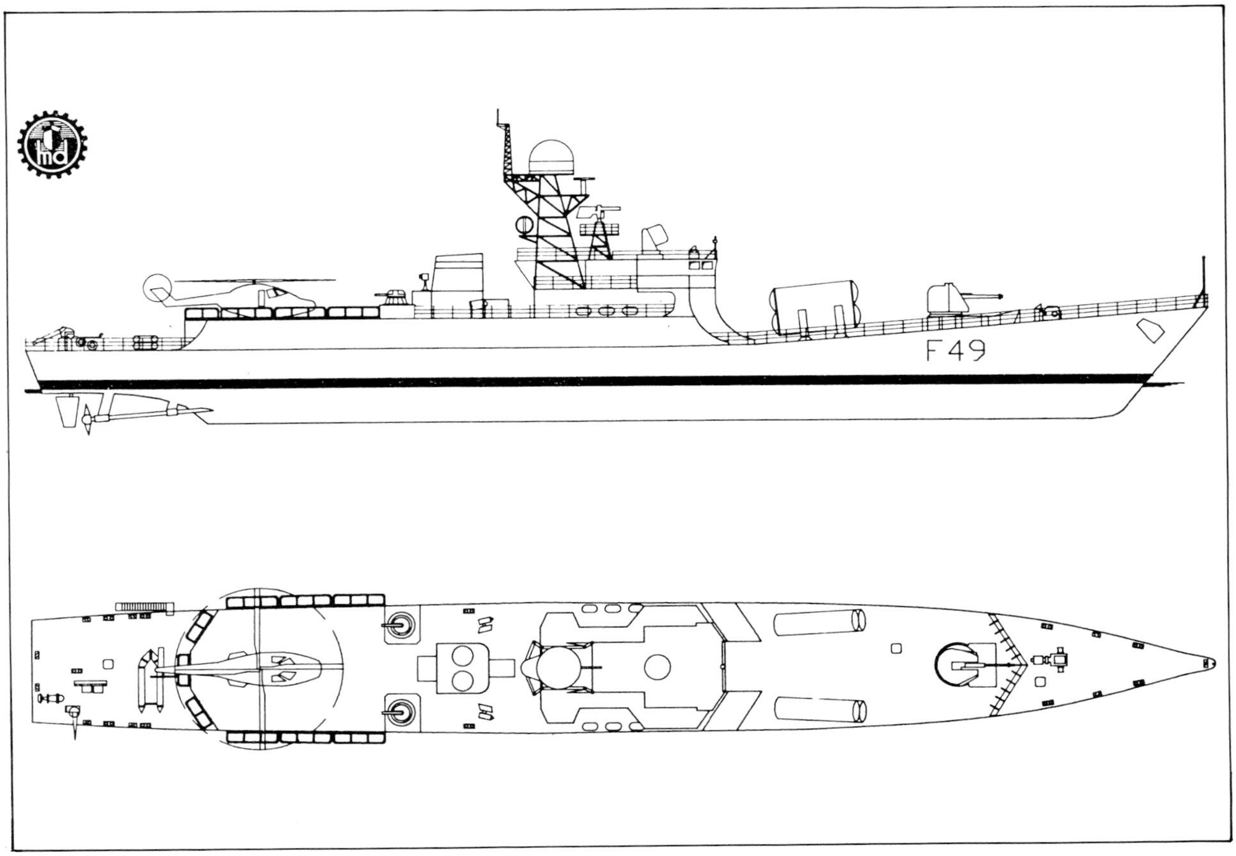


## C(iii). Eastern European Nations

**USSR.** Western estimates suggest that defence spending in 1989 fell by about 4–5 per cent in real terms, with procurement down by 6–7 per cent, and reductions up to 10 per cent are estimated for 1990; actual spending is still much higher than published Soviet figures. An official 2 per cent contraction in the economy in 1990 may have been as high as 10 per cent. While spending on conventional land and air forces has been reduced, there is no sign of corresponding budget reductions in strategic arms modernisation or naval forces, and naval personnel has not been cut. Surface ship types have been curtailed – no cruiser under construction was laid down later than 1986 – but more submarines were launched in 1990 than in 1989 (ten against nine). The naval air arm continues to press ahead, although the eventual total of large carriers is uncertain. The carriers *Tbilisi, Riga* and *Baku* were renamed after famous naval officers or ships, symbolising the steady disintegration of the centralised Soviet State.

Other eastern European navies have ships and equipment of Soviet pattern; some ex-*Volksmarine* ships may be sold further east, but in general post-Warsaw Pact trends are unclear.

## C(iv). Middle East

**Israel's** two HDW/IKL submarines, cancelled in November for budgetry reasons, were reinstated after the Gulf war, with funding from FMS.

**Egypt**. After cancellation of much foreign debt, the Navy may buy second-hand foreign tonnage, but the acquisition of ex-*Walrus* and ex-*Oberon* was reconsidered. **Saudi Arabia** may order another six SRMH.

*The Indian missile corvette* Khukri, *first of a planned twelve; the type is offered for export.*

## C(v). Pacific Rim ('PACRIM') and Indian Ocean

**(a) China's** defence budget for 1990 was $6.13b. The navy is looking at proposals for a carrier; the shipyards are occupied with frigates of improved types building for Thailand.

**India.** The new NF Government set 1990–91 defence spending at $9.27b, less than 4 per cent of GNP, 16.7 per cent of total government spending and up by 8.6 per cent (inflation 7.7 per cent). The Navy received $1.27b. Spending in 1991–92 was to increase by 4 per cent, an actual increase of $577m. New programmes in hand including the carrier and more 'Tarantul I' missile corvettes. Increasing political instability and economic weaknesses are clouding the future of the ambitious naval expansion programme.

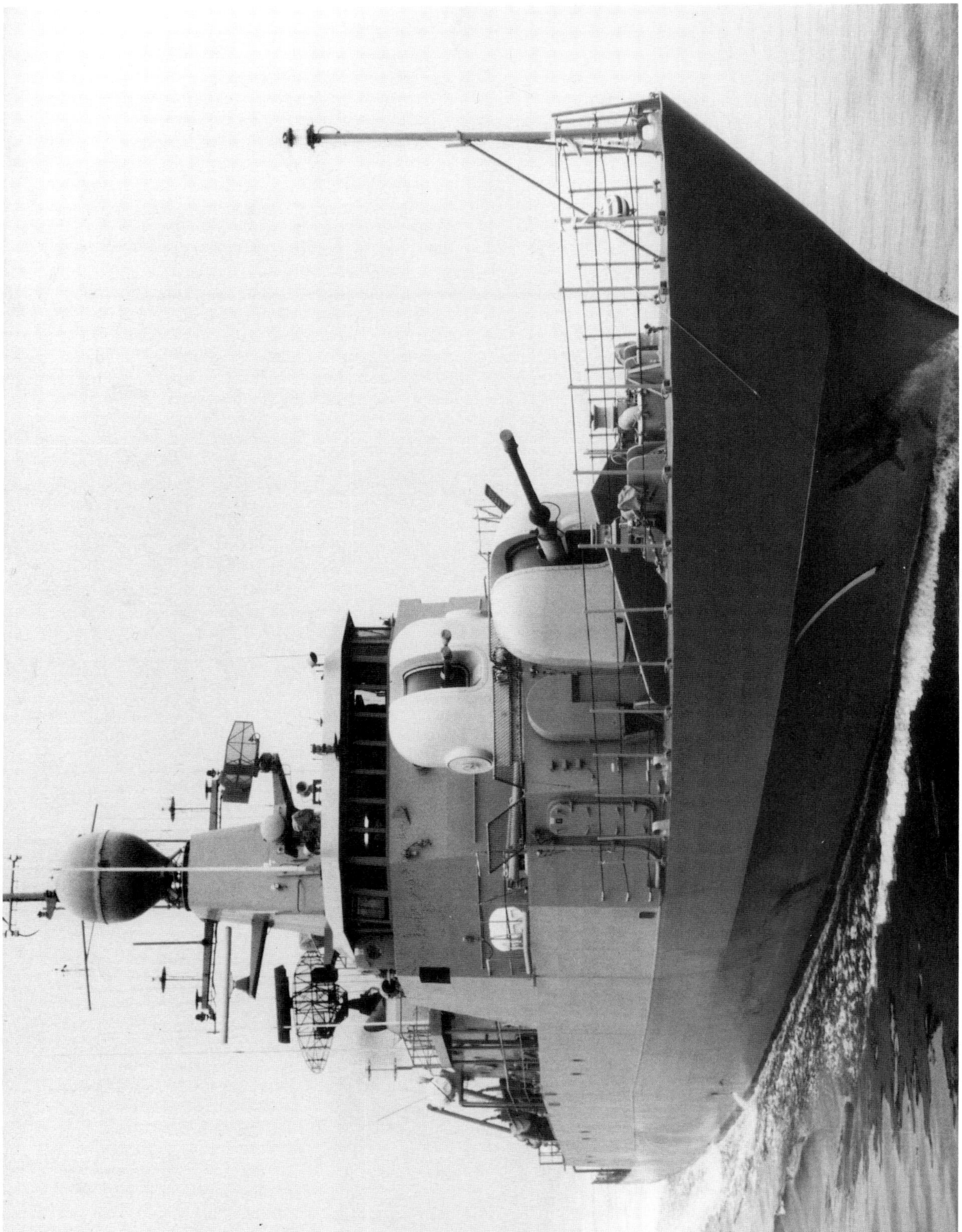

*The Thai missile corvette* Rattanakosin. *The weapons suite, remarkable for a ship displacing under 1000t at full load, comprises Harpoon SSM, Albatros/Aspide SAM, Phalanx CIWS, Mk 32 ASW TT and three calibres of guns.* (Tacoma)

# *LESSER NAVIES*

**South Korea's** modernisation programme includes the KDX destroyer (due to start mid-1991), new submarines, and minehunters based on an Italian design. **Taiwan**. The requirement for 6 light frigates, to follow the FFG-7 class, remains unfilled; more submarines are wanted, and the MCMV force needs renewal. **The Philippines** may receive ex-American warships for extending the Subic Bay Naval Station lease; negotiations began with an Australian shipyard for six 396-ton FAC(G). **Thailand** is purchasing an amphibious assault ship (with a disaster relief function) at a cost of about $210m; construction will be from 1991 to 1994. **Malaysia's** submarine contract went to Kockums. It provided for two new T96 boats, with the old *Draken* class boat *Vargen* as training ship and *Delfinen* for spares. The submarine competition was, however, reopened in April 1991. Yarrow is poised to win a contract for two ASW frigates, part of the Anglo-Malaysian defence deal. **Brunei** reopened its competition for three 1000-ton OPV, as the October 1989 order with Vosper Thornycroft was not confirmed. **Indonesia** plans a new frigate class; talks with China and with Western shipbuilders were reported, but an indigenous design may be preferred. **Myanmar (Burma)** took delivery of six Chinese 'Hainan' class patrol boats in January 1991 as part of a $1b arms deal. **Pakistan's** differences with America on its 'non-nuclear' status held up FMS purchases of frigate helicopters. The tripartite minehunter contract is not yet signed. The **New Zealand** budget was cut by a real 8 per cent to $792m, without affecting the ANZAC frigate project; the logistic support ship for the Ready Reaction Force was deferred and one *Leander* class may be sold. A curious Soviet offer of surplus warships for New Zealand wool was declined.

## C(vi). Latin America

**Argentina's** navy continues to face funding problems, effectively suspending new construction, but Fincantieri was awarded a contract to refit the carrier, and may build a new Antarctic supply ship. **Brazil** proposes to refit its carrier and, although the diesel submarine programme is lagging, very long-term SSN plans progress. **Chile** began purchasing and modernising Batch 3 *Leanders*, and is talking to RDM about three or four *Moray* class submarines (see page 215). **Venezuela** will modernise its *Lupo* class frigates, and also plans an OPV programme of at least six 800-ton vessels.

## C(vii). Africa

A West German delegation cleared **South Africa** of clandestinely building German-design submarines, but the Federal public prosecutor was given permission to investigate HDW/IKL for suspected transfer of submarine drawings.

# D. WARSHIP BUILDING

## D(i). New Designs and Principal Orders

**Multinational.** Following the collapse of the NFR 90 project, western European nations are collaborating on future AAW frigates and associated weaponry. A 'Joint Statement of Need' for a common Anglo-French frigate was signed in London on 1 March 1991, while the Netherlands, already cooperating with Spain on new fast combat support ships, has signed frigate Memoranda of Understanding with that country and with Germany.

**(a) United States.** The *Seawolf* submarine (SSN-21) and DDG-51 programmes were cut back, the former severely; one boat will be purchased annually, beginning in FY91, for a class total of ten or eleven; three or four DDG-51 will be purchased annually, in place of five. Savings should total $5–$7b in FY91 through FY94 (Table 2 includes details of cuts in major programmes).

*The Brazilian carrier* Minas Gerais *is due to enter modernisation in 1991. A 35,000–40,000t replacement is 'under consideration'.* (USN)

▲
*The future* Ville de Quebec, *CPF-03 ready to launch at MIL-Davie's Levis, Quebec yard, 16 May 1991.* (MIL-Davie/LYNCAN Photo)

*RFA* Fort George *photographed after launch at Swan Hunter's Tyne shipyard, 1 March 1991. Sister ship* Fort Victoria's *engine room was slightly damaged by a terrorist bomb at Harland and Wolff's Belfast shipyard, 9 September.* (Swan Hunter)
▼

▲ *The Dutch frigate* Karel Doorman *on first sea trials, 1 October 1990, without the Signaal SMART 3D radar antenna. The 16 Sea Sparrow VLS launchers are prominent on the port side of the hangar.* (KM de Schelde)

**(b) United Kingdom.** The delayed order for the SSBN *Vigilant*, placed on 13 November, will put back entry into service by six months; the fourth boat, not yet ordered, will also be late, putting back the phasing-out of Polaris. Problems in software integration for the weapons systems are also causing slippage in the programme. The Dowty-SEMA and Racal SSCS (Surface Ship Command System) for the Type 23 frigates will not be fitted until 1995 at the earliest.

**(c) Canada.** The hulls of the *Halifax* class continue at least two years behind schedule; as their EH-101 helicopters will not be ready until 1994, alternatives are being investigated. Unidentified turbulence at high speeds is causing excess noise. Later units will not be lengthened.

**(d) Netherlands.** *Karel Doorman* began sea trials without the Signaal SMART 3D radar; because of software delays, the fully automated command and control systems will not be ready until 1992–93.

*Ecuador's corvette* Esmeraldas, *first of six. Similar ships were delivered to Libya and built for, but not delivered to, Iraq.* (CNR) ▼

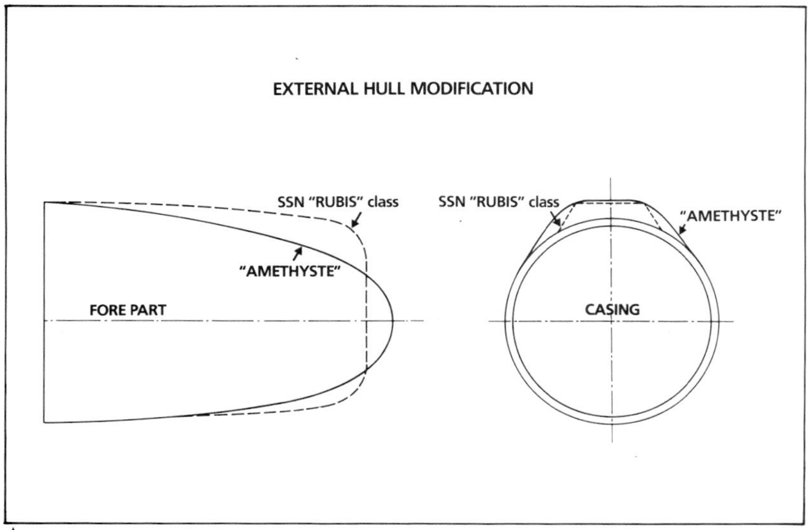


*Diagram showing external modifications in the* Amethyste *batch (SNA 5–8) of the* Rubis *class. The first four emphasised the ASUW role, SNA 5–8 are optimised for ASW warfare.* (DCN)

**(e) Greece.** Cuts in the investment programme at Hellenic Shipyards, Skaramanga, may delay building of the last three *Ydra* class Meko 200 frigates.

**(f) Turkey.** The fifth and sixth Meko 200 frigates will be longer than the first four, with CODOG instead of CODAD propulsion.

**(g) France.** The third pair of *Floreal* class patrol frigates was ordered in January 1991.

**(h) Australia.** *Collins*, the first Kockums 471 submarine, was laid down in 1990; the first ANZAC frigate is scheduled for construction between 1993 and 1996.

*An artist's impression of the French BAMO type minehunter/sweeper with GRP catamaran hulls. The first-of-class* Narvik *is due to complete in 1994.* (DCN)

*The French patrol frigate* Floreal *on builder's sea trials; main armament and most sensors are not yet fitted.* (GEC Alsthom) ▲

*The Venezuelan frigate* General Soublette. *Venezuela's six* Lupo *class will be extensively modernised; eight similar ships are in the Italian and Peruvian navies, but four built for Iraq languish in Italian ports.* (CNR) ▼

*Soviet 'Grisha I' class light frigate (USSR classification MPK = small anti-submarine ship). Around 80 'Grisha' variants are in service, 18 with the KGB, and production of 'Grisha V' continues.*

**(i) USSR.** Analysis of satellite photographs now suggests nuclear propulsion for the 75,000-ton carrier *Ul'yanovsk*, as no boiler uptakes have been observed. It is believed she will have catapults; the air group may include the Yak-38 'Forger', the Su-27 'Flanker' and the MiG-29 'Fulcrum'. The new destroyer 'Balcom 12' will be an uprated *Udaloy*, with twin 130mm guns replacing single 100mm guns, and an improved AAW suite. The third 'Sierra' class submarine is lengthened by 3m ('Sierra II').

**(j) Iraq.** Although 'freed for delivery', modifications and new technology requested by Iraq kept the ships of the 1981 order in Italy. Small Iraqi crews remained on board during the Gulf conflict, under supervision and with movements restricted.

**(k) India.** INS *Delhi*, first of a 6000-ton indigenous DDG class, was launched at Mazagon Dock, Bombay, in February; details of weapons and sensors are not yet available.

*Plan and elevation of the Indian OPV* Sukarya*; three were ordered in South Korea in 1987, and four in India. This Korea Tacoma 'Neptune' design has a similar hull to the South Korean* Ulsan *class frigates.*

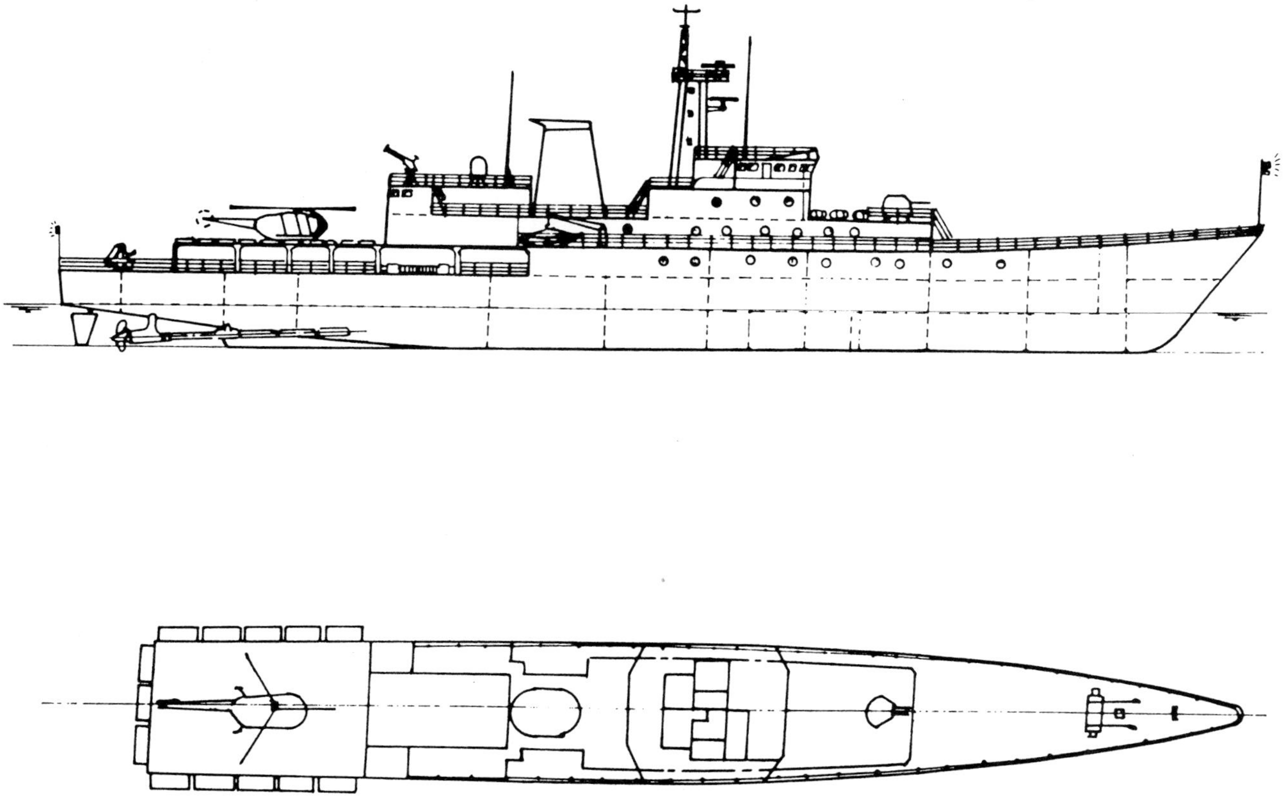

## Table 3. *NEW AND RECONSTRUCTED FRIGATE TYPES*

| *Country* | *Canada* | *Netherlands* | *Thailand* | *USSR* |
|---|---|---|---|---|
| Class | 'Tribal' TRUMP | *Karel Doorman* | *Chao Phraya* | *Neustrashimy* |
| No in class | 4 | 8 | 2 | 3+? |
| Builder(s) | – | K M de Schelde | Shanghai | Kaliningrad |
| Reconstruction | MIL Davie | – | – | – |
| Building dates | – | 1985–1995 | 1989–1991 | 1985–? |
| Reconst dates | 1987–*c*1994 | – | – | – |
| Displacement (max) | 5100t | 3320t | 1702t | 3800t |
| Lxbxd(max), metres | 129.8 × 15.2 × 6.6 | 122.3 × 14.4 × 4.3 | 103.2 × 10.8 × 3.1 | 130 × 15.5 × 5.6 |
| Missiles | SM-2MR VLS | 8 Harpoon<br>Sea Sparrow VLS | 8 Ying Ji | 6 SS-N-X<br>2 CADS-N-1 |
| Guns | 1–3in/62<br>1–20mm CIWS | 1–3in/62<br>1–30mm CIWS<br>2–20mm | 4–3.9in/56 (2x2)<br>8–37mm (4×2) | 1–3.9in/70 |
| ASW | 6–12.75in TT | 4–12.75in TT | 2 RBU 1200 | 1 RBU 12000 |
| Aircraft | 2 Sea King | 1 Lynx | – | 1 Ka-27 |
| Machinery | COGOG | CODOG | Diesel | Gas Turbines |
| Max SHP/BHP | 50,000 | 37,550 | 32,850 | 110,000 |
| Speed (kts) | 29+ | 28 | 28 | 30 |

*Note:* Two further units of the Thai *Chao Phraya* class will replace 2–3.9in/56 (1×2) with helicopter + platform.

### D(ii). Ships entering service during the year

These are listed in Table 3 (the figures for the Soviet Union and China are approximate).

The Soviet carrier *Admiral Kuznetsov* (ex-*Tbilisi*) was commissioned in January 1991, but has yet to exit the Black Sea. The air wing may all stow in the hangar, suggesting only 20–24 fixed wing aircraft and 4 or more helicopters. Important new types running sea trials included USS *Arleigh Burke* (DDG-51), the Canadian frigate *Halifax*, the Dutch frigate *Karel Doorman*, the Thai frigate *Chao Phraya* and the Soviet frigate *Neustrashimy*, formerly 'Balcom 8'. The Japanese *Harushio*, the Dutch *Zeeleeuw* and HMS *Upholder*, all lead-ships of new diesel submarine classes, commissioned during the year.

(Note: Tables 4 and 5 list data on certain new and reconstructed frigates, and on the above submarines).

*Launch of* Ursula *at Cammell Laird, Birkenhead, 28 February 1991. Cammell Laird was put up for sale in October; if no buyer is found, it will close when the* Upholder *class is complete* (VSEL)

## Table 4. *NEW SUBMARINE TYPES*

| *Country* | *Japan* | *Netherlands* | *UK* |
|---|---|---|---|
| Class | *Harushio* | *Walrus* | *Upholder* |
| No in class | 6 | 4 | 4 |
| Builder(s) | Mitsubishi, Kobe<br>Kawasaki, Kobe | RDM | VSEL, Barrow<br>Cammell Laird |
| Building Dates | 1987–1995 | 1979–1993 | 1983–1993 |
| Dived Displacement | 2750t | 2800t | 2455t |
| Lxbxd, metres | 80.0 × 10.8 × 7.8 | 67.7 × 8.4 × 6.6 | 70.3 × 7.6 × 5.5 |
| Missiles | | Sub-Harpoon (from TT) in all | |
| T Tubes | 6–21in | 4–21in | 6–21in |
| HP | 7200 | 6910 | 5400 |
| Subm speed (kts) | 20+ | 20 | 20 |

## Table 5. *NEW SHIPS ENTERING SERVICE, 1 APRIL 1990 TO 31 MARCH 1991 (USSR, CHINA IN 1990)*

| *Type* | *USA* | *USSR* | *UK* | *France* | *China* | *India* | *Japan* | *Italy* |
|---|---|---|---|---|---|---|---|---|
| CV (large) | – | – | – | – | – | – | – | – |
| CV (medium) | – | – | – | – | – | – | – | – |
| CV (small) | – | – | – | – | – | – | – | – |
| BB | – | – | – | – | – | – | – | – |
| CAH | – | – | – | – | – | – | – | – |
| CG | CG-61<br>CG-63<br>CG-65 | 1 *Slava* | – | – | – | – | – | – |
| DD | – | 1 *Sovremenniy* | – | – | – | – | 1 | – |
| FF (fleet) | – | 1 'Krivak III' | 1 Type 23<br>1 Type 22 | – | – | – | 2 | – |
| (escort) | – | 6 'Grisha V' | – | – | – | 2 | – | 3 |
| SSBN | SSBN-736 | 1 'Delta IV' | – | – | – | – | – | – |
| SSGN | SSN-750<br>SSN-753 | 2 'Oscar II' | – | – | – | – | – | – |
| SSN | SSN–754 | 2 'Akula'<br>1 'Sierra II'<br>1 'Victor III' | *Talent* | – | – | – | – | – |
| SS (all) | – | 3–4 'Kilo' | *Upholder* | – | 1 | 1 | 2 | – |

*Note:* One or more of above 'Kilos' may be for export.

## Table 6. *APPROXIMATE USN DELETIONS, 1990–92*

| *Type* | *FY90* | *FY91* | *FY92* |
|---|---|---|---|
| *SSBN* | *2* | *2* | *2–3* |
| *SSN* | *3 Permit*<br>*3 Skipjack* | *6 Permit*<br>*2 Sturgeon*<br>SSN-685 | *? Permit*<br>*? Sturgeon* |
| CV | *Coral Sea* | – | *? Midway* |
| BB | – | *New Jersey*<br>*Iowa* | *? Missouri*<br>*? Wisconsin* |
| CGN | – | – | *Truxtun* |
| DDG | *2 Coontz*<br>*8 Charles F Adams* | *3 Coontz*<br>*8 Charles F Adams* | *? Coontz*<br>*? Charles F Adams* |

**Note:** The deletions programme has been affected by the Gulf conflict.

HMCS Algonquin, *DDH-283 steams for Halifax, December 1990.* Algonquin *is the first of the four 'Tribal' class to complete TRUMP, and left MIL Davie in Levis-Lauzon to beat the freeze-up of the St Lawrence River. Final work was completed at MIL's subsidiary, M & M Manufacturing, Dartmouth, NS, and is scheduled to begin builder's trials on 4 June, before being handed over to the Canadian navy in July. TRUMP is now two years behind schedule.* (Litton/LYNCAN Photo)

## D(iii). Reconstructions

**(a) United Kingdom.** *Edinburgh* was refitted with a single Phalanx CIWS between the Sea Dart launcher and the 4.5in gun, making space for lightweight Seawolf either side of the funnel.

**(b) Canada.** The 'Tribal' TRUMP programme is about two years behind schedule. *Algonquin* completing in 1991; the radar and fire control fit is believed not to make full use of SM-2MR missile potential.

**(c) Other reconstructions** may be summarised more briefly. Refits for the Australian *Oberon* class submarines were delayed; one boat is presently refused diving clearance. Fincantieri has been given an initial contract to modernise ARA *25 de Mayo*'s machinery; further progress is delayed by lack of money. The refitted Chilean frigate *Lynch* has MM-40 tubes amidships; the Israeli Barak PDMS will replace the MM-38 canisters on the fantail, allowing a larger helicopter.

## D(iv). Fleet Depletions (decommissionings, transfers, etc)

Noteworthy items in this category are summarised below.

**(a) United States.** Table 6 shows USN disposals for FY90, FY91 and FY92 (proposed). A detailed sales list of ships and equipment is being prepared; ships withdrawn may be sold to allies. *Forrestal* will replace *Lexington* as training carrier; *Midway* will follow *Coral Sea* out of service, and *Ranger* may be withdrawn without entering SLEP.

**(b) United Kingdom.** The following withdrawals were announced 31 July: *Conqueror* (due for refit), *Odin, Onslaught, Phoebe*, while *Challenger* was to be sold to commercial interests, and chartered back if needed. *Aurora* was broken up (BU) in July, *Euryalus* BU in September as planned sales overseas did not proceed; *Achilles* sold to Chile as *Ministro Zenteno*; sinking of *Arethusa* as target delayed, but *Hul Vul* (ex-*Naiad*) was sunk in explosive trials, 24 September. *Warspite* and *Churchill*, both nearing ends of very expensive refits, are to be scrapped, in part because of age-related cracks found in their PWR 1 P1 reactors' primary cooling circuit (announced November). This defect is believed to be present in all British submarines with the reactor, including the four *Resolution* class; however, Polaris boats spend much less time at speed than fleet submarines.

*HMS* Conqueror *at Devonport. On 31 July, it was announced that* Conqueror *is to be scrapped early, as part of RN's contribution of £170m to cut £600m from defence overspending (not, officially, part of 'Options for Change').* (DML) ▲

*HMS* Challenger, *the RN's Seabed Operations Vessel, was decommissioned in autumn 1990 for sale to a commercial company; the RN would be able to charter this expensive, much modified and little-used white elephant if needed. No buyer reported to mid-1991.* (MoD) ▼

**(c) France.** *Le Redoubtable*, the first French SSBN, withdrawn in February 1991, will be used for trials of equipment for the SNLE-NG class. Two more *Commandant Rivière* class frigates were sold to Uruguay.

**(d) USSR.** The disposal of older warships continued apace. Some 70 submarines, half nuclear powered, were effectively withdrawn in 1990–91; all *Sverdlovs* have gone, and the first of the 'Kresta I' and 'Kynda' classes have joined several 'Kashins' on the scrap lists.

**(e) India.** *Chakra*, the first Indian SSN, was returned to Vladivostock in January 1991 after three years' loan, without extension or replacement; factors include the high maintenance cost and possibly technical difficulties. India is interested in building its own SSN under the Advanced Technology Vessel Programme (ATVP).

*Soviet 'Victor I' nuclear-powered attack submarine. At least one of these boats has been withdrawn; production of the latest derivative, 'Victor III', may cease in 1991.* (USN)

*The French cruiser* Colbert, *scheduled to remain in service until 1997, may now pay off in 1993.* (ECP Armées)

## E. NAVAL WEAPON SYSTEMS

Salient developments in naval weapon systems are listed below.

### E(i). Anti-Surface Missiles, including Ballistic Missiles

**(a) United States**. An official report expressed doubt about the safety of the Trident II (D5) missile, as the propellant can be accidentally detonated, and the warhead core would be unshielded from the resulting fire. Testing of the Block III Tomahawk AGM-109 began; changes include an uprated powerplant, new cruise and terminal guidance systems, and better timing. Up to 200 Norwegian Penguin Mk 2 ASM will be acquired for SH-60B Seahawk helicopters.

**(b) United Kingdom.** For budgetry reasons, the UK put back delivery of the first Trident D5 missiles from USA; delays in the new A90 production plant may affect warhead production for the second and later boats.

### E(ii). Maritime Aircraft

**Multinational.** The development phase of the NH 90 helicopter, the French – Italian – German – Dutch replacement for the Lynx and AB 212, has begun; its in-service target is *c*2000.

**(a) United States.** The very advanced, mainly composite A-12 Avenger was cancelled on 7 January, because of managerial and technical problems and cost overruns; while a replacement airframe (AX) is being identified, 60 existing A-6s will get new wings and a new, more capable F/A-18 is to be developed. Funding for the Navy's Advanced Tactical Fighter (ATF) variant was deferred until at least FY97, more F-14D being requested as a stopgap. Congressional insistence ensured that the tilt-rotor V-22 Osprey survived another year, but DoD will continue to support cancellation and oppose funding requests. The order for 125 Lockheed P-7A land-based ASW aircraft, the follow-on to the P-3 Orion, was cancelled because of R&D and cost problems. The USMC is to upgrade its Harrier II aircraft to the radar-equipped Harrier II Plus; a trilateral MoU to share costs was signed with Italy and Spain.

**(b) United Kingdom.** The MoD evaluated rival bids to manage final development and initial production of the EH 101 Merlin ASW helicopter; proper management is essential to keep the programme on cost and schedule. The RN will accept below-specification endurance but will insist on low frequency active dipping sonar. Merlin first landed on *Norfolk* in November; flying trials will begin aboard in June 1991.

**(c) Italy.** The purchase of STOVL aircraft for *Garibaldi* was authorised; two TAV-8B Harriers acquired in 1991 under a FMS deal will be followed by 16 radar-equipped Harrier II Plus from 1992 to 1996. The first shipboard trials for the EH 101 helicopter took place aboard *Maestrale*.

**(d) France.** The naval Rafaele, first of a possible 86, will begin deck trials in *Foch* in 1992; it will have nuclear capability. Plans to buy at least four E-2C Hawkeye AEW aircraft may be hit by spending cuts.

**(e) Spain.** The eleven EAV-8B Harrier II will be upgraded to Harrier II Plus standard from 1994, while seven new Harrier II Plus are to be purchased.

**(f) USSR.** A total of 670 Soviet Air Force planes have been transferred to the Navy since 1988, mainly in the Baltic area. The navalised Su-27 will be operational in 1991, but its MiG-29 counterpart is not yet ready. A side-by-side two-seat Su-27 has been undergoing sea trials; while ostensibly a trainer, this configuration would be suitable for a strike/reconnaissance variant. A new ASW seaplane, the A-40 Albatros, will replace the Be-12 'Mail' and the Il-38 'May'.

### E(iii). Anti-Aircraft and Anti-Missile Warfare (AAW)

**Multinational.** NAAWS and FAMS were the acronyms for the rival systems intended to counter highly-manoeuvrable supersonic missiles with low radar cross-sections. NAAWS (USA, Canada, Netherlands) envisaged two system levels, the interim – based on an improved, vertically-launched Sea Sparrow – and the fully compliant, using a new Mach 3 missile, while FAMS (France, Italy, UK, W Germany) involved a naval point-defence system based on the Aster 15 missile and an area defence version based on the Aster 30 (UK LAMS). Spain monitored both programmes closely. In early 1991 the USN terminated R&D funding for NAAWS, saving over $20m in FY92, but leaving a future local AAW defence gap. FAMS, however, went ahead, contracts being signed for advanced development of Aster 15, Aster 30 and the British LAMS. Continued US funding for the US-German RAM missile-based CIWS is uncertain.

**(a) United Kingdom.** Pending entry into service of LAMS, BAe is to uprate Sea Dart with a new IR fuse. The first firing of VLS Seawolf took place from *Norfolk* on 31 July. The Commons Defence Committee criticised the VLS procurement programme; it was difficult to integrate the system's complex software, and problems in turning the missile towards the target after vertical launch were noted.

**(b) France.** The Matra Mistral was first successfully tested at sea, from Sadral in *Cassard*. Norway will be the first customer to use the twin-round Simbad launcher, developed for FAC and MCMV.

➤ *The second Type 23 frigate,* Argyll, *on builder's trials and to commission 31 May 1991, will be followed into service in June by the first Swan Hunter ship,* Marlborough. *(*Yarrow*)*

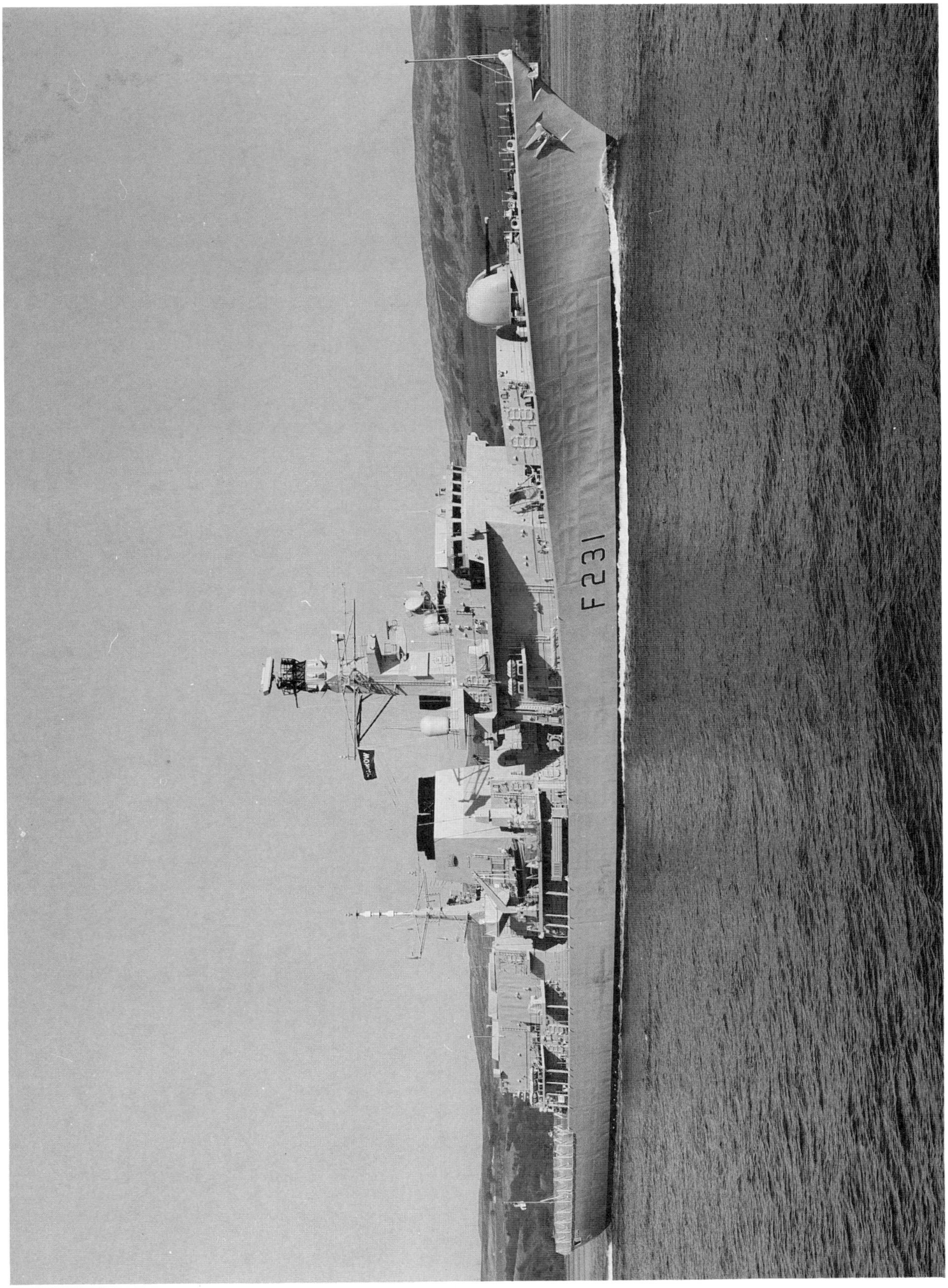

## E(iv). Anti-Submarine Warfare (ASW)

ASW is still considered the first fighting priority of the USN and RN, and acoustic systems developments receive most money. Low frequency dipping sonars will be fitted in shipborne helicopters of both navies, while the RN invited tenders to upgrade its submarine sonars, retaining passive intercept and ranging capability and adding active intercept sonar systems.

*The Meko 360 frigate* Almirante Brown *headed Argentine's contribution to the multinational Gulf force. Meko technology enabled a 40mm mounting to be replaced in just one day en route.* (Blohm & Voss)

## E(v). Guns

**United States.** The Block 2 development of the Phalanx CIWS is likely to have the twin GE 25mm Gatling gun or the quadruple Tround breechless gun (IOC expected *c*2000); the 30mm Signaal Goalkeeper CIWS has an 'extremely remote' chance of selection, although in US live trials it successfully destroyed a variety of ASUW missiles, including multiple Harpoon and Exocet.

## E(vi). Other Weapon Systems

Two American nuclear submarines will be equipped to allow 10–12 USN SEALS (equivalent to RN SBS) to deploy from submarines offshore; Maritalia's 3GST9 midget submarine is being evaluated as a SEAL transport.

# F. NAVAL EVENTS

## F(i) Areas of Conflict and Naval Actions

### THE GULF

Iraq's occupation of Kuwait on 2 August included the use of naval units offshore; with the exception of one FPB 57 and one TNC 45 FAC, all Kuwait's naval and coastguard ships were seized by the invader.

**(a) 'Desert Shield'.** As the situation became threatening, US warships in the Gulf joined hastily arranged exercises with UAE on 23 July (US ships present in area were the HQ ship *La Salle*, one destroyer and four frigates). Reinforcements came from the USS *Independence* carrier battle group (CVBG), on station in the North Arabian Sea. The *Saratoga* CVBG and the battleship *Wisconsin* left USA on 6 and 7 August and entered the Red Sea on 22 August; *Saratoga* had been due to replace *Eisenhower* in the Sixth Fleet, but the *Eisenhower* group was retained, and partly redeployed through the Suez Canal, the carrier passing through on 8 August. The *John F Kennedy* CVBG was under way from the US by 25 August and four MCMV were transported by heavy lift ship. The *Midway* arrived in October to replace *Independence* in the Gulf, but the latter, like the *Eisenhower*, remained for the time being, pending arrival of further US reinforcements announced in mid-November: three more carriers, *Theodore Roosevelt, America* and *Ranger*, a second battleship, *Missouri*, and their escort groups.

Britain's Armilla patrol comprised *York, Battleaxe* and *Jupiter*, joined by *Gloucester* on 15 September. Three MCMV, initially sent to the eastern Mediterranean, went on to the Gulf, and, with *Herald* as Command Ship, were based at Bahrain from 7 September. The three original warships were relieved by *London, Brazen* and *Cardiff* in September/October; in support were RFA *Olna, Diligence, Orangeleaf* and *Fort Grange*. *Ark Royal* sailed for exercises in the Mediterranean on 10 January, arriving on station with *Manchester, Sheffield, Olmeda* and *Regent*, but relieved the US carrier watching Libya, and operated with USS *Virginia, Philippine Sea* and *Spruance* before returning to Britain in April.

The French carrier *Clemenceau* landed its aircraft and, loaded with over forty army helicopters, left Toulon with escorts on August 13, remained at Djibouti from August 22 to 28, then headed into the Gulf zone and spent time there before being diverted to the Saudi Red Sea port of Yanbu to unload the helicopters (September 23 to 25). *Clemenceau* returned to Toulon on October 5. Press reports stated that French naval aircraft were too few, old and unreliable to operate alongside the USN.

Other NATO navies sent destroyers, frigates, minecraft and support ships to the eastern Mediterranean, Red Sea and Gulf area; weapon, decoy and communications fits were added or augmented as necessary, the Canadian ships in particular receiving rapid and extensive modifications. Unity of purpose in NATO did not submerge older rivalries; Greece only contributed one frigate to the multinational force and Turkey, while readying two frigates for the Gulf, sent a naval force to patrol off Cyprus for fear of Greek Cypriot military action. Of non-NATO nations, Argentina and Australia also contributed warships. US officers were allowed to join Soviet surface ships patrolling the Gulf, to cooperate in RF communications links and to work out joint action procedures should war break out, but the USSR did not participate actively in the blockade or the war.

HMS Brave *was one of four Type 22 frigates in the theatre during hostilities;* Brilliant, *the first warship with Wrens embarked on active, did not see action.* (MoD) ▲

RFA Sir Galahad *and the four other RFA logistic landing ships were employed in supplying British troops in 'Operation Granby'. 142 chartered ships were also used, only 8 British flagged.* (MoD) ▼

USS Wasp *(LHD-1), first of a class of five, replacements for the* Iwo Jima *class. The USN's amphibious assault ships carry AV8-B Harriers in addition to helicopters;* Nassau *(LHA-4) operated Harriers in 'Desert Storm'.* (Litton)

The first interdiction of an Iraqi ship was on 4 September, when marines from USS *Goldsborough* boarded the inward-bound freighter *Zanubia* and escorted her into a Gulf-state port; she was released after 24 hours. In total, 26,343 challenges were issued, with 994 subsequent boardings and 51 diversions. The vast majority of boardings took place in the northern Red Sea, only 83 in the Gulf.

**(b) 'Desert Storm'.** The shooting war began during the night of 16–17 January. Initially, heavy missile and air strikes were launched on strategic targets, including air bases; in the second phase emphasis was switched to attacks on Iraqi sea and land forces, to obtain sea area denial. 291 Tomahawk TLAM-C and TLAM-D SLCM were launched from around twenty surface ships and two submarines (52 missiles in first attack, 196 by Day 3), with a high degree of accuracy. *Louisville* fired the first submarine-launched Tomahawk against a land target on 19 January; *Pittsburg* fired from the Mediterranean over Turkey to a target in northern Iraq. A total of seven Stand-Off Land Attack Missiles (SLAM), an air-launched Harpoon derivative still in the operational evaluation stage, was delivered, the first two by A-6E Intruders from *John F Kennedy* on 18 January. At the end of hostilities, the carriers *Midway, Ranger, Theodore Roosevelt* and *America* operated in the Gulf, with *John F Kennedy* and *Saratoga* in the Red Sea and *Forrestal* in support in the eastern Mediterranean. Once fighting began, US, UK, Australian, Canadian and Dutch warships rotated as escorts under US tactical command; only USN, RN and Saudi warships were involved in actual shooting.

In all, US naval aircraft launched 18,624 sorties to 6 March, of which 36 per cent were strike missions, 30 per cent fleet defence/CAP and the remainder support; some 3000 tons of bombs were delivered; the proportion of missions flown against sea targets was very small. Naval strike aircraft flew 23 per cent of the total strike missions, in exact proportion to their numbers in the theatre. Seven naval and eight Marine Corps aircraft were lost.

Even with ex-Kuwaiti units, Iraq's naval strength was slight. Poorly-handled missile-armed fast attack craft posed a fairly negligible threat to allied shipping, some 1200 haphazardly-strewn mines were more serious; an amphibious landing would require the elimination of both. The fast attack craft – and indeed all Iraqi units – proved very vulnerable to bomb, gun and rocket attacks by US strike aircraft, reinforced by RN Lynx helicopters firing Sea Skua missiles. Detailed accounts of naval operations conflict; in poor visibility, command ships were sometimes confused by a number of simultaneous engagements.

On 19 January USS *Nicholas* engaged Iraqi positions on oil platforms, and on 1 February probably sank a patrol boat and damaged two others. The tanker and support ship *al Mutanabbi* was badly damaged by Intruders on 23 January and its three 'Winchester' class hovercraft destroyed. A patrol craft laying mines was sunk by a Harpoon from a Saudi warship. On the following day, a minelayer went down after an Intruder attack, with 3 dead and 22 prisoners. Soldiers from Qaruh island fired on allied forces rescuing survivors, so the island was taken, with 29 more prisoners. An AM-39 missile strike failed when the attacking force was intercepted by allied fighters; the missile was jettisoned harmlessly out of range.

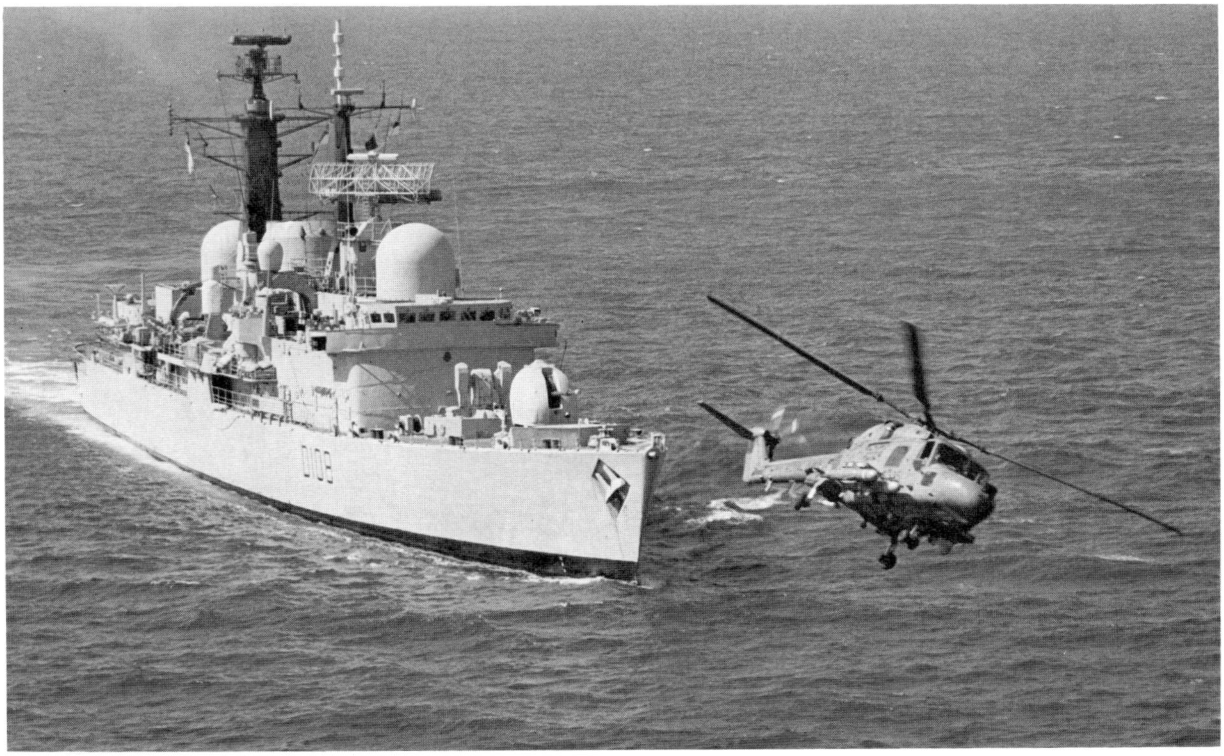

*HMS* Cardiff *and Lynx helicopter in the Gulf.* Cardiff's *Lynx scored several successes with Sea Skua missiles; helicopter targets included fast attack craft, T-43 minelaying minesweepers, 'Polnochny' class LSLs and 'Zhuk' class patrol boats.* (MoD) ▲

*RFA* Diligence *served as Forward Repair Ship in the Gulf in 1987–89 and from September 1990; she assisted with temporary repairs to the mined US cruiser* Princeton. (MoD) ▼

Late on 29 January, seventeen small craft were attacked by US helicopters and jets, as well as Lynx from *Gloucester, Brazen* and *Cardiff*. Five boats were sunk and twelve damaged, of which four were later beached. Next day, repeated attacks by up to sixteen aircraft and the three Lynxes sank or set alight six or more FAC(M), including at least two ex-Kuwaiti TNC 45 (one by *Gloucester's* Lynx). By 2 February, some sixty-five Iraqi and ex-Kuwaiti ships and craft of all types were claimed sunk or disabled; during the conflict, the RN sank 12 with 26 Sea Skuas.

The missile threat eliminated, allied minecraft could clear channels to the Kuwaiti mainland. Phase 3, inshore operations, began on 4 February, when the battleship *Missouri* opened fire on shore targets, using her Pioneer RPV drone to spot fall of shot; her sister *Wisconsin* took over on 7 February. At 4.40am local time on 18 February, USS *Tripoli* (LPH-10) hit a contact mine, blowing a large hole in the hull 5ft below the waterline on the forward starboard bow, badly damaging the keel and injuring four crew members. The ship continued under her own power. Some 2½ hours later and 10nm distant, USS *Princeton* (CG-59), while manoeuvring (reportedly at 25kts) to protect US and UK MCMV from possible 'Silkworm' attack, was severely damaged by the almost simultaneous detonation of two influence mines – probably Italian Mantas, with 235kg charge (one under stern, one 300m off starboard bow); the resulting shock wave and air bubble nearly broke the hull in two, buckling and cracking the superstructure. Helicopter pilots reported a 'large crease' on the flight deck and 'rippling' along the starboard quarter; 50 per cent of the power was lost, with the aft gun and VLS missile system inoperative; three injured crew members were treated on RFA *Argus*, modified as a primary casualty receiving ship. *Princeton* was withdrawn next day and docked in Dubai for 2 weeks' temporary repairs.

**(c) 'Desert Sabre' and after.** The land battle was begun by the guns of the *Missouri* and *Wisconsin* at 0100 GMT on 24 February, threatening an amphibious landing that never materialised (68,000 US Marines were ashore for the land fighting, 17,000 in the amphibious force); the ceasefire came 100 hours later, at 0500 GMT on 28 February. Two 'Silkworm' missiles fired at *Missouri* on 25 February were engaged by *Gloucester* with two Sea Dart missiles. One 'Silkworm' passed low over *Cattistock* and was intercepted by a Sea Dart about four miles short of the battleship; the other splashed in the sea. After the ceasefire, RN MCMV and US minesweeping helicopters started clearing the channels to Kuwaiti ports, and the first, to Shuibah, was opened on 12 March. The clearing involved much 'finger touch' searching by divers, including a RAN team, as oil contamination hampered usual methods. A few details of the activities of eighteen US submarines were released in March: they helped secure Mediterranean sea routes, were employed in survelliance and reconnaissance, and, like the RN *Otus* and *Opossum*, participated in special operations.

**(d) Conclusions.** The Gulf operations provide a classic example of the strategic exercise of sea power. Two US carriers were on station by 7 August, ensuring that troops and aircraft could be landed in Saudi Arabia without risk of interference by Iraq. The initial blockade, declared 6 August, lacked 'teeth' for enforcement, but by the time that the use of force, if necessary, was approved on 25 August, an international fleet of some seventy warships from almost every Western nation had assembled in the Red Sea and Gulf; the blockade quickly became total. As it became clear that sanctions alone would not produce a rapid withdrawal from Kuwait, the military build-up ashore and afloat was greatly increased; some five million tons of supplies, ammunition and fuel (80 per cent of the total) went to Saudi Arabia by sea without 'let or hindrance'. When the Security Council ultimatum expired on 15 January, 'all necessary means' were in position and ready for action.

The USN's major tactical problem was lack of an equivalent to the Air Force's CAFMS, a computerised flight management system, leaving it unable fully to participate in coordinating the daily air strike programme. The problem of initial losses resulting from low altitude flying was solved by changing strike tactics, while flexibility in launching strikes increased when the four carriers could move safely into the northern Gulf. Communications with allies was by the secure Link 11 network, but with non-NATO and Soviet vessels by standard VHF radio and visual signalling.

HMS Exeter *refuelling. Four Type 42 destroyers provided 40 per cent of upfront air defence for the four American carriers and two battleships in the northern Gulf.* (MoD)

# *THE REST OF THE WORLD*

**(a) Africa.** Tribal warfare in Liberia and Somalia led to the collapse of central authority, and to the evacuation of foreigners from the respective capitals. As insurgents closed on Monrovia, foreign fishing boats were seized by rebel coastguard gunboats, and their crews held ashore. On 5 August, US Marines from USS *Saipan*, part of the Landing Force, Sixth Fleet, took over the Embassy compound to evacuate American (and other) diplomats and civilians by helicopter. Nigeria and other West African states, acting under ECOWAS, assembled a joint peacekeeping force to intervene in the stricken city. Some 4000 men, mostly Nigerian and Ghanaian, were landed from the Nigerian LST *Ambe*, covered by the FAC(M) *Damisa* and other units, on 24 August. In January 1991, foreign nationals were flown from Mogadishu to the US helicopter carrier *Guam* and the French naval supply ship *Jules Verne* offshore.

**(b) Indian Ocean.** In July, major Sri Lankan Government offensives against Tamil Tiger forces in the north of the island included naval cordons offshore, to prevent insurgents escaping by sea.

**(c) Baltic.** Sweden noted more sightings of foreign submarines within territorial waters in 1990 than in 1989; on five occasions ASW weapons were fired, but no intruder was forced to surface.

**(d) Arctic.** MV *Greenpeace*, sent to stop Soviet nuclear tests on Novaya Zemlya, was seized by men from the KGB frigate *Imeni XXVII Sezda KPSS* in October, and released with the crew at Murmansk after being held for six days. Four activists landed by inflatable boat reported, erroneously, very high radioactivity levels ashore.

*The survey ships* Herald *(nearer camera) and* Hecla *in the Gulf;* Hecla *left UK in January to relieve* Herald *as MCM Support Ship. Modifications included an enlarged flight deck for Lynx and an ad-hoc 'sanctuary' for use in event of chemical warfare.* (MoD)

*Almost in the sights is a 'Hunt' class MCMV; five were in the Gulf when hostilities began; 270 mines had been cleared by mid-March.* (MoD)

*The Nigerian frigate* Otobo *is being converted to an OPV for EEZ patrols by Fincantieri. Sister ship* Dorina *sank in 1987 after hull was badly corroded during fumigation; although raised, she exists only as a hulk.* (Vosper Thornycroft)

## F(ii). Major Casualties at Sea, 1 April 1990 to 31 March 1991

(a) An explosion and a fire damaged USS *Midway* (CV-41), 125nm off the east coast of Japan, killing 2 and injuring 16, 20 June; the ship returned to Yokosuka under her own power.
(b) The Indian frigate *Andaman* foundered in heavy weather about 150 miles off Visakhapatnam, 21 August, with the loss of 14 lives.
(c) A steam valve ruptured in the boiler room of USS *Iwo Jima* (LPH-2) off Bahrain, killing 10, 30 October.
(d) The Philippine patrol boat *Nueva Viscaya* sunk in a typhoon in October, with 3 missing.
(e) The fishing trawler *Antares* sank when her fishing gear was snagged by HMS *Trenchant* in the Firth of Clyde on 22 November, with the loss of 4 lives. The submarine had previously been in a mock battle with a frigate, part of the 'perishers' course. The accident recalled other episodes, twelve officially since 1979, but fishermen allege at least 36 deaths by NATO and Soviet submarines since 1982. In October, the High Court ordered the MoD to hand over the logs of any RN submarines within 20 miles radius when the fishing boat *Inspire* sank off Fishguard with the loss of three lives in September 1988.
(f) 21 US servicemen were drowned when the ferry *Tuvia*, returning libertymen to *Saratoga*, capsized off Haifa, Israel on 22 December.

## F(iii). Footnotes.

(a) Leif Larsen, much-decorated hero of the wartime 'Shetland Bus' and a leader of the 1942 'chariot' attempt on the German battleship *Tirpitz* at Trondheim, died on 12 October, aged 84.
(b) As a result of Congressional pressure on the Defense Department, the captain and crew of the USS *Pueblo* (AGER-2), captured by North Korea in January 1968 and imprisoned for 11 months, received prisoner-of-war medals, May 1990.
(c) In November, the well-established but mysterious crash-landing of a RN Sea King 4 flying from HMS *Invincible* near Punta Arenas, Chile, during the Falklands War, was explained. The helicopter had been ferrying an SAS advance party to attack Argentine mainland bases. The main attack, by about 70 SAS troops in two Hercules, was cancelled hours after take off because surprise had been lost.
(d) Funding hitches will delay the start of the Dutch–Soviet attempt to lift the sunken submarine *Komsomolets*, using a specially constructed salvage ship, until mid-1992.

## G. MISCELLANEOUS

(a) Serious environmental pollution resulted from naval activities at both ends of the globe. Moscow stated that the cause of a major marine disaster at Severodvinsk, near Arkhangelsk, was leakage of toxic rocket fuel from a naval storage tank; in Antarctica the hull of the Argentine naval auxiliary *Bahia Paraiso*, wrecked in January 1989, was still spilling fuel.
(b) Yachts caused problems in two tense areas. In May, an Israeli gunboat opened fire on Jordan's Royal Yacht with King Hussein on board, Red Sea; Israeli rules on firing were revised. In July, Irish Prime Minster Haughey's private yacht *Celtic Mist* was searched by a regular RM patrol in Carlingford Loch, between Northern Ireland and the Republic; LE *Orla* was moved into the area 'on routine fishery protection and security duties'.
(c) Following protests by animal rights activists, a New England company declined to supply another dolphin to the USN to be trained as an underwater sentinel for the Trident SSBN base at Bangor, Wa.

## H. STOP PRESS

The following revised schedule for delivery of the ships of the Canadian frigate programme was supplied by Thomas G Lynch.

### *REVISED DELIVERY SCHEDULE FOR CPF*

| *CPF No* | *Name* | *Number* | *Delivery Date*[1] |
|---|---|---|---|
| 01* | *Halifax* | 330 | June/July 1991 |
| 02* | *Vancouver* | 331 | early 1992 |
| 03** | *Ville de Quebec* | 332 | early 1993 |
| 04* | *Toronto* | 333 | August 1992 |
| 05** | *Regina* | 334 | December 1993 |
| 06** | *Calgary* | 335 | September 1994 |
| 07* | *Montreal* | 336 | September 1993 |
| 08* | *Fredericton* | 337 | May 1994 |
| 09* | *Winnipeg* | 338 | January 1995 |
| 10* | *Charlottetown* | 339 | September 1995 |
| 11* | *St John's* | 340 | March 1996 |
| 12* | *Ottawa* | 341 | September 1996 |

* Built by Saint John Shipbuilding Limited, St John, NB.
** Built by MIL Group Limited Inc, MIL Davie, Levis, Quebec.
[1] Delivery date is not commissioning date.

### *DELIVERY OF FRIGATES IN CHRONOLOGICAL ORDER*

| *CPF No* | *Name* | *Number* | *Delivery Date* |
|---|---|---|---|
| 01* | *Halifax* | 330 | June/July 1991 |
| 02* | *Vancouver* | 331 | early 1992 |
| 04* | *Toronto* | 333 | August 1992 |
| 03** | *Ville de Quebec* | 332 | early 1993 |
| 07* | *Montreal* | 336 | September 1993 |
| 05** | *Regina* | 334 | December 1993 |
| 08* | *Fredericton* | 337 | May 1994 |
| 06** | *Calgary* | 335 | September 1994 |
| 09* | *Winnipeg* | 338 | January 1995 |
| 10* | *Charlottetown* | 339 | September 1995 |
| 11* | *St John's* | 340 | March 1996 |
| 12* | *Ottawa* | 341 | September 1996 |

*Notes:* As can be seen, starting in 1992, the ships should be delivered to the navy at the rate of two–three per year. Because of early delays in the construction process, SJSL will be delivering (07) *Montreal* before MIL Davie deliver (05) *Regina*, and (08) *Fredericton* before (06) *Calgary*.

# INDEX

Italicised page numbers refer to illustrations and diagrams. An illustrated page may also carry relevant text.